# Exploring Psychological Research Methods

*Prepared by the course team*

*(The course team would like to thank the authors of the methods booklets which formed the basis for this book: Peter Banister, Troy Cooper, Dan Goodley, Jacqui Hastewell, Wendy Hollway, Rebecca Lawthom, Martin Le Voi, Dorothy Miell, Graham Pike, Ann Phoenix, Kathleen Robinson, Kerry Thomas, Carol Tindall, Jane Tobbell, Margaret Wetherell, David Williams. And special thanks to Graham Pike and Dorothy Miell for their role as editors.)*

This publication forms part of an Open University course DSE212 *Exploring Psychology*. Details of this and other Open University courses can be obtained from the Student Registration and Enquiry Service, The Open University, PO Box 197, Milton Keynes MK7 6BJ, United Kingdom: tel. +44 (0)870 333 4340, email general-enquiries@open.ac.uk

Alternatively, you may visit the Open University website athttp://www.open.ac.uk where you can learn more about the wide range of courses and packs offered at all levels by The Open University.

To purchase a selection of Open University course materials visit http://www.ouw.co.uk, or contact Open University Worldwide, Michael Young Building, Walton Hall, Milton Keynes MK7 6AA, United Kingdom, for a brochure. tel +44 (0)1908 858785; fax +44 (0)1908 858787; email ouwenq@open.ac.uk

The Open University
Walton Hall, Milton Keynes
MK7 6AA

First published 2007



Edited and designed by The Open University.

Typeset by Pam Callow, S & P Enterprises (rfod) Ltd.

Printed in the UK by Bell & Bain Ltd.,Glasgow

SUP 92397 2

3.1

MIX
Paper from responsible sources
FSC® C007785
FSC www.fsc.org

# Contents

CHAPTER 1 Introduction to research methods 1

CHAPTER 2 Correlational studies and experiments 43

CHAPTER 3 Variables, measurement and descriptive statistics 77

CHAPTER 4 Graphs and distributions 105

CHAPTER 5 Testing hypotheses 129

CHAPTER 6 Inferential statistics 163

CHAPTER 7 The experimental project 189

CHAPTER 8 Qualitative research: an overview and examples 241

CHAPTER 9 Doing thematic analysis 281

CHAPTER 10 The qualitative project: from research design to analysis 313

CHAPTER 11 Writing up your qualitative research report 357

Glossary 379

Index 393

Acknowledgements 401

CHAPTER 1

# Introduction to research methods

## Contents


| | | | |
|---|---|---|---|
| | **Aims** | | **2** |
| 1 | **Introduction** | | **2** |
| 2 | **From epistemology to data** | | **5** |
| 3 | **Seeking objectivity** | | **11** |
| | 3.1 | Features of objective data | 11 |
| | 3.2 | Measuring people: the research goals of those who seek objectivity | 12 |
| | 3.3 | The need for statistics | 17 |
| | 3.4 | Thinking about methods | 19 |
| 4 | **Exploring subjectivity** | | **20** |
| | 4.1 | Features of subjective data | 20 |
| | 4.2 | Understanding people: the research goals of those who explore subjectivity | 20 |
| | 4.3 | Thinking about methods | 29 |
| 5 | **Ethics** | | **32** |
| | 5.1 | Informed consent | 33 |
| | 5.2 | Anonymity rather than confidentiality | 34 |
| | 5.3 | Right to withdraw from the research | 35 |
| | 5.4 | Feedback and debriefing of research participants | 35 |
| | 5.5 | Ethical issues when researching with children | 38 |
| 6 | **Conclusion** | | **39** |
| 7 | **References** | | **42** |

## Aims

This chapter aims to:

- explore the research process, particularly the interrelatedness of questions, claims, data and evidence (as introduced in the cycle of enquiry in the Introduction to Book 1)
- introduce the differences between quantitative and qualitative methods
- present some of the ways in which quantitative and qualitative methods are used by researchers who are either pursuing objectivity or exploring subjectivity
- show you how *different* methods reflect different ways of gaining *different* forms of knowledge.

## 1 Introduction

Welcome to *Exploring Psychological Research Methods*. Over eleven study weeks this book will help you to learn how psychological research is conducted, by providing information about the research methods and analytical techniques used by psychologists working in a variety of fields. One of the main goals of this book is to prepare you to conduct psychological research yourself, and indeed two of your assignments (TMAs 03 and 05) will involve completing research studies and writing them up. Although the second of these assignments will represent the end of your research journey within this course, we very much hope you will continue and take the opportunity to expand your skills as a psychological researcher at one of our associated research project courses (DXR222 *Exploring Psychology: Project* or DZX222 *Exploring Psychology: Online Project*) and through other Open University psychology courses.

We hope you find the prospect of conducting research yourself exciting, and that you will enjoy it and find it very useful. Of course, there are a number of skills you will need to develop in order to research psychology successfully, as well as quite a bit of information you will need to learn. In reading this book it is worth bearing in mind that working through the material more than once can be very beneficial. So if you haven't understood a concept after your first read through of a particular section or chapter, try rereading the material, or even coming back to those detailed points once you have read and understood the broad framework being described. As we shall be introducing you to many different terms associated with the research process, and using these in later chapters, we have defined what we consider to be the most important terms in a glossary at the end of the book – please refer to this glossary if you are uncertain about the meaning of a term. This glossary is also available on the course website.

It's also worth bearing in mind that even the greatest researchers do not remember every detail of every procedure; instead, they refer to methods books a great deal – so keep this one handy when conducting your own studies. In fact, given that conducting your own research is a key element of both this and our other courses, you might like to keep all your methods materials (this book, the *SPSS Booklet*, your project work and computer printouts) together in one 'methods' file.

Information about research, from broad approaches to descriptions of individual studies, is a key feature throughout DSE212. We hope you will find that the more detailed information provided in this book will assist your understanding of the research covered in the other course material. In fact, it is impossible to learn about psychological topics and psychological perspectives without *simultaneously* thinking about the evidence for their theoretical claims. For example, in the chapter you have just read (Book 1 *Mapping Psychology*, Chapter 1, 'Identities and diversities') you have seen two examples of 'featured methods'. These are methods that are central to the investigation of identity and they have been set out in boxes, partly to draw your attention to their importance for the chapter, but also to highlight their importance as *types* of method that you need to be familiar with. As you read through the chapters in Book 1 you will find more featured method boxes presented in relation to particular psychological topics or perspectives. In this way you will learn the details of methods alongside discussion and argument about how to ask questions in psychology, and about which kinds of data are acceptable as evidence. Importantly, what you learn about methods will also be valuable for evaluating the evidence currently available on particular issues.

You will already have read (in Section 2.3 of the introductory chapter of Book 1) that researchers always work on the basis of particular sets of theoretical assumptions. However, these are not always spelled out or discussed explicitly. So researchers might rely on certain theoretical assumptions implicitly and by virtue of their location – in time and in a culture, a society, a particular university or interest group where a specific set of theoretical assumptions has become accepted. For example, the approaches that are referred to as following the scientific tradition (e.g. biological and cognitive psychology) often do not discuss or make explicit their perspective. This is partly because they make use of what is known as the positivist model. This involves a perspective based on gathering quantifiable and objective data and which is well established as it has been the dominant model used in researching the natural sciences.

In contrast, some researchers very carefully and explicitly discuss and develop the theoretical assumptions that they see as fundamental for the topics they address and the questions they ask. For example, some of the approaches that are more focused on subjectivity, such as social constructionism, do involve an explicit discussion of the perspective being used. This is partly because social constructionism is a relatively new perspective which differs significantly from the traditional scientific, positivist model. It is concerned with making assumptions about how knowledge is produced through psychological research visible, and with challenging those assumptions.

Whether it is made explicit or not, research is always conducted within a context that is made up of theoretical assumptions about the subject matter (e.g. what kinds of question should be asked, and what kinds of topic can be studied); and the ways in which it should be studied (i.e. what methods can give us the best insight into these topics). This context, which represents a specific set of theoretical assumptions, is referred to using several different terms, including 'paradigm' and 'theoretical framework'. In this course we shall use the term perspective, which simply refers to a particular set of theoretical assumptions about the subject matter. The perspective adopted by a researcher will therefore influence which topic they study and how they study it.

The link between the perspective adopted by a researcher and the types of question they ask, the methods they employ and the analysis they use is explored throughout the course books. The *embeddedness* of questions, methods and analysis within a perspective was first discussed in the introductory chapter of Book 1 when the cycle of enquiry was introduced. This embeddedness is something that you need to keep in mind throughout the course, because it underpins an understanding of how methods have to be chosen so as to be appropriate to what is being studied. As the cycle of enquiry shows us, the perspective taken will determine what concrete shape and form the 'questions', 'claims', 'evidence/data', 'evaluation', and 'theory development' will take.

From the above discussion we hope it is apparent that, as well as detailed information about how to collect or analyse data, understanding research methods involves an appreciation of the broader framework in which research is conducted. Think of this first chapter as enabling you to get a 'bird's-eye view' of psychological methods so that you can begin to map them. As is often the case, it is only when you can 'get above' the detail and look down on the range of psychological methods as a whole that you will be able to make sense of the diversity. You will have plenty of opportunity to fill in the details later as you work through the course. In this first methods week we would like you to stand back a little and get a view of the range of psychological research methods – how they differ from each other and the ways in which they are similar.

# 2 From epistemology to data

We'll begin our bird's-eye overview of the broader frameworks within which psychological research is conducted by defining a few key terms.

- **Epistemology** is the 'theory of knowledge'. It refers to the principles of what can be known and how we can know it; that is, how we can find out about it.
- **Methodology** is the 'theory of methods'. It refers to the overall theoretical rationale and the principles that define how a research question, a set of methods, and data are embedded within a perspective.
- **Methods** are certain research techniques and tools for gathering and/or analysing data.
- **Data** are the concrete details; the 'measures' that are collected, gathered or produced when applying a method. Data can come in virtually any shape or form; for example, behaviour, inner experiences, material data or symbolic data.

It can be very easy to get these terms confused, as they describe related constructs, and it might help to think of them as operating at different levels. This means that epistemology operates as a broad framework that underpins the methodology employed, which in turn decides which methods are used, and therefore what types of data are collected. These four terms encapsulate the basic building blocks of psychological research (and indeed of any kind of research). They will accompany you throughout your methods training and will be explained and exemplified in more detail below and throughout this book. So do not worry if things might appear complex at this point, they will become clearer as you progress through the course.

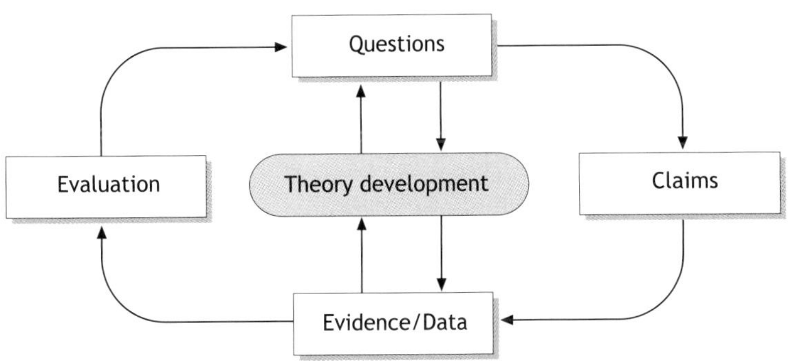


**Figure 1.1** The cycle of enquiry

In the Introduction to Book 1 you started to learn about the overall process of research, including the cycle of enquiry (see Figure 1.1, taken from the Introduction to Book 1). You have also been given a basic grounding in four kinds of data that psychologists use: behaviour, inner experiences, material and symbolic (see Book 1, Introduction, Section 2.2). In addition, you have been introduced to a range of methods used in psychology to collect and/or analyse data, albeit briefly: experiments, questionnaires, interviews, psychological tests, observations, and meaning and language-based methods such as content analysis and discourse analysis (see Book 1, Introduction, Section 2.3). Yet crucially, as outlined above, research questions, methods and the kinds of data gathered are always embedded within a specific perspective. This perspective informs what kinds of question are relevant and can be asked, what kinds of method will be seen to deliver useful data, and how these data need to be analysed to deliver the appropriate kind of evidence. See Table 1.1 for a reminder of the types of data that tend to be associated with different methods.

**Table 1.1 Methods and data types outlined in Book 1, Introduction**

| Method | Data type |
|---|---|
| Experiments | Behaviour and material data. |
| Questionnaires | Self reports on behaviour; accounts of inner experience. |
| Interviews | Accounts of inner experience; language used as symbolic data. |
| Psychological tests | Self reports of behaviour and responses to simple, standard questions. These reports are from the respondent's viewpoint but the ideas for them are imposed by the test. |
| Observations | Behaviour in particular settings; sometimes records of what is said and how it is said. |
| Meaning and language-based methods | Diary entries; conversations; published text sources |

The general term that captures the overarching rationale (the theoretical principles) according to which the research is conducted is *methodology*. Altogether, the research questions, the methods and the types of data form the basics of *methodology* – literally the 'science' of methods – or the theory of methods.

This is why the same method can feature in different methodologies. For example, data collected from interviews could be used in a quantitative research project that relies on content analysis (e.g. counting how often certain words appear) as a way of analysing the data. However, data from interviews could also be used in a qualitative research project that uses discourse analysis (i.e. analysing how meaning is constructed and negotiated by the speakers). Yet these two research projects would be embedded in very different perspectives; that is, they relate to very different theoretical assumptions and views about the best ways to try to understand and explain people, their behaviour and their experience. Hence they would also be asking very different research questions. Content analysis makes sense within a perspective which places value on 'objectivity' and thus needs quantifiable data, and which assumes that counting the prevalence of words or phrases will give us an insight into how people communicate. In contrast, discourse analysis is situated within a perspective that considers language as productive and accordingly is interested in finding out about the processes whereby people construct meanings socially and individually. Counting the prevalence of words would not make sense within this perspective. Hence the two approaches might use similar methods but they differ hugely with regard to their *methodology*.

In this sense we can say that methodology is the rationale according to which the research question and the methods are embedded in the perspective. So methodology is concerned with how to choose the methods that are appropriate to the questions being asked, knowing how to start thinking about what data to collect, how to design a study to collect those data, and then what to do with the data to convert them into research evidence. Evidence is then used to create new psychological knowledge; for example, to build theories of how memory works or of how we construct our identities. Yet again, depending on the overall perspective we are relying on, a theory of how memory works could be based on material data, using brain-imaging techniques to locate areas in the brain that are active when memory tasks are performed (scientific tradition). Alternatively, we could also build a theory of how memory works based on symbolic data, analysing conversations and interactions of people collaboratively constructing memories and what these memories mean to them in everyday life (hermeneutic tradition). Obviously the two resulting theories of memory would be embedded within very different perspectives and would make very different assumptions about what 'memory' is and what can be known about it. Hence, they would differ fundamentally in their assumptions about what should be considered relevant research questions and relevant evidence, as would their assumptions about how this evidence should be gathered. Thinking about the different ways in which evidence is gathered and used to build and develop theories (the principal questions of what can be known, what is considered to count as 'evidence', and how it can be explored) is called *epistemology* – literally the 'science' of knowing, or the 'theory of knowledge'.

The kinds of data outlined in Table 1.1 differ on the important dimension of *objectivity–subjectivity*. This links to another crucial feature of methodology – namely the overall aim of the research. This aim will be very different depending on whether the researchers wish to focus on objectivity or to focus on subjectivity.

## Activity 1.1

In Chapter 1 of Book 1 you were introduced to the work of a number of psychologists, including Kuhn and McPartland, Erikson, Marcia, Tajfel and Gergen. Have a look back through the chapter and take a few minutes to see if you can identify the different kinds of data that each of these researchers used. For each type of data, try to work out if the focus is on objectivity or subjectivity. The clue is to consider whether the data are from an outsider viewpoint (pursuing objectivity) or an insider viewpoint (exploring subjectivity). Later on in this chapter, we shall focus on different research studies in more depth to develop a greater understanding of methodology.

Where researchers work at gaining objective data, it is because their goal is to establish knowledge about human behaviour and experience which would be true for anybody who shares similar characteristics (such as age or gender) doing that action or having that experience in the same circumstances. In addition, these researchers use methods that should yield the same results whoever the researcher is. Because of this, researchers who work in the scientific tradition aim to formulate statements or laws about human experience and behaviour, often of cause and effect, which are generalisable. The focus of this type of research is generally on collecting large amounts of data from a number of people and analysing these data statistically in ways which will identify their common features and/or the differences between the groups studied. This is referred to as the scientific tradition and researchers in this tradition use quantitative methods, often conducting experiments but also using questionnaire and observational studies.

In contrast, where researchers work at gaining subjective data, it is because they aim to build knowledge which is based on an understanding of how people construct, perceive and exchange meanings which then guide, and can thus explain the way they act and make sense of the world around them. Hence, their overall aim is to explore and understand subjectivity – that is, personal experience and meanings. This is called the hermeneutic tradition and researchers draw on a range of qualitative methods, including discourse analysis and other meaning and language-based methods.

Since objective and subjective approaches to psychological research have such different goals, researchers in these two traditions sometimes engage in heated debate about how best to investigate psychological issues. However, as you saw in Book 1, Chapter 1, and will encounter again in later chapters, experimental methods (such as those used to examine Social Identity Theory) and hermeneutic methods (such as those used in social constructionist perspectives) have *both* contributed to our understanding of particular psychological phenomena (such as identities). Many psychologists, although not all, feel that both objective and subjective approaches contribute to psychological understandings. For example, some psychologists who use experiments now also interview their research participants or record what they have to say about the research topic. The two approaches are summarised in Box 1.1.

### 1.1 Two broad approaches to research

#### What is the goal of the research?

*Seeking objectivity.* To explain using general statements or laws, often of cause and effect. In order to have a *general* statement or law in psychology, everyone must agree on what is being said, everyone must 'see' the same things, and definitions must be definite. One way to achieve this kind of clarity and consensus is to *measure and use numbers* – which everyone can agree on. So this type of research primarily makes use of quantitative methods to try to ensure objectivity.

*Exploring subjectivity.* To explore meanings – sometimes in relation to individuals and sometimes in relation to the ways that language creates meaning. Here, there is no attempt to be objective in the strict sense, because it is subjectivity and meanings that are at the heart of what is being studied. However, interpretations and results will always be embedded into theory, must be argued carefully and need to relate explicitly to the data collected in order to form plausible interpretations that can be shared by a research community. This is called the hermeneutic approach, and it uses qualitative methods.

## Activity 1.2

As you have seen, one important distinction in psychological methods is between research which seeks to make generalisable claims and research which seeks to understand people in more depth. Imagine that you have been asked to carry out research into the experiences of OU students studying *Exploring Psychology*. Spend a few moments thinking about how you might carry out the research. What type of data would you wish to collect? How might you collect the data? Think

**about the different ways in which you might carry out the research from either an objective or a subjective perspective. What would be the strengths and weaknesses of each approach?**

### Comment

You may have considered a number of different ways of carrying out such research. Perhaps you considered conducting an interview with a group of students at one of your tutorials, where you would allow them to speak freely about their experiences – hence you would use a qualitative method. Alternatively, you might have thought about posting a questionnaire to an online discussion group, message board or forum, asking students to click on 'agree' or 'disagree' to a list of statements about their student experience – hence you would use a quantitative method. There are many other possibilities that you could have considered – too many for us to give you a definitive list here – and this reflects the diversity of methods within psychology.

Although there are considerable differences between quantitative and qualitative research (these will be explored in detail in the next section), it is important to remember that to conduct either successfully requires considerable skill and knowledge on the part of the researcher. In addition, both must be conducted with care and thoroughness. Just because research is not conducted in a laboratory and does not involve analysis of numbers and the pursuit of objectivity, it does *not* follow that the standards adopted by the researcher in approaching their study are any less rigorous.

Before we examine the differences between quantitative and qualitative research, it is worth mentioning one more similarity that the two share. Regardless of whether it is quantitative or qualitative, research must involve data. As you saw in Table 1.1, data can take many different forms, such as scores on a test or a dialogue between two people, but all data will be based (in broad terms) on something that a researcher has seen, heard or otherwise sensed. For example, a researcher in a laboratory experiment may see the words recalled and written down by a participant, or the researcher in an interview study may hear the words spoken by the participant. This reliance on what can be 'sensed' is referred to as the empirical approach, and empirical evidence is that which is based on some form of experience – such as that gained through experimentation, observation, surveying or interviewing. Empirical evidence also includes material data gained from technological apparatus which 'senses' some aspect, usually physiological, of the participant. This would include data gained from imaging technology, such as MRI and PET scans, and also from measuring such things as heart rate or blood pressure.

The definition of the empirical approach is therefore quite encompassing and you may feel as if *all* research must be empirical. However, there are ways of researching that are not based on empirical data, and these would include attempting to explain phenomena solely through reasoning and theorising.

### Summary Section 2

- Epistemology is the understanding of broad frameworks that are central to all stages of the cycle of enquiry. They establish the methodology to be used, which is central to decisions about which methods are used and the type of data to be collected.
- Ideas about the overall rationale of the research process, research methods, and types of data form the basics of methodology.
- Different methods will be chosen depending on whether the goal is to collect objective or subjective data.
- Researchers who follow a scientific tradition collect objective data and aim to make generalisable claims, often about cause and effect. By way of contrast, researchers who work in the hermeneutic tradition collect subjective data and aim to understand meanings and particular people in depth.

# 3 Seeking objectivity

## 3.1 Features of objective data

When psychologists adopt an objective approach, their data are usually defined in some way. For example, psychologists seeking objectivity usually collect both behavioural and material data. Behavioural data are concerned with measures such as responses – for example, how quickly people can distinguish between two stimuli presented very briefly on a screen, or how accurately they can remember a list of words. The data produced in these examples would be response times and number of words remembered. Material data are concerned with measuring, for example, electrical activity in a particular region of the brain or the amount of sweat produced while completing a task.

The data collected in these behavioural and material examples are agreed measures, in that when researchers collect the data they *already know* the format of what they are collecting. Because there are agreed measures, what they 'find' doesn't have to be negotiated with other researchers (or with the participants), because they all 'see' the same thing – the same computer record of brain activity, the same stopwatch record, the same number of words remembered. Such approaches use an outsider viewpoint with the aim of allowing measures to be agreed between researchers – and so making it possible to be objective.

Another important feature of these types of data is that they are almost always *quantitative*, in that there is a quantity that can be measured. The number of words, amount of time, volume of sweat are all measurable quantities. They have values that can vary, and so are known as variables. You will find that experiments are the main method used in quantitative research, but behaviours can also be studied using other methods, such as observation and questionnaires, and correlational studies can also be conducted, which you will read about in Book 1, Chapter 5, 'The individual differences approach to personality', and in the next chapter of this book.

## 3.2 Measuring people: the research goals of those who seek objectivity

Research that focuses on objectivity has the goal of generalisation. It aims to establish general laws or statements which apply widely across participants and across different, specified conditions.

Insofar as the aim of this type of research is to describe and explain what exists in the world in as accurate a way as possible, you can see that within this tradition it is extremely important that researchers strive for objectivity. The processes of research – design of studies, the type of data to be collected and the collection of those data – must all be as objective as possible. Also, as another part of 'being objective', researchers attempt to remove their personal or cultural values, preconceptions and prejudices from the research process. There are well-established techniques for helping researchers to maximise objectivity. For example, concepts, theories and hypotheses (statements of what the researcher expects the results of the study to be) need to be stated in terms that are very clearly defined. All the researchers involved have to agree how to record the data. This may seem a simple matter. However, it is often difficult to record even the simplest human behaviour accurately and consistently.

### Activity 1.3

Some psychologists have studied smiling in social interactions. Think about how you would define a smile so that other people would always record a particular expression as a smile. Spend no more than two minutes jotting down the characteristics you would use to record a 'smile' reliably.

### Comment

If a smile is defined as a stretching of the mouth sideways, then this can be applied to a range of facial expressions that most of us could reasonably agree to be a smile. But when does a smile shade into a grin or a laugh? How fleeting can an expression be and still count as a smile? Can we reliably distinguish a grimace or a leer from all smiles? Can we agree on what constitutes a smile with people from other cultures? Researchers might well perceive smiles to be different in friendliness, genuineness or intensity, but decide that all these can be treated as *equivalent* smiles for the purposes of a particular study and the 'smiles' can then be counted. However, the researchers are likely to have to practise to make sure that they are recording the same thing in the same ways.

Some of these problems are overcome by focusing on behaviours that are measured on standard instruments where there is no room for disagreement, such as number of words remembered or number of points allocated – as in Tajfel and colleagues' experiment on social categorisation (see Book 1, Chapter 1, Section 4.1). A particular instance is worked through in Box 1.2.

### 1.2 An example of seeking objectivity in research: the 'social categorisation' experiment

You may recall the classic 'social categorisation' experiment from Book 1, Chapter 1 (Section 4.1, Box 1.4). This was carried out by Tajfel *et al.* (1971) in Bristol, with 14- and 15-year-old schoolboys as participants. The experiment demonstrates how the use of an agreed measure can help to produce objectivity in the research process. Tajfel and his colleagues wanted to find the answer to the question of whether being a member of a group is enough in itself to promote favouring of the 'ingroup' and hostility against the 'outgroup'. Since it is difficult to gain a clear and generalisable answer to this question from studying social groups in everyday life, they devised a laboratory experiment.

Conducting such a study in a laboratory requires some creativity in working out how intergroup discrimination can be measured (that is, operationalised) and how researchers can demonstrate that any discrimination they find is related to group membership and nothing else. Tajfel and his colleagues decided that they would measure 'favouring the ingroup' by seeing how many points the boys would allocate to someone they were told belonged to their group and to someone they were told belonged to the other group. The number of points allocated is an objective measure in that all the researchers (and anybody who reads their work) can agree that two points is more than one point and can recognise which group is allocated more points. The finding was that boys allocated more points to the ingroup than the outgroup, and statistical analysis showed that the favouritism to the ingroup was unlikely to have occurred by chance. Because they used objective measures, Tajfel and his colleagues were able to generalise their findings (i.e. to formulate a general statement about group processes) rather than interpreting them as only relevant to a particular boy.

When designing studies, or even just reading about them, it is important to consider the details of the method(s) used. In interpreting the findings of Tajfel *et al.*'s study (1971), the *random allocation* of the boys to the different groups and the way the groups were presented to the participants were both important. Whilst the boys believed that they had been allocated on the basis of artistic taste, their allocation to groups was in fact entirely random and unrelated to their artistic preferences. Tajfel *et al.* could conclude that such allocation to a group was enough to produce ingroup favouritism, as there was no real difference between the members of each group. As you read more about the experimental method in psychology you will soon realise the importance of randomly allocating participants to different groups or conditions. For the moment, let's look more closely at the procedures that Tajfel *et al.* put in place.

In writing about their research Tajfel *et al.* listed six criteria that they felt were important in artificially creating the 'minimal groups' used in their social categorisation study. These criteria are summarised below:

1. There should be no interaction between the participants, either in the ingroup or outgroup or between the groups.
2. The anonymity of group membership should be preserved.
3. There should be no instrumental or rational link between the criteria for intergroup categorisation and the nature of the ingroup and out-group responses requested from the participants.
4. The responses given by the participants should not have any useful or practical value to them as individuals.
5. A strategy of responding in terms of favouring the ingroup which is also detrimental to the outgroup should be in competition with a strategy based on more 'rational' principles, such as obtaining maximum benefit for all.
6. The responses given by the participants should be made as important as possible to them. The responses should consist of real decisions about the concrete distribution of rewards and/or penalties to others, i.e. the response should not be evaluative.

*(Adapted from Tajfel* et al. *(1971, pp. 153–4))*

You may wish to reflect on each of these criteria in turn and consider why it was important in the creation of the 'minimal groups'. Here, though, we are going to focus on point number (3): that there should be no instrumental or rational link between the criteria for intergroup categorisation and the responses requested from the groups. So how did Tajfel *et al.* (1971) suggest to the boys that they were being allocated to groups in a meaningful way, whilst actually allocating them randomly? In Chapter 1 of Book 1 you were told that the boys had been informed that they had been allocated to each group on the basis of whether they preferred the paintings of Klee or Kandinsky. In reality, the procedure was more complex than this. If you are unfamiliar with the work of Klee and Kandinsky, it might be worth searching for these artists on the internet to look at some of their art. Relevant here is that both artists adopt an abstract style of painting (i.e. they use patterns, colours and shapes rather than paint actual scenes or recognisable objects).

Tajfel *et al.* (1971) selected twelve coloured slides: six showing reproductions of paintings by Klee and six by Kandinsky. A point to note is that one criterion for the selection of the paintings was that the signature of the artist should not be visible on the paintings. The names of the artists were written on the blackboard and the boys informed that they would be asked to express their preference between the paintings of 'two foreign modern painters, Klee and Kandinsky'. The boys were then shown the paintings in twelve successive pairs and after each pair the boys had to tick a box to indicate their preference. The pairs of paintings were shown in different combinations and, indeed, some of the combinations consisted of two reproductions by the same painter. At no time were the boys told whether the reproduction paintings were by Klee or Kandinsky. The boys were then assigned randomly to the 'group preferring Klee' and the 'group preferring Kandinsky'.

Although the allocation of the boys to each of the groups was entirely random, the procedure that Tajfel *et al.* (1971) used to convince the boys that their assignment to groups was based on something that they had 'in common' with each other and that was 'different' to the other group was quite complex. However, note that there was still no instrumental or rational link between the groups that the boys thought they belonged to (Klee or Kandinsky) and the responses that they were required to give in terms of the points awarded to each group. Their apparent differences in aesthetic preference should not have been a rational criterion for favouring one group over another – as might have been the case if the groups were divided up along existing social categories with meaning for the boys (e.g. supporters of particular football teams). In addition, as the boys never awarded themselves points or shared ingroup points, Tajfel *et al.*'s design also meets their fourth criterion listed above: that there should be no 'utilitarian value' to each participant when responding. Put simply, there was nothing of practical value to be gained by a 'Klee' boy giving another 'Klee' boy more points, or a 'Kandinsky' boy fewer points. Without considering these factors right from

**the start, in the design of their study, Tajfel *et al.* would not have been able to make the conclusions that they did based on their data. It is therefore crucial to give careful consideration to your methods throughout the research process, and, as you will see, this is just as true in qualitative as it is in quantitative research.**

One of the advantages of objectivity is that it provides a means for everyone – researchers, participants and the public at large – to agree with what they 'see' because it is an accurate version of what is actually there (it is worth noting that this 'advantage' would be contested by many qualitative researchers). It also allows other researchers to attempt to replicate the studies conducted by previous researchers, which is a key technique for determining whether the results obtained were valid. For example, suppose that a researcher found that more information about a staged crime could be obtained by asking participants to recall starting at the end and working backwards through what happened, rather than recalling events in the order in which they occurred. If the researcher took the results of this experiment to the police and recommended that they change the way they interview witnesses, it would be reasonable for the police to expect the academic community to attempt to replicate this finding before they changed their interviewing practice. This is because a single study can never provide compelling evidence by itself: the researcher may have made a mistake in analysing the data; the measurement used may have been inaccurate; the people who participated in the study may not have been a representative sample; or there may have been something unusual about the particular experimental setting (e.g. the nature of the staged crime). Indeed, there are any number of factors which could mean that the results obtained from just one study should not be taken at face value. Instead, it is necessary for the study to be replicated before the results should be relied upon. The need for replicability is why it is so important for researchers to record and report the *precise* procedure they used in their study extremely carefully, as the details given in their research report must be sufficient to allow other researchers to carry out the same study using exactly the same methods. (We will emphasise this point again when providing guidance on writing up your own experimental project in Chapter 7 of this book.)

However, in practice, objectivity in science (and especially in psychology) is often reached through negotiation. For example, you saw earlier that psychology researchers may have to negotiate, test and agree in advance what will be counted as a 'smile', since smiling is a behaviour which will take slightly different forms for different people and may last for only brief moments. Other types of data can be more truly objective. For example, when response times are recorded as data there is less of a problem since everyone can agree that the time recorded on a reliable watch or a computer is an accurate measure.

## 3.3 The need for statistics

We have mentioned previously that much of quantitative research sets out to explain psychological phenomena in terms of general laws, for example explaining how people can attend to two things at once or how children remember words. This means that in these two examples the population we are interested in are people or children. Researchers are not in a position to conduct their research on *all* people or *all* children, so they collect data from a small subset (called a sample) of the population they are interested in. They seek to generalise the findings from the sample to the population from which they were drawn.

Obviously it is extraordinarily unlikely that researchers will be in a position where they could test the entire population they are interested in and indeed the only time this tends to happen is when studying clinical populations with a rare disorder. Not being able to test an entire population leads to two issues that researchers must overcome. The first is generalisability and the second is determining whether any effects discovered are 'real' or not.

Generalisability is important if we want the results of a study to be relevant to the entire population we are interested in, rather than limit our conclusions to the sample of people in the study. Just as it is usually not possible to test the entire population of interest, it is also not possible to define the key characteristics of this population with any accuracy. This means it is necessary to take a *random* sample of the population. If the sample is not selected randomly, then the researcher may be introducing a form of bias into the selection and it will not be possible to generalise. For example, quantitative psychological research has often been criticised for not sampling randomly from the general population, but instead only sampling from undergraduate psychology students. Strictly speaking, this means that the results of any statistical tests conducted should not be generalised beyond the population of psychology students.

One way of helping to ensure that the results of a study can be generalised is to have a large sample, as including more participants in the research will tend to make the sample more representative. However, simply using 200 psychology students rather than 30 does not overcome the criticisms about generalisability levelled at a lot of experimental psychology research, and it is important to pay close attention to who the participants were, when reading research papers.

The issue of generalisability extends beyond having a representative sample, as it is also important that other factors do not prevent the results from being generalised. Perhaps the most important of these factors is the 'situation' used in the research, such as where the study takes place and what the participants are asked to do. To illustrate this issue, ask yourself the following question: 'Would I be happy being flown in a plane by a pilot that had only ever practised in a flight simulator?' Unless you have a particularly strong trust in technology, the answer is probably 'No' (or something stronger in tone but equivalent in meaning!). The equivalent in psychology is to ask the question, 'Can experiments conducted in a laboratory using artificial stimuli ever truly represent situations from the *real* world?' For the results of a study to be relevant and applicable to the 'real' world, the situation used in the research must have ecological validity (this has nothing to do with whether it is legitimate to save endangered species!). This means that the physical space, stimuli and task used in a study must match as closely as possible the real-world experience that is being modelled. In other words, if you are going to study pilot behaviour using a flight simulator, it had better be a *very* realistic flight simulator indeed (including weather fluctuations, unanticipated turbulence, co-pilots suffering from food poisoning, unexpected technical problems with the aircraft, and irate and nauseous passengers complaining about the fish dinner which you are just beginning to wish you hadn't eaten).

The second issue which arises from studying only a sample, rather than the entire population, is that we have to work out whether the results of a study are 'real', or simply down to choosing a poor sample. If we could study every person in the population, we could be certain that any differences we found were real differences. However, if we can only include a sample of the population in our study, it is quite possible that any differences we find are down to the specific sample. For example, if we found that, on average, 10-year-old children responded more quickly to a stimulus than did 5-year-old children in a study that had tested the response times of *every* 5- and 10-year-old child, we could safely conclude that 10-year-olds had quicker response times than 5-year-olds. But what if we could only test twenty children of either age? What we need is some means of using the data obtained from the sample of children to make estimates about what the data would look like if we could test the entire population. In addition, we also need some means of determining whether the difference between our two samples (such as a sample of 5-year-olds and 10-year-olds) is a difference that would occur if we *could* test the entire population or one that is down to the specific samples we have selected. As we shall see in later chapters, researchers use statistics both to make estimates about populations and to determine whether differences between samples are 'real' or a product of the specific samples chosen. Statistics are therefore an important and integral component of research which seeks objectivity.

## 3.4 Thinking about methods

Psychologists adopting a quantitative approach place great importance on objective data that can be measured or counted. In the Tajfel et al. study described in Box 1.2, for instance, the researchers counted the number of points that the boys awarded to each group. Throughout Book 1 you will encounter many more experimental studies which emphasise measurement and (in various ways) counting. For example, Chapter 3 'Three approaches to learning' provides examples of experiments carried out with animals and humans to help understand behaviour and learning, and Chapter 6 'Perception and attention' demonstrates how researchers have used the experimental approach to investigate how people perceive and attend to their surroundings. When you read about them you will see that the experiments are very different, since they are asking different questions, but they do have an important feature in common: in all these studies the researchers tried to minimise subjectivity and maximise objectivity.

### Summary Section 3

- Psychologists who seek objectivity usually collect behavioural or material data and use an outsider viewpoint.
- Objective data are usually defined in advance and then measured or counted: this is quantitative research. The data are quantified and the analysis is usually statistical.
- Research that focuses on objectivity is research that has the goal of generalisation.
- The experiment is the method most commonly used by those seeking objectivity.

# 4 Exploring subjectivity

## 4.1 Features of subjective data

When inner experiences are to be studied, and also when symbolic data are the focus, what is being studied are people's social interactions and subjectivity – their personal experiences and meaning. Data collection is not strictly standardised and data are not measured. Instead, data are explored for their *qualitative* nature (e.g. qualities of people's experiences or thoughts) and the data collected are usually descriptive.

## 4.2 Understanding people: the research goals of those who explore subjectivity

Those who explore subjectivity start with insider viewpoints. This means that the researcher is trying to capture (as far as this is possible) the experience of participants in the research. So, at the level of the raw data, there will be as many variations in the data as there are participants – because each participant has their own meanings. These meanings are constructed from the participant's personal experience, their own unique view of the world, and their psychic reality (i.e. their own perception of what is real or true). Take again the example of a smile. A researcher studying the place of smiles in communication might need to observe and note the slightly different *meanings* of smiles in the contexts in which they occur – a seductive smile, a friendly smile, a sarcastic smile, and so on. This aim would be quite different from the aim described in Section 3.2, Activity 1.3. In the hermeneutic tradition the aim would *not* be to find ways to make all smiles 'equivalent'. In contrast, describing the *differences* between smiles, and their meanings within a certain context and for certain individuals, would be the goal (in this case the *number* of smiles would be completely irrelevant, so the quantitative approach of counting 'smiles' would be inappropriate).

Researchers who are interested in capturing the subjective nature of psychological phenomena attempt to gain access to the meanings attached to these phenomena. To do so, often they set about becoming immersed in particular contexts or social situations with particular groups. People are seen as social beings and as creating, and being created by, their understandings of the world around them. This expresses the ontological assumptions that underpin perspectives that explore subjectivity.

Generally speaking, ontology is the theory of existence. In the context of psychology, ontology refers to the nature of existence as a human being, i.e. what constitutes a person. We shall look at ontology further in Chapter 8 of this book. The researcher is responsible for using methods and analyses that explore the meanings people understand, create and express. In Book 1, Chapter 1, you saw examples of how social constructionists study subjectivity through social constructions of meanings, using language as their data. This approach is discussed in Box 1.3.

### 1.3 An example of exploring subjectivity: research from a social constructionist perspective

Section 5 of Chapter 1 in Book 1 introduced the notion of social construction and discussed what it means in relation to identity. You may remember that social constructionists conceptualise identities as being socially constructed (as opposed to occurring naturally) as we go about our everyday lives. As a result, they are relational, constructed in language and affected by the discourses available within society. Identities are viewed as shifting over time and from context to context. They are therefore provisional, dynamic, and historically and culturally specific, rather than fixed. In addition, they are multiple, de-centred and changeable, rather than singular, centred and stable.

It follows from this that research done from a social constructionist perspective aims to understand social processes in the particular context in which they arise at a particular time for a particular person. Rather than attempting to generalise the findings of research from an objective, outsider viewpoint, the focus is instead on subjective, insider accounts. Therefore, it is not surprising that social constructionists see the analysis of language as a crucial research tool.

Section 5 of Chapter 1 in Book 1 demonstrates this focus on language and meanings in three ways common to social constructionist research. First, it considers how the choice of particular, familiar terms constructs the way in which we see the world (using the example of 'terrorist' versus 'freedom fighter'). This demonstrates how subjective accounts are produced by social understandings. Second, the section pays close attention to Kenneth Gergen's brief autobiographical account of his switch from using pens to computers. It uses his subjective account to analyse what he has to say and in doing so demonstrates that identities are constructed (rather than naturally occurring), embedded in social relations, change over time, are a resource we can use in our interactions and are produced in the stories we tell about ourselves. Finally, the section uses analysis conducted by Stuart Hall to explore the ways in which identities are multiple, de-centred (rather than unitary and core) and involve power relations. In this third example, it was Hall's subjective account of other people's subjectivity that was analysed, rather than the other people's own subjective accounts.

The final section (Section 6, Chapter 1, Book 1) then applies all three kinds of subjective analysis of language to a consideration of identity and disability. It thus discusses the power of language to construct disability in negative ways and to construct 'disabling environments', and it uses first person accounts from people with various physical impairments, as well as discussing the analysis from a research project on children and disability.

It is by conducting qualitative analysis of these sorts of subjective accounts that it is possible to demonstrate that identities are context-bounded, relational, change over time and are produced in language for particular people.

In examples such as those in Box 1.3, researchers choose to focus as far as possible on the subjectivity of the data – its meaning for the individual concerned. They are, in effect, trying to see and think about the data 'through the eyes of the other'. Nonetheless, many researchers who focus on subjectivity and study meanings *also* want to examine processes and make comparisons between groups of people. In such cases, the inner experiences of a participant cannot be compared with others unless and until the researcher does something with the data to *negotiate and create equivalencies*. As we shall see shortly, an example of this can be found in The Twenty Statements Test where personal responses to the question '*Who am I?*' were collected and sorted into *categories* by the researchers, enabling generalisations to be made about the most frequent categories used by people. Another similar example is semi-structured interviews, where individuals are asked to talk about or 'narrate' particular domains of inner experience (see Book 1, Chapter 1, Box 1.2). The material that is recorded and transcribed is rich in diversity and meanings but, after the event, these data can be *simplified* by identifying 'themes'. The researcher sorts the participants' free responses into categories (e.g. themes such as 'connectedness' or 'separation' in a study of the impact of early relationships on identity). This process requires the researcher to decide which of the participants' ideas and statements (insider viewpoint) can be treated as equivalent: sufficiently the same to belong in the same category, where the categories and the search for equivalencies or themes come from the researcher (outsider viewpoint).

Qualitative research is not associated with a single method. Tesch (1990) identified twenty-six varieties of qualitative methods in the *hermeneutic* tradition (and we will explore three commonly used methods in Box 1.4).

The methods in the hermeneutic tradition, and indeed the hermeneutic tradition itself, are not limited to psychological research and in fact have been more traditionally associated with other social science disciplines such as sociology and anthropology.

As noted earlier, before the inner experiences of a participant can be compared to others, the researcher must negotiate and create equivalencies. An excellent example of this can be seen in Box 1.1 Featured Method The Twenty Statements Test (see Book 1, Chapter 1, Section 1.2).

In The Twenty Statements Test the researcher asks each participant to respond freely to the question '*Who am I?*' Although the data are generated by the research participants themselves (and so are essentially insider data), the very process of collecting and interpreting the data inevitably introduces an outsider viewpoint. For example, in The Twenty Statements Test, the questions generated personal responses, but researchers collected these and sorted them into what they (the researchers) deemed to be equivalent categories. This enables some transferability of findings, for example about which are the most frequent categories used by people.

## Activity 1.4

Here are a set of responses to The Twenty Statements Test given by young people with ages ranging from 10 to 18 years. Spend about ten to fifteen minutes identifying types of categories mentioned and sorting the responses into these categories. Can you identify any broad differences in the self descriptions of younger children and adolescents?

*I am a boy. I have blue eyes. I have brown hair. I love* 'The Simpsons'. *I don't like maths. I am a good swimmer. I am friends with Jack. I am tall for my age. I am friendly. I am good at music. I love animals. I am 9 years old.*

*My name is *. I am a girl. I am 11 years old. I like English and science. I have brown eyes. I have long hair. I am best friends with Kimberley. I am sister to Katie. I am from Northern Ireland.*

*My name is *. I am 14. I am a Sagittarian. I am usually honest. I am taller than most girls in my class. I don't believe in God. I like The Red Hot Chilli Peppers. I don't like dance music. I am ambitious. I am sometimes talkative and sometimes quiet. I am a vegetarian. I am female. I am a human being. I'm not very pretty.*

*I am male. I am a brother. I am a psychology student. I am tired. I am a socialist. I work at Pizza Hut. I am permanently broke. I am an agnostic. I am sociable. I am me. I am a brother and a son. I am an individual. I am ambitious.*

## Comment

One category you may have noted was 'physical characteristics', which included the responses:

*I am a boy.*

*I am a girl.*

*I have blue eyes.*

*I have brown eyes.*

*I am tall for my age.*

*I am taller than most girls in my class.*

*I'm not very pretty.*

You are likely to have found that there are a range of categories which can be used to deal with self-descriptions. You may have also found that you altered or revised your categories as you went through the exercise, perhaps because the data did not seem to 'fit' the categories you were using. You may have found that some statements crossed categories or could be interpreted in different ways; for example, 'I'm not very pretty' could be categorised as a physical descriptor (like 'I have blue eyes'), as a peer-comparator (like 'I am taller') or as an emotional evaluation. This process of revising is a characteristic part of analysing qualitative data as you try to let the meaning emerge from the data rather than imposing your own preconceived ideas upon it.

You may also like to compare the categories you have devised with those of other researchers. The Twenty Statements Test was used by Montemayer and Eisen (1977) with 9- to 18-year-olds to gain insight into how they saw themselves at different ages (their 'self-concepts'). They found that descriptions could be placed in several different categories including reference to embodiment or appearance ('I have blue eyes'/'I am tall'), references to likes/dislikes ('I like maths/English'), to beliefs ('I don't believe in God'), social roles ('I am a student') or personality traits ('I am honest'). They argued that self-descriptions undergo a change from childhood to adolescence from those which are primarily physical to abstract qualities such as ideologies and beliefs. Older adolescents are also more likely to make reference to the social roles they fulfil. In an earlier study, Kuhn and McPartland (1954) found that, on average, children aged 7 years gave five answers relating to social roles whereas undergraduates gave an average of ten. Here the qualitative data obtained from The Twenty Statements Test had been transformed into quantitative form by counting the numbers of statements in each category. This allowed Kuhn and McPartland to make comparisons between the self-concepts of different age groups. However, whilst this transformation has the advantage of allowing numerical comparison, it loses some of the richness which is available when the data are in the original qualitative form.

As might be expected, *qualitative methods* are used to gather various forms of *qualitative data* that will then be subjected to *qualitative analysis*. However, unlike quantitative research approaches (which clearly map out distinct stages: of stating a hypothesis, designing a study, collecting data and analysing those data), qualitative research does not involve working through stages. Instead, the researcher may move back and forth between research questions, collecting and analysing data in an iterative process. Take the following example: a researcher wants to understand how childhood experiences have affected participants' lives and devises a series of interview questions to ask them. As the interview progresses, the participants raise a variety of issues and points that are personally important but which were not considered by the interviewer at the outset of the research. For instance, the interviewer might have devised a list of issues around early childhood to explore with a participant, but during the interview it may become apparent that adolescent experiences are more important for this participant. The open nature of the interview provides a space and place for participants to introduce issues and experiences that *they* see as crucial to an understanding of *their* life story. Here the interview questions (method) are informed by the experiences talked about by the participant (emergent data), which then raise further points to explore (a refining of the research question and method). This refining of the method (e.g. asking additional questions) can then be applied to subsequent interviews to explore the emergent findings with other participants. This highlights the iterative nature of much qualitative research.

Let us now look at some of the ways in which qualitative researchers analyse the material they collect (see Box 1.4). We will return to this in detail in Chapter 8 of this book, but for now it would be useful to gain some general understanding of qualitative analysis.

## 1.4 Qualitative analysis

In experimental research projects, precise statements called hypotheses are formulated before the data collection begins. In qualitative research, one or more research questions are posed that may later be added to and/or developed further from the material collected and/or emergent findings. Given the complexity and diversity of qualitative methods and analyses, it would be impossible to present a comprehensive overview here, but for illustration we shall outline three methods and three ways of analysing particular types of qualitative data:

### Qualitative analysis of observation

The method of observation can involve being a participant in a particular group or community, or it can involve covert or overt non-participant observation (where the observer is not a member of the group or culture they are observing). Observation is potentially an extremely rich and complex source of data, and some form of record is made (for example field notes or a video or audio record) for later analysis.

Observational field notes are diverse in format. Their precise content is determined by the observational focus. For example, a researcher might use observation to explore eye contact in interactions from a study on helping behaviour in public contexts. The observations might vary from observations of an individual to group observations where the researcher is a participant observer.

The notes made during the observation are descriptions of what is observed but which need subsequently to be carefully *analysed* and *interpreted* by the researcher. For example, is a particular smile an indicator of familiarity, a 'put down' or a sexual 'come on'? The information obtained may be analysed into common themes or patterns observed. Schatzman and Strauss (1973, pp. 99–103) identify three types of note taking: 'observational notes' (the who, what, when, where and how of human activity); 'theoretical notes' (interpretations, inferences, hypotheses and conjectures); and 'methodological notes' (the timing, sequencing, stationing, stage setting and manoeuvring of research). They state that the 'model researcher starts analysing very early on in the research process' so that initial analyses can help to refine later observations (p. 110). This is, of course, related to the issue of emergent findings discussed earlier.

### Qualitative analysis of interview material

Interviews can be conducted with individuals, with focus groups, or as part of clinical practice. They can be structured (around a set of questions set by the interviewer), semi-structured (where the interviewer has specific topics they want to explore, but is free to do so in any order and with the exact questions free to vary in the way they are worded) or open interviews (with both questions and answers emerging primarily from the participant as the researcher exclusively wants to explore the participant's reality and therefore does not want to impose a structure – for this reason the term 'unstructured interviews' is often used).

Interview material is perhaps the most commonly collected form of subjective data because interviews are the most commonly used qualitative method. If interview accounts are to be analysed qualitatively they are usually transcribed (i.e. translated from their recorded form into a full written account of what both the interviewer and the participant have said). The data are then explored in detail often by reading and rereading the transcript and/or listening to the interview repeatedly. The analysis undertaken may be thematic analysis (which is the subject of Chapter 9 of this book, and which you will have a chance to try in your qualitative methods project later in the course), discourse analysis, narrative analysis or grounded theory. Qualitative approaches aim to base analysis on the participant's experience, so the researcher needs to become familiar with the account, aiming to step inside the participant's world, to see things from his or her perspective. Patterns of meaning then emerge from the data, but interpretations of the data are shaped by the researcher. For example, an interview on the subject of bereavement might produce issues such as coping, denial, coming to terms with new identities. However, using the participant's own words, ideas such as anger, loss, rejection or blame might be elicited. The precise meanings surface from the participant's account.

### *Discourse analysis of newspaper articles*

Discourse analysis is both a method and a form of analysis. Discourse is the term given to spoken and written communication, and discourse analysis involves analysing these forms of communication. Discourse analysts choose to study naturally occurring talk and text from conversations, newspaper articles, magazines, policy documents or political speeches. They take the view that language is functional: it is used by people to achieve certain things, such as persuading or justifying. The aim of discourse analysis is to establish how people construct and present accounts in language.

As explained earlier, a key principle of the hermeneutic tradition is the constructive role of language. Discourse analysis encourages us to consider and reconsider how ideas in the world are constructed through the use of language. For example, we might want to review how people with disabilities are talked about in newspaper articles. If we were to find that some language use tended to centre around the notion of the 'sufferer with disabilities', then this would raise questions about how dominant ideas (i.e. discourses) connected with disability tend to construct a version of disability as something that is related to suffering. We might then want to question *why* such ideas dominate our society. We might find, for example, that people with disabilities do not feel that they 'suffer' as a result of their impairments but that what we had initially interpreted as 'suffering' (as represented in the media) reflects a society where 'disabled people' are not sufficiently considered in ergonomic design, and so are impeded in going about their normal lives. We might also look for alternative ideas about disability; for example, representations of disability as a social problem caused by a society that excludes people with impairments, rather than a personal problem of the person with the impairment. There are many levels at which we could examine this issue, and analysis in this example views language as more than just a medium for communication: language is seen as a key constructive facet of social life (Potter and Wetherell, 1987).

From Box 1.4, and indeed the discussion throughout this section, it should be apparent that qualitative methodology can involve a range of methods and ways of analysing data. We shall finish this section by moving from the bird's-eye view of research based on exploring epistemology and methodology with which we started, to look in more detail at a qualitative study involving discourse analysis of an extract from the BBC *Panorama* interview, broadcast on 20 November 1995, between the journalist, Martin Bashir and the late Diana, Princess of Wales. They have been talking about her post-natal depression following the birth of Prince William. The analysis on pages 30 and 31, prepared by Elizabeth Stokoe from Loughborough University, shows the rigour and complexity involved in conducting discourse analysis. The data have been transcribed using a particular system commonly used by discourse analysts.

### Key to transcript notation

Pauses are timed to the nearest tenth of a second. Underlining means emphasis; colons mean elongation or stretched sound; up and down arrows indicate marked pitch shifts. Breathiness is indicated by 'h's in parentheses, in and out-breaths are represented by rows of 'hhh's. Talk that is noticeably quieter is enclosed by degree signs (°); more degree signs means talk is whispered. Louder talk is written in capital letters. Closing or 'final' intonation is indicated by a full stop; continuing intonation by a comma; and questioning intonation by a question mark. Speeded-up talk is enclosed by '> <' signs. Equals signs means that the 'units' of the turn are 'rushed through' as a way of keeping the conversational floor. 'Cut off' sounds are indicated by a dash.

As Stokoe points out, what we can see from this brief example is that while talk transcribed and analysed this way looks pretty complicated, the aim of analysis is to explicate what members of a culture understand about their interactions and construct as 'reality' – as displayed in the way they build and respond to each other's turns at talk. If you have ever had a conversation with someone – a friend, parent, partner, boss – and thought afterwards 'What did they mean?', 'Why did they say that?', 'I don't believe that's what really happened', 'Well, she would say that, wouldn't she?', you are already a kind of discourse analyst!

## 4.3 Thinking about methods

Psychologists who explore subjectivity have many different methods for carrying out research and, concomitantly, many different ways of analysing the data. The researcher is considered to have an impact on the data produced and the analyses done to a much greater extent within qualitative research than in quantitative research. For this reason, when you carry out your qualitative project later in the course, you will be asked to carry out a reflexive analysis exploring just this issue. This means standing back from the research itself in order to reflect on *your* role as the researcher, and the influences that you might have brought to your analysis and interpretation of the data. It is important to remember that qualitative researchers do not adopt the scientific method because they are interested in subjective, rather than objective, processes. However, the research process and the analysis of data within qualitative research must be as rigorous as that found within a quantitative approach. Exploring subjectivity does *not* mean that you can simply base your conclusions on your own opinions or personal views. You must be able to support your arguments and conclusions with evidence from your data.

### Summary Section 4

- Psychologists who work in the subjective tradition collect insider accounts and symbolic data using a range of qualitative methods.
- The goal of qualitative research is to explore and understand people's subjective experiences and meanings. The focus is frequently on the analysis of language. The focus on meaning and subjective experience in qualitative research make it part of the hermeneutic tradition.
- Some researchers who study subjectivities and meanings wish to make comparisons between groups and/or study processes. To permit this, some simplification of data is required. A common form of simplification involves finding categories or themes in the data.
- Qualitative research is frequently an iterative process, rather than consisting of discrete stages.

**Extract from BBC *Panorama*, broadcast on 20.11.95, between the journalist, Martin Bashir, and the late Diana, Princess of Wales. They have been talking about her post-natal depression following the birth of Prince William.**

```
B: WHAT effect: did the depression have on your ma:rriage.
      (1.8)
D: .pt well it gave everybody: hh a wonderful: (0.2) new la:bel.
   Hh is- Diana's:: unstable. (0.4) .hh an' Diana's: um (0.3)
   mentally imba:lanced. .hh an' unfortunately that seems to have
   STu:ck.=>on an' off.< over the years. ((smiles))
      (1.9)
B: Are you saying: (0.2) th't that label stuck within your
   marri:age,
      (0.9)
D: I think people u:sed it
      (1.2)
D: °An' it stuck.°
      (0.4)
D: °°Yes.°° ((nodding))
      (2.3)
B: According to:: (0.4)↓press reports (1.2) it was suggested th-
   that it was around this time (0.3) things became so difficult
   that you: (0.7) actually tried to injure your°self.°
      (0.5)
D: M(h)m.
      (0.5)
B: Is that tru:e,
D: >Mm<= Hhh↑When no one: (0.2) li:stens to you. or you fe:el no
   one's listenin' to you, .hh all sorts of things start to
   happen.=for instance you have so much pa:in inside yourself
   .hhh that you:. try an'- hurt yourself on the outside cos you
   want help. .hh but it's the wrong help you're asking for. .hh
   people see it as crying wolf: or attention seeking, .hh an'
   they think because you're in the me:dia all the time you've
```

1. Discourse analysts focus on how speakers and writers 'put together' or 'construct' their talk and texts to accomplish particular kinds of 'action'. In this extract, Bashir's first turn does 'questioning' and Diana's first turn does 'answering'. But Bashir and Diana could have built their turns in any number of different ways, using any number of different words and phrases. Discourse analysts ask questions like, "What action is being done here? Why has this wording been used? Why does this action happen here? What else could have happened? Are speakers direct or do they imply things? How are events and persons described? What does the use of one word/phrase rather than another imply? How are events, experiences, characters and so on produced as objective or subjective, 'natural', 'factual' or biased? How do speakers get to talk about things suited to their own agenda? How do speakers avoid appearing motivated or one-sided? What kind of stance do speakers take – first person or third person? Why do pauses occur where they do? Why are some words uttered with emphasis, and others whispered?"

2. Note how Bashir formulates his opening and follow-up questions, about the effect of Diana's post-natal depression. The activity of 'marriage' involves two parties: 'husband' and 'wife'. Diana (the 'wife') is present, and so Charles (the 'husband') is implied by the term. But neither Bashir nor Diana name Charles directly. Instead, Diana talks about "everybody" and "people", which allows the audience to infer that Charles called her 'unstable' and 'imbalanced', but without Diana saying so directly.

3. Discourse analysts pay attention to what look like tiny pauses and gaps within and between turns – they often indicate some 'trouble' in the interaction. So, for example, long gaps before Diana answers questions display some difficulty with them.

Diana's voice gets softer and softer as she talks about 'people' calling her 'unstable', which infuses her answer with evaluation – the 'labelling' done by 'people' is upsetting.

4. Bashir's question introduces a new topic. Notice the way he constructs and delivers his question about Diana's self-harming. First, the pauses indicate this is a tricky question to ask. Second, he doesn't ask it bluntly (e.g. "So, did you self-harm?"), but rather builds up slowly, recruiting 'press reports' as evidence – it is public interest, not Bashir's nosiness motivating the question. News and political interviewers often ask questions this way, voicing other people or reports to maintain a neutral 'footing' when posing critical points. Third, Bashir supplies a candidate account for Diana's behaviour – 'things became so difficult' – within his question, suggesting that self-harm was caused by external events rather than Diana's unstable personality. The question is therefore not so neutral – but sympathetically asked.

5. Diana's confirmation of self-harm is minimal ("mm" not "yes"), and she 'rushes past' this to begin the long account, apparently something she's happier to talk about than the visceral details of her behaviour. She talks in general ("you") not personal ("I") terms; so she depicts herself as understandable as an example of anyone in general, doing and reacting like anyone might normatively do – i.e., she is not *personally* accountable!

```
   got enough attention. =inverted commas. .hhh (0.3) but I was
   actually crying out cos I wanted to get b(h)etter. (0.4) in
   order to go forward and continue my duty and my role as: .hh
   (0.4) wife: mother: Princess of Wa:les, .HHH so:: I uh- yes I
   did. (0.3) inflict s- up-on myself. (0.7) I didn't li:ke
   myself.=I was asha:med because I couldn't- cope with the
   pre:ssures.
     (1.0)
B: Wha:t did you actually do.
     (0.7)
D: W(h)ell I j(h)st hu(h)rt my arms an' my l(h)egs,
     (0.7)
D: And: I .hh (0.2) work in environments now where I see s- women
   doing similar things. (0.4) and I'm able to .nh understand
   completely where they're co:ming from.
     (1.7)
B: What was your husband's reaction.
     (0.8)
B: To this,=when you: (.) began to injure yourself °in this
   way.°=
D: =↑Mm. .hh (0.3) well I didn't actually always do it in front
   of him. .hhhh um::: (0.8) but obviously anyone. (0.3) who
   loves someone would be very conce:rned about it.
     (1 6)
```

6. In the middle of her turn, Diana constructs a possible critical response to her self-harming - that she was 'attention seeking', quoting what other people might say about her having "enough attention.=inverted commas". This rhetorical contrast functions to 'inoculate' against such a criticism (Potter, 1996), and make a contrast with the 'actual' – 'real' and 'factual' – reasons for her actions and their consequences.

7. At the end of her lengthy account, Diana formulates its upshot – "so:: I uh- yes I did ..." – treating it as oriented to answering Bashir's previous question. So, instead of simply confirming the truth of the press reports' claim that she self-harmed, Diana uses the 'answer' slot that follows Bashir's question to do some further business – to give a context for her actions, to talk more broadly about them, but also avoid talking in a detailed way about the specifics of them. And note that she still has some trouble saying what she did: her admission starts and stops, sounds hesitant and abbreviated: "I did. (0.3) inflict s- up-on myself.".

8. Bashir asks a follow-up question that is more direct than his previous one – and requests 'actual' details about the behaviour which Diana has avoided in her previous account. After a pause, Diana answers very 'breathily'. But while her turn does the action of 'answering', its content is again quite vague, and includes none of the potentially gory aspects one might expect in an account of self-harm. So, for example, rather than use words like 'cut' or 'slash' she says "hu(h)rt" – a more general, less gruesome term. Precise selection of one word over another is crucial for what the speaker is doing!

9. As we saw earlier, Diana answers Bashir's questions in a way that allows her to follow a particular trajectory – so she answers questions about self-harm minimally and instead talks about how her experience entitles her to better understand other ordinary women and do her duties as "wife: mother: Princess of Wa:les".

10. Bashir's final question is about Charles's reaction to his wife's self-harm. Note that 'Charles' can be referred to in a number of different ways (e.g. 'Prince of Wales', 'husband', 'Charles', 'the Queen's son', 'farmer', 'environmentalist', 'sportsman' etc.) – so the fact that Bashir refers to him as "your husband" here makes his reaction in *this* rather than any other role relevant – 'husbands' have particular duties and obligations of care, love, and concern for 'wives'.

11. Diana does not respond immediately to Bashir's question, at the first point at which she could, so Bashir reformulates it. Diana's answer is formulated in general terms – "anyone" would be 'concerned'. While this could describe Charles's reaction, it noticeably does not include his name – instead we're left with the logical inference that if Charles doesn't love Diana, then he's not in the category of 'anyone' who would be concerned...'

# 5 Ethics

Ethics is one of the most important aspects of any form of research and should be considered in detail before embarking on any research project regardless of scope, scale or methodology. Ethical issues are enormously complex and inextricably linked with personal morals and wider societal values. You were introduced to ethics in psychology in the Introduction to Book 1.

### Activity 1.5

Descriptions of two psychological studies are provided below. For each study try to generate a list of any ethical issues you think might have been overlooked by the researcher.

*Study 1*

In this study the researcher was interested in determining whether the presence of a weapon affected eyewitness memory. As the researcher was currently teaching two undergraduate classes, they decided to stage an event in which a masked man ran into the classroom and stole a laptop. For the first class the masked man carried a combat knife, with which he threatened the researcher, while for the second class he was unarmed. To keep the situation realistic (i.e. to add ecological validity), neither class was told that the staged robbery would take place. The researcher was worried that the students from the first class might tell the second class that a robbery would occur, and that it would not be real, so the lecturer allowed the first class to continue believing that the event was real after the class had finished. The lecturer sent the students from the first class to another room to 'wait to be interviewed by the police' so that they could not tell the second class what had happened.

*Study 2*

In this study, two researchers were interested in exploring identity formation within criminal gangs in an inner city. Previous research on this topic had noted the reluctance of gang members to talk freely to researchers, so the researchers decided to approach a gang 'undercover' and not reveal their true identity. Using a hidden recorder they recorded gang conversations for several weeks, which they later transcribed and analysed. As they were worried about possible reprisals, they contacted the gang members before publishing a report of the research to guarantee that anything they had said would be treated as confidential.

Once you have made your two lists of ethical issues, put them to one side for a moment. We shall revisit them in the next activity, after we have looked further at ethical issues in research.

A fundamental tenet of ethically conducted research is that of showing respect for participants, and indeed the use of the word 'participant' is seen as being more respectful than the use of the word 'subject' that you will see in many twentieth-century psychology texts. In addition, by using the term 'participant' rather than 'subject' we are acknowledging that the people we gather data from are an active part of the research process.

You have seen that the British Psychological Society's (BPS) *Code of Ethics and Conduct* published in March 2006 is based on four ethical principles which make up the main areas of responsibility for practitioner and research psychologists (see Book 1, Introduction, Box 2). These are respect, competence, responsibility, and integrity. Each of these principles is described in a statement of values. All research, whether qualitative or quantitative, has to conform to ethical guidelines. To help researchers, the BPS has issued a supplementary paper called *Ethical Principles for Conducting Research with Human Participants*. In the rest of Section 5, as an illustration of the importance of reflecting on ethical issues, we shall concern ourselves with those which relate most directly to the treatment of research participants.

## 5.1 Informed consent

Psychologists conducting research are required to negotiate the terms of their research with their participants to ensure that the participants understand what is happening. The paper *Ethical Principles for Conducting Research with Human Participants* argues that all research should be thought about carefully in terms of the impact it might have on the participants. In order to protect the participants, the researcher should consider as far as possible the study from the participants' standpoint and should think carefully about potential risks to their physical health, psychological well-being, personal values and dignity. This means that the researcher should ask their participants from the start about factors which might lead to a risk of harm, including risks related to the participants' own personal circumstances.

Researchers should then ensure that their participants are given as much opportunity as possible to understand the nature, purpose and anticipated consequences of taking part in the research. (Specific guidance is offered regarding the issue of deception.) This issue of consent is not an easy one as it is not just a case of telling your participants what you are going to do and getting them to say yes or no. Informed consent requires that participants understand what they are really agreeing to, what will happen to the data and how they will be used.

All research has an aim and any participant who contributes to that research has a right to know what the aim is. It is therefore important that the researcher explains:

- what is being done
- why it is being done
- how it will be done
- how the data will be handled
- who will see the data
- how the final research will be presented
- who will have access to the research.

How a researcher achieves this should be given a great deal of consideration. It is usual to write a consent form so that the participant can indicate that the above points have been explained to them. The participant is asked to read and sign it, indicating that they understand and consent. Care should be taken to ensure that the form is written in clear and unambiguous language, avoiding technical jargon.

It should also be noted that consent does not simply take place at the start of the research process. Instead, it should be seen as an ongoing process in which the researcher should continue to negotiate with their participant (for example, by asking a participant for consent to use transcripts after they have been produced).

Gaining consent is also an important issue in observational research. When collecting observational data the researcher should restrict research which involves observing public behaviour to situations in which people being studied would reasonably expect to be observed by strangers.

## 5.2 Anonymity rather than confidentiality

Your participant has the right to expect that, should they so wish, their identity will not be revealed in the research write-up or to anyone else. However, you cannot promise them that the information will be *confidential*, because it is likely that a number of other people will see it. You can, however, promise them that it will be *anonymous*. Anonymity does not just mean leaving their name out. In qualitative research, for example, it may be that a participant could easily be identified by reference to the experiences discussed. If this is the case, the researcher should remove these clues prior to a third party seeing the data. If you cannot promise anonymity, consent for disclosure should be sought from the participant.

## 5.3 Right to withdraw from the research

As part of your wider duty to protect your participants, you should also inform them, from the first contact, that they are free to withdraw from the research and that this freedom is not affected by issues of payment or any other agreements made. In interviews, you should also make it clear that they do not have to answer questions put to them and you may decide together when you are negotiating consent that some areas or topics may be 'off limits'. This is important in interviewing, as the interview process may be more stressful than either of you had envisaged, or topics might come up which your participant had not intended to discuss, and they should feel free to stop if this is the case. They should also be free to withdraw their data from the research prior to or after analysis. Some (but not all) qualitative researchers believe that participants should be given the opportunity to read through the raw data that have been collected. It may be that they were not aware of what they revealed about themselves and, retrospectively, they do not want the information to be made public. As a researcher you must accept this no matter how inconvenient it is. Obviously, it is difficult for participants to withdraw from research: they may feel that they are letting the researcher down or making a fuss. The researcher needs to enable the participant to withdraw while reassuring them that they will suffer no adverse consequences from withdrawing.

## 5.4 Feedback and debriefing of research participants

Researchers have an obligation to debrief their participants at the end of their participation, which fulfils a number of important functions, including that it serves to identify if the participant has experienced any harm or discomfort during the research. It is also used to discuss with them the outcomes of the research and to answer questions they may have. Researchers need to be careful when discussing outcomes of the research with their participants, as they may be sensitive to what they perceive as evaluative or critical statements. In qualitative research it seems reasonable that participants should see the analysis so that they know how the researcher has interpreted their contribution. It is therefore sometimes advocated that the analysis should be taken back to the participant for their thoughts on the interpretations made. If the participant does not agree with the researcher, it raises the thorny ethical question of who owns the data and the interpretation – the researcher or the participant. It is often argued that ethically we do not have the right as researchers to impose our own values and meanings on our participants' experiences without their consent.

*You may want to think about the notion of self-knowledge. Some theoretical traditions, such as psychoanalytic theory (see Book 1, Chapter 9), argue that self-knowledge is partial and any understanding of the self on the part of the participant would reflect this. Hollway and Jefferson (2000) argue that it could, therefore, be damaging to participants to see certain research interpretations of what they have said or done. On the other hand, the data gathered reflect only a small part of the participant's thoughts and experiences, so any interpretations made by the researcher are necessarily limited by the knowledge acquired.*

In the process of analysing data, there is always a potential for misrepresentation. For example, think about all the times you have heard people argue that they were 'quoted out of context' and their meaning was distorted. A researcher needs to think carefully about how they will handle this. As we shall emphasise in Chapter 10, part of the analytical technique in qualitative research is to acknowledge the contribution the researcher makes from her/his point of view, and this is also important from an ethical point of view.

## Activity 1.6

Reread the descriptions of the two psychological studies described in the previous activity and for each study try to generate a new list of any ethical issues you think might have been overlooked by the researcher, based on the BPS ethical guidelines. **Now would be a good time to look through these – you might wish to just scan the *Code of Ethics and Conduct* but you must read through carefully the supplementary paper on *Ethical Principles for Conducting Research with Human Participants*, even if you have read them previously. You can find a link to these on the course website. You will also need to look at these again when conducting your own project work for TMAs 03 and 05.**

Once you have generated your two new lists, compare them to your original lists.

### Comment

What you may well find is that your first lists contain fairly commonsense points such as:

*Study 1*

- It is wrong for a researcher to arrange a situation that might cause participants considerable anxiety (such as brandishing a combat knife near them).
- It is wrong to make people think they have seen a crime when they have not, especially as they might waste police time reporting it and therefore be open to prosecution.

*Study 2*

- It is wrong to lie to people in order to gain their trust.
- It is wrong to record people without their knowledge.

These (and many others) are good points, but you may find that your second list, using the advice outlined here from the BPS *Ethical Principles for Conducting Research with Human Participants*, contains additional points such as:

*Study 1*

- The participants were not told anything about the research, so the researcher did not obtain informed consent.
- The participants were not given the right to withdraw. In fact they were deceived and 'tricked' into participating and never realised that they were actually participating in research.
- By allowing the participants to believe the crime was real even after it had finished, the researcher failed to debrief them and provide them with information about the study.
- The researcher failed to show the participants respect by treating them in this way, particularly since the researcher paid no attention to the possible physical or psychological harm that the anxiety of being a witness to this 'crime' might have caused.

*Study 2*

- By working 'undercover', the researchers denied the opportunity for participants to give their informed consent and their right to withdraw – which many may well have done, given the experience of previous researchers.
- The researchers should not have promised that any information provided would be treated confidentially; instead, they should have explained that it would be anonymous.
- The researchers potentially colluded with criminal acts committed by the gang. This, therefore, appears to breach the principles of responsibility and integrity.
- It is not clear from the description, but it does not look as if the researchers gave appropriate feedback on the research once it was completed. If the researchers did do this then they should make it clear; if they did not then they have made another unethical decision!

In comparing your two sets of lists you will hopefully find that the BPS *Ethical Principles for Conducting Research with Human Participants* has made you think of additional issues that did not occur to you before. It may also have given you a formal framework for thinking about the issues that *did* occur to you when you first considered the ethics of these studies.

## 5.5 Ethical issues when researching with children

The ethical issues discussed above raise special problems when doing research with children. Partly in recognition of this, it is not now possible in the UK to conduct research with children, or in settings where there are children, without having a police check by the Criminal Records Bureau (CRB). Researchers who are CRB-cleared and who do research with children first need to acknowledge the power relationships that exist between adults and children. In many societies, adults teach and children learn. Doing research with children reverses this relationship in a sense, in that researchers are asking children to share their experiences with them and tell them what they think. Child participants are entitled to the same sort of respect as adult participants. This means researchers need to gain consent, respect anonymity, maintain the right for child participants to withdraw, and give feedback. It can be difficult to achieve informed consent with young children. How does one explain what might be complex research aims to a child? Can children appreciate what it means to agree to take part in a research study? It is difficult to provide general answers to these questions because how one explains the project will depend on the child and the situation. In any event, researchers *must* get the consent of the child's parent or guardian and, if at all possible, the consent of the child. Researchers should also be sensitive to the child's behaviour during the research process. It may be that because of the power relationships discussed above the child does not admit to experiencing distress. The researcher must be vigilant and if the child is uncomfortable bring the activity to a close. Again, in giving feedback researchers must show respect for both the child and the parent. There are many other issues that arise from doing research with children; however, we will not go into these issues here, especially as you will not be conducting research with children on this course.

### Summary Section 5

- This review of ethical issues in research should stimulate you to think about the effect that research may have on your participants.
- Psychological researchers must work within ethical frameworks such as those set out by the British Psychological Society.
- As far as is possible, researchers need to think about consequences from the participants' point of view.

# 6 Conclusion

Doing research requires a series of choices that bring with them a set of challenges. Psychologists may take different perspectives and have differing epistemologies and methodologies. In addition, data can be collected and analysed in a variety of ways depending upon the specific research question or hypothesis being addressed. Furthermore, in collecting data, the methods and analyses used often reflect the particular assumptions and views of the researchers on how best to research psychological issues. In other words, they may be trying to use objective data to establish general laws about people, or they may be using subjective data to explore the meanings that an individual or a group of individuals assigns to a particular event or set of circumstances. All of these issues are explored further in the chapters that follow.

Later in the course you will have the opportunity to explore both types of research in practice, by carrying out two projects. The first of these is an experimental project and you will be required to gather objective data and analyse it quantitatively. The second project adopts a qualitative approach and you will carry out a thematic analysis of interview data. As you carry out the projects it may be helpful to reflect on the distinctions made here between the different methods and types of analysis. Also, you will be reading about many specific research studies as you work through the rest of DSE212. For each new study you encounter, try to consider what kind of data it collects and what aims the researchers had in embarking on that way of studying the phenomenon in question.

So far, the different methods have tended to be considered as operating within a dichotomy: data are *either* objective *or* subjective. However, some data, such as individual responses to The Twenty Statements Test (discussed above), are essentially qualitative but can be categorised and coded for use as quantitative data (depending on the research perspective). This raises questions about the nature of data and also asks a bigger question about whether distinctions are always clear within psychology. In reality, very little in psychology is absolutely clear-cut, as humans are difficult to study. As you work through the course this will become apparent, but for now it is worth considering a specific example in terms of the data psychologists might collect, so that you are aware of some of the wider issues when thinking about types of data and how they are used as evidence.

When considering material data, a particularly exciting growth area within psychology is that of neuropsychology. As you may recall from the Introduction to Book 1, neuropsychology makes use of brain-imaging techniques to explore evidence about structures in the brain and brain functioning. Positron Emission Tomography (PET) is an example of this, and you may be familiar with the term PET scans. Indeed, there will be an opportunity to learn about these later in the course (in Book 1, Chapters 4 and 8). Relevant here, when considering the use of data, is that PET scans seem to be rooted in the scientific tradition (and hence objective) since the images obtained through the scanning process rely on the quantitative measurement abilities of the PET scanner (an objective measure with no personality, opinions, prejudices, etc.). However, the outputs of the scan are visual images and these need to be interpreted by the psychologist. This interpretation, while seeking to be objective, may nonetheless be influenced by the psychologist's own knowledge, experience, interests, concerns and perceptiveness.

We have covered a lot of material in this chapter and introduced quite a few new concepts and terms. The activity below should help you check your understanding of the material we've covered.

## Activity 1.7

For this activity you have to decide which key elements tend of be associated with the scientific and hermeneutic traditions: do this by assigning the text on the right (labelled with an 'A' and a 'B') to the appropriate column in the table. Don't look at the page opposite until you've completed this activity. The first row, to do with methodology, has been completed to help show you what to do.

| | **Scientific** | **Hermeneutic** | |
|---|---|---|---|
| Methodology | B | A | A – Qualitative<br>B – Quantitative |
| Aims | | | A – Seeks generalisable laws<br>B – Seeks in-depth understanding |
| Types of questions | | | A – Testable hypotheses driven by theory<br>B – Questions and theory are grounded in the data |
| Methods | | | A – Insider approach. Emphasises subjectivity, interpretation and reflexivity<br>B – Outsider approach. Emphasises objectivity, standardisation and replicability |
| Data | | | A – Symbolic, meanings, personal experience<br>B – Behavioural and material |

## Comment

A completed version of the table has been provided below so that you can check your answers.

| | Scientific | Hermeneutic | |
|---|---|---|---|
| Methodology | B | A | A – Qualitative<br>B – Quantitative |
| Aims | A | B | A – Seeks generalisable laws<br>B – Seeks in-depth understanding |
| Types of questions | A | B | A – Testable hypotheses driven by theory<br>B – Questions and theory are grounded in the data |
| Methods | B | A | A – Insider approach. Emphasises subjectivity, interpretation and reflexivity<br>B – Outsider approach. Emphasises objectivity, standardisation and replicability |
| Data | B | A | A – Symbolic, meanings, personal experience<br>B – Behavioural and material |

## References

Hollway, W. and Jefferson, T. (2000) *Doing Qualitative Research Differently*, London, Sage.

Kuhn, M.H. and McPartland, T.S. (1954) 'An empirical investigation of self-attitudes', *American Sociological Review*, vol. 19, pp. 68–76.

Montemayer, R. and Eisen, M. (1977) 'The development of self conceptions from childhood to adolescence', *Developmental Psychology*, vol. 13, pp. 314–19.

Potter, J. and Wetherell, M. (1987) *Discourse and Social Psychology: Beyond Attitudes and Behaviour*, London, Sage.

Schatzman, L. and Strauss, A.L. (1973) *Field Research: Strategies for a Natural Sociology*, Englewood Cliffs, NJ, Prentice-Hall.

Tajfel, H., Billig, M., Bundy, R.P. and Flament, C. (1971) 'Social categorization and intergroup behaviour', *European Journal of Social Psychology*, vol. 1, pp. 149–77.

Tesch, R. (1990) *Qualitative Research: Analysis Types and Software Tools*, London, Falmer Press.

# Correlational studies and experiments

## Contents

Aims 44

1 Introduction 44

2 Correlational studies 45
2.1 What is correlation? 45
2.2 Correlation coefficients 50

3 Experiments 54
3.1 What is an experiment? 54
3.2 Independent and dependent variables 58
3.3 Quasi-experiments 63
3.4 Confounding variables 64
3.5 Experimental design 66

4 Final word 72

References 72

Answers to activities 73

# Aims

This chapter aims to:

- introduce you to two types of quantitative studies, namely correlational studies and experiments
- familiarise you with scatterplots and correlation coefficients
- explain what an experiment is and outline issues relating to experimental design.

In this study week we also introduce you to SPSS (see Chapter 1 in the *SPSS Booklet*).

# 1 Introduction

In Chapter 1 a distinction was made between two fundamentally different approaches to research in psychology: there is research that *seeks objectivity* and research that *explores subjectivity*.

### Activity 2.1

See if you can write down the main features of these two approaches. Think about their goals, their methods and the kinds of data they use. Revisit Chapter 1 if you need to.

In this and the next few chapters we shall focus on just one approach and consider research that aims to be objective and to explain psychological phenomena in terms of general laws. The researcher almost always uses an outsider viewpoint because an insider viewpoint is about subjectivity and virtually rules out attaining objectivity. The kinds of data used are almost always either material (e.g. hormone levels, sweat produced on the skin) or behavioural (e.g. decision times, the score on a test). Sometimes systematic self-reports of inner experience are used in questionnaires such as anxiety inventories or personality tests.

Objectivity is basic to the kind of research that sets out to establish general laws that apply across people and across time and situations, and/or to arrive at statements of 'cause and effect'. What is objectivity and why is it so important? Everyone, the researchers and those who read the reports of the research, must be able to agree on the definitions used, on what is happening and on what is being measured. Clarity and consensus (as far as this is possible) are what is needed throughout the research process. Remember the example in Chapter 1 of observing 'smiles'. Effort has to be put in to ensure, as far as possible, that everyone agrees in advance on a definition of what constitutes a smile, and that everyone 'sees' the same thing. This is the approach that characterises the scientific tradition and the search for 'truth' insofar as this is possible. One way to maximise clarity and consensus is to use measurements and numbers, and this is what *quantitative research* sets out to do.

In this chapter we shall explore two types of studies conducted by quantitative researchers: correlational studies and experiments. Not covered here is the use of observations by quantitative researchers (this is discussed on other psychology courses). We shall start by looking at the featured method outlined in Box 5.3 in 'The individual differences approach to personality', the Book 1 chapter you have just studied. Here you read that researchers look for patterns or correlations in the responses to questionnaire items.

# 2 Correlational studies

## 2.1 What is correlation?

Correlational studies are basically a way of investigating relationships between two or more variables. (You may remember from Chapter 1 that things which vary, such as amount of time or number of words, are called variables.) If we have a theory that frustration and aggression are linked, we might predict that as frustration increases, aggression will too. Equally, we might predict that as frustration increases any self-ratings of happiness may decrease. Since the two variables are 'tied together' like this, they are said to vary together, to co-vary, co-relate or *correlate* as it is referred to in statistics.

In Book 1, Chapter 5 you were introduced to several areas where the relationship between variables was important. With personality tests, it is important that the test is repeatable. The chapter introduced you to the term 'test reliability', which is defined as 'the extent to which a test gives the same result for an individual over time and situation' (Box 5.2). So two personality measurements, taken at different times with the same personality questionnaire, need to agree very strongly and that agreement (called test-retest reliability) is measured via *correlation*. Similarly, when looking to see how much personality is inherited, one approach taken is to compare the personality scores of monozygotic (identical) twins. If a personality trait is mostly inherited then the scores for twins should be very strongly correlated: if one twin has a high score, so should the other twin.

Let's take a close look at an example of a correlational study in which a researcher was interested in the effects of tiredness on cognitive function in newly qualified medical staff. It was predicted that the more tired the person, the more mistakes he or she would make.

Twenty adult students were recruited from a large teaching hospital and asked to participate in the research. As part of their training and assessment, the students were asked to make a diagnosis of a test case (the same patient was seen by all twenty participants) at some point during a sixteen-hour working day. As the participant made their diagnosis, the researcher recorded how long it had been since their shift began. The diagnoses were checked by a senior member of the medical staff, who recorded the number of errors made in each case.

At the end of the study, the researcher had the following data concerning two variables:

- the number of errors made in the diagnosis by each of the twenty students
- the length of time that had passed (when a diagnosis was made) since the beginning of that student's shift.

## Activity 2.2

We present fictitious data for the two variables in Table 2.1 below. Can you spot a pattern?

**Table 2.1 Number of errors made in a diagnosis and length of time since beginning of shift**

| Student | Number of errors | Length of time (in hours) |
|---|---|---|
| 1 | 1 | 2 |
| 2 | 3 | 6 |
| 3 | 5 | 8 |
| 4 | 8 | 12 |
| 5 | 2 | 5 |
| 6 | 4 | 6 |
| 7 | 3 | 4 |
| 8 | 1 | 4 |
| 9 | 6 | 5 |
| 10 | 7 | 9 |
| 11 | 4 | 4 |

| | | |
|---|---|---|
| 12 | 5 | 5 |
| 13 | 8 | 10 |
| 14 | 1 | 3 |
| 15 | 9 | 9 |
| 16 | 2 | 1 |
| 17 | 2 | 1 |
| 18 | 8 | 9 |
| 19 | 5 | 4 |
| 20 | 4 | 5 |

Your answer to the activity above is likely to have been that larger numbers of errors tend to be paired with longer lengths of time since the beginning of the shift, or that as one variable increases so the other variable tends to increase as well. It is much easier to spot any such pattern when the data are in the form of a graph. The way to represent graphically how two variables are related is through a *scatterplot*. To produce a scatterplot (by hand), you first draw two axes, each one representing one of your two variables. To examine the relationship between the numbers of errors made by each student doctor ('Errors') and the length of time since they started their shift ('Time'), we need to allocate each variable to one of the axes. Normally, the variable being measured is allocated to the y-axis but because this is a correlational study we have measured two variables and either one can be allocated to the y-axis. We suggest placing the 'Time' variable on the x-axis (the horizontal line along the bottom of the graph) and the 'Errors' variable on the y-axis (the vertical line along the side of the graph) (see Figure 2.1).

You can now plot the data from Table 2.1 on the graph. For instance, the data for the first participant were 1 for 'number of errors' and 2 for 'length of time', so we would place a point on the graph so that it was in line with '2' on the 'Time' axis and '1' on the 'Errors' axis (see Figure 2.2).

Filling in the scatterplot with the data from the remaining nineteen participants produced the graph in Figure 2.3.

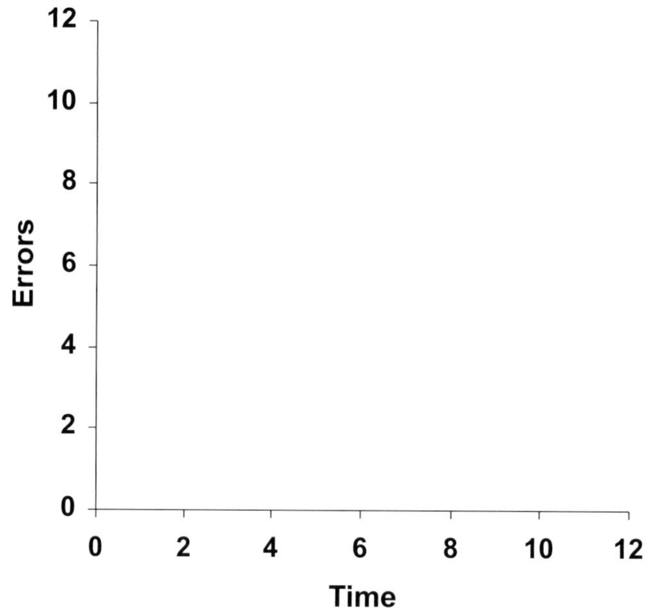


**Figure 2.1** Axes for a scatterplot

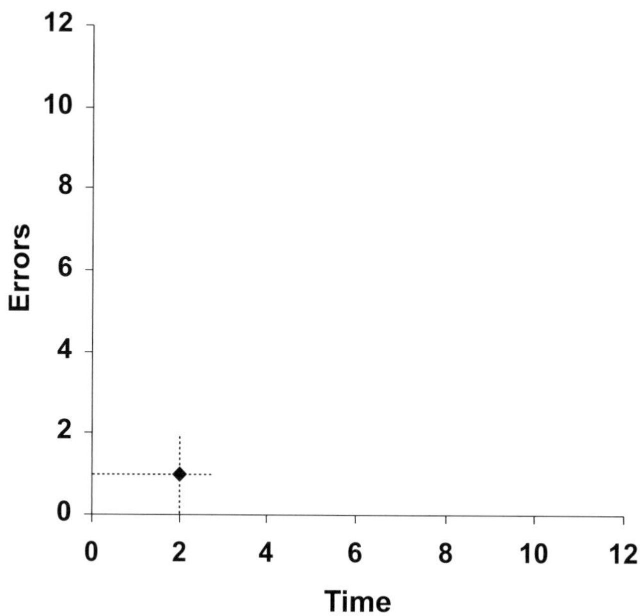


**Figure 2.2** Scatterplot containing a single data point

From the scatterplot in Figure 2.3, we can see how the two variables of 'Time' and 'Errors' are related. Although the relationship is not very clear, the pattern of points on the scatterplot slopes upwards from bottom left to top right, so it appears that there is a tendency for the number of errors to increase as the time since the shift started increases.

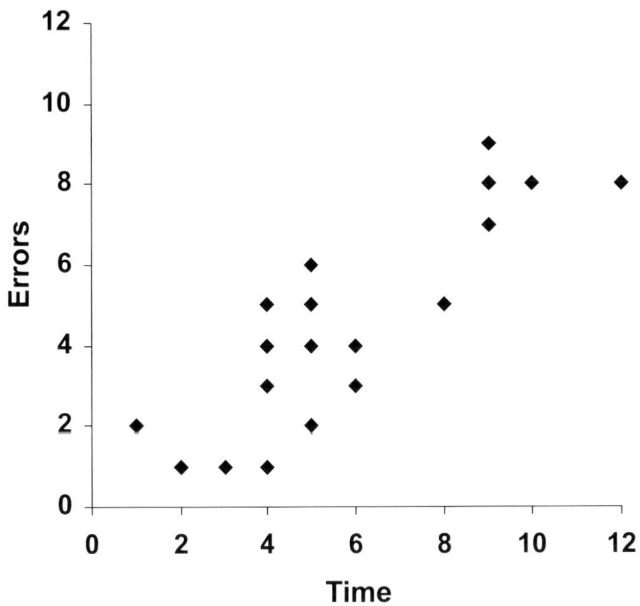


**Figure 2.3** Completed scatterplot

### *Activity 2.3*

Table 2.2 shows the data from a different study that considered the relationship between ageing and word recall. Again the data are fictitious. Draw a scatterplot by hand, place the 'Age' variable on the x-axis and the 'Word recall' variable on the y-axis. Describe the pattern you observe. Compare your scatterplot and description with the one provided at the end of the chapter.

**Table 2.2 Number of words recalled and age of participant**

| Participant | Word recall | Age (in years) |
|---|---|---|
| 1 | 25 | 42 |
| 2 | 5 | 80 |
| 3 | 15 | 59 |
| 4 | 18 | 45 |
| 5 | 9 | 78 |
| 6 | 12 | 69 |
| 7 | 24 | 45 |
| 8 | 16 | 50 |
| 9 | 8 | 75 |
| 10 | 11 | 55 |

## 2.2 Correlation coefficients

Whilst we can look at a scatterplot and get an idea of the direction of slope and how close the points are to falling along a straight line, we need to obtain an accurate and objective measure of the correlation. *Correlation coefficients* provide a numerical measure of the extent to which the two variables are related; they are expressed as a number between −1 and +1.

If our correlation coefficient is a positive number, between 0 and 1, then we say that the correlation is positive, or that the relationship between the variables is positive. A positive correlation shows that one variable increases at the same time as the other does. In other words, as one variable increases so does the other or as one variable decreases so does the other. The pattern of points on the scatterplot will slope upwards from bottom left to top right. For example, this is the pattern we saw when we plotted number of medical students' errors in diagnosis against length of time on shift(see Activity 2.2).

If our correlation coefficient is a negative number, between −1 and 0, then we say that the correlation is negative, or that the relationship between the variables is negative. A negative correlation means that one variable increases at the same time as the other decreases. In other words, as one variable increases the other decreases or as one variable decreases the other variable increases. The pattern of points on the scatterplot will slope downwards from top left to bottom right. For example, this is the pattern we saw when plotting word recall against age (see Activity 2.3).

The magnitude of the number tells us how strong this relationship is. A value of 1 shows a perfect positive correlation, a value of −1 a perfect negative correlation, and a value of zero shows that there is no relationship between the two variables at all (see Figure 2.4).

You can see that the size (or magnitude) of the correlation coefficient is directly related to whether the points plotted fall on a straight line, fall roughly on a straight line or are completely random. If the points form a perfectly straight line, then the correlation coefficient will be either 1 or −1 depending on which direction it is sloping in. However, if the points are completely random, so that they appear distributed almost equally across the graph, then the correlation coefficient will be 0.

In reality, correlation coefficients are rarely exactly 1, −1 or 0, but instead fall somewhere in between, as displayed in Figure 2.4. A coefficient of 0.8 or above or −0.8 and below would certainly be seen as a very strong

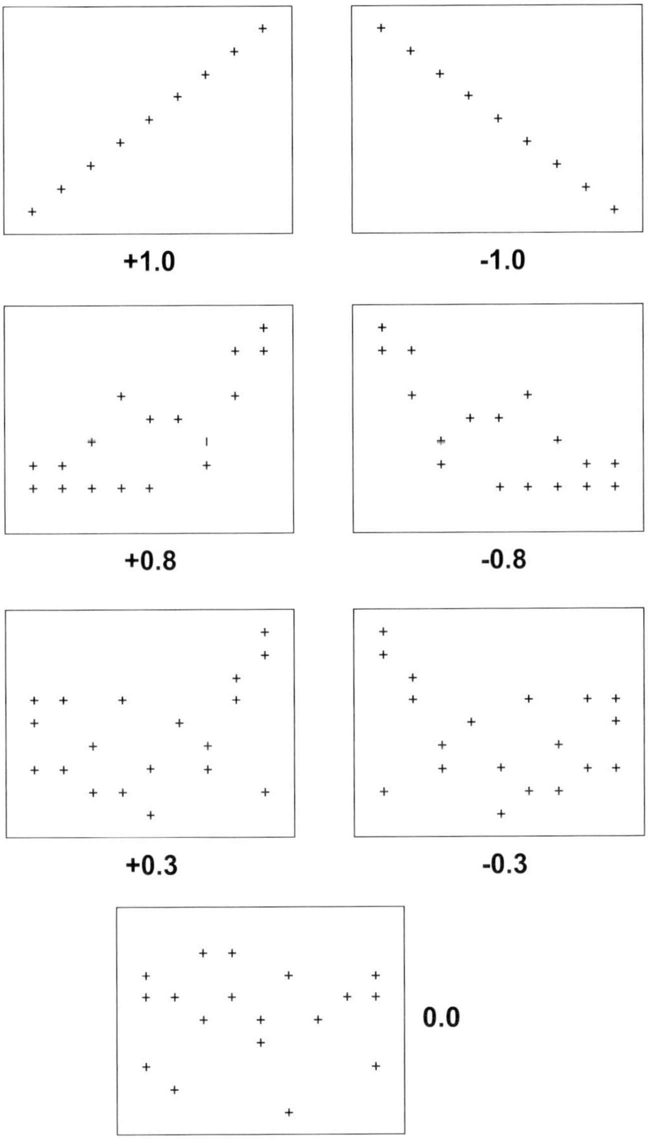


**Figure 2.4** How correlation coefficients relate to scatterplots

relationship. Indeed, Cohen (1988) suggests that a coefficient of 0.5 (or –0.5) would mean a strong relationship whilst one of 0.3 or –0.3 would mean a medium relationship. So, the magnitude of the correlation coefficient tells us about the strength of the relationship between two variables.

### Activity 2.4

Decide whether there might be a positive, negative or no correlation for the following:

1. the relationship between the amount of clothing worn and the number of ice creams sold
2. the relationship between motivation to achieve and academic success
3. the relationship between amount of time spent reading and hair length
4. the relationship between lung cancer and smoking.

For suggestions, see the end of the chapter.

---

An important point to note about a correlation coefficient is that it can only tell us how strongly related two variables are. As we've said above, saying that there is a correlation between two variables is simply saying that the values of the two variables X and Y co-vary in some way. There can be many different explanations of why this is the case, including the following:

- Changes in X cause changes in Y.
- Changes in Y cause changes in X.
- Changes in some third variable, Z, independently cause changes in X and Y.
- The observed relationship between X and Y is spurious, a coincidence, with no causal explanation at all.

Since the existence of a pattern and of a correlation coefficient cannot tell us which explanation is valid, it is important to note the following:

*Correlation is not causation*

So, there may well be a weak positive correlation between our motivation to achieve and academic success, but which leads to the other? Is it that academic success is a *result* of a higher level of achievement motivation or does academic success lead to a higher level of achievement motivation? There is undoubtedly a relationship between the number of items of clothing that people are wearing and the number of ice creams sold. But does this mean that reducing the amount of clothing we wear makes us buy icecreams? Of course it doesn't. In this case, there is definitely a third variable, how hot it is, which is causing the changes in both variables. When conducting correlational studies, it is important to bear in mind that the changes to the variables you are observing could be due to another variable altogether.

It could also be the case that, although there appears to be a relationship between two variables, the observed correlation is entirely spurious and due to chance alone. An example of this might be a correlation between rainfall in Sweden and the performance of shares on the Dow-Jones index. You can imagine that if you compared enough variables with share performance, you would eventually find one that correlated very well. However, it would be a brave investor indeed who sank all their capital in shares on the basis of a rainy day in Stockholm.

So, remember, correlation does *not* equal causation. Why do we bother then with correlational studies if we cannot assume any causal link between the variables? The answer is that in order to allow us to determine a cause and effect relationship between our variables, we would need to conduct an experiment. This would entail the *manipulation* of one of the variables and sometimes this is just not possible. For example, conducting an experiment to establish a causative relationship between lung cancer in humans and smoking would require us to randomly allocate people to two groups and make one of the groups smoke cigarettes. Such a study would be extremely unethical and also impractical (how would you stop the non-smoking group from smoking or make the smoking group smoke?). Correlational studies do not require as great a level of intervention as experiments, meaning they can be used in many circumstances where it would be impossible to conduct an experiment. For instance, reflect back on the use of twin studies to explore heritability, outlined in Book 1 *Mapping Psychology*, Chapter 5. It would be impossible to conduct an experiment in which the experimenter could manipulate genetic relatedness.

## Summary Section 2

- Correlational studies investigate relationships between two or more variables.
- Scatterplots allow us to see any relationship graphically.
- There may be a positive relationship so that as one variable increases, the other variable also tends to increase.
- There may be a negative relationship so that as one variable increases, the other variable tends to decrease.
- Correlation coefficients provide a numerical estimate of the extent to which two variables are related, and will range from −1 to +1.
- Correlation is not causation.

# 3 Experiments

### Activity 2.5

Why not test how much you already know about experiments? See if you can fill in the gaps in the following sentences:

> *An experiment is an artificial set-up designed to investigate ________ and effect. The experimenter aims to control all possible ________ and keep all but one of them ________. Then one variable – the ________ variable – is manipulated in a controlled way and its effect on behaviour is measured via the ________ variable.*

If you get stuck, you could go back to Book 1, Chapter 3 ('Three approaches to learning') and look again at the Featured Method Box 3.1: *Experiments I: The importance of control and manipulation*. For answers, see the end of the chapter.

## 3.1 What is an experiment?

You will already have read about several experiments so far in this course; for example, the social categorisation experiments by Tajfel *et al.* (1971) in Book 1 Chapter 1, the 'hide-and-seek' experiment by Chandler *et al.* (1989) in Chapter 2, and the work on instrumental conditioning in Chapter 3 on 'Three approaches to learning'. Think back through some of the experiments you have read about and try to work out what features they have in common. Below are the things we came up with when thinking about these features:

- The researcher created a situation.
- The researcher tried to control this situation in certain ways.
- The researcher set out to manipulate something to see what effect this might have.
- The researcher recorded or measured something to determine this effect.
- Rather than look at the effects of lots of things at once, the researcher tended to select just one or two things.

As you can see, the first thing that occurred to us was that all the examples of experimental studies involved a situation that was created by the researcher. Sometimes this situation was in a laboratory, a *laboratory experiment*, such as the experiments described in Book 1, Chapter 6, on perception and attention (which you will soon start reading) and sometimes it was in a more naturalistic environment, such as a classroom, a *naturalistic field experiment*. By 'create a situation' we mean that the researcher attempted to manipulate circumstances so that they could study whatever it was they were interested in. So rather than take a series of taxi journeys in the hope of observing how drivers attend and react to a pedestrian in the road, a researcher would (via a simulator) create a situation in which the driver was confronted with a pedestrian.

Implicit in the researcher creating a certain situation is that they are attempting to control what happens. This control has two aspects. First, the researcher controls the situation so that the phenomena they are interested in studying are introduced, and second, they attempt to remove anything else that might get in the way. For instance, in our driver/pedestrian example, the researcher might control how fast the car is travelling when the pedestrian steps out and also ensure that all the participant drivers are experienced and alert.

The creation of a specific situation and attempted control of what happens in this situation are both integral parts of an experiment. (It is important to remember that, as the experimenter is controlling the situation, they have a responsibility to safeguard the well-being of their participants.) Of course, some experiments will be more controlled than others, but even if the researcher is working in a naturalistic setting, they will still be trying to control what happens in important ways. This makes experiments very different from correlational or observational studies, in which the researcher does not necessarily play any part in proceedings beyond measuring the variables or recording what happens.

### Activity 2.6

A researcher would like to conduct an experiment to look at the effect of teaching style on students' learning of psychological research methods. Can you think of anything they should control?

For suggestions see the end of the chapter.

Another integral part of an experiment is that the researcher manipulates one thing to see what effect it has on another. This entails the researcher setting out to introduce a specific change to one thing and then measuring something else to see the effect. We shall look at this manipulation and measurement in more depth in Section 3.2. For now, we will concentrate on the fact that the researcher is only manipulating 'one thing'.

By now we hope you are aware that human psychology is immensely complicated and that our behaviour is governed by the interaction of complex social and environmental factors with our internal thought processes. You can imagine that this makes studying any one specific aspect of our psychology very complicated. Consider the research question 'How do we remember words?', and think for a second about how complex this question actually is. For example, it could be that:

- Different types of words are remembered in different ways.
- Our memory is affected by our motivation for learning the words.
- The social situation we are in when shown the words could affect our memory.

In fact, we could probably fill several pages just off the tops of our heads with things that could affect memory for words.

Now imagine trying to answer that research question 'How do we remember words?' by conducting a psychological study. To provide a complete and comprehensive answer to the question would require you to be able to study and understand the effect that every conceivable variable might have on our memory for words. Obviously, this would not be possible in any single study. But how many different things could we study at once?

Let's take the three factors that we identified above and see if we could study aspects of them in a single study. Our study would need to look at different types of word, so we could give participants a list of nouns, adjectives and verbs. Our study would need to look at motivation, so we could tell some of our participants that they will get a financial reward for every word they remember. And our study would need to look at the social situation, so some participants could sit in isolation and some in small groups. But, if we manipulate word-type, motivation and social setting in a single study, how will we know which of these is the cause of any effects that we see?

To use an analogy, if your car, which at first won't start does so after you change both the spark plugs and the starter motor, you won't know which was the cause of the original problem. A better strategy would be to change one component at a time so that you will know where the fault lay. It might also be better to look at just one thing at a time in our psychological study of memory so that we will know that any effects observed will be due to the factor we are currently studying.

Studying one thing at a time is therefore a central part of the experimental approach. Although psychologists make use of statistical techniques that do allow more than one thing to be manipulated at once, methodically researching one aspect of psychology at a time tends to be a guiding principle in experimental design.

You may be able to see a problem with this approach. For instance, what if motivation and social setting have no discernible effect on their own, but they do in combination? For example, a financial reward may only be motivating when the participant is on their own, but not when they are part of a small group. Although the use of certain statistics does allow more than one thing to be studied at once, it is still true that an experimental approach may not be particularly suitable for studying complex forms of behaviour.

In addition, it may occur to you that, because experimenters create a controlled situation and introduce a manipulation, experiments cannot be used to study naturally occurring human behaviour. In fact, the experimental situation is in itself a specialised type of social situation, so there is a sense in which it is then hard to generalise to other social situations. Just because a participant in an experiment can remember more nouns than verbs, for instance, it doesn't necessarily mean that the same is true of a child in a classroom

So experiments, which we will define as systematic and controlled studies in which a researcher attempts to determine the effect that one variable has on another, can have their problems and limitations. However, as you will see throughout this course, they have played and continue to play a prominent and important role in psychology.

## Activity 2.7

**Stop reading for a few minutes and think about the following two research problems. Can you think of any problems using the experimental method to explore either of these?**

1 **How juries reach decisions.**

2 **How productivity in the workplace can be improved.**

## Comment

In the case of (1), there is the issue that those serving on real juries are making a decision that will affect a person's life. We can explore jury decision making by asking participants to form mock juries, and hence manipulate variables such as the defendant's race or sex. However, our participants are not likely to feel the same pressure or responsibility as a real jury; whatever decision they reach it will not have comparable consequences to the one reached by a real jury.

In the case of (2) you may have heard about the 'Hawthorne effect' – the notion that behaviour changes as a result of being observed. For example, we might explore the effect of music on productivity in the workplace by placing one group of workers in a room with music and another group in a different room without music. However, both groups will be aware that their performance is being measured and so may increase their work rate. In addition, by regrouping them we may have changed group dynamics and the social elements of work which can affect job satisfaction and motivation and hence alter productivity.

## 3.2 Independent and dependent variables

In our discussion so far, we have mentioned 'manipulation' and 'recording/measuring'. Let's look at these further. If you think about all the experiments that you have read about, it is possible to describe them in the following way:

- The researcher manipulated one thing.
- The researcher measured what effect this manipulation had on something else.

This means that at the heart of every experiment are two things that vary, hence two variables. The first is caused to vary by the researcher. This could be:

- a variation in the instructions given; for example, one group is told to memorise a passage and another group just to read it
- a variation in the stimuli given to the participants; for example, one group sees faces the right way up and another sees them upside down
- a variation in the nature of the task; for example, one group of participants is asked to push a button as soon as they hear a klaxon and another group to say the word 'Now' as soon as they hear a klaxon.

Whatever the exact nature of the manipulation, in every case the researcher is introducing a variation to the thing that they are interested in studying. We call the variable that is manipulated by the researcher the *independent variable*. This is often shortened to IV. You can think of it as being the variable that is *independent* from any others, leaving it free to be manipulated by the researcher.

So we now have a technical term for the variation introduced by the researcher, but how does the researcher see what effect their manipulation has? The answer is that they see what effect the manipulation has by measuring or recording a second variable. This variable therefore needs to be something that is likely to be affected by the manipulation of the independent variable. Returning to the above examples of independent variables, this could be:

- the number of words later recalled from the passage by the two groups
- the number of faces later recognised by the two groups
- the response time between the klaxon and the participant pushing the button/saying 'Now'.

Whatever the exact nature of what is actually being recorded, in every case the researcher is measuring one variable to see how it was affected by the independent variable. We call the variable that is being measured the *dependent variable*. This is often shortened to DV. You can think of it as being the variable whose variation is *dependent* on the manipulation introduced by the researcher; in other words, it is dependent on the independent variable.

One way of seeing an experiment, therefore, is as a study of cause and effect. We have one variable, the IV, which causes an effect in a second variable, the DV. The researcher manipulates the IV and this causes an effect in the DV that the researcher then measures.

## Activity 2.8

To check your understanding of IVs and DVs, descriptions of psychological studies have been provided below. In each case, try to work out what the IV and DV are. The first example has been done for you and the answers to the others can be found at the end of this chapter.

1 Researchers have investigated the effect of taking cannabis on driving. An experiment has been conducted in which the amount of cannabis taken by the participants was systematically manipulated by the researcher, to be either a high dose or a low dose, to see what effect it had on driving behaviour.

 The IV = amount of cannabis taken

 The DV = driving behaviour

2 The Home Office wanted to know whether identification of suspects at video identification parades was different from that at traditional, live identification parades. They asked a psychologist to conduct an experiment to investigate this. The psychologists showed forty participants a staged crime and a week later asked half to identify the suspect from a video identification parade and half from a live identification parade. The psychologist recorded whether each participant identified the suspect or a 'foil'.

3 A psychologist was studying musical creativity in children. They recruited thirty 10-year-olds and asked half of them to compose a piece for the recorder by themselves and the other half to compose in groups of three. Each piece of music was rated for creativity by the researcher.

4 A researcher wanted to find out if the emotive nature of a word affected how memorable it was. They produced a list of fifty words, half of which were highly emotive (e.g. 'love', 'war' and 'passion') and half of which were non-emotive (e.g. 'table', 'place' and 'carpet'), and asked twenty participants to read and remember the words. Ten minutes after reading the words, each participant was asked to recall as many of the words as they could remember.

In Studies 2 and 3 in Activity 2.8, the manipulation of the IV clearly led to there being two groups of participants (e.g. in Study 2, there was a video identification parade group and a live identification parade group). The IV that was manipulated in Studies 1 and 4 also led to two categories, but these corresponded to the cannabis dose (high or low) or the type of word (emotive or non-emotive) rather than two separate groups of participants.

We shall look in more detail at these two different forms of experiment in Section 3.5, but for now we need a way of describing the sub-categories of the IV that can be used regardless of whether the manipulation leads to groups of participants, groups of words or groups of anything else for that matter.

The technical term that is used to describe the groups formed by the specific manipulation introduced by the IV is *conditions*. In all four studies described in Activity 2.8, the IV contains two conditions. These are:

Study 1 – high dose condition and low dose condition.

Study 2 – video identification parade condition and live identification parade condition.

Study 3 – individual composition condition and group composition condition.

Study 4 – emotive word condition and non-emotive word condition.

In theory, an IV can have any number of conditions. However, there are statistical tests that are designed for IVs with just two conditions, and it is these that we shall be looking at in this course. So, although you should bear in mind that IVs can have many conditions, all the experiments we shall be analysing (including the one you will be conducting) will have just two conditions.

Sometimes in research we are interested in studying the introduction of a novel item. For example, clinical psychologists may want to know whether a new drug will work, so the two conditions they need to study are one in which participants are given the drug and one that is identical to this except that the participants do not receive the drug. Likewise, a forensic psychologist may want to know whether a new police interviewing technique works, so they would need one condition in which the new technique was used and one that was identical to this in all respects other than the fact that the new technique was not used.

When an experiment uses this type of design, we refer to the condition in which the novel item has been introduced as the *experimental condition* and the condition that is identical to this, except that the novel item was not introduced, as the *control condition*. For example, we might wish to investigate whether alcohol has a negative effect on manual dexterity. We would design our experiment so that there was an experimental condition which involved giving participants alcohol and a control condition which did not involve giving participants alcohol. In one condition a possible 'cause' is present (the experimental condition) and in the other this 'cause' is absent (the control condition), thus allowing us to investigate whether there is a causal relationship between alcohol and poorer manual dexterity.

The nature of the control condition is critical in experiments. The control and experimental conditions have to be identical in all aspects except for the 'cause' that we wish to study. For example, we would want to test participants in the same room, at the same time of day and give them identical instructions. Often the control condition is the *absence* of the thing you want to see the effect of (e.g. music vs. no music; drug vs. no drug). However, sometimes you will want to compare a 'new' thing with an 'old' thing (e.g. new video identification vs. old live identification). In this case the control condition is not simply the absence of the thing you are interested in – for example, it would not be meaningful to have a 'no identification' condition: what could you measure? There are also other cases where *absence* is inappropriate; for example, when comparing males and females or children and adults. The key point is that your control condition should be a meaningful basis for comparison with your experimental condition.

Another aspect to consider concerns the way we allocate participants to each condition. People vary enormously in many characteristics or attributes that are beyond our control and often difficult or impossible to measure. To ensure that these differences do not adversely affect our experiment, we would use *random allocation* of participants to conditions. This means that as far as possible these characteristics or attributes (e.g. motivation or intelligence) should be spread evenly across conditions.

The control condition also has to compensate for any side effects caused by the nature of the manipulation introduced. For example, our clinical psychologist could not simply have a group of patients that received the new drug and a group that stayed at home. As well as not receiving the drug, the second group of patients would also not have attended the hospital/laboratory and would not have been injected (or swallowed a pill etc.). As expectations are a very powerful psychological force, it could be the case that any effects seen in the experimental condition were due not to the drug but to the fact that the participants went to a laboratory and were given an injection and so *expected* to be affected. So, as these are important differences that could affect the DV, our control condition needs to contain them, too.

In fact, expectations are such a powerful force that it is often (particularly in drug studies) necessary for participants in both the experimental and the control conditions either to all think that they are receiving the drug or to not know whether they are receiving it or not. Those who do not receive the drug are given what is known as a placebo, which is essentially a harmless substance that will have no effect. The power of expectation can be seen in many studies that report a *placebo effect*, in which the participants in the control condition experience the apparent effects of the drug.

The process of not informing the participants whether they are receiving the real drug or not is known as *single-blind testing*. It is also necessary to keep this information from the person responsible for administering the drug to the patients, otherwise they could unintentionally provide verbal and non-verbal cues that could have an effect on the participant. If neither the participant nor the administrator is aware who is getting the drug and who the placebo, we say that the study is employing *double-blind testing*.

Whether single-blind or double-blind testing is employed, it is important for our control condition to provide an accurate *baseline measure*, against which we can measure our experimental condition. In the drug study, the control condition should provide a baseline measure of how participants might be affected by everything in the experimental condition except for the effects of the drug itself.

Baseline measures tend to be very important in studies that are looking to see whether the introduction of a new item, such as a drug or interview technique, leads in some way to an improvement. For example, if we were to assess the impact of a new teaching strategy on young children's mathematical ability, it would be very important to find out how mathematically proficient the children were before the introduction of the new strategy. This initial test of their ability would be the baseline measure.

### Activity 2.9

The following are brief descriptions of three fictitious experiments. See if you can spot what is wrong with the design of each experiment. Each one relates to a particular issue mentioned in this subsection.

1 To investigate the effect of caffeine on concentration, an experimenter gave one group of women cups of coffee and then a simple maths test, and a second group of women cups of tea and then the same maths test. Participants were instructed to complete as many maths questions as possible in a ten-minute period.

2 To explore the influence of music on group performance, a researcher asked students on a music course to work together to complete a complex puzzle whilst listening to Beethoven's Ninth Symphony, and students on a maths course to do the same task without listening to any music.

3 To research the effectiveness of a new treatment for depression, an assistant clinical psychologist gave one group of depressed patients the new drug and another group a placebo. She then interviewed each patient after three months of treatment to measure their level of depression.

See the end of the chapter for our answers.

## 3.3 Quasi-experiments

Inherent in our definition of an experiment was the idea that the researcher *manipulates* a variable, this being the IV. The implication of this is that if the researcher does not *manipulate* the IV, then the study cannot be an experiment.

Consider the following description of a study, and try to work out if it is an experiment or not:

> *An OU researcher was interested in how tutors of different sex behaved at residential school. The researcher attended two residential schools in Durham, and recorded the number of hours that the male tutors spent socialising and the number of hours that the female tutors spent socialising.*

Is this study an experiment? It certainly appears to have a DV, as the researcher recorded the number of hours the tutors spent socialising. But what about the IV? This appears to be 'the sex of the tutor', but the researcher cannot be said to have manipulated this. Instead, we have a situation in which we have a causal variable, sex of tutor, and a variable that we are recording to see the effect, hours spent socializing, but not a variable that was directly manipulated by the researcher.

If we consider the four experiments that were described in Activity 2.8, we can see that, as well as directly manipulating the IV, the researcher was also able to randomly allocate participants to each condition. However, in the study currently being discussed, the researcher could not randomly allocate participants as being either male or female, instead condition allocation was determined by an existing characteristic.

If the researcher is unable to randomly allocate people to each condition, and so did not *directly* manipulate the IV, we say that the study had a *quasi-experimental design*. Any study that is looking at the effects that an existing characteristic such as sex, age, height, IQ or a personality trait has on another variable will have a quasi-experimental design.

### Activity 2.10

A health psychologist would like to investigate whether regular exercise has a positive effect on reducing the number of sick days recorded in the workplace. She could recruit participants and allocate one group to the experimental 'exercise' condition, and another group to the control 'no exercise' condition. Then, at the end of a two- or three-year period, she could look at their record of sick days. If she did this, she would have conducted a 'true experiment', as she would have complete control over the independent variable, and random allocation of participants to each condition would ensure that no other variables affected her results. However, there are ethical issues preventing such an experiment (e.g. telling people not to exercise!). The health psychologist therefore has to proceed with a quasi-experimental design involving one group of participants who have been exercising regularly and another group who have not been exercising. Can you think of how this might impact on the conclusions that she could draw?

See the end of the chapter for our suggestions.

As you saw in Activity 2.10, in some instances it would be possible to randomly allocate participants to each condition, but the manipulation inherent in the IV would then cause some ethical or other serious problem. For example, if we wanted to investigate neural activity in murderers compared with a control group, we could not split a group of people into two groups, and then ask one of these groups to commit murder! The same problem is experienced by medical researchers, who cannot give one group of participants a specific medical condition or force one group of people to start smoking. Although the distinction between experiments and quasi-experiments is important, it is not one we will dwell on any further here, as the data from both experiments and quasi-experiments are analysed by the same statistical tests.

## 3.4 Confounding variables

If an experiment is a study that looks at the effect that the IV has on the DV, then a good experiment is one in which the only thing that affects the DV is the IV. In reality, such control over what happens is just not possible – at least not in a psychological experiment. No matter how much the researcher strives to control the experiment, there will always be things that affect the DV which are not the IV. Some of the time these variables will have an equal effect on all the conditions. Although this may act to increase or decrease our DV, we don't have to be too concerned about this, as any difference *between* the conditions will remain. However, it is a considerable problem if a variable (other than the IV of course) has more effect in one of the conditions than it does in the other. In such a case, the researcher might conclude that their IV was having an effect on the DV when in reality it was another variable altogether that was having the effect. Any variable, other than the IV that has a systematic effect on the DV so that one condition is affected more than another is called a *confounding variable.*

For example, when looking at the effect of a particular teaching style on learning, there are a host of factors that will affect learning, such as motivation and intelligence. However, by randomly allocating participants to different conditions we hope to even out any effect they have. Through good experimental design we aim to eliminate or control for confounding variables; if we do not, then we will end up with findings that have been *confounded.* For example, when looking at the effect of a new strategy to teach reading, unless we use the same teacher to teach the standard strategy and the new strategy, or unless we have carefully matched our teachers in terms of teaching ability, experience and all other relevant criteria, then any effect we observe may not be because of teaching style but because of the personal characteristics of the teacher.

### Activity 2.11

Decide whether each of the following may result in a confounding variable:

1. An experimenter allocates female participants to the experimental condition and male participants to the control condition.
2. An experimenter allocates the first twenty participants to volunteer to take part in his study to the experimental condition and the next twenty participants to the control condition.
3. An experimenter collects the data for the experimental condition in the morning and for the control condition in the afternoon.

See the end of the chapter for our answers.

When designing an experiment, a researcher will try to ensure that no confounding variables occur. When we were discussing what an experiment is in Section 3.1, it was suggested that one central criterion is that the researcher attempts to control the situation both to introduce the variable they are interested in studying and to remove any other variable that might 'get in the way'. Thus, a good experiment is one where the researcher has managed to remove all confounding variables so that the only variable remaining that can affect the DV is the IV itself. To achieve this situation, the researcher must introduce *controls* that will limit or remove the effects of any confounding variables.

Let's look at an example. In an experiment to test the effect of cannabis on driving, the participants were tested three times, once with a placebo, once with a low cannabis dose and once with a high dose. If participants were all given these conditions in the same order, there is the possibility that this could become a confounding variable. Each time the participant performed the task, they were in a sense being provided with a chance to practise it. Therefore, we would expect that the participant would get better at the task each time they were asked to perform it. In this case, the effects of practise would become a confounding variable and could even lead to a result that suggested cannabis improved driving. To stop this from happening, the researcher took steps to counterbalance the *practise effect* by making sure that participants did the three conditions in different orders. Here, the confounding variable was practise and the control introduced was *counterbalancing*.

Practise effects are a common form of confounding variable. Another common form of confounding variable is individual differences. If the participants in one condition are different in some important respect from those in the second condition, then it is likely that these individual differences will affect the DV. Avoiding practise effects and individual differences is an important aspect of experimental design, and one we shall look at in more depth in the next section.

### Activity 2.12

Which of the following statements are correct? (Our answers are at the end of the chapter.)

1 The independent variable is manipulated by the experimenter.

2 The independent variable is measured by the experimenter.

3 The independent variable is the causal factor in our 'cause and effect' relationship.

4 The independent variable is a measure of the effect in our 'cause and effect' relationship.

5 The dependent variable is the causal factor in our 'cause and effect' relationship.

6 The dependent variable is the outcome measured by the experimenter.

7 The dependent variable is manipulated by the experimenter.

8 The dependent variable is the effect in our 'cause and effect' relationship.

9 Confounding variables are other factors that might affect the result, and confuse the picture we are getting from these results.

10 It is important to have some confounding variables in an experiment.

11 It is important to try to control as many confounding variables as possible in an experiment.

## 3.5 Experimental design

In designing an experiment, we want to maximise the potential effect of our IV and minimise the potential effect of any and all confounding variables. Previously, we emphasised the importance of randomly allocating participants to experimental conditions, and we saw that practise effects and individual differences can act as confounding variables. Indeed, the decision as to whether the same or different participants complete each condition is perhaps the most critical one you will need to take. In fact, this element of experimental design is so important that psychology experiments tend to be classified into one of two categories based on the allocation of participants to conditions. These are described next.

## Types of experimental design

### *Between-participants design*

This design is also known as independent groups, independent samples or independent measures. In this design we use *different* participants in each condition. Where possible we split the participants up randomly; for example, by tossing a coin for each and putting those with a 'head' into one group and those with a 'tail' into the other. However, this is not always possible when, for instance, we have a quasi-experiment – there are different participants in each condition but they are allocated on the basis of an existing characteristic.

### *Within-participants design*

This design is also known as repeated measures or paired-samples. In this design, each of our participants will take part in both of the conditions. This design is often used in 'before and after' situations, where we want to look at the effect of a particular change.

## Important elements of experimental design

We shall now look at some of the more common problems that need to be avoided in designing a good experiment, and some methods of dealing with them.

### *Practise effects*

As we have seen, each time a participant performs a task, they will tend to get better at it. Thus, regardless of the IV we are manipulating, we should expect participants to perform better in the second condition than in the first. There are two main ways of dealing with practise effects. The first is to change the order in which participants do the conditions, so that some do condition 1 then condition 2 and some do condition 2 then condition 1. The second is to have different participants in each condition.

### *Order effects*

Practise effects are one example of an order effect, as by using the conditions in the same order for every participant a possible confounding variable is introduced. As well as the order of the conditions, it is also important to bear in mind the order in which any material is presented, particularly when using a within-participants design. For example, if you are presenting word lists that contain different types of word, you should be careful that the order of these is either randomised or counterbalanced. Counterbalancing is the process whereby we control the order in which conditions and material are presented, so that if one participant sees condition 1 first, the second participant will see condition 2 first, and so on.

### *Differences between participants*

Usually referred to as individual differences, differences between participants are perhaps the main problem that psychologists have to deal with. A physicist in the UK can heat a metal to 1000 °C and be sure that a US researcher heating the same type of metal to the same temperature will find the same effects. The same cannot be said of human participants. Humans and human behaviour are extremely complicated and it is simply impossible to design an experiment in which all your participants will react in the same way. There are two principal ways of reducing the effects of individual differences. The first is to make sure your sample is large enough to overcome the differences between individuals, and to randomly allocate to each condition, if using a between-participants design. The second is to use the same participants in each condition and hence use a within-participants design.

### *Differences in a participant over time*

Just as a UK and US physicist can expect to get the same results, the UK physicist will expect to get the same result with their piece of metal tomorrow as they did today. Not so the psychologist. Just as there are differences between individuals, there are differences in the same individual over time. Just because your participant behaves one way today, it does not mean that they will behave the same way tomorrow. One way of dealing with this is to use different participants in each condition, although you then have the problem of individual differences. It is best, then, to use sufficient participants so that their average behaviour overcomes differences over time.

### *Demand characteristics*

In short, people try to be helpful. When we are conducting our experiment we want the participant to respond 'naturally' and not try to work out what the researcher wants them to do and then try to do that. So, demand characteristics are where the participant responds as they think they are supposed to and not as they would do usually. One way to limit demand characteristics is to have different participants in each condition. That way, each individual participant has less chance to work out what specific effect the experimenter is looking for.

### *Experimenter effects*

Although the researcher often plays a central role in the experiment, by recruiting participants, providing instructions and conducting the experiment itself, they should try to remain objective and dispassionate. Basically, the researcher should try not to influence the outcome of the experiment. If the researcher does exert an influence, even if they are not conscious of doing so, then they are introducing experimenter effects. When conducting an experiment you should be careful to give the experimental instructions in a standard way that does not favour a certain outcome, and try not to give away any verbal or non-verbal cues that might influence the participants. You may remember that earlier in the chapter we talked about double-blind testing. This is an excellent way of avoiding experimenter effects: if the experimenter does not know what condition the participant is in, then he or she cannot influence them. You should also be aware that it is impossible to be 100 per cent objective and that you will have an influence on the results you obtain.

### *Habituation*

The more you present a stimulus to a participant, the more they will become used to it. This can be particularly important in drug studies, where the effects the participant experiences after the fiftieth dose may well be considerably less than those they experience after the first dose. Habituation can also affect any experiment where the same stimulus or task is presented many times. For example, if we were studying attention by presenting a large red warning triangle on a computer screen whilst a participant was typing, we might expect their twenty-fifth response to be quite different from their first. The obvious way to avoid habituation is not to use an excessive number of presentations/tasks/doses. This can often be helped by having different participants in each condition.

### *Fatigue effects*

If your experiment goes on for a long time, your participant will get tired and a tired participant may well respond in a different way from an alert one. Fatigue can be especially problematic in studies conducted with young children, who may only be able to concentrate for a few minutes. Again, the obvious way to avoid fatigue is not to have long experiments, and again this can be helped by having different participants in each condition so that no one participant has to complete the whole experiment.

## Advantages and disadvantages of different experimental designs

When deciding how to design an experiment in order to overcome the above problems, you need to weigh up the likely impact of each on your results. You can use a within-participants design ensuring that the same participants are in each condition, which, for example, can minimise individual differences. Alternatively, you can employ a between-participants design so that different participants are allocated to each condition, which, for example, can overcome practise effects. Both designs have advantages and disadvantages, and there are some situations where only one design is really practicable. Our degree of control over potential confounding variables also differs between the two designs. Table 2.3 provides a summary of the advantages of each design. You will also discover that the use of within- or between-participants designs determines the statistical test we can use to analyse the data from our experiment and indeed how to lay out the data in statistical software such as SPSS.

**Table 2.3 Comparison of between- and within-participants designs**

| Between-participants | Within-participants |
|---|---|
| Less chance of practise and fatigue effects.<br>Less need to worry about counterbalancing.<br>Often the only choice when conducting a quasi-experiment. | Requires less time and effort as fewer participants have to be recruited.<br>Can reduce the effects caused by individual differences.<br>Often the only choice when comparing individuals' performances against baseline measures. |

## Activity 2.13

Below are descriptions of five psychological studies. In each case, state whether the design used is within- or between-participants (our answers are at the end of the chapter). You can also try to spot the IV and DV, if you want.

1 A developmental psychologist conducted an experiment to compare the response times of 5-year-old and 10-year-old children. Each child was asked to push a button on a computer keyboard every time a large blue square appeared on the screen.

2 Twenty participants were recruited by a researcher who was studying whether taking an exam increased levels of stress. Ten participants were asked to complete a maths-based test and ten participants were asked to read a magazine article. After this task, all the participants completed an Anxiety Inventory, which yielded a score indicating stress levels.

3 A researcher conducted an experiment to see whether moving faces would be recognised more accurately than static images of faces. Thirty participants were shown a videotape containing eighteen faces, nine of which were shown turning from side to side and nine of which were static. Ten minutes after watching the video, the participants were shown a photo-array of thirty-six faces and asked to pick out any they had seen on the video.

4 It has been suggested that small groups of people tend to make more 'risky' or 'extreme' decisions than individuals. A researcher recruited thirty people and gave them descriptions of five court cases that required a financial settlement. Each participant first worked on their own to arrive at an amount and then formed a group of ten participants and arrived at a group decision as to the amount of the settlement.

5 It is a commonly held belief (at least in the advertising community) that people are more likely to buy a product if it is presented by an attractive person. To test this belief, a researcher constructed adverts for a new brand of toothpaste. In half the adverts the person using the toothpaste was rated as 'very attractive' by a panel of ten judges and in the other half the toothpaste-user was rated as 'of average attractiveness' by the judges. The researcher showed fifty people one of the adverts involving a 'very attractive' person and another fifty people one of the adverts involving a person 'of average attractiveness'. All were asked to give a score of between 1 (very unlikely) and 10 (very likely) to indicate how likely they would be to buy the toothpaste.

## Summary Section 3

- An experiment is a study in which the researcher sees the effect that the IV (independent variable) has on the DV (dependent variable).
- The IV is the variable that is manipulated by the researcher.
- Manipulating the IV will lead to the formation of different conditions.
- The DV is the variable that is measured by the researcher.
- A confounding variable is any variable, other than the IV, which affects the DV in one condition more than another.
- The researcher attempts to limit the effects of confounding variables by introducing controls and through the design of the experiment.
- A between-participants design is one where different people take part in each condition.
- A within-participants design is one where the same people take part in each condition.

# 4 Final word

We have looked at two methods in this chapter: correlational studies and experiments. These both seek to be objective, and the kinds of data used are almost always either material or behavioural. The main difference between the two methods is that correlational studies can involve the *measurement* of two or more variables without any kind of intervention, whereas carrying out an experiment involves deliberately *manipulating* one variable (the independent variable) to see what effect this has on another variable (the dependent variable).

| **Terms you should be familiar with (remember the glossary at the end of this book):** | |
|---|---|
| Correlation | Random allocation |
| Correlation coefficient | Placebo |
| Scatterplot | Single-blind and double-blind testing |
| Cause and effect | Baseline measure |
| The independent and the dependent variables | Quasi-experiment |
| Experimental and control conditions | Confounding variables |
| Between- and within-participants designs | Counterbalancing |

**Now it is time to turn to the first chapter in the *SPSS Booklet*. We will introduce you to this statistical package and you will find out how to run SPSS and open different types of files.**

# References

Chandler, M., Fritz, A.S. and Hala, S. (1989) 'Small-scale deceit: deception as a marker of two, three, and four-year-olds' early theories of mind', *Child Development*, vol. 60, pp. 1263–77.

Cohen, J. (1988) *Statistical Power Analysis for the Behavioural Sciences* (2nd edn), New York, Academic Press.

Tajfel, H., Billig, M., Bundy, R.P. and Flament, C. (1971) 'Social categorization and intergroup behaviour', *European Journal of Social Psychology*, vol. 1, pp. 149–77.

# Answers to activities

### Activity 2.3

Here is our scatterplot of the data in Table 2.2:

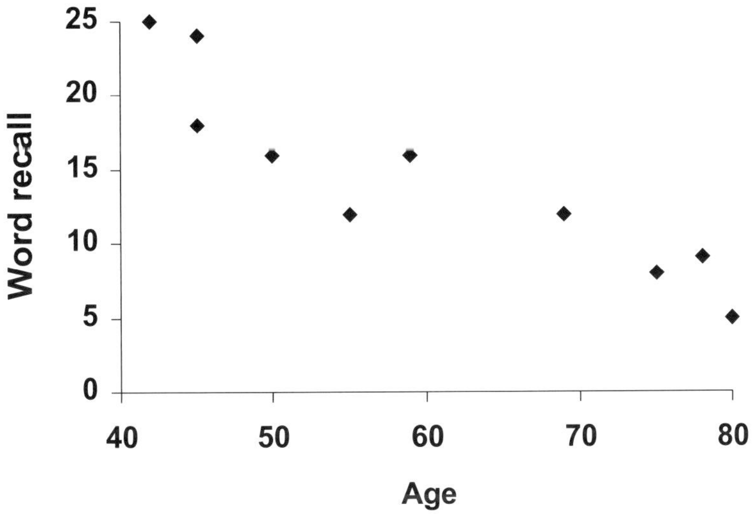


The pattern of points on the scatterplot slopes downwards from top left to bottom right, so it appears that there is a tendency for older participants to recall fewer words.

### Activity 2.4

1 We would suggest a negative correlation between amount of clothing worn and the number of ice creams sold. It is likely that fewer items being worn would be paired with a greater number of ice creams being sold.
2 We would suggest a positive relationship between achievement motivation and academic success. It is possible that a higher level of achievement motivation will be paired with greater academic success; however, there will, of course, be other variables affecting academic success so we would expect the correlation to be weak.
3 We would suggest that there is no relationship between amount of time spent reading and hair length as we cannot think of any reason why these two variables should co-vary.
4 We would suggest a positive relationship between lung cancer and smoking. Studies have suggested that the incidence of lung cancer increases with the number of cigarettes smoked.

### Activity 2.5

> *An experiment is an artificial set-up designed to investigate* ***cause*** *and effect. The experimenter aims to control all possible* ***variables*** *and keep all but one of them* ***constant****. Then one variable – the* ***independent*** *variable – is manipulated in a controlled way and its effect on behaviour is measured via the* ***dependent*** *variable.*

### Activity 2.6

The researcher might want to control how much understanding of psychological research methods the students already possessed and ensure that they didn't learn about methods outside of the experimental setting. He or she might also want the same tutor to teach methods using different teaching styles.

### Activity 2.8

2 IV = type of identification parade (either live or video)
DV = identification of the suspect/foil
3 IV = composition method (either alone or in a small group)
DV = creativity rating
4 IV = emotive nature of words (either highly emotive or non-emotive)
DV = recall of words.

### Activity 2.9

With (1), the experiment does not include a control group, a no-caffeine group, so the experimenter will not be able to infer a causal relationship between caffeine and concentration. With (2), there is no random allocation to each condition so that the presence and absence of music is not the only difference between the two groups of participants; indeed, the students in the two groups are studying different subjects. With (3), there is no double-blind testing – the person administering the drug and interviewing each patient knows whether the patient is in the drug or the placebo condition. There is also no baseline measure of depression against which change could be measured.

### Activity 2.10

The health psychologist might find that the number of sick days is lower for the group that regularly exercises than for the group that does not exercise. But can she conclude that the difference in the number of sick days is because of the exercise? There may be a host of other factors which also differed between the two groups participating in the study. For example, those exercising may be more health-conscious and therefore have a better diet. Those not exercising may have less time for themselves, either because of family commitments or because they work longer hours and may therefore be under more stress. You might have thought of other factors, such as age, prior injury, income, etc. If possible, the health psychologist could select her two groups of participants very carefully so that they are matched in terms of all these other things.

### Activity 2.11

All three may result in a confounding variable. In terms of (1), there is evidence suggesting that males and females may differ in the strategies they employ to complete certain cognitive tasks, so to rule out any possible effect due to sex, it is always best to control for sex of participant. (Of course, if the experimenter were randomly allocating participants to conditions, this shouldn't be an issue.) With (2), we can't rule out motivation as a confounding variable here – the first twenty participants to volunteer may well be more motivated or willing to take part than the second set of twenty participants. In terms of (3), there is evidence that time of day may affect performance, so it is best to control for this as a possible confounding variable.

### Activity 2.12

1 The independent variable is manipulated by the experimenter. TRUE
2 The independent variable is measured by the experimenter. FALSE
3 The independent variable is the causal factor in our 'cause and effect' relationship. TRUE
4 The independent variable is a measure of the effect in our 'cause and effect' relationship. FALSE
5 The dependent variable is the causal factor in our 'cause and effect' relationship. FALSE
6 The dependent variable is the outcome measured by the experimenter. TRUE
7 The dependent variable is manipulated by the experimenter. FALSE
8 The dependent variable is the effect in our 'cause and effect' relationship. TRUE
9 Confounding variables are other factors that might affect the result, and confuse the picture we are getting from these results. TRUE
10 It is important to have some confounding variables in an experiment. FALSE
11 It is important to try to control as many confounding variables as possible in an experiment. TRUE

## Activity 2.13

1 Between-participants
IV = age of child (either 5 or 10)
DV = response time

2 Between-participants
IV = task completed (either maths test or article reading)
DV = stress score on Anxiety Inventory

3 Within-participants
IV = presentation of face (either moving or static)
DV = recognition accuracy on photo-array task

4 Within-participants
IV = type of decision (either individual or group)
DV = amount of settlement

5 Between-participants
IV = attractiveness of toothpaste-user (either 'very attractive' or 'of average attractiveness')
DV = score indicating likelihood of buying toothpaste

CHAPTER 3

# Variables, measurement and descriptive statistics

## Contents

Aims 78

1 Variables and measurement 78

1.1 Levels of measurement 80

1.2 Continuous vs. discrete vs. categorical variables 82

2 Descriptive statistics 85

2.1 Measures of central tendency 87

2.2 Measures of dispersion 93

2.3 Generalising from the sample to the population 98

2.4 Describing data with statistics 99

References 101

Answers to activities 102

## Aims

This chapter aims to:

- explore in more detail variables and their measurement
- introduce you to descriptive statistics including measures of central tendency and spread.

In this study week we also show you how to obtain descriptive statistics using SPSS (see Chapter 2 in the *SPSS Booklet*).

---

**Activity 3.1**

(a) Drawing on the part of Chapter 6 'Attention and perception' that you read this week, find an example of a laboratory experiment and a study in a naturalistic setting.

(b) What are the values of carrying out experiments in a laboratory and in naturalistic settings?

See the end of this chapter for suggestions.

---

In Chapter 2 of this book we introduced you to two different methods employed by researchers *seeking objectivity*. These methods involve the gathering of evidence through measurement. This chapter will explore in more detail the issue of measurement and introduce you to descriptive statistics.

## 1 Variables and measurement

Think back to the social categorisation experiment conducted by Tajfel *et al.* (1971), discussed in Chapter 1 of this book. They were trying to establish a general statement relating 'group membership' to 'hostile/favourable behaviour to those in the outgroup/ingroup'. For their laboratory experiment they manipulated 'cause' (i.e. being in one group and not being in another group) and then measured the 'effect' (i.e. hostile behaviour towards members of the outgroup and favourability to the ingroup members). How might you set about measuring hostile/favourable behaviour? It could be measured in a variety of ways, including recording verbal abuse and observing body language. As Tajfel *et al.* were conducting quantitative research and trying to establish cause and effect, they found a way to quantify and measure hostile/favourable behaviour. Their first step was to define hostile/favourable behaviour *in the context of the experiment* in a way that would allow precise measurement. So they chose to define hostility/favourability in terms of the number of points allocated (points that could be traded in for money). We introduced you to the term *operationalise* in the introductory chapter in Book 1 *Mapping Psychology* as meaning to define concepts and make them usable in practice – hostility/favourability was operationalised as the number of points awarded. You might feel that this measure is a very simplified version of the dimension hostility/favourability, but it is this simplification that allowed the researchers to arrive at a consensus. Devising a simple index like this to yield numerical data and maximise objectivity is commonplace in psychology. Everyone can agree that four points awarded is more than one point, so the numbers allowed comparisons to be made between the numbers of points allocated to the ingroup and the outgroup. Similarly, in a memory experiment it is relatively easy to make comparisons between two groups when 'memory' is operationalised as the 'number of words remembered' or 'time taken to remember a set of words'.

By devising this index of hostility/favourability, Tajfel *et al.* (1971) created a variable, in fact a dependent variable. You might be able to think of several different ways of measuring hostility/favourability, so when designing a study it is important to think very carefully about what it is that you want to measure and how you are going to measure it. When designing their studies, researchers consider these four issues.

## The validity of the measure

Are the researchers measuring what they think they are measuring? This is relatively straightforward to establish when measuring reaction time or taking physiological measures, but it is more problematic when using questionnaires to measure personality or attitudes (see Chapter 5 of Book 1 for more on the issue of validity). One particular type of validity is ecological validity, the extent to which a study reflects naturally occurring or everyday situations. This is of particular concern when conducting laboratory experiments, as we need to consider whether the behaviour we are measuring inside the laboratory reflects the behaviour that would be measured in other settings.

## The reliability of the measure

Will the measuring instrument used by the researchers (e.g. a memory test) always produce the same set of results under the same conditions? This is an important consideration when devising questionnaires.

### Measurement error

What is the discrepancy between the numbers the researchers use to represent what they are measuring and the actual value of what they are trying to measure? Think of the temperature of your oven; it will rarely be the exact temperature that you programmed or set the dial to. Similarly, your bathroom scales are unlikely to measure your weight with 100 per cent accuracy (unless very expensive or carefully calibrated). In psychology, we can minimise measurement error by collecting material data (e.g. physiological measures). Most vulnerable to measurement error are indirect measures that may be influenced by other factors such as social pressures (e.g. self-report measures).

### The analysis of the data

How will researchers analyse the data they collect? When designing an experiment and thinking about measurement, it is important to be clear about the type of data being gathered, so that it can be analysed in a meaningful way. We shall look at type of data in more detail next.

## 1.1 Levels of measurement

### Activity 3.2

Think about what you would measure to explore the following:

(a) change blindness

(b) mate selection amongst men and women

(c) automatic and controlled processing.

#### Comment

(a) You have read about change blindness in Chapter 6 of Book 1. In a naturalistic field study, Simons and Levin (1998) measured whether or not pedestrians noticed a change in the person they were talking to. An alternative would be to show participants in a laboratory a video or series of slides depicting some sort of scenario where a change is introduced. Again you would record whether or not they noticed a change.

(b) You have read about mate selection in Chapter 2 of Book 1. One possible design would be to provide male and female participants with a list of characteristics and ask them to rank these in order of preferences (this would be a quasi-experiment as you are not actually manipulating the IV, sex of participant). You would then be looking at differences between men and women in terms of how they ranked these characteristics.

(c) You have read about automatic and controlled processing in Chapter 6 of Book 1. In many of the experiments mentioned there, response time taken to complete a particular task was measured, such as how long it took participants to complete the task in studies of the Stroop effect. If you had thought about the Stroop effect, you might also have considered an alternative measure, such as the number of errors made.

In the research examples in Activity 3.2, different devices were used to measure something and what was measured differed according to how the dependent variable was operationalised. Data can be measured at four levels: nominal, ordinal, interval and ratio (these generally correspond to what the numbers in the data set represent). In example (a) in Activity 3.2, participants either noticed or did not notice a change. In order to record this numerically, we could assign a '1' to when they did notice and a '0' to when they didn't. However, these numbers are completely arbitrary (we could just as easily have decided to assign a '0' to when they did and a '1' to when they did not notice), and are simply a shorthand for the labels 'participant noticed the change' and 'participant didn't notice the change'. We refer to data measured at this level as *nominal*.

In the case of example (b) in Activity 3.2, participants were asked to rank the order of the characteristics they would prefer their mate to possess. In order to record their responses numerically, if there were ten characteristics, we could assign '1' to the characteristic they most preferred, '2' to the second most preferred, and so on until '10' was assigned to the least preferred characteristic. Alternatively, we could assign '10' to the characteristic they most preferred, '9' to the second most preferred, and so on. What matters here is that the numbers indicate an order. So if '1' is 'best' then we can assume that '2' is more preferable than '4'. What we cannot assume is that '2' is *twice* as preferable as '4', just as we cannot assume that the athlete who finished first in a race did so in half the time taken by the athlete who came second. We refer to data measured at this level as *ordinal*.

In the case of example (c) from Activity 3.2, participants are asked to complete the Stroop task and their response time is measured. Here the numbers in the data set have *all* the properties of numbers, in that '2' is twice as much as '1' and half as much as '4'. In other words, both the order of the numbers and the intervals between them are important. Thus, the intervals between 30 seconds, 29 seconds and 28 seconds, etc. are all equal. We have used a scale (time) to measure the dependent variable, and equal intervals represent equal differences in what we are seeking to measure. If, in addition, the scale we are using for our measurement contains a true 0 (i.e. the '0' means complete absence of the property being measured), then the ratios of values will be meaningful. This is indeed the case with example (c), so that 40 seconds is twice as much time as 20 seconds. We refer to data measured at this level as *ratio*. If it does not contain a true 0, such as when we measure temperature using the Celsius scale (0 °C doesn't mean a complete absence of heat, it is just the point at which water freezes), then data measured at this level is referred to as *interval* (and this means that you can't say that 30° is twice as hot as 15°).

*Note:* You will find later on that in terms of statistical analysis, data measured at interval and ratio levels are treated as equivalent. However in terms of *interpretation*, it is important to bear in mind whether the data were measured at the ratio or interval level. For example, if measured at the interval level, you could not conclude that one group performed twice as well as the other group in an experiment.

## 1.2 Continuous vs. discrete vs. categorical variables

We have seen that there are four levels of measurement and these tell us about how we can use the numbers we record. These numbers might just act as labels, they might tell us about order or they might give precise information about amount. The level of measurement we use will depend on the variable itself, and an important distinction is made between continuous, discrete and categorical variables.

If we are measuring response times, height, weight or temperature, then these would be *continuous variables* because the variables can take any value between the lowest and highest points on the scale; that is, the values can vary continuously. Some continuous variables can be measured precisely using a scale. This often happens with material data: for example, measuring hormone levels. Behavioural data can also be measured over a continuous scale. An example is the measurement of response time (time in seconds). A continuous variable must be able to produce data of absolutely any value (including decimal places).

Variables that can only produce certain values, such as only integers (whole numbers), are referred to as *discrete variables*. An example is the measurement of extraverted behaviour in personality research which is a score on a test scale. Also, whilst the variable 'time taken to recall a word list in seconds' would be continuous, the variable 'number of words recalled correctly' would be discrete. For the first variable, it is theoretically possible that a participant's response time could be absolutely any number (e.g. 5.3908765 seconds or 10.7893536 seconds), whilst for the second variable the participant's response could only be an integer (e.g. 6 words or 12 words).

In reality, response time is usually measured at most to the nearest millisecond and could therefore be considered a discrete variable. In some respects, then, there can be a degree of similarity between discrete and continuous variables, and indeed the distinction between continuous and discrete variables is also not a particularly useful one in deciding how to analyse data statistically. Instead, when deciding which statistical test to use, as you will see in Chapter 6, a more important consideration is whether there is a definite and ordered relationship between the numbers produced, as when measuring data at ordinal, interval or ratio levels. For instance, a response time of 3.4 seconds is *less* than a response time of 4.5 seconds, and a participant who recalled 15 words recalled *more* words than one who recalled 12. With ordinal level data, this relationship may be opposite to the actual magnitude of the numbers; for example, a confidence scale may use the number '1' to represent 'Very confident' and the number '10' to represent 'Very unconfident', but there is still a definite and ordered relationship.

Likewise, another important aspect to consider in terms of statistical analysis is whether the variable is being measured at the nominal level. Such a variable is often termed a *categorical variable*. Simple examples of categorical variables are: sex, handedness, political affiliation and religion. A rather more complicated example of a categorical variable from Book 1, Chapter 1 is eye colour; that is, 'being in the falsely attributed "bad" blue-eyes group' or 'being in the falsely attributed "good" brown-eyes group'. A categorical variable therefore produces data that tell us about which category a participant was in.

As categorical variables are measured at the nominal level, they do *not* maintain a definite and ordered relationship between the numbers produced. For example, by assigning the number '1' to 'female' and the number '2' to 'male', we are not implying that women are somehow more or less than men. Instead, the number is simply being used as a label and the assignment of a particular number to a particular category is arbitrary (for instance, we could equally label 'males' as '1' and 'females' as '2').

### Activity 3.3

Classify the following as continuous, discrete or categorical and identify the level of measurement involved:

(a) 'BSc (Hons) Psychology', 'BA/BSc (Hons) Social Sciences with Psychological Studies', 'BA (Hons) Philosophy and Psychological Studies'.

(b) 'Pass 1', 'Pass 2', 'Pass 3', 'Pass 4', 'Fail'.

(c) A percentage mark on a multiple choice test.

(d) The time a student spends writing a TMA essay.

See the end of the chapter for answers.

Whilst measurements and numbers are common to all quantitative methods, you are probably already sensing that numbers are not quite so straightforward and transparent as many people think. A central part of the quantitative research process is therefore *making sense of the numbers*, and that means being clear about what was measured and how it was measured.

It is because 'numbers' are not transparent, but have to be made sense of, that quantitative research uses statistics. What is it about statistics that is so important? There are several reasons why we use statistics. As we saw in Chapter 1, statistics are necessary as usually we cannot conduct research on entire populations, but must instead use samples. Statistics are also very useful as they allow us to describe and communicate numerical findings in standard and often pictorial ways – and to do this we use *descriptive statistics*. Although describing the data collected is important, it is equally important that we are able to make decisions about what the numbers we collect actually mean, and what conclusions can be drawn (safely) from the measurements and numbers that the research has generated – and to do so we use *inferential statistics* (because they allow inferences to be made from numerical findings). Let's first explore descriptive statistics in the rest of this chapter. We will introduce you to inferential statistics in Chapters 5 and 6.

## Summary Section 1

- When designing a correlational study or an experiment, variables are defined (operationalised) in certain ways.
- It is important to reflect on whether their measurement has validity and reliability, on whether there might be any measurement error, and on how the data will be analysed.
- There are several levels of measurement: variables can be measured at nominal, ordinal, interval and ratio levels.
- There are different types of variables: continuous, discrete and categorical variables.
- Statistics can be divided into descriptive and inferential statistics.

# 2 Descriptive statistics

Quantitative research generates numbers – often large quantities of numbers, and it is easy to be overwhelmed with numerical findings. Sometimes the numbers that are generated in a study are referred to as a data set and descriptive statistics provide methods and conventions that enable researchers to 'see' and describe, summarise and communicate their data sets to other researchers.

### Activity 3.4

You probably already know something about descriptive statistics; every day the media bombard us with numbers. Write down any ways you can think of in which numbers and data are presented to us in everyday life.

In response to Activity 3.4, you might have thought of a graph, as these are often used in everyday life and are a useful way to summarise and present data. Suppose an educational researcher used current Open University records to find out about the ages of people who study at the University. The data could be lists of the numbers of people currently registered who fall into each of the following age groups: up to 25, 26 to 30, 31 to 35, 36 to 45, 46 to 55, 56 to 65, 66 and above. Counting the frequency of people in each group would give seven numbers. A pie chart could be drawn to show the different sizes of 'slices of the pie' (seven slices in all) that

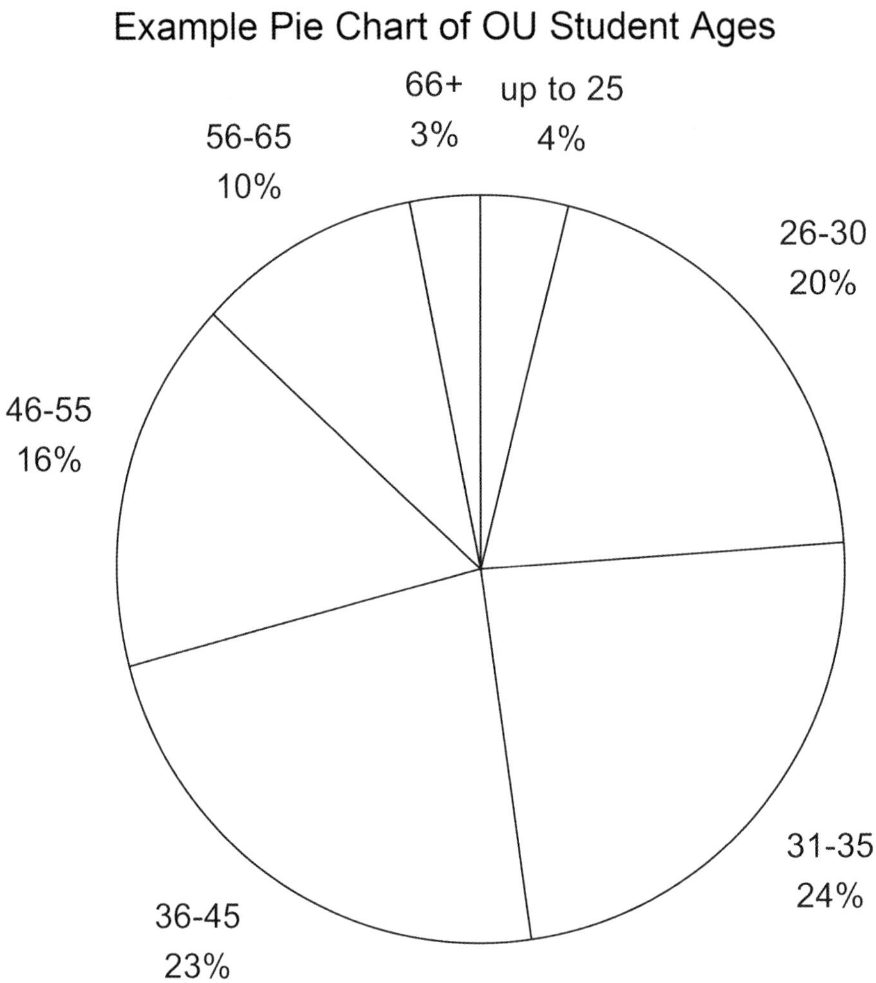


**Figure 3.1** Example of a pie chart

represent the percentage of the total number of registered students in each age group (see Figure 3.1).

Another type of graph, a histogram, would present the same data, but not as percentages of the total. Instead, the actual numbers (frequencies) of students in each age group would be represented by the height of a bar on the graph (see Figure 3.2). We shall look at how to construct such a graph in the next chapter.

In your list of everyday examples of descriptive statistics you might also have included the terms 'average' or 'mean'. These and other descriptive statistics are explained in Section 2.1. But if a researcher were to summarise the findings of a study by giving only the *mean* value of the data collected, a great deal of information would be lost. Every variable (by definition) can take on a range of values and the extent of this range is important information. The researcher studying the ages of OU students might count the frequency of students who are 22 years old, 23 years,

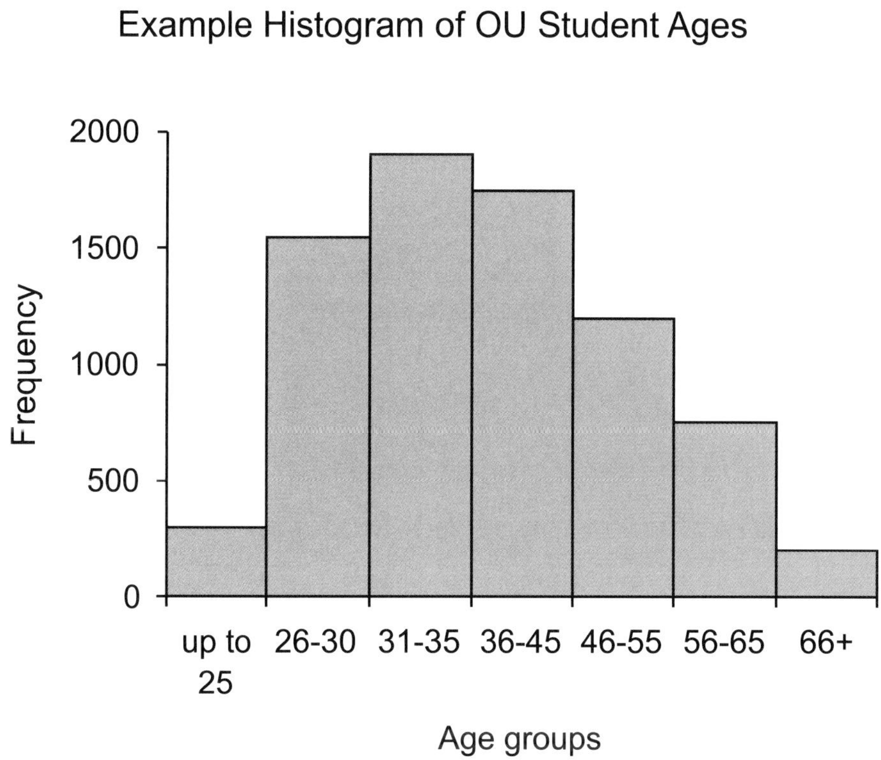


**Figure 3.2** Example of a histogram

24 years, etc., right up to 80 years or more. The range of these scores (which is the difference between the highest and lowest scores) is potentially interesting. You will learn about a similar statistic called standard deviation in Section 2.2.

## 2.1 Measures of central tendency

Below is a description of a basic psychological study:

> *A team of psychologists wanted to look at how children's memory for words changes as they get older. After obtaining the relevant permissions from parents, school and children, they recruited thirty children, ten children from each of three different age groups (4–5, 7–8 and 10–11 years). Each child was read a specially constructed word list containing twenty concrete nouns that they would be familiar with (e.g. 'tree' and 'table') and asked to repeat each word after the researcher. Three minutes after being read the list, each child was asked to recall all the words they could remember from the list by saying each word aloud.*
>
> *The psychologists carefully recorded how each child responded to the recall task. As the psychologists knew what words were on the original*

*list, they were able to tell how many words the child recalled correctly and how many they recalled incorrectly (i.e. words that were not on the original list). The psychologists then put all the data from the study in a table (see Table 3.1).*

**Table 3.1 Performance on a recall task by age of child**

| Age group | No. of words recalled correctly | No. of words recalled incorrectly | Age group | No. of words recalled correctly | No. of words recalled incorrectly |
|---|---|---|---|---|---|
| 4 to 5 | 4 | 5 | 7 to 8 | 7 | 2 |
| 4 to 5 | 6 | 2 | 7 to 8 | 8 | 0 |
| 4 to 5 | 4 | 3 | 7 to 8 | 9 | 2 |
| 4 to 5 | 5 | 2 | 7 to 8 | 8 | 0 |
| 4 to 5 | 3 | 0 | 7 to 8 | 9 | 0 |
| 4 to 5 | 6 | 0 | 10 to 11 | 10 | 0 |
| 4 to 5 | 3 | 3 | 10 to 11 | 12 | 1 |
| 4 to 5 | 6 | 3 | 10 to 11 | 12 | 1 |
| 4 to 5 | 4 | 2 | 10 to 11 | 13 | 0 |
| 4 to 5 | 3 | 1 | 10 to 11 | 11 | 0 |
| 7 to 8 | 7 | 1 | 10 to 11 | 14 | 1 |
| 7 to 8 | 9 | 0 | 10 to 11 | 13 | 0 |
| 7 to 8 | 10 | 1 | 10 to 11 | 13 | 1 |
| 7 to 8 | 6 | 1 | 10 to 11 | 12 | 0 |
| 7 to 8 | 12 | 1 | 10 to 11 | 10 | 0 |

We need to be able to summarise the data from *each* age group in a way that makes comparison *between* age groups easy to perform. One way to do this would be to add up the number of words recalled correctly by the children in each age group. Doing this gives us totals of 44 for the 4 to 5-year-olds, 85 for the 7 to 8-year-olds and 120 for the 10 to 11-year-olds. From these figures we can see that the older children recalled more words correctly than the younger ones. Are these totals sufficient to describe the data though? Let's think about what they *don't* tell us:

- We don't get any sense of how an individual child performed.
- We can't tell whether all the children recalled a similar number of words correctly or whether there were large differences in the number of words recalled by each child.

Also, total scores are fine as long as the number of children in each group is the same. If we had used thirty children in the youngest group and only ten in the others, we could never directly compare the totals. In other words, we need a way of describing the data that is not dependent upon the size of the sample.

So, what we need is a method of summarising the data that allows a direct comparison between the groups, even if they have unequal numbers of children in them. Can you think of a simple way to do this? One answer is to divide the total score by the number of children in that group. That way, if the group contains a large number of children, the total score will increase, but we will then divide it by a larger number to compensate for this.

You may recognise this particular form of descriptive statistic, as it is regularly used to summarise data and is referred to as an average. Actually, there is more than one way to calculate the average, and this particular method is known as the *mean*.

To recap, the mean score is calculated by:

- adding all the scores together
- dividing by the number of scores.

We could calculate a mean score for all the data collected. This would entail adding all the scores together and then dividing this total by the number of scores, in this case 30. This would give us:

$$4+6+4+5+3+6+3+6+4+3+7+9+10+6+12+7+8+9+$$
$$8+9+10+12+12+13+11+14+13+13+12+10=\mathbf{249}$$

$$\frac{249}{30}=\underline{\mathbf{8.3}}$$

So, the mean number of words recalled correctly by all the children in the study was 8.3. We can now use this method of calculation to work out the mean scores for each age group. To do this we just add up all the scores in that group and divide by the number of scores (in this case, 10). Let's do this now:

### 4- to 5-year-olds:

$$\text{Mean score} = \frac{(4+6+4+5+3+6+3+6+4+3)}{10}$$

$$=\underline{\mathbf{4.4}}$$

### 7- to 8-year-olds:

$$\text{Mean score} = \frac{(7+9+10+6+12+7+8+9+8+9)}{10}$$

= **8.5**

### 10- to 11-year-olds:

$$\text{Mean score} = \frac{(10+12+12+13+11+14+13+13+12+10)}{10}$$

= **1.2**

The mean scores we have calculated give us a simple and direct method of comparing different groups of data and also tell us something about the performance of individual children. In this case, we can see how many words were recalled on average in each age group.

### *Activity 3.5*

Calculate the means for the following data sets:

(a) 10; 5; 8; 10; 9; 12; 15; 14; 7; 10

(b) 18; 2; 19; 18; 18; 4; 14; 12; 15; 10

(c) 4; 2; 9; 3; 10; 7; 6; 32; 4; 3

See the end of the chapter for answers.

There are two other commonly used methods of calculating an average score, these are the *mode* and the *median*. To calculate the mode, all you have to do is see which value occurred the most frequently. As it is possible that two or more values occurred with equal frequency, it is possible that the mode will be two or more numbers. Below we calculate the mode score for each age group in our study of children's memory for words:

### 4- to 5-year-olds:

Mode score = three 3s, three 4s, one 5 and three 6s = **3, 4 and 6**

### 7- to 8-year-olds:

Mode score = one 6, two 7s, two 8s, three 9s, one 10 and one 12 = **9**

### 10- to 11-year-olds:

Mode score = two 10s, one 11, three 12s, three 13s and one 14 = **12 and 13**

To calculate the median score, we first put all the scores in order and then work out which score is in the middle. If there are an even number of scores, then there will be two numbers in the middle, so we simply take the midpoint between them (i.e. add them together and divide by two). Calculating median scores can be time-consuming to do by hand (although you can give it a go if you want), but SPSS will produce them for us.

We make the median scores:[1]

### 4- to 5-year-olds:

Median score = 3 3 3 4 **4 4** 5 6 6 6 = **4**

### 7- to 8-year-olds:

Median score = 6 7 7 8 **8 9** 9 9 10 12 = **8.5**

### 10- to 11-year-olds:

Median score = 10 10 11 12 **12 12** 13 13 13 14 = **12**

We refer to the mean, mode and median as being measures of *central tendency*, which basically means that they tell us what the *central* scores in our sample *tended* to be. This makes them a very useful method by which we can estimate what the scores in the population might be. The specific sample of data was collected, after all, in order to draw conclusions about the population.

Why are these measures of central tendency a useful estimate of the population? We have seen that adding all the individual scores together to form a total score is not useful, as it is dependent upon the size of the sample and bears no resemblance to the score that any one individual could obtain. There is also an obvious problem in choosing the score from just one individual to be an accurate estimate of the wider population – which would you choose? Choosing either the lowest or highest score would hardly be a good estimate, and simply choosing the *value* that was in the middle of the range obtained would not take any account of the frequency with which individual values occurred. Instead, we need a single figure, calculated from the data in the sample, that tells us what the

[1] As there are an even number of values in each group, we have put the middle two values in **bold** type. The median score is calculated by adding these two numbers together and dividing by two.

average score was. The average score calculated from the sample data is always going to be our most accurate method of estimating what the average score of the population is.

So, by calculating the mean, mode or median we are able to derive a single descriptive statistic that is the most accurate estimate of what the average score in the wider population might be. The mean, mode and median are referred to as *point estimates* of the population.

You can see that although the figures we calculated for the mean, mode and median for the data from the study on children's recall are very similar, they are not exactly the same. The reason for this is that the three methods of calculation are sensitive to different aspects of the data as a whole.

### Activity 3.6

Calculate the modes and the medians for data sets below which are the same as those in Activity 3.5:

(a) 10; 5; 8; 10; 9; 12; 15; 14; 7; 10

(b) 18; 2; 19; 18; 18; 4; 14; 12; 15; 10

(c) 4; 2; 9; 3; 10; 7; 6; 32; 4; 3

How do these compare with the mean? See the end of the chapter for answers.

The mode is obviously sensitive to whether most participants tended to obtain one of the scores in the middle. If we had collected data in which lots of people had recalled either most of the words or very few of the words, the mode would have been very different. For instance, if lots of children in our study of memory for words had recalled just 1 word correctly, then the mode would also have been 1 regardless of whether other children had recalled 14, 15 or 16 words. So the mode will only be similar to the mean score if the majority obtained scores near the mean and few people obtained the more extreme low or high scores.

The median is not sensitive to the magnitude of the more extreme scores. For instance, if the child in the oldest group who recalled 14 words (the highest score) had actually recalled all 20, the median would not have been affected and would still be 12. Similarly, if the two children who scored 10 (the lowest score) had actually scored 0, the median would still be 12.

Which measure of central tendency is reported will depend on the type of data collected. If the data are measured at the nominal level, then it is not possible to calculate either a mean or a median but it is possible to say which category had the highest frequency count. If the data are measured at ordinal level or if there are extreme scores that are extraordinarily high or low – these are known as *outliers* – then often the median is reported. With interval and ratio data, the mean is usually reported. The mean score is the preferred measure of central tendency as it is sensitive to the *actual* values obtained. It is therefore the descriptive statistic that is most often used to describe data and is also the basis of more complex statistical analyses (which we will look at in Chapter 6). Having said that, the relationship between the mean, mode and median is useful in telling us whether any peculiarities in the data exist (such as lots of people obtaining scores distant from the mean).

## 2.2 Measures of dispersion

There are two things that need to be accounted for in describing the data from the study of children's memory for words presented at the start of Section 2.1. These are:

- We need to get a sense of how an individual child performed.
- We need to be able to tell whether all the children recalled a similar number of words correctly or whether there were large differences in the number of words recalled by each child.

Our measures of central tendency take care of the first of these, but what about the second? We know that the mean scores for each age group were 4.4, 8.5 and 12, but these do not tell us anything about how spread out or *dispersed* the data in each age group were.

As an example, let's look at a simpler set of data (labelled A) that only contains five scores, these being:

(A) 12 14 15 16 18

$$\text{Mean} = \frac{(12 + 14 + 15 + 16 + 18)}{5}$$

$= \underline{\mathbf{15}}$

However, 15 is also the mean of the following five scores in set B:

(B) 2 3 15 27 28

$$\text{Mean} = \frac{(2 + 3 + 15 + 27 + 28)}{5}$$

$= \underline{\mathbf{15}}$

So, if we were just relying on the mean to describe our data, we would describe both sets of data as being the same, even though they are evidently quite different. Looking at the difference between the two sets of data, it is apparent that the scores are more closely clustered around the mean in the first set, and more widely dispersed in the second.

As well as the mean, we also need to describe how spread out the individual scores are if we are going to provide a useful description of our data. We refer to the form of descriptive statistic that tells us how 'spread out' the data are as a *measure of dispersion*. There are a number of different methods available for calculating the measure of dispersion, and by far the simplest is the *range*.

To calculate the range, we simply take the smallest value in the data set away from the largest. For our two simple data sets, A and B, the ranges would be:

(A) 12 14 15 16 18

Range = (18 – 12) = **6**

(B) 2 3 15 27 28

Range = (28 – 2) = **26**

Using the range to describe these two sets of data reveals that the second contains more widely dispersed scores than the first. However, there is a problem with relying on the range that we can demonstrate by using a new set of data (set C):

(C) 2 14 15 16 28

Range = (28 – 2) = **26**

Calculating the range for set C reveals that it is identical to the set B above (and the mean for set C is also identical to the mean for set B). But the actual scores in sets B and C are quite different. Although the highest and lowest scores in both sets are the same, the remaining scores in set B are far more different from the mean than the remaining scores in set C are. The problem with the range, therefore, is that it *only* tells us about the highest and lowest scores and nothing about those in between.

What we need to do instead is somehow to calculate a measure of how dispersed the scores are that takes account of every score in the data set, not just the highest and lowest. One way to do this would be to take each individual score away from the mean score. This would provide us with a new piece of data telling us how each individual score *deviated* from the mean. (The actual calculations for some of the measures of dispersion are quite complicated and certainly fiddly to do. You will *not* be required to do these calculations by hand, or indeed remember exactly how to do so.) We could then find the mean of these deviations, which would provide us with a single value describing the average deviation of each score from the mean score. This is where things can get tricky to understand as we are talking about the mean deviation from the mean (and this involves using the word 'mean' quite a lot). Working through an example might help, so let's return to data set A:

The individual scores were:

12 14 15 16 18

and the mean score was **15**

To find out how each score *deviated* from the mean score, we need to subtract the mean score from each individual score:

(12 – 15) = –3

(14 – 15) = –1

(15 – 15) = 0

(16 – 15) = 1

(18 – 15) = 3

We now have five new values that represent the deviation of each individual score from the mean score. But we want to end up with just a single value that will tell us about the dispersion of the scores. We have already seen that the best way of summarising a set of scores as a single value is to calculate their mean. Doing this here will tell us by how much on *average* each individual score varied from the mean score (or the mean deviation from the mean if you will). We refer to this measure as the *mean deviation*. Let's try calculating the mean deviation for data set A:

Our deviation scores were: –3 –1 0 1 3

We now need to add these together and divide the total by the number of values (5):

–3 + –1 + 0 + 1 + 3 = 0

and 0 divided by 5 = **0**

Oh dear, we've ended up with 0 and that does not seem to be a particularly useful measure of how dispersed the scores were. Because the mean is a measure of central tendency, it will usually be the case that half our deviations will have negative values and half will have positive values. As adding positive to negative is going to result in the deviations cancelling each other out (–5 + 5 = 0), our mean deviation score is often going to be zero.

Therefore, we have to find a way of getting rid of the fact that some deviations are positive and some negative. One way we do this is to calculate the square of the deviation. Squaring a number involves multiplying that number by itself and, because a negative number multiplied by a negative number equals a positive number (−4 × −4 = 16), and a positive number multiplied by a positive number equals a positive number (4 × 4 = 16), this acts to make all numbers positive. Let's try doing this on the set 'A' deviation scores:

−3 × −3 = 9

−1 × −1 = 1

0 × 0 = 0

1 × 1 = 1

3 × 3 = 9

Now we can calculate the mean of these squared deviation scores in the sure knowledge that we won't end up with 0. The mean of the squared deviation scores is referred to as the *variance*. It is called this because it tells us about how the individual scores in the set of data vary in relation to the mean. Let's calculate the variance of data set A:

### Variance of A:

$$\frac{(9+1+0+1+9)}{5}$$

$= \underline{\mathbf{4}}$

Although we have now avoided ending up with a 0, unfortunately there is another problem with using the variance as a measure of dispersion. Despite this, variance is an extremely important statistical concept and although you will not be dealing with it in any great depth on this course, you will encounter it in other psychology courses, particularly DXR222 and DZX222 (the residential school and online courses associated with DSE212). 'What's the problem with the variance?' we hear you ask. Don't worry, we only have to do one more thing to our calculations and we'll arrive at a measure of dispersion that we can use sensibly. First, though, let's work out what the main problem with the variance is.

Let's look again at the actual scores in data set A. The individual scores were:

12 14 15 16 18

The mean was 15 and the variance was 4.

Can you spot why the variance is not a particularly useful measure of dispersion? The answer is that there was not a single score in the data set that was more than 3 away from the mean, yet the variance was 4! We want our measure of dispersion to tell us at a glance how the individual scores tended to vary. Having a measure that produces a value which is greater than the difference between any of the individual scores and the mean is therefore not that useful.

The problem lies in the fact that we squared the deviation scores (these were the mean score minus each individual score). By squaring the deviation scores, we've created numbers much larger than the actual deviations. So, if we made the deviations too large by squaring them, we can make them an appropriate size by finding the square root. You find the square root of a number by working out what number, when multiplied by itself, will result in the original number (or by pushing the square root [√] button on your calculator to save yourself a lot of time). The square root of 25 is therefore 5, as $5 \times 5 = 25$. The square root of 36 is 6 and the square root of 16 is 4.

Fortunately, we do not have to find the square root of each deviation. Instead, all we have to do is find the square root of the variance. We can work out that the square root of the variance we calculated for data set A is:

Variance = 4

Square root of variance = **2**

We refer to this new measure of dispersion (the square root of the variance) as the *standard deviation*, and it is the accepted descriptive statistic to use in order to describe how spread out scores are, particularly with data measured at interval or ratio level. For ordinal data, the range may be more appropriate.

Looking at the individual scores in data set A, we can see that a value of 2 is a much better indication of how the scores tend to vary from the mean. The largest deviation from the mean is 3 (15 to 12 or 15 to 18), but there are also scores that deviate from the mean by just 1. With deviations of 1 and of 3, a value of 2 seems spot-on in telling us what the standard deviation of the scores was.

To recap, calculating the standard deviation involves:

- finding the deviation scores (each individual score minus the mean)
- squaring the deviation scores (multiplying each deviation score by itself)
- calculating the mean of these squared deviation scores (this is the *variance*)
- finding the square root of the variance

and it provides us with a standard value indicating how the individual scores tended to deviate from the mean.

### Activity 3.7

As you have already calculated the mean for the data sets below, why not have a go at calculating the standard deviations.

(a) 10; 5; 8; 10; 9; 12; 15; 14; 7; 10

(b) 18; 2; 19; 18; 18; 4; 14; 12; 15; 10

(c) 4; 2; 9; 3; 10; 7; 6; 32; 4; 3

See the end of the chapter for answers.

---

Now that you've had a go at calculating the standard deviation in Activity 3.7, you might be relieved to hear that throughout the rest of this course you will not be asked to calculate the standard deviation by hand or even be required to remember how to do this. We have worked through the necessary steps so that you can get an idea of what the standard deviation is and how it represents the dispersion of the data. The main thing to remember is that the standard deviation is the accepted measure of dispersion to use on data such as we have been looking at here.

## 2.3 Generalising from the sample to the population

In Section 2.2, we showed you how to calculate the standard deviation for a particular sample of scores and you practised this in Activity 3.7. You may recall from Chapter 1 that in most quantitative research we want to generalise from the sample to the population. To do this, we use a concept known as *degrees of freedom* (df) which is often defined in terms of the number of scores whose values are free to vary. Howell (2002, p. 56) explains degrees of freedom in the following way:

> *Assume that you have in front of you the three numbers 6, 8 and 10. Their mean is 8. You are now informed that you may change any of these numbers, as long as the mean is kept constant at 8. How many numbers are you free to vary? If you think that you are free to vary all three numbers, you are wrong. If you change all three of them ... the mean almost certainly will not equal 8. Only two of the numbers can be freely changed if the mean is to remain constant. For example, if you change the 6 to a 7 and the 10 to a 13, the remaining number is determined; it must be 4 if the mean is to be 8.*

To explain this by analogy, if there are three urns and you know there is one of coffee, one of tea and one of hot chocolate, how many of these have to be labelled so that you can correctly obtain the type of drink you want? Only two need to be labelled: by knowing what two urns contain you will then also know what the third must contain (e.g. if one is labelled 'tea' and one is labelled 'coffee', then the remaining one must contain the hot chocolate).

As you have seen above, all but one of the scores are free to vary. This makes our degrees of freedom equal to the number of scores minus 1 (df = N – 1).

In the case of calculating the standard deviation for the sample of data in the simple data set A in Section 2.2, we divided by the number scores, i.e. by 5. If we wanted to generalise from that sample to the population then we would have divided by N – 1, i.e. by 4. For Activity 3.7, you divided by the number of scores (i.e. by 10) and the standard deviations you calculated should have been those shown in the answers to this activity at the end of the chapter. If you want to estimate the standard deviation for the population, then you would divide by the degrees of freedom (i.e. N – 1), in this case by 9. This will give you different figures for the standard deviations of the scores, as shown in Table 3.2.

**Table 3.2 Sample and population standard deviations from Activity 3.7**

| Scores from Activity 3.7 | Sample standard deviation | Population standard deviation |
|---|---|---|
| Set (a) | 2.90 | 3.06 |
| Set (b) | 5.73 | 6.04 |
| Set (c) | 8.39 | 8.81 |

Notice that the population standard deviations are larger than the sample standard deviations. This allows for more variation in the population scores than is present in our sample.

When estimating standard deviations for the population from a sample, degrees of freedom will always be N – 1. For other statistics, degrees of freedom may be calculated differently. However, you will be pleased to know that SPSS always calculates the correct degrees of freedom for you.

## 2.4 Describing data with statistics

We have now worked out a method of describing many sets of data, no matter how many scores they contain, using just two values. These values are:

- Mean – which is a measure of central tendency and tells us what the average score was.

- Standard deviation – which is a measure of dispersion and tells us how spread out the scores were in relation to the mean.

It is very important that you include *both* these measures when describing the data you will collect in your project work, as we need to know both what the average score was and how varied the actual scores were in relation to this average.

Of course, there are some types of data where it would be pointless to calculate either the standard deviation or the mean. As mentioned previously, if we had measured the data at the nominal level – for instance, recording whether the participant was male or female and coding the women as '1' and the men as '2' – then calculating the mean and standard deviation would not be possible. Instead, we would simply summarise by stating how many instances of each category there were (e.g. there were 17 men and 24 women).

## Summary Section 2

- Descriptive statistics summarise numerical data sets.
- Measures of central tendency include the mean, mode and median.
- The mean is considered the best measure of central tendency. However, the median is often used if the data set contains outliers or if the data are measured at the ordinal level. The mode is used if the data are measured at the nominal level.
- Measures of dispersion include the range and the standard deviation.
- The range is the simplest measure and is the difference between the largest and the smallest score in the data set. The range is often used with data measured at the ordinal level.
- The standard deviation takes account of all of the scores and provides an indication of how dispersed they are.
- Degrees of freedom is a statistical concept used when generalising from a sample to a population. When estimating the standard deviation for the population, degrees of freedom is calculated as $N - 1$.

| **Terms you should be familiar with:** |
|---|
| Validity |
| Ecological validity |
| Reliability |
| Measurement error |
| Nominal level of measurement |
| Ordinal level of measurement |
| Interval level of measurement |
| Ratio level of measurement |
| Continuous variables |
| Discrete variables |
| Categorical variables |
| Descriptive statistics |
| Mean |
| Mode |
| Median |
| Range |
| Standard deviation |
| Degrees of freedom |

**Now turn to Chapter 2 in the *SPSS Booklet*. You will see how to enter data and obtain descriptive statistics using SPSS.**

# References

Howell, D.C. (2002) *Statistical Methods for Psychology: Fifth Edition*, CA, Duxbury.

Simons, D.J. and Levin, D.T. (1998) 'Failure to detect changes to people during real-world interaction', *Psychonomic Bulletin and Review*, vol. 4, p. 644.

Tajfel, H., Billig, M., Bundy, R.P. and Flament, C. (1971) 'Social categorization and intergroup behaviour', *European Journal of Social Psychology*, vol. 1, pp. 149–77.

# Answers to activities

## Activity 3.1

(a) The dual-task studies of attention described in Box 6.2. involve experiments conducted in the laboratory. The study of change blindness described in Box 6.1 is an example of a study conducted in a naturalistic setting.

(b) Laboratory experiments allow variables to be controlled. This means the experiments can be replicated more easily. Naturalistic field experiments allow the researcher to investigate phenomena in a real-life setting.

## Activity 3.3

(a) You may be studying DSE212 as part of a degree. 'BSc (Hons) Psychology', 'BA/BSc (Hons) Social Sciences with Psychological Studies', 'BA (Hons) Philosophy and Psychological Studies' are three different OU degrees listing DSE212 as a core course (at the time of writing). The degree which students might link to is a categorical variable, and the numbers assigned to each degree in the data set would represent categories. The level of measurement is nominal, as the three different degrees have no ordered relationship.

(b) DSE212, like many other Level 2 courses, has four pass levels and a fail. Result graded on completion of the course is a discrete variable as it involves only certain values (e.g. there is no Pass 3½) and the level of measurement is ordinal as the values can be put into a meaningful order (e.g. a Pass 2 is a better result than a Pass 3). Note that level of measurement is *not* interval as the intervals between the grades are not the same. For example, the fail grade has 40 points (0–39 per cent) whilst Pass 4 has 15 points (40–54 per cent).

(c) Assessing performance on a multiple choice test that provides a percentage score is defining performance as a discrete variable, as only certain points are possible. For example, with 25 questions the only points available would be 0 per cent, 4 per cent, 8 per cent and so on; with 50 questions the points would be 0 per cent, 2 per cent, 4 per cent and so on. The level of measurement is ratio as 0 per cent means that no correct answers were given and it is meaningful to say that 80 per cent is twice as many correct answers as 40 per cent.

(d) The time taken to write a TMA essay is a continuous variable as, if measured precisely enough, it could produce any value (e.g. 15 hours, 23 minutes and 34.9872299386 seconds). The level of measurement is ratio as there is a true zero (no time at all – if the student did not do the TMA!) and it is meaningful to say that 2 hours is half the time spent as 4 hours.

## Activity 3.5

The means are (a) 10; (b) 13; (c) 8.

## Activity 3.6

The modes are (a) 10; (b) 18; (c) there are multiple modes: 3 and 4.
The medians are (a) 10; (b) 14.5; (c) 5.
The mean, median and mode for data set (a) are all identical.

For data set (b) the median is slightly higher than the mean, and this is because it is less sensitive to the two low scores. The mode is much higher because the most frequent score in this relatively small data set is the second highest score.

For data set (c) the median is quite a bit lower than the mean. This is because this data set is rather odd with one very peculiar high score – extraordinarily high or low values are called outliers. There is no single mode.

## Activity 3.7

To two decimal places, the standard deviations are (a) 2.90; (b) 5.73; (c) 8.39.

# CHAPTER 4

# Graphs and distributions

## Contents


| | | |
|---|---|---|
| **Aims** | | **106** |
| **1 Graphs** | | **107** |
| 1.1 | Histograms | 107 |
| 1.2 | Bar graphs | 112 |
| **2 Distributions** | | **116** |
| 2.1 | Normal distribution | 116 |
| 2.2 | Non-normal distributions | 123 |
| **Answers to activities** | | **127** |

## Aims

This chapter aims to:

- explore different ways of representing data graphically, including histograms and bar graphs
- introduce you to normal and non-normal distributions.

In this study week we also show you how to obtain histograms and bar graphs using SPSS (see Chapter 3 in the *SPSS Booklet*).

### Activity 4.1

We have introduced you to a number of terms which represent criteria for evaluating research studies. Can you match the following criteria with the correct definition?

The criteria are:
*validity, reliability, ecological validity, generalisability.*

The definitions are:

- The extent to which a measure or test gives the same result for an individual over time and situation.
- The extent to which a measure or test actually measures what it claims to.
- The extent to which research findings may be applied to a larger population or to other situations.
- The extent to which a study reflects naturally occurring or everyday situations.

Answers are given at the end of the chapter.

In the previous chapter you were introduced to descriptive statistics which provide numerical summaries of data sets; these are very useful in that they can transform a large amount of data into just a few numbers that tell us what those data are like. However, such statistics are often accompanied by graphs which can make it even easier to understand the data. We've already introduced you to scatterplots in Chapter 2 and in the last chapter included an example of a pie chart and a histogram. In this chapter we explore histograms in more detail and introduce you to bar graphs, as both are frequently used in quantitative research.

# 1 Graphs

## 1.1 Histograms

Any variable will have a characteristic distribution and you can discover the distribution of a given variable empirically by taking a large number of measurements and then plotting the distribution of these samples. You do this by plotting graphically the values you recorded and how many people got each value. This graphical summary is known as a histogram.

A histogram is produced by putting each of the values you have recorded along the x-axis (the horizontal line on a graph). In the study concerning recall by children of different ages (discussed in Chapter 3), values were recorded that could be any number between 0 words recalled correctly and 20 words recalled correctly (we won't worry about incorrect responses just yet). The y-axis is used to represent the number of occurrences there were of each value in this study (i.e. how many participants recalled that number of words). We call the number of occurrences of each value the *frequency*, which is why a histogram is also known as a *frequency distribution*.

If we use SPSS to construct the histogram, then everything will happen automatically, but if we were drawing it ourselves there would be some decisions to make first. The first thing we need to decide is the range of values that will be on the x-axis and the y-axis. Let's return to the data from the study described in the previous chapter.

Remember that the psychologists wanted to look at how children's memory for words changes as they get older. They showed children from three different age groups a word list and recorded how many words each child recalled correctly and how many they recalled incorrectly. Looking at the data from all thirty children (see Table 4.1 overleaf), we can see that no child correctly recalled fewer than 3 words or more than 14 words. Therefore, the range of values on the x-axis only need go from 3 to 14. You can include all possible values, even those that were not obtained by any of the participants, in order to show the range of *possible* scores, but this can sometimes lead to a graph with lots of blank space and where the data are harder to see as they are bunched together.

Again, looking at the data from all thirty children we can see that there were no more than 4 children who recalled any particular number of words correctly. For example, 4 children recalled 6 words correctly and 4 children recalled 12 words correctly. In other words, the frequency ranged

**Table 4.1 Performance on a recall task by age of child**

| Age group | No. of words recalled correctly | No. of words recalled incorrectly | Age group | No. of words recalled correctly | No. of words recalled incorrectly |
|---|---|---|---|---|---|
| 4 to 5 | 4 | 5 | 7 to 8 | 7 | 2 |
| 4 to 5 | 6 | 2 | 7 to 8 | 8 | 0 |
| 4 to 5 | 4 | 3 | 7 to 8 | 9 | 2 |
| 4 to 5 | 5 | 2 | 7 to 8 | 8 | 0 |
| 4 to 5 | 3 | 0 | 7 to 8 | 9 | 0 |
| 4 to 5 | 6 | 0 | 10 to 11 | 10 | 0 |
| 4 to 5 | 3 | 3 | 10 to 11 | 12 | 1 |
| 4 to 5 | 6 | 3 | 10 to 11 | 12 | 1 |
| 4 to 5 | 4 | 2 | 10 to 11 | 13 | 0 |
| 4 to 5 | 3 | 1 | 10 to 11 | 11 | 0 |
| 7 to 8 | 7 | 1 | 10 to 11 | 14 | 1 |
| 7 to 8 | 9 | 0 | 10 to 11 | 13 | 0 |
| 7 to 8 | 10 | 1 | 10 to 11 | 13 | 1 |
| 7 to 8 | 6 | 1 | 10 to 11 | 12 | 0 |
| 7 to 8 | 12 | 1 | 10 to 11 | 10 | 0 |

from 0 to 4. This means that the range of values on the y-axis only need go from 0 to 4. The structure of the histogram would therefore look like that shown in Figure 4.1.

We can now fill in the actual data. The way to do this is to calculate the frequency of each value, which simply involves counting how many children recalled 3 words correctly, how many recalled 4 words correctly and so on all the way to how many children recalled 14 words correctly. This will give us the frequency of each value. We then just plot this number on the histogram. For instance, looking at the table you can see that 2 children recalled 7 words correctly. We would therefore draw a bar against the value 7 on the x-axis that stretched to the 2 point on the y-axis. This bar has been drawn in on the histogram shown in Figure 4.2.

Now we just need to do the same thing for all the other values. Doing this gives us a histogram that looks like the one shown in Figure 4.3 (see page 110).

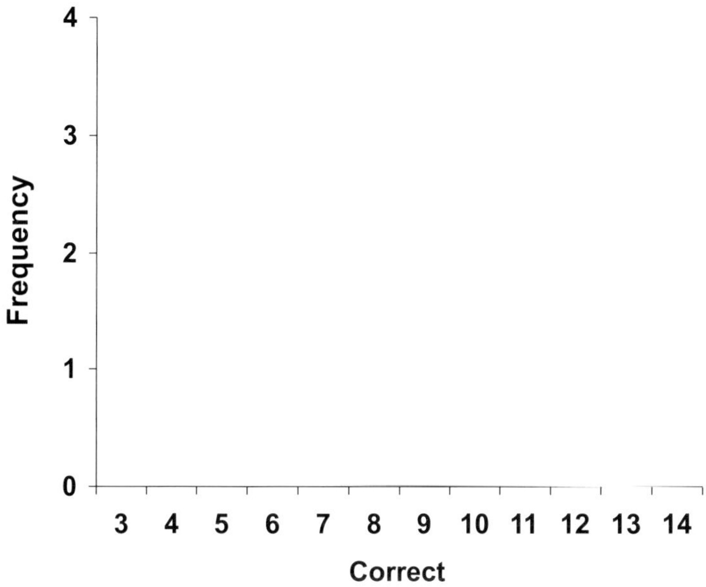


**Figure 4.1** Axes for histogram

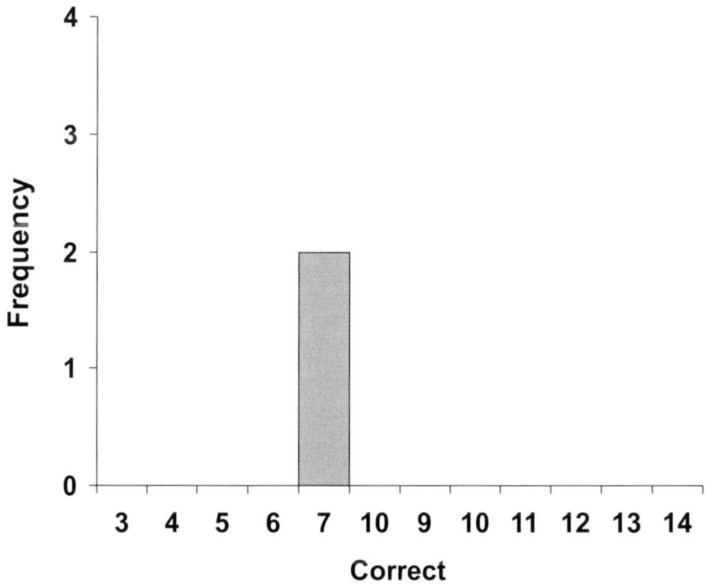


**Figure 4.2** Histogram with one bar

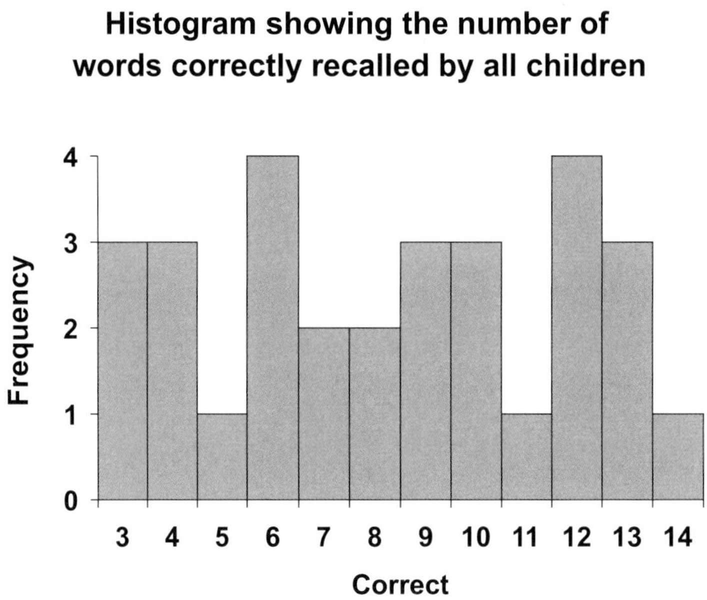


**Figure 4.3** Completed histogram

What do histograms tell us about the data? From just looking at the display we can readily see the following:

- the range of values of the data
- which values have the lowest and highest frequencies, and hence the modal value(s)
- how symmetrical the distribution of the data is
- whether there are gaps where no values were observed
- whether there are any data values that are markedly different from the rest.

### Activity 4.2

Try constructing a histogram on the axes below for the following data set:

3; 4; 4; 5; 5; 5; 6; 6; 6; 7; 7; 7; 7; 7; 8; 8; 8; 8; 8; 8; 9; 9; 9; 9; 10; 10; 10; 11; 11; 12

The data were collected in a dual task study of attention which recorded the number of errors made by participants.

Don't forget to give your histogram a title.

**Title:**

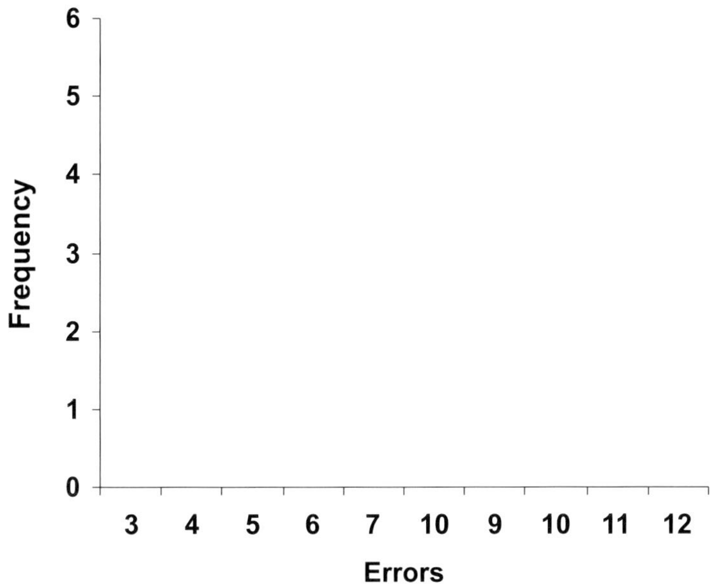


See the end of the chapter for an example of such a histogram.

---

Although constructing the histogram by hand in Activity 4.2 probably did not take you too long to do, imagine that you had 3000 participants instead of 30, that their scores ranged from 0 to 20 and that the frequencies varied from 0 to 800. Constructing the histogram for such data would take you considerably longer. Luckily, as you will see, SPSS can produce a histogram for us very quickly with just a few button clicks regardless of the amount of data involved.

Although histograms are a very good way of displaying the frequency with which each value occurred, there are some things that they are not so good at. First, they are mainly a way of presenting the data that were collected from a specific sample, and what we are really interested in doing is making estimates regarding the entire population. The first step towards this is to combine the individual data that were collected together using a statistic such as the mean.

Another problem that we can see in the histogram depicted in Figure 4.3 is that it does not give us a very good idea of how the children in the different age groups performed. In fact, it does not actually contain any information about the child's age. What we need, therefore, is a graph that shows us how the children in *each age group* performed.

Before we can begin to construct such a graph, we have to decide upon a way of describing the data in each age group. One answer would simply be to construct three histograms, one for each age group. Although this might be practical in the case of our present study, you can imagine that if we had recorded five types of data and had ten age groups, that displaying fifty histograms could be problematic. In addition, it is not that easy to see at a glance how different groups performed by comparing histograms. A useful and common way of comparing groups is to consider their means, which can be easily represented on a bar graph.

## 1.2 Bar graphs

We have established that in order to compare different groups we need to calculate descriptive statistics that summarise the data in that group and the best method of doing this is to use the mean and standard deviation. We have just looked at histograms, which are graphical representations of dispersion that illustrate the extent to which scores are spread out. Now we want to look at graphical representations of the mean. A simple way of doing this is to plot the mean score from each group as a bar. Although bar graphs contain information only about the mean score for each group and not about the associated standard deviations, they are a very good method of showing the differences between groups and are widely used.

As with a histogram, a bar graph has an x-axis and a y-axis. The x-axis is used to represent the different groups and the y-axis the mean score. Figure 4.4 shows the axes that would be necessary to represent the data from our children's memory study example.

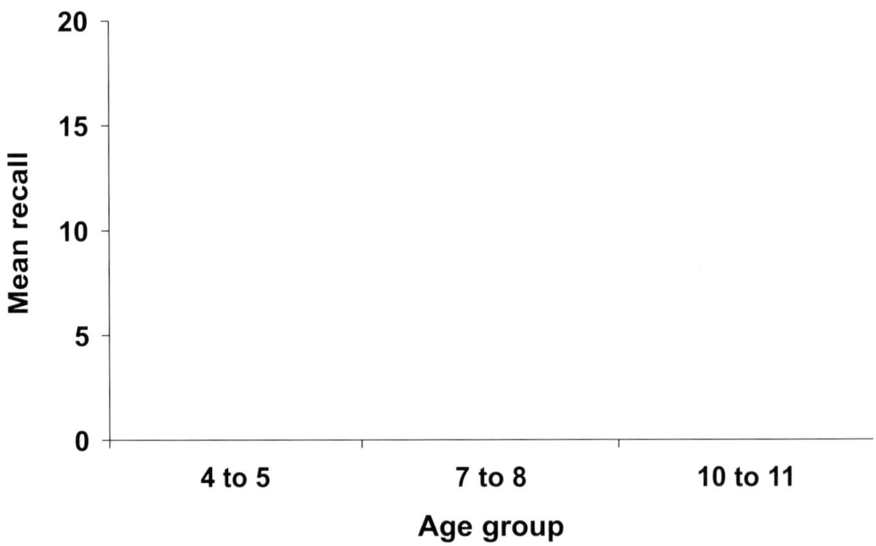


**Figure 4.4** Axes for bar graph

Now we have drawn our two axes, we can begin to plot the data. To do this, we simply find out what the mean for each group is and draw a bar against that group's position on the x-axis that stretches to the relevant value on the y-axis. For instance, the mean number of words recalled correctly by the children in the 4 to 5 age group was 4.4. We can therefore draw a bar against the label '4 to 5' on the x-axis that stretches to '4.4' on the y-axis – see Figure 4.5.

Next, we simply do the same for the other two groups, so that our bar graph looks like Figure 4.6.

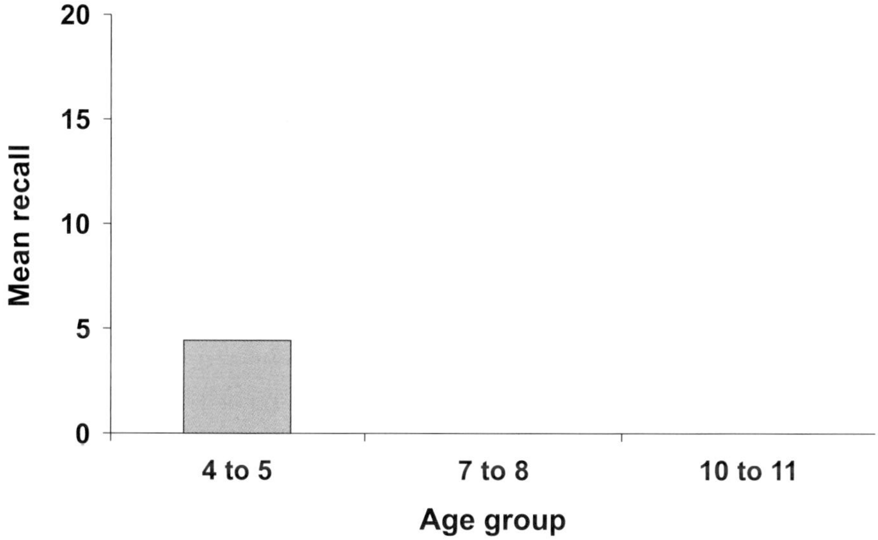


**Figure 4.5** Bar graph with one bar

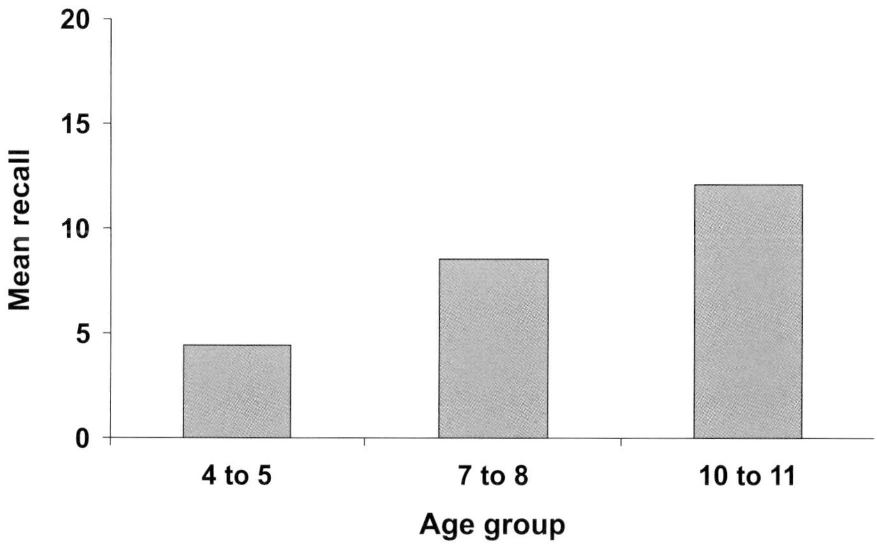


**Figure 4.6** Bar graph with all bars

From the graph in Figure 4.6 we can clearly see how the three groups of children differed in the number of words they correctly recalled, with the youngest recalling the least and the oldest the most.

As well as providing a way of displaying the mean score for each group of children for one variable, bar graphs can also be used to display the means for each group for two or more variables. In the original description of our children's memory study, it stated that the researcher recorded not only the number of words recalled *correctly* by each child, but also the number they recalled *incorrectly*. Incorrect recall corresponded to a child recalling a word that was not present on the original list.

We can display these incorrect recall scores on the same graph as the correct recall scores, so that we can compare both variables simultaneously across the different age groups. The first step in doing this is to calculate the mean number of words recalled incorrectly by each age group. These means are:

### 4 to 5-year-olds:

$$\text{Mean} = \frac{(5+2+3+2+0+0+3+3+2+1)}{10}$$

$$= \underline{\mathbf{2.1}}$$

### 7 to 8-year-olds:

$$\text{Mean} = \frac{(1+0+1+1+1+2+0+2+0+0)}{10}$$

$$= \underline{\mathbf{0.8}}$$

### 10 to 11-year-olds:

$$\text{Mean} = \frac{(0+1+1+0+0+1+0+1+0+0)}{10}$$

$$= \underline{\mathbf{0.4}}$$

We can now plot these mean incorrect recall scores on our bar graph in Figure 4.7. In order to distinguish the mean correct recall scores from the mean incorrect recall scores, we have used darker and lighter shades of grey for each bar. The two shades representing the two types of recall score are shown in a 'legend'[1] at the bottom of the graph.

[1] The 'legend' is a key that tells you which colours/shades/patterns, etc. have been used to represent which pieces of information on the graph. Here you can see that the light grey bars are used to represent correct recall, whilst the dark grey bars have been used to represent incorrect recall.

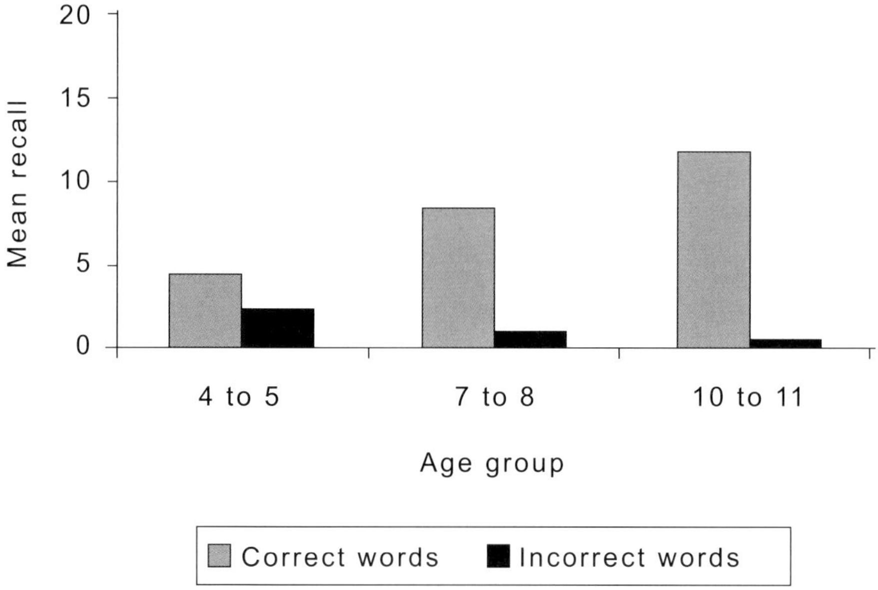


**Figure 4.7** Bar graph with two variables

We can clearly see from the graph above that not only do children recall more words correctly as they get older, but they also recall fewer words incorrectly. Before we finish with bar graphs, and before you get a chance to produce some using SPSS, there is just one more thing we need to add. Every graph should contain a title that explains to the reader what the data being displayed are. It is common practice to give the main title as 'Figure 1', so that the graph can be easily referred to in the text, and

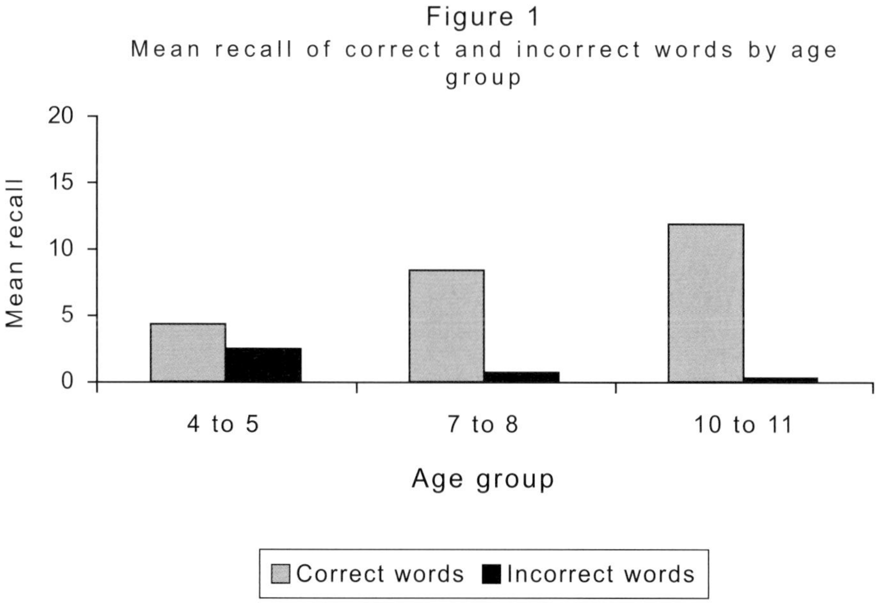


**Figure 4.8** Adding titles to a bar graph

a subtitle that explains what the data are. For instance, we can now supply the titles to the bar graph we have just constructed, as shown in Figure 4.8 (see previous page).

When producing a graph, you should always make sure that you use a suitable title and that the axes are appropriately labelled. A key or 'legend' may also be needed in some cases.

### Summary Section 1

- Histograms and bar graphs are often used in reports of quantitative research.
- Histograms display the frequency with which each value in a data set occurred.
- Histograms show how symmetrical the distribution of the data is, the range of values, and whether there are any gaps or any outliers.
- Bar graphs display differences between groups or conditions; each bar represents the mean from a particular group or condition.

**This would be a good point to turn to your computer and the *SPSS Booklet*. Work through Chapter 3 to see how you can use SPSS to produce histograms and bar graphs. If it is more convenient, then you can do this at a later point in your study week.**

# 2 Distributions

## 2.1 Normal distribution

Quantitative research generates numbers, and often large quantities of numbers. It is easy to be overwhelmed by the sheer volume of numbers in the data sets. Descriptive statistics provide methods and conventions that enable researchers to 'see' and describe, summarise and communicate their data.

We have introduced you to several ways of summarising and describing numbers in data sets, using measures of central tendency and measures of dispersion as well as different types of graphs. In Chapter 3 we explored measures of central tendency: the mean, mode or median. We might expect that when we collect data few people will obtain either very low or very high scores and the majority will have scores closer to our measure of central tendency.

But is it right to expect our data to conform to this expectation? Should we expect few participants to get extreme scores and most to get scores in the middle of the range of values? Thankfully the answer to these questions is 'Yes' or at least 'Usually yes', especially when we measure something that is naturally occurring. The distribution of our data will tend to have few extreme values and more central values.

Let's look at some examples of simple, naturally occurring phenomena to show that this holds true. First, let's think about how tall people are. Without worrying about statistics, think about the height of the people you know. You should find that you know few very tall people, few very short people and quite a few people of around average height. The same should also be true of weight and shoe size.

It seems as if data relating to physical attributes hold true to our expectation, but what about psychological attributes? Intelligence is very hard to gauge or measure, but you probably know very few highly intelligent people and very few people of well below average intelligence. Personality types can also be hard to gauge, but most people tend not to have extreme personalities. We could continue our thinking throughout the realms of psychology and virtually all the concepts we could think of would match this model.

As this regular spread of data is so common, it has been given a specific name and is called the *normal distribution*. Figure 4.9 (overleaf) shows some graphical representations of the normal distribution. As you can see, there is more than one curve that can be considered normally distributed. From the graphs you can see that this type of distribution has certain characteristics, and these will be true for all data that are normally distributed. These characteristics are:

- The distribution is described by a smooth curve.
- The curve is symmetrical.
- The curve is 'bell' shaped.
- The highest point of the curve corresponds to the mean score.
- The 'tails' of the curve gradually approach the x-axis, but never actually touch it (as in theory they are infinitely long).

So, with normally distributed data, few of our observed values will be at the extremes and most will be clustered around the mean. In fact, the frequency with which each value occurs should rise steadily towards, and fall steadily away from, the mean.

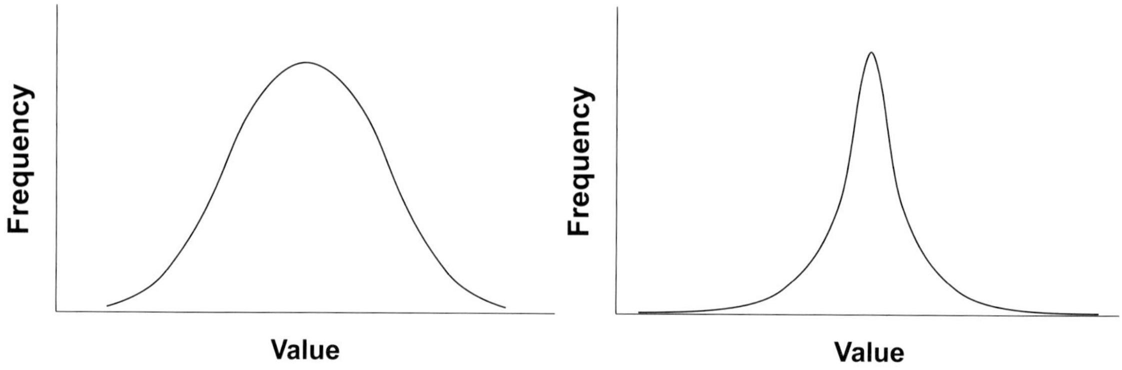


**Figure 4.9** The normal distribution

### *Activity 4.3*

Reflect back on the histogram you drew for Activity 4.2. What could you say about the distribution of these data? See the end of the chapter for our comment.

Before we look further at how we can make use of the normal distribution, let's consider the expectation that if you collect a sufficient amount of data, you will tend to end up with a normal distribution. This implies that if we don't collect much data, the distribution will not be 'normal' and also that the more data we collect, the more it will conform to the normal distribution. Let's look at an example of this.

A researcher was interested in the amount of time participants took before they gave up on a certain task. The task in question was to join three houses (A, B, C) to three different utilities (1, 2, 3) by drawing lines between them (see Figure 4.10). However, the participant had to draw the lines so that they never crossed. Each participant was given a copy of the figure and asked to complete it as per the instructions. The researcher recorded how long it was before they gave up (try the task yourself if you want[2]).

To start with, the researcher gave the task to five participants, who produced the following times (in seconds): 60, 220, 290, 330, 640. Plotting these figures produces the histogram shown in Figure 4.11.

The dispersion of data clearly bears no resemblance to the normal distribution.

[2] The task is actually impossible to complete. Nevertheless, some participants will keep trying for a very long time and some don't believe the researcher even when they're told it's impossible and will keep on trying!

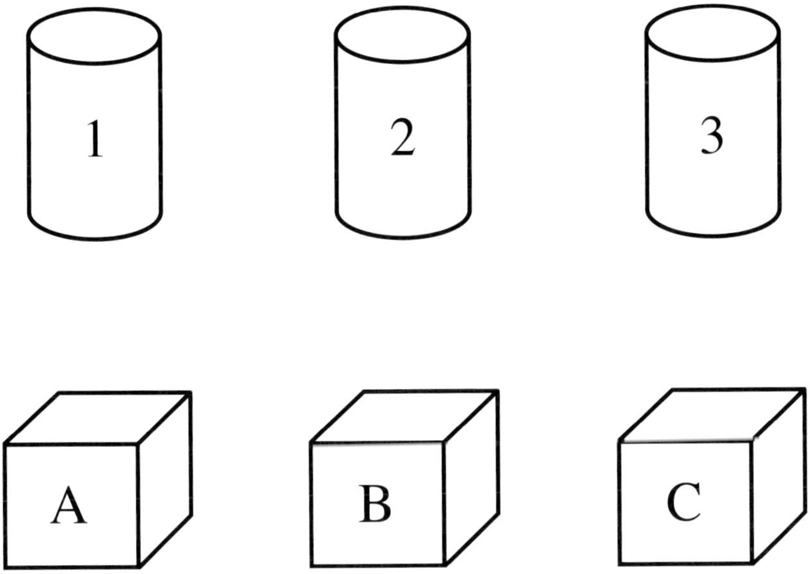


**Figure 4.10** Joining houses to utilities task

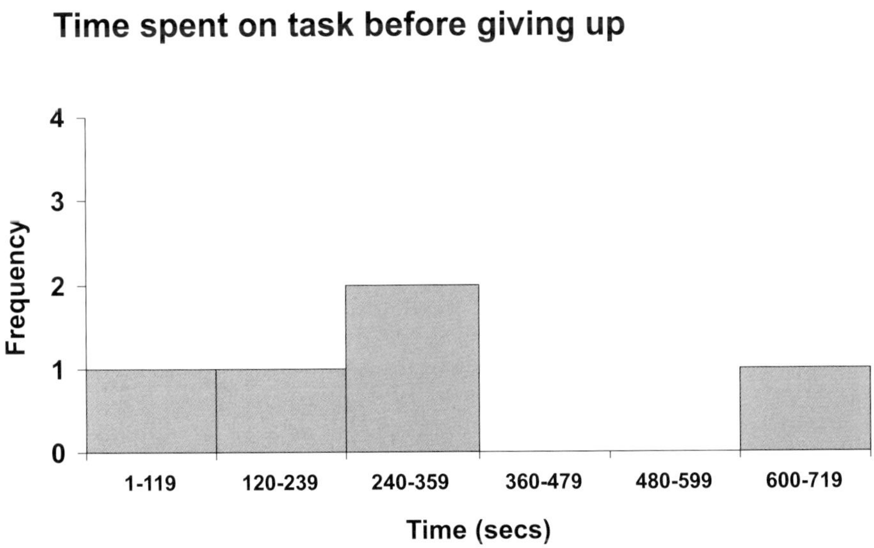


**Figure 4.11** Histogram of times from five participants

The researcher conducted the study on a further five participants. Adding their times to the original five produced the histogram shown in Figure 4.12.

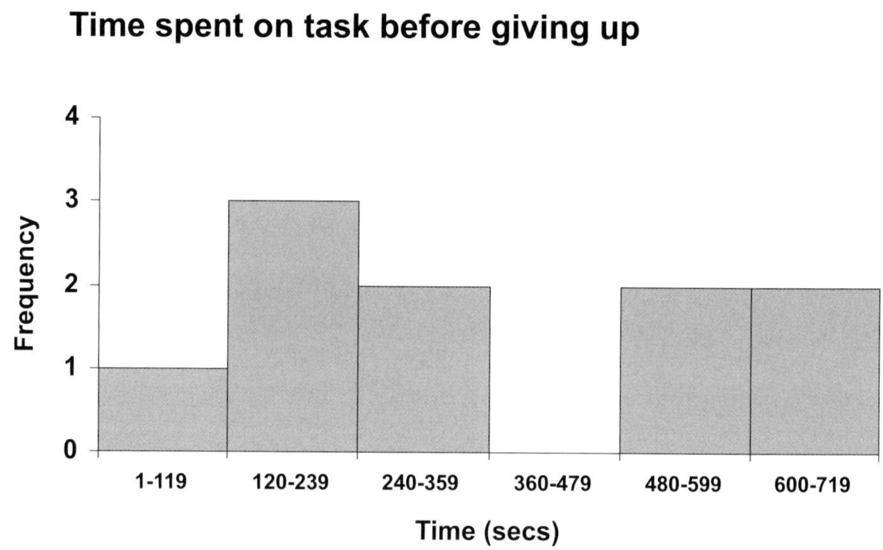


**Figure 4.12** Histogram of times from ten participants

The dispersion of these data also does not look too much like the normal distribution.

The researcher then conducted the study on a further twenty participants and when these data were added to the original ten participants, the resulting histogram looked like Figure 4.13.

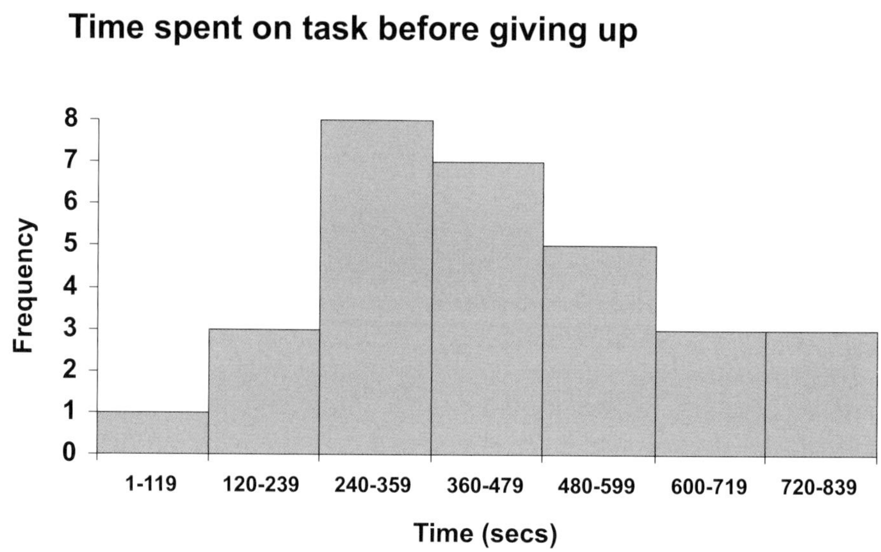


**Figure 4.13** Histogram of times from thirty participants

The dispersion of the data is now beginning to resemble the normal distribution more, and there are relatively fewer extreme values compared with the number of values in the centre of the range of scores.

In order to find more participants, the researcher visited an Open University residential school and managed to find an additional thirty people who volunteered to participate in the study. The final histogram of all the data looked like Figure 4.14.

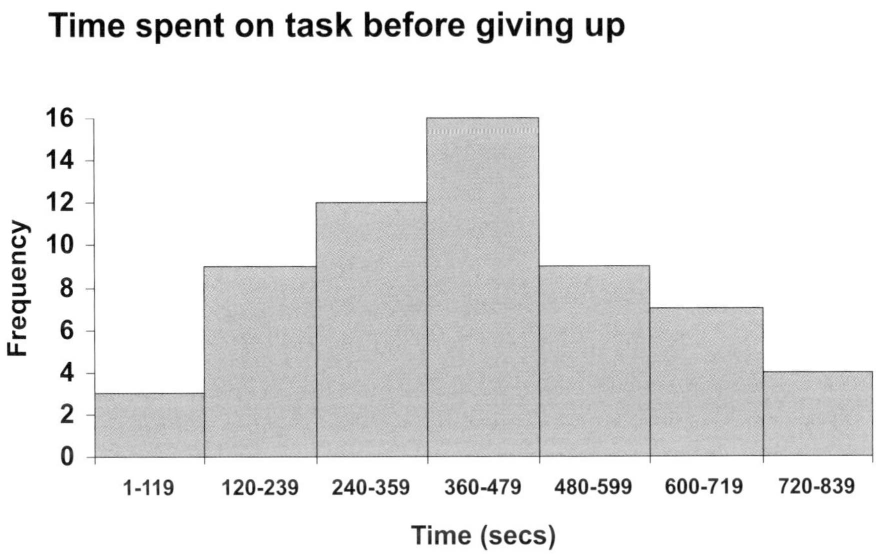


**Figure 4.14** Histogram of times from sixty participants

The final histogram contains data taken from sixty participants and you can see that the dispersion of these data has become more and more like the normal distribution as more participants were added in. However, the final shape of the distribution is *not* symmetrical, is *not* a smooth curve and is *not* a perfect 'bell' shape. So although the dispersion has some properties in common with the normal distribution, such as fewer extreme scores and more central scores, it is far from being a perfect example.

It is actually extremely rare for the data we collect to look exactly like a normal distribution, unless we collect a very large amount. Indeed, the important issue is not whether our sample of data is normally distributed, but whether the population it is drawn from is normally distributed. From the figures above, you can see that as we increase our sample size the dispersion of data becomes more and more like the normal distribution. If we found some way of testing the entire population, it is likely that the data would be almost perfectly normally distributed.

### Activity 4.4

Compare the following two histograms. What do they tell you about the distribution of scores in these samples?

**Histogram A**

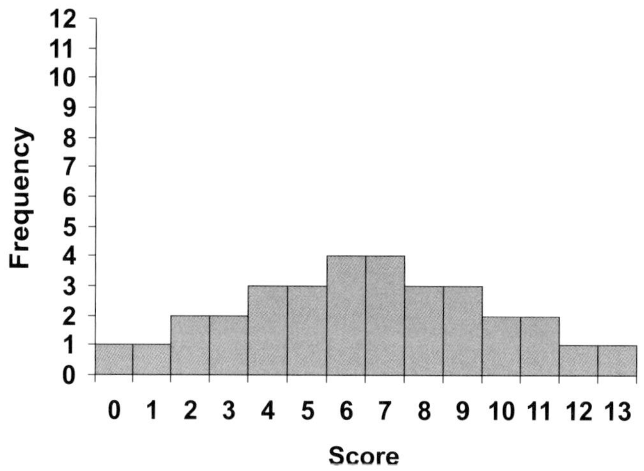


**Histogram B**

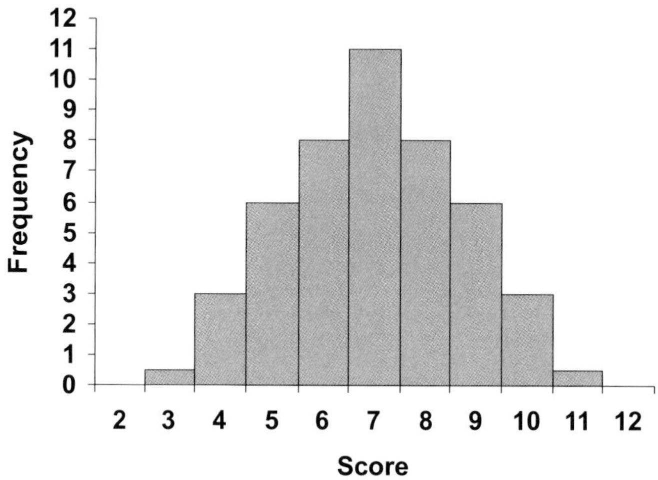


See the end of the chapter for comment.

The normal distribution is a very important statistical concept. As we shall see in Chapters 5 and 6, knowing how the data from a population are dispersed allows us to calculate some very useful statistics. Before that, however, we will look at some of the ways in which distributions can vary.

## 2.2 Non-normal distributions

As indicated in Section 2.1, the characteristics of a normal distribution are that it is symmetrical, that there are few extreme scores and that the majority of scores cluster around the mean score. However, non-normal distributions can occur (and regularly do occur) that deviate from these characteristics in important ways.

One common form of non-normal distribution arises when the 'peak', which corresponds to the most frequently occurring scores, is not in the centre of the distribution. This means that there was a greater range of scores to one side or the other of the 'peak', which has resulted in a longer 'tail' being produced on one side. When this happens we say that the distribution is skewed.

There are therefore two different forms of skewed distribution. The first corresponds to a long tail to the right with the peak on the left. This means that there will be a greater range of values that are higher than the mean than there are that are lower. For example, if the mean percentage score on a test is 10 per cent and the range of scores is from 0 per cent to 100 per cent, then 9 per cent of the possible values will fall below the mean and 89 per cent of the values will fall above it. This is known as *positive skew*. Conversely, if there are a greater range of values that are less than the mean, this will produce a longer tail to the left with the peak to the right. This is known as *negative skew*.

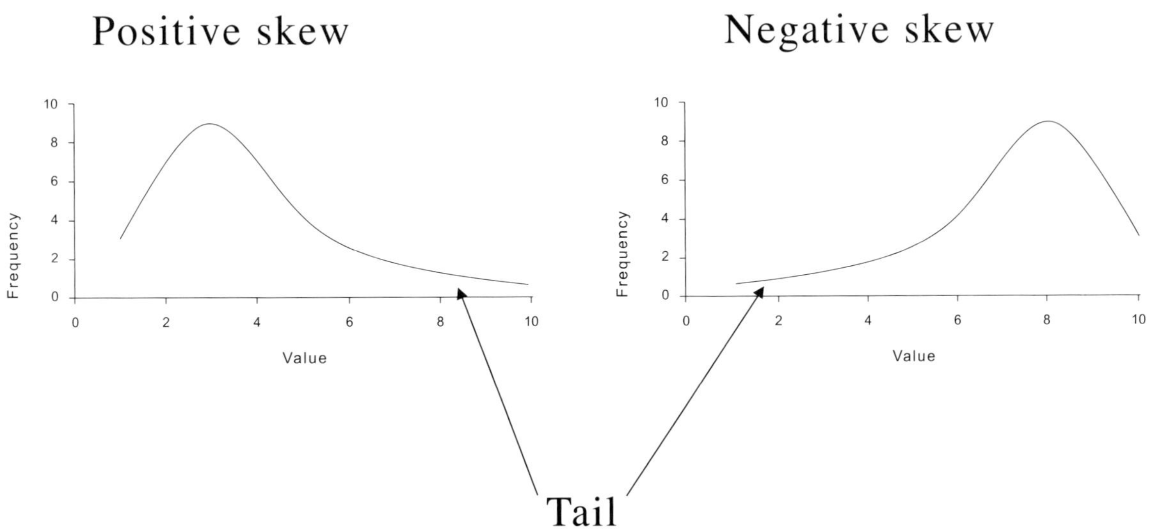


**Figure 4.15** Positive and negative skew

The graphs in Figure 4.15 demonstrate positive and negative skew. Most of the data you collect will tend to be either slightly positively or negatively skewed. If your data are too skewed, however, you cannot really use the mean as a reliable measure of central tendency, as it will be altered by the presence of the 'tail' of the distribution. Instead, it is best to use the median, as this will better reflect the value obtained for the majority of participants.

Positively skewed data can result from using a scale in which the majority of participants will produce responses toward the bottom. For instance, if we made a word-recall task too difficult, we might find that lots of people get very low scores, but that a few did manage to get higher scores. Negatively skewed data can arise from making a task too easy, so that scores tend to be 'bunched' near the top of the range of possible values.

### *Activity 4.5*

Which of the two histograms below is positively skewed and which is negatively skewed?

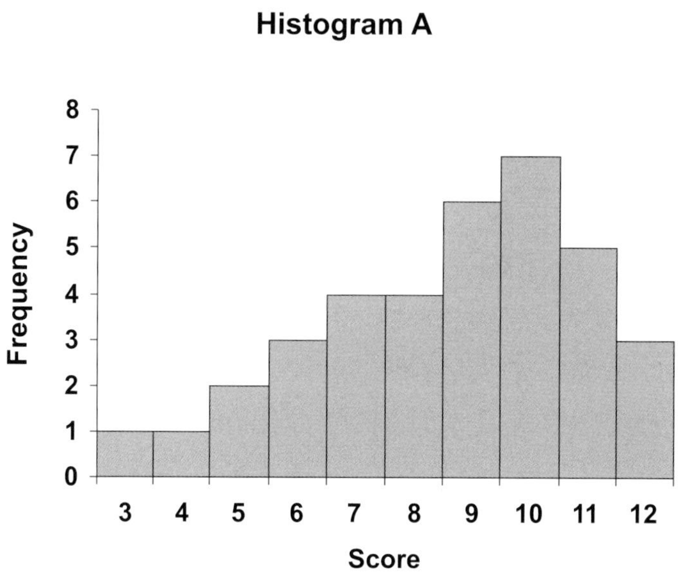

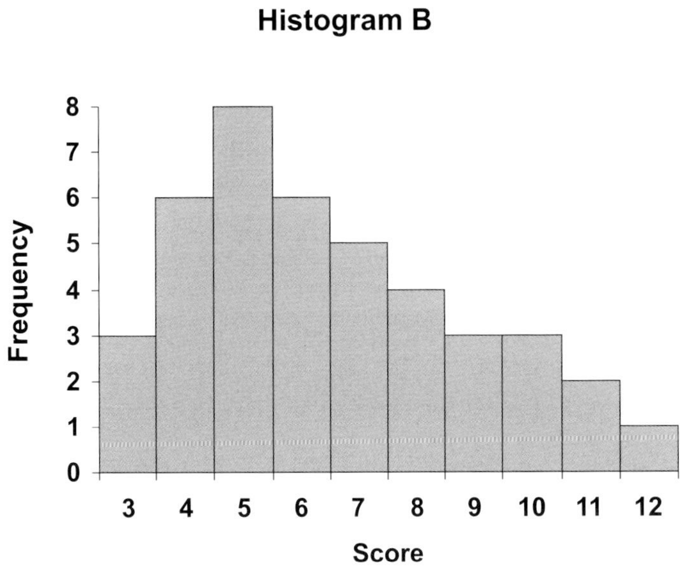


See the end of the chapter for the answer.

As well as skewed distributions, there are distributions that look even less like the normal distribution. Consider the spread of data we would get if we recorded the hair length of everyone in the UK. Would it be normally distributed? Well, it would certainly be true that few people would have extremely long hair and few extremely short hair, but what about the rest? We would probably find that as men tend to have shorter hair and women tend to have longer hair, our distribution would look like Figure 4.16.

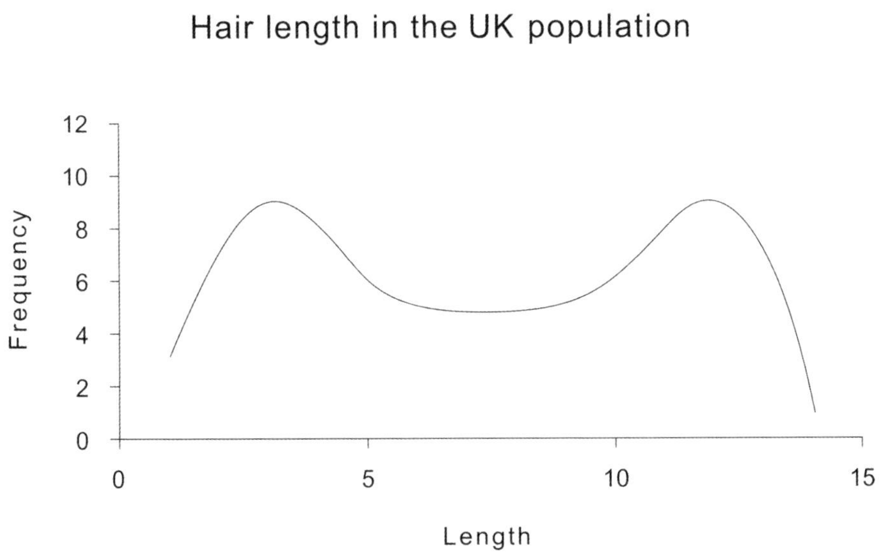


**Figure 4.16** A bimodal distribution

In this distribution, there are quite a few people with reasonably short hair, quite a few with reasonably long hair, but not so many with intermediate length hair. In a way, the shape is like two normal distributions with different means that have been joined together. If you think about it, this is exactly what has happened. If we plotted male hair length and female hair length separately, we might get something like the normal distribution in each case.

We call the distribution in Figure 4.16 a *bimodal distribution*. The reason for this is that if we calculated the mode, we would find it had two values corresponding to each 'peak' in the histogram. The mode would be a better measure of central tendency for this distribution, as the mean and the median would be values in the middle that did not occur as frequently as the values corresponding to the peaks.

So the shape of the distribution can tell us which is the most appropriate descriptive statistic to use and it is also essential to the calculations of some of the more powerful statistical tests that we will look at later, in Chapter 6. Plotting a graph of your data can therefore be a good first step to analysing them, as you will then be able to see how they are distributed.

## Summary Section 2

- Many of the variables measured in psychology have a regular spread which is called the normal distribution.
- In terms of statistical analysis, it is important to consider whether the sample of data collected in a study is drawn from a population which is normally distributed.
- Non-normal distributions include positively or negatively skewed and bimodal distributions.

| **Terms you should be familiar with:** |
| --- |
| Histograms |
| Bar graphs |
| Normal distribution |
| Positive and negative skew |
| Bimodal distribution |

# Answers to activities

## Activity 4.1

| | |
|---|---|
| Reliability | The extent to which a measure or test gives the same result for an individual over time and situation. |
| Validity | The extent to which a measure or test actually measures what it claims to. |
| Generalisability | The extent to which research findings may be applied to a larger population or to other situations. |
| Ecological validity | The extent to which a study reflects naturally occurring or everyday situations. |

## Activity 4.2

Your histogram will look something like the following:

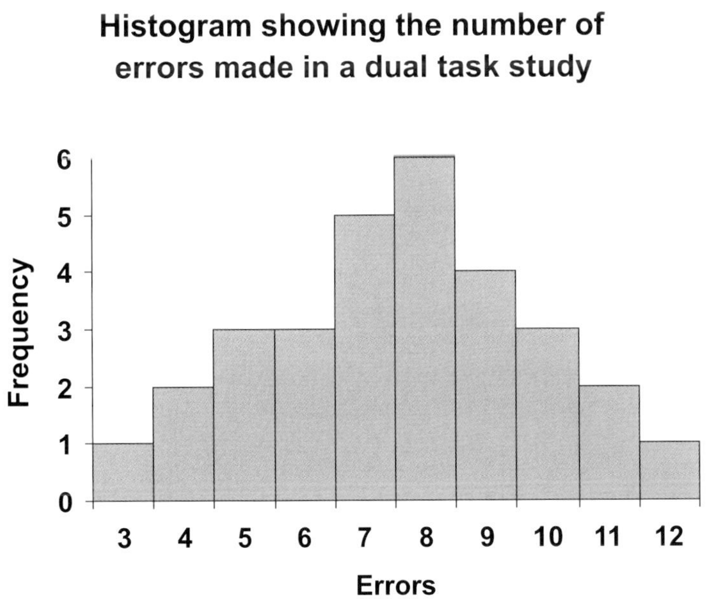


## Activity 4.3

This histogram you drew in Activity 4.2 does resemble the normal distribution.

## Activity 4.4

Both samples are normally distributed, but Histogram A is flatter and wider than Histogram B; the standard deviation will therefore be larger compared to Histogram B.

## Activity 4.5

Histogram A is negatively skewed and Histogram B is positively skewed.

# Testing hypotheses

## Contents

| | | |
|---|---|---|
| | Aims | 130 |
| 1 | Introduction | 130 |
| 2 | Sampling error | 133 |
| 3 | Sampling distribution | 136 |
| 4 | The basis of statistical testing | 138 |
| 5 | Confidence intervals | 140 |
| 6 | Hypotheses | 148 |
| 7 | Hypothesis testing | 154 |
| | Answers to activities | 161 |

# Aims

This chapter aims to:

- introduce you to important concepts underpinning inferential statistics
- consider the possibility of introducing error due to sampling and explore what is meant by sampling distributions and how they underpin statistical tests
- explore the importance of the confidence interval and error bar chart
- explain the role of hypotheses, including the null and the research hypotheses, and hypothesis testing.

In this study week we also show you how to obtain confidence intervals and error bar charts using SPSS (see Chapter 4 in the *SPSS Booklet*).

# 1 Introduction

In Chapter 1 we discussed why we need statistics and described how statistics allow us to overcome the fact that we cannot test the entire, relevant population and that instead we select a random sample from that population. We have now reached the point in the course where we will return to this issue and explore in more detail how statistics can be used to make inferences and generalise our results beyond the sample of participants in our study. Statistics are a phenomenally useful research tool, but can sometimes be a little tricky to understand. If you are finding it difficult to grasp any of the concepts we introduce in this chapter, remember the advice we gave in Chapter 1 and try either rereading the text or reading the whole section through first and then come back to the part you are finding difficult to grasp.

To help you further we have included a summary in Box 5.1 of the key information from Sections 2 to 5, which deal with statistics (in Sections 6 and 7 we explore the different types of hypotheses and hypothesis testing). The information in this summary is what you really need to take away from Sections 2 to 5, and if you find any of the detailed description confusing, it might be helpful to return to this box. By reading the summary now you should gain a good overview of what we shall be describing in more detail throughout Sections 2 to 5 and this should in turn help you to work through these sections more effectively.

## 5.1 Summary of key points underlying statistics

Below we provide a summary of each of the next four sections, which demonstrates how it is possible to use samples of populations both to make estimates about those populations and to determine whether there is a statistical difference between two samples. In other words, by working out the mean score and standard deviation from the sample used in a study, we can then estimate what the mean score of the broader population is. And, by working out the mean score and standard deviations from two samples used in a study (which often correspond to two conditions in an experiment) we can then determine (with the help of statistical tests) whether they are statistically different. Thus, if we have conducted an experiment and want to work out if there is a difference between our conditions, the first step is to work out the mean and standard deviation for each condition and to then use inferential statistical analysis to see if this difference is statistically different.

It would obviously be much easier if we could simply look to see whether there was any difference in the means from the conditions in our study and base our conclusions on this. We will now look at why this is not possible and what we can do instead.

### Sampling error

- By selecting a sample, rather than testing the entire relevant population, we introduce what is known as sampling error into our study, namely that the mean and standard deviation of the sample will be different from the mean and standard deviation of the broader population from which the sample was taken.
- It therefore follows that if we select two samples from the same population we should also expect the means and standard deviations of these samples to be different from one another.

### Sampling distribution

- Increasing the size of the sample tends to bring its mean and standard deviation closer to that of the broader population.
- Another way of estimating the mean and standard deviation of the broader population is to take multiple samples from the same population.
- If we plot the means of enough multiple samples on a graph, then we would see that they form a normal distribution (we refer to this graph as the sampling distribution of the mean).

### The basis of statistical testing

- As we know the sampling distribution of the mean forms a normal distribution, we can work out what means to expect when we take samples from this population.

- Thus, if we take two samples and both their means are similar to the population mean, we can conclude that both samples are taken from the same population.
- However, if the two sample means are sufficiently different, we conclude that they are from different populations; that is, that they are statistically different.

### *Confidence intervals*

- The steps outlined above involve knowing what the population mean is, which is not possible to do with 100 per cent accuracy unless we test the entire population.
- Instead, we can use a statistical technique, which uses the sample mean and the sample standard deviation to estimate a range of possible values that we are almost certain the population mean falls within.
- This range is known as a confidence interval and the specific calculations used in determining the confidence interval allow us to be 95 per cent certain that the population mean falls within the range of values specified – which is why the statistic is known as a 95 per cent confidence interval.
- 95 per cent confidence intervals can be displayed numerically, by stating the upper and lower values in the range, or graphically, by drawing lines above and below the mean that correspond to these upper and lower values.

So statistics allow us to overcome the fact that we are only testing a sample and not the entire population, although there will always be some uncertainty in the results of statistical tests – after all, they are only estimates. We will now explore the steps described above in more detail.

By now you've probably realised that in this chapter we will be introducing you to a number of important concepts. The first relates to the fact that when we conduct research we almost always use samples of individuals from the population of interest. Say, for example, that we are interested in the usefulness of a particular reading programme designed for children with dyslexia. We are unlikely to be in the position of having sufficient funds to ask all children with dyslexia to participate in our study, so instead we use a sample and then hope to generalise the findings from this sample to the population of children with dyslexia. But are the values derived from the sample the same as those that would result from testing the entire population? In the next section we shall see that it is possible to answer this question and that there is always some degree of error involved when we sample (known as sampling error).

# 2 Sampling error

When designing and conducting an experiment, the aim is to investigate whether the independent variable (IV) affects the dependent variable (DV). Imagine you are a researcher conducting an experiment to see whether an anxiety workshop helped students who were about to sit an examination. At the end of the experiment you will have collected scores from an Anxiety Inventory from fifteen students in a control group and from fifteen students in the anxiety workshop group. But now what? How can you tell whether the IV had the predicted effect on the DV?

One thing you could do would be to look through all the data and see if you think the scores from the control group were higher than those from the workshop group. But it is very unlikely that you would be able to *reliably* say whether there is a difference between the two conditions. In addition, remember that you are attempting to pursue an objective means of conducting research which will definitely be ruined if you have to rely on your own opinion as to whether there is a difference or not.

Fortunately, as we have seen in previous chapters, there are descriptive statistics that can be used in order to provide certain estimates from our sample. You can calculate the mean for each condition, which provides a measure of central tendency, and the standard deviation, which provides a measure of dispersion. Let's say, then, that the mean score on the Anxiety Inventory was 25.3 for the control group and 21.8 for the anxiety workshop group. If there were only thirty people in the entire population and you have tested them all, then as the mean for the workshop group was lower than the mean for the control group you could safely conclude that the anxiety workshop reduced anxiety in the examination.

But you did not test the entire population, only a (relatively small in this case) sample of it. Can you think of any other reasons why the means from the two conditions might be different, other than the potential effects of the IV?

The following might help you think along the right lines. Imagine a team of five market researchers have been employed by Supermarket A and that their main job is to check how much Supermarket B is charging for its products. If the researchers were extremely diligent, very quick on their feet and had a very high boredom threshold, they could go to Supermarket B every day and check every single price. From this they could work out the mean price charged by that supermarket for its products. This overall mean price would correspond to the population mean in this case. For the purpose of this example, let's say that the mean price of all the products in the supermarket (i.e. the population mean) is £2.74.

However, an alternative, lazier and more realistic method would be to select a basketful of products and calculate the mean price for just that basket. The basket of products would be equivalent to a sample. The problem with this method is that the mean price of the sample would be dependent upon the particular products you chose to put in the basket. If you filled your basket with a *different* load of products each day, you would expect to find that the mean price of the products in the basket was also *different* each day. Even if you were careful to choose the same *type* of product each day (e.g. one type of cheese, one type of cat food), the means would still be different. Our researchers (being more realistic and lazy than they are diligent and quick on their feet) decide to use sampling to estimate the average price of the items in Supermarket B. Each researcher fills a basket with similar items and then calculates the mean price of the products they have picked up. This then gives them five sample means of:

£2.55 £1.89 £3.04 £2.89 £3.09

So the mean prices of the baskets of products (the samples) will tend to differ from one another. Also, we can clearly see that the mean price of each basket also differs from the mean price of all the products in the supermarket (the population), as none of the baskets had a mean price of £2.74. In short, the sample means differ both from one another and from the population mean.

The same is true of human participants. The mean of a sample will be dependent on the people we select. If we repeat an experiment several times over, the mean will vary. Even if we try very hard to select entirely random samples, it is still likely that the mean of one sample will tend to differ from the mean of another sample, and these will also differ from the population mean. To return to the question 'Can you think of any other reasons why the means from the two conditions might be different, other than the potential effects of the IV?', the answer is that we would expect them to differ because they are different samples. In a between-participants design, the participants in one group are not the same people as the participants in the other group and therefore represent a different sample of the population. As they are different samples, we should expect their means to be different, too. In Chapter 2, we talked about the importance of randomly allocating participants to conditions in the hope that things like motivation, speed of processing, alertness, intelligence, etc. will influence performance in both conditions equally. It is because of the influence of factors like these that we find differences in the means between samples. In a within-participants design, we also would not expect the same participants to perform in exactly the same way twice, even if the task were identical. For example, the participants' tiredness, motivation and interest may vary over time.

As we cannot control or know in advance by how much our sample means will differ from one another, we can say that this difference is a *variability that is due to chance.* We will aim to design an experiment very carefully to control for any variability brought about by possible confounding variables (e.g. order, practise, fatigue), but there will be some variability that we cannot control, for that is brought about by natural differences between people. In other words, by taking just a sample and not testing the entire population, we are inevitably going to introduce a certain amount of *error* (variability that is not caused by the manipulation of the IV) into our sample statistics. As this error is a naturally occurring consequence of using samples rather than using the whole population, we refer to it as *sampling error.*

So far, we have looked at sampling error in relation to experiments. It is, however, also important when we conduct correlational studies and wish to explore possible relationships between several variables. Think back to our example, introduced in Chapter 2, of student doctors and the relationship between the number of errors made in a diagnosis and the length of time that had passed since the student's shift had started. If we had two samples of student doctors who diagnosed the test case, it is extremely unlikely that the two scatterplots showing the relationship between 'errors in diagnosis' and 'time since shift started' will be identical. The larger the sample we take from the population of student doctors, then the greater the likelihood that our findings will reflect the population accurately.

The important questions we need to ask, therefore, are:

- *In experiments:* whether the difference in our two conditions is indicative of a real difference caused by our IV, or whether it is simply due to sampling error.
- *In correlational studies:* whether the relationship between two variables is indicative of a real relationship, or whether it is simply due to sampling error.

These are the questions that the statistical tests we shall be looking at in the next chapter are designed to answer.

## Summary Section 2

- The statistics we calculate are based on data from a sample, not an entire population.
- We would expect different samples to perform differently.
- Therefore, by taking just a sample we introduce variability or error into our sample statistics and this is called sampling error.

# 3 Sampling distribution

In this section we shall look at one of the basic concepts that underlie the use of statistical tests. One way of reducing sampling error can be to increase your sample size. This is because the mean you calculate for the sample will be affected by the specific elements in the sample and particularly by any extreme values. For example, using our shopping basket example you can see that if you chose just three items, and one happened to be very expensive, the mean would then be much higher than the overall population mean (in this case the mean price of all products in the supermarket). If we chose ten items, however, the presence of one expensive item would not have such a marked effect, and the sample mean would be a better reflection of the population mean. In short, an extreme value will have a greater effect on the mean of a smaller sample than it will on the mean of a larger sample.

By increasing the sample size, we are making our sample more like the population, so the sample mean should be a better match for the population mean. You can imagine that there is likely to be little difference between the mean price from a sample consisting of 90 per cent of the products in the supermarket and the mean price of the entire population of products. However, it could well be the case that there is a large difference between the mean price calculated from a sample of 5 per cent of the products and the mean price for the entire population. Likewise, in the stress measured in the control and anxiety workshop groups, you would expect the mean calculated from a sample of one million people to be a better match for the population mean than that from a sample of twenty people.

Although the size of the sample is very important, and generally we should aim for the largest sample we can manage, there are difficulties with relying solely on this method of combating sampling error. First, it is entirely possible that the mean calculated from a sample of just two people could be a perfect match for the population mean. For example, if our shopping basket contained one item worth £1.74 and a second item worth £3.74, the sample mean would be £2.74 and match the population mean exactly. In this case, adding in more items would actually tend to increase the amount of sampling error. Second, we can only guess at what the actual population mean might be, so in reality we would never know how much sampling error we had, no matter how large the sample.

Although we can never be 100 per cent certain what the actual population mean is, and therefore how much sampling error we have, we can begin to estimate these using statistics.

Rather than simply increasing the number of people/items in our sample, what would happen if we took more than one sample? Our market researchers adopted this method by each selecting a different basket of products; meaning there were five samples. The mean price of the products in each basket was:

£2.55 £1.89 £3.04 £2.89 £3.09

As we saw before, there is considerable variation between these sample means and also between them and the population mean (which was £2.74). But, what if we were now to take the mean of all the sample means?

This would give us a new mean price of:

$$\frac{(£2.55 + £1.89 + £3.04 + £2.89 + £3.09)}{5}$$

$= \underline{\textbf{£2.69}}$

As you can see, the mean of all the individual sample means is quite a good estimate of the overall population mean. In fact, it is a better estimate than any of the individual sample means in this case. So, we can get a reasonably accurate estimate of what the population mean might be by repeatedly sampling the population and finding the mean of these samples.

If we were to take an infinite number of such samples, and plot each sample mean on a histogram, it would look like Figure 5.1.

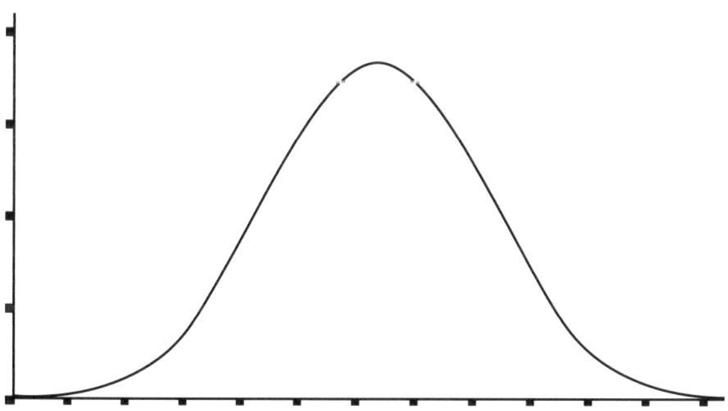

**Figure 5.1** Sampling distribution of the mean

Do you recognise the shape of this graph? It is a normal distribution. When you think about it, a normal distribution is exactly what we would expect to find. Most of our samples will produce a mean that is not too far from the population mean and few of our samples will produce a mean that is a long way from the population mean. Consider the sample supermarket baskets. Most of these baskets will tend to produce a mean price that is approximately the same as the population mean, and few will produce a mean price that is either a lot more or a lot less than the population mean.

When we plot a histogram of the individual statistical values that we have calculated from each sample, we say that we are plotting the sampling distribution of that statistic. In the example above, we were calculating the mean of each sample, so the graph was therefore the *sampling distribution of the mean*.

### Summary Section 3

- Increasing the sample size may reduce sampling error. However, we would still need to estimate how much sampling error there is.
- One way to do this would be to repeatedly sample the population and find the mean of these samples.
- If we repeatedly sampled the same population and plotted each sample mean, the histogram would show the shape of a normal distribution.
- Such a histogram would illustrate the sampling distribution of the mean.

## 4 The basis of statistical testing

Sampling distributions are the basis for all statistical tests and therefore are a very important concept. The reason they are so important is that they allow us to predict what values we should and should not expect to obtain for any given statistic under a set of predefined conditions. In the supermarket prices example, once we know what the population mean is, we can estimate that we are unlikely to obtain a sample mean of over £4 or under 50p (we shall show you how to arrive at such estimates in Section 5). As we know what range of values to expect for any sample mean that is drawn from this population, we are then in a position to determine whether our sample is actually drawn from that population. Basically, if the sample mean is within a certain range of the population mean, we can conclude that that specific sample was indeed drawn from the population in question. However, if the sample mean is outside this range, meaning it is unlikely to occur, we can conclude that the sample is unlikely to have been drawn from the population in question. In addition, we are also in a position to be able to tell whether two samples are drawn from the same population or from different populations.

At the moment, this might seem like rather an odd thing to want to know. However, let's consider an example experiment in which a psychologist is interested in whether 'social factors affect the perception of pain'. The experiment consists of varying the sex of the person administering a 'pain test' (so that half the participants are tested by a male researcher and the other half by a female researcher) and recording the amount of pain that the participant reports experiencing using a ten-point scale. What we want to know is whether the difference between our two conditions (male researcher or female researcher administering test) is just due to sampling error or whether our IV is really having an effect on our DV (i.e. the sex of the researcher is really causing the participants to report different levels of pain).

If the difference between the two conditions is just due to sampling error, then we are in effect saying that all the participants in the experiment are from the same population. This would mean that there was no difference between the conditions other than that caused by sampling error. Basically, although there is some difference in the means, both are inside the range that we would expect to find for samples of this population. This means that the IV is not really affecting the DV, that the sex of the researcher is not really affecting the amount of pain that the participants report experiencing. Instead, the difference is just because we have two slightly different samples.

However, if the participants in one condition are really behaving in a different manner from those in the other condition, then we can no longer consider them to all be part of the same population. Remember, population does not (necessarily) refer to the entire population of the country or of the world. Instead, population in this context is limited to those people who match the criteria we are studying. We therefore define our population as all those people who share the key characteristic or behaviour in which we are interested. But how does this relate to our social factor/pain perception study? The point is that if our IV (sex of researcher) has no effect on the level of pain reported by participants (DV), then we can consider all the participants, regardless of which condition they were in, to be part of the same population. Any difference we observe in the means of each sample (in this case the sample is the people in one condition) is therefore only due to sampling error.

However, if the sex of the researcher (IV) is really having an effect on the perception of pain (DV), then we have discovered a key characteristic that can define a population. To put it another way, if people really do behave differently according to whether the researcher is male or female, then we have two *separate* populations – people reporting pain to a female researcher and people reporting pain to a male researcher.

So, if we can tell whether two samples are from the same population or from different populations, we are in a position to know whether our IV did affect our DV, or whether any difference we observe is simply due to sampling error. This is the basis of how statistical tests operate and how they work out whether the difference between our conditions is due to our IV or just to sampling error.

### Summary Section 4

- Sampling distributions allow us to predict the values we should and should not expect for a particular statistic (such as the mean) under certain conditions.
- If the sample mean is within a certain range of the population mean, then we can conclude that the specific sample was drawn from the population in question.
- If we have two samples, then we can conclude whether they are from the same population or from two different populations.
- Making such a conclusion allows us to see whether our IV did affect our DV or whether any difference we observe is just due to sampling error.

## 5 Confidence intervals

So, let's just recap: if we have designed an experiment with two conditions we can use statistical tests to work out whether any difference between them is likely to be due to sampling error. If sampling error is an unlikely explanation then we can instead conclude that the two conditions contained samples taken from different populations. This is another way of saying that our IV did lead to a difference between the two conditions.

Let's just go though this logic point by point:

- A sample mean is dependent on the specific values that were used in its calculation.
- Because of this, it is likely that a sample mean will be different from the population mean.
- It is also likely that one sample mean will be different from other sample means.
- The difference between the sample mean and the population mean is due to sampling error.
- The difference between two sample means taken from the same population is also due to sampling error.

- If we take a large number of samples and plot their means on a histogram, we produce the sampling distribution of the mean.
- This will be a normal distribution.
- We know the shape of the distribution so, once we know the population mean, we can tell the likelihood of obtaining a specific sample mean.
- There will be a greater chance of obtaining a sample mean close to the population mean than one further away from the population mean.
- If two sample means are both reasonably close to the population mean, we can conclude that they are both taken from that population.
- If the two sample means are not both reasonably close to the population mean, we can conclude that they are from different populations.
- We can use this to see if the IV in an experiment is actually affecting the DV.
- Each condition in the experiment can be considered to be a sample.
- If the two sample means are from the same population, then any difference between them is due to sampling error.
- If the two sample means are not from the same population, then the IV is having an effect on the DV.

The above is the logic involved in telling whether there is a real difference between two conditions, or whether the difference is just due to sampling error. It is undoubtedly tortuous to follow, but even if you do not follow every step, you should be aware that:

- To see if the IV is having an effect on the DV, we test to see whether the two samples (corresponding to our two conditions) are from the same population.

Looking back through our chain of logic, can you see any problems? First, if we are actually to conduct a test based on this approach, we would have to find an accurate and reliable way of assessing whether a sample mean was 'reasonably close' to the population mean. A more important problem can be found in the following step:

- We know the shape of the distribution so, once we know the population mean, we can tell the likelihood of obtaining a specific sample mean.

The first part of this point is OK. We know that the sampling distribution of the mean will always result in a normal distribution. But what about the second part? How can we possibly know the population mean? In addition, if we are actually going to go out and find the population mean, why bother messing around with sample means at all?

The problem here is that we need to know what the population mean is in order to be able to tell how likely it is that a sample came from that population. But the reason we are using samples is that it is usually impossible to test the entire population. Even our supermarket researchers are going to have a hard time working out the mean price of every item in the shop, but our researcher who is studying the effects of the sex of the researcher on pain perception cannot possibly test the entire population of the planet!

Instead, we need to find some way of working out what the population mean is, without actually having to physically test the entire population. You may well be thinking to yourself that this is surely impossible. In fact, if you think that working out the exact population mean from just a sample is impossible, then you have a good understanding of what we have covered so far. Without actually recording data from every person (or item) in the relevant population, we can never be 100 per cent confident what the population mean is. However, it is possible to estimate a range of values that we are reasonably confident the population mean will fall within.

The sample mean is a *point* estimate of the population mean in that it provides just a single value. In reality, we cannot know whether the actual population mean is higher, lower or the same as our sample mean. However, we can use statistics to make an estimate as to the range of values that we are confident the population mean falls within. As this is a range of values, we refer to it as an *interval* estimate, rather than a point estimate.

Remember, though, that we cannot be 100 per cent confident that the population mean falls within this range. For example, we could have been very unlucky and included a large number of extreme values (ones much higher or lower than the population mean) in our sample. As we are not certain that the population mean actually does fall within the interval we are estimating, we refer to the range of values as the *confidence interval.* The way to think of this measure is that we are confident, but not certain, that the population mean falls within the interval (i.e. range of scores) specified.

The best way to calculate the confidence interval is to put your data into SPSS and let it work out the values. To be honest, the way in which confidence intervals are calculated can get a bit confusing (and you don't ever need to calculate them by hand on this course). The important thing is that you know that the confidence interval is the range of values that we can be confident the population mean falls within. You will not be tested on how to calculate confidence intervals. Indeed, it is possible to understand their function without knowing how to calculate them. We will not go into all the details involved in the calculations here, but will briefly describe how the calculations work. Underlying all the calculations is the normal distribution, which statisticians find very useful for modelling the variation observed in lots of phenomena, including human behaviour. Statisticians have therefore fully explored the properties of the normal distribution. In particular, they have calculated the area underneath the bell-shaped curve in very precise amounts. In fact, these calculations are so precise that it is possible to take any part of the normal distribution curve and know very accurately indeed the size of the area underneath. As the area under the curve represents the entire population being studied, a section will represent a specific proportion of the population. In short, once we know that data are normally distributed, we can work out very precisely what range of values to expect and how likely it is that any particular value or range of values will occur.

When we plot the sampling distribution of the mean, which is *always* a normal distribution, the mean value of all the individual samples should correspond to the exact centre of the curve, which is also its highest point. Remember that the mean calculated from taking lots of samples tends to be a very good estimate of the actual population mean.

We have also seen in Chapter 3 that to describe a sample of data we also need to specify the standard deviation. The standard deviation tells us how dispersed or spread out the data were compared with the mean. Just as it is possible to calculate the standard deviation for a single sample, we can also calculate it if we have taken many samples. In this case, the standard deviation will tell us how dispersed or spread out our samples were, compared with the mean of all the samples.

Normally distributed data will have the same properties in terms of how the data are spread out compared with the mean. In fact, as the curve is perfectly symmetrical, the points that are 1 standard deviation above the mean and 1 standard deviation below the mean will be at the same points on the curve on opposing sides of the mean. Likewise, the points corresponding to 2 times the standard deviation and 3 times the standard deviation will also always be at the same points on the curve either side of the mean. We refer to these as *standard deviation points*, so that:

1 standard deviation point = the standard deviation multiplied by 1

2 standard deviation points = the standard deviation multiplied by 2

3 standard deviation points = the standard deviation multiplied by 3.

See Figure 5.2 for an example.

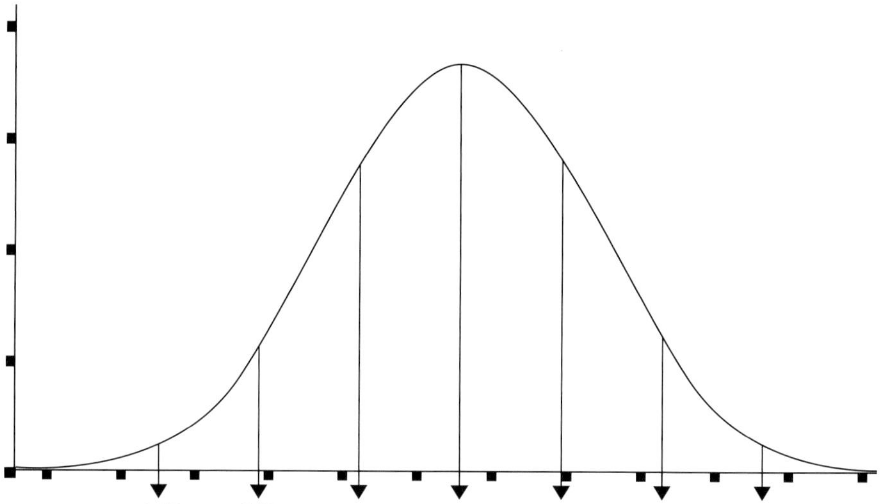


**Figure 5.2** Standard deviation points

The fact that each standard deviation point will always be at exactly the same point of the normal distribution curve is very useful in predicting which values are likely to occur and which values are not. From Figure 5.2 you can see a large majority of the data falls within 2 standard deviation points and virtually all the data falls within 3 standard deviation points. In fact, we know (because someone else with far more time than either you or us for such things has worked it out and put the values in a readily available table) that:

- 68.26 per cent of the data fall within 1 standard deviation point either side of the mean.
- 95.44 per cent of the data fall within 2 standard deviation points either side of the mean.
- 99.74 per cent of the data fall within 3 standard deviation points either side of the mean.

So, simply because the data are normally distributed we know that 95.44 per cent of values will fall within 2 standard deviation points of the mean. Another way of looking at this is that we can be 95.44 per cent confident that any value chosen at random will fall within this range. However, using a phrase '95.44 per cent confident' is a little clumsy. Instead, the convention is to use 95 per cent confidence intervals. Using the same table that we used to arrive at the values above, we find that:

- 95 per cent of the data falls within 1.96 standard deviation points of the mean.

So, a 95 per cent confidence interval implies that we can be 95 per cent confident that a value chosen at random will fall within this range.

When we collect multiple samples of data in order to calculate the sampling distribution of the mean, the 95 per cent confidence interval will tell us that we can be 95 per cent confident that the mean for any sample will fall within 1.96 deviation points of the population mean (or at least the mean of all the sample means, which is a very good approximation of the actual population mean). Turning this on its head, we can be 95 per cent confident that the population mean will fall within 1.96 standard deviation points of the sample mean.

Ah, this is the statistic we are after! We accept that we can never know for certain what the population mean is, but the above calculations allow us to be 95 per cent confident that it will fall within a certain range (either 1.96 standard deviation points above or below) of the sample mean. Let's just recap on the calculations involved.

First, we need to plot the sampling distribution of the mean – oh dear! If you remember, the sampling distribution of the mean requires us to take a very large number of samples and we don't really want to have to do this. In fact, we really only want to take one sample and use this as the basis for *all* of our statistics. Maybe there's a short cut. What information did we *really* need from the sampling distribution of the mean? Thinking about it, we really only need to know what the standard deviation associated with the mean of all the samples was. Once we know this, we can just multiply it by 1.96, and we can then be 95 per cent confident that the population mean will fall within a certain range of the sample mean. (We will show you how that range is calculated shortly.)

So, what we need is some way of calculating the standard deviation associated with the sampling distribution of the mean. Luckily, there is a short cut for estimating this figure. In fact, the standard deviation of the sampling distribution of the mean is so important in calculating statistics that it has been given its own name (mind you, it could just be that 'the standard deviation of the sampling distribution of the mean' was too much of a mouthful even for statisticians). We call it the *standard error.*

The standard error is calculated by dividing the standard deviation of our sample by the square root of the sample size. So, if we measure the height of a sample of twenty-five women, we might find the following:

mean = 160 cm

standard deviation = 4.65

sample size is 25, so the square-root of the sample size = 5 (as 5 × 5 = 25)

$$\text{standard error} = \frac{(4.65)}{5} = \underline{\mathbf{0.93}}$$

To work out the 95 per cent confidence interval for these data, we simply multiply the standard error by 1.96 (as 95 per cent of the data falls within 1.96 standard deviation points of the mean):[1]

95 per cent confidence interval = 0.93 × 1.96 = **1.82**

So we can be 95 per cent confident that the population mean will fall within 1.82 of the sample mean, i.e. it is **160 cm ± 1.82** (the symbol '±' means 'plus or minus').

The usual way of specifying confidence intervals is to state the *lower bound* and *upper bound*. The upper bound corresponds to the sample mean plus the figure we calculate and the lower bound corresponds to the sample mean minus the figure we calculate. Thus, for the example above we would say:

### 95 per cent confidence interval for mean:

Lower bound = (160 cm − 1.82) = **158.18**

Upper bound = (160 cm + 1.82) = **161.82**

It is also possible to display confidence intervals graphically using an *error bar chart*. This is produced by representing the mean score as a single point. Lines are then drawn above and below this point to represent the upper and lower bounds of the confidence intervals. For example, if we were producing a graph of the above data, we would place a point at 160 cm to represent the mean score, draw one line extending upward by 1.82 to represent the upper bound and one line extending down by 1.82 to represent the lower bound. To help you see where these lines finish, a second line is then drawn at right angles (see Figure 5.3).

One point to note about the confidence interval calculations is that at one stage we divided by the square root of the *sample size*. It follows from this that our confidence interval will be a smaller range of values for large samples than it will for smaller samples. This means that we can make a better estimate of the population mean from larger samples.

So we are now in a position to estimate what the population mean is, based on just one sample of data. Remember, estimating the population mean is important as we know that if two samples are from the same population, any difference between them is due to sampling error and not the effects of the IV.

[1] Using the figure of 1.96 taken from the normal distribution to calculate confidence intervals is an approximation only. The more accurate method of calculating confidence intervals makes use of the '*t* distribution' and takes account of the sample size. This is the method used by SPSS, which means that there may be a very slight difference between the values that you would calculate by hand and those produced by SPSS.

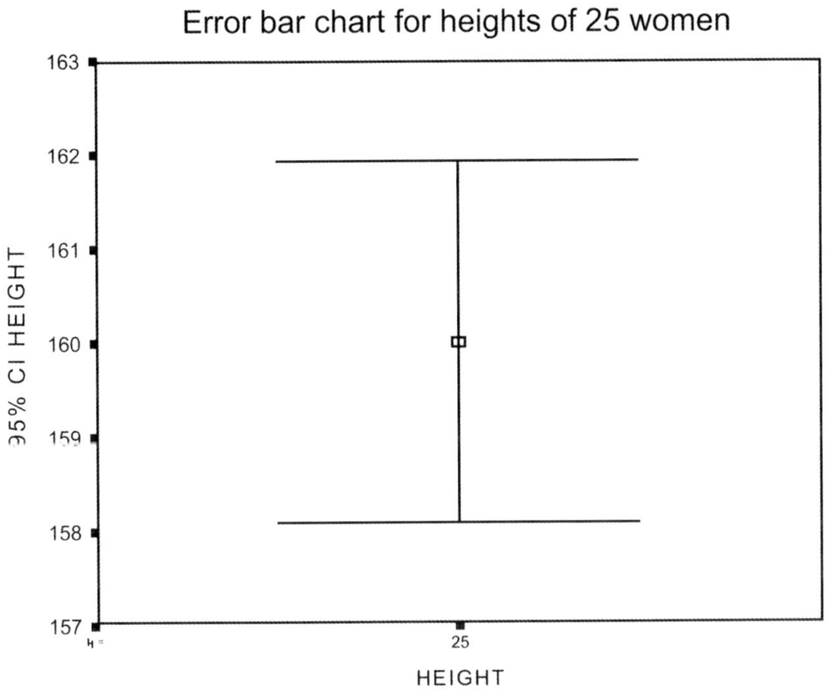


**Figure 5.3** An error bar chart

As we said before, the important thing is that you know what confidence intervals are, not the calculations involved. If you can follow the way in which we calculated the 95 per cent confidence intervals, it should aid your understanding, but the important thing is to know what they are and why they are useful. To recap then, a 95 per cent confidence interval is calculated from a sample mean and is the range of scores that we can be 95 per cent confident the population mean falls within. It is useful as it allows us to judge whether two samples are from the same or different populations.

## Summary Section 5

- As it is not usually possible to find out what the population mean is, we have to estimate a range of values that we are reasonably confident the population mean will fall within.
- This range of values is referred to as the confidence interval.
- If the data are normally distributed, then 95 per cent of the values will fall within 1.96 standard deviation points of the mean.
- To work out the 95 per cent confidence interval, we need to calculate the standard error which is the standard deviation of the sampling distribution of the mean.
- Confidence intervals can be displayed graphically using error bar charts.

### Activity 5.1

You have been introduced to lots of terms so far in this chapter; see if you can fill in the blanks below:

(a) We call the histogram of the means of a large number of samples of the same population the ______________________________ of the mean.

(b) The sample mean is a ________________ estimate.

(c) We refer to the range of values that our population mean falls into as the ________ interval.

(d) ______ per cent of the data falls within 1.96 standard deviation points of the mean.

(e) The standard error is calculated by dividing the ________________ of our sample by the ________________ of the sample size.

See the end of the chapter for answers.

**This would be a good time to turn to Chapter 4 of the *SPSS Booklet*. Work through the chapter to see how you can use SPSS to produce confidence intervals and error bar charts. If it is more convenient, then you can do this at a later point in your study week.**

## 6 Hypotheses

It is sometimes possible to get so wrapped up in the way that certain statistics are calculated that you lose sight of why you are calculating them. Psychologists do not spend their time calculating standard errors and confidence intervals (or even getting SPSS to calculate them) just because they like dealing with numbers (though come to think of it, we know a couple of colleagues who do this). Instead, these statistics are just tools that can be used to help us find out more about psychology. Here, we need statistics in order to tell whether the difference between two conditions in an experiment is due to sampling error or the effect of the IV.

Previously, we have looked at what an experiment is and some of the issues surrounding experimental design. We said that the point of an experiment is to see what effect the independent variable (IV) has on the dependent variable (DV). Of course, in reality we are interested in the effect that a specific IV has on a specific DV and our choice of variables will be based on the research question we are addressing.

Usually our research question will be broader than can be tested in a single experiment. For example, our psychologist who was interested in how the perception of pain can be mediated by social factors might pose the research question: 'How do social factors affect the perception of pain?' It is hard to see how we could design an experiment that would provide an answer to this question. For one thing, there are an enormous number of social factors, far more than could be studied in even a very complex experiment. In addition, an experiment could never properly answer a question based on 'how' something happens. After all, the experiments we have looked at so far simply involve seeing *whether* the IV affects the DV, and not *how* it might do this.

It is true that if we took the results of a number of experiments, we could begin to work out in more depth how social factors affect pain perception, but this would require us to interpret and theorise well beyond the scope of any one experiment. What we need, therefore, is a way of stating a more specific version of the research question, which is based on existing findings and theory and which also lends itself to being tested in an experiment. In other words, we need an intermediate step that will allow us to work out which specific IV and DV we need to employ in our experiment.

We refer to this specific formal statement as a *hypothesis*. Returning to our study of how social factors affect pain perception, the researcher needs to state a hypothesis that can be tested in an experiment and which therefore makes explicit what the IV and DV are. Such a hypothesis might be something like: 'The sex of the researcher administering the test will affect the participants' rated perception of pain.' Here we have a specific statement that lends itself to being studied in a single experiment and that makes the IV (the sex of the researcher) and the DV (participants' rated perception of pain) very clear.

You can see that there is a clear structure to this hypothesis. It is a statement which predicts that the IV will have an effect on the DV. Alternatively, if conducting a correlational study, it will be a statement which predicts that there will be a correlation between two variables. A hypothesis that predicts that there will be an effect or a correlation is referred to as a *research hypothesis* (we use the term research hypothesis, but it is sometimes referred to as the alternative hypothesis, or for an experiment the term experimental hypothesis is often used).

But the research hypothesis is not the one that is actually *tested* in the experiment. In the last section, we saw that the way to see if the IV is affecting the DV is to determine whether the observed difference is due to sampling error. If the two samples (corresponding to the two conditions) are taken from the same population, then any difference between them is due to sampling error. When you think about it, as we are testing to see whether the two samples are from the same population, our hypothesis needs to be one that states that there will not be a difference. The same applies to correlational studies; to see if there is a relationship between variables is to determine whether the observed relationship was due to sampling error.

There are also more philosophical reasons for not testing the research hypothesis, which have to do with the 'method of contradiction'. Basically, although it is possible to demonstrate that a hypothesis is definitely false, we can never 'prove' that one is 'true'. A classic example of the method of contradiction is the test of the statement 'All dogs have four legs'. If we went to the park and observed a hundred dogs, all of which had four legs, could we accept our hypothesis as being definitively true? The answer is we couldn't, and even if we increased our sample size to 5000 dogs, there would still be a chance that somewhere there is a dog with three legs. However, if when we went to the park we saw a dog with either one, two or three legs (or even five legs!), we could definitely state that our hypothesis was false.

Returning to our study of social factors and pain perception, imagine that we conduct the experiment and find that the group with the female researcher reported experiencing more pain than the group with the male researcher. On the basis of this result, can we definitely state that the sex of the researcher affects pain perception? For this to be true, our result could not possibly be due to anything other than the IV. Unfortunately, and especially in psychology, there will always be the possibility that something other than the IV is causing the observed effect. Critically, it is also the case that we never test the entire population in psychology experiments and so can never be 100 per cent certain that our sample is representative. For example, it could be that the difference between our conditions was just because the participants in the female researcher condition had a lower pain threshold than those in the other condition.

So, instead of testing the research hypothesis, we test what is known as the *null hypothesis*, which in the case of an experiment states that the IV will *not* affect the DV. In other words, the null hypothesis is predicting that our two samples are from the same population and that any difference between them is due to sampling error. If conducting a correlational study, the null hypothesis states that there is no relationship between the variables and that any observed relationship is due to sampling error.

If, once we have calculated the relevant statistics, we find that there is a marked difference between our samples that is not due to sampling error, we can *reject the null hypothesis*: basically, the statement that there is no real difference between our conditions, or alternatively that our two samples are from the same population, is false. If conducting a correlational study we find, once we have calculated the relevant statistics, that there is a marked relationship between the variables, then we can reject the null hypothesis.

If our statistical tests show that there is not a sufficient difference between our conditions – that the two samples could be from the same population – then we accept the null hypothesis. This means that we are accepting that our samples are drawn from the same population and therefore that there is no difference between the conditions. However, it does not necessarily follow from this that the null hypothesis is 'true'.

For example, what if the effect that the IV had on the DV was only small and only *appeared* to be sampling error. Just as we can never be sure that all dogs have four legs simply because our sample of a thousand dogs all had four legs, we can never be completely certain that two samples that appear to be from the same population actually are from the same population.

Exactly what to conclude in studies where it was not possible to reject the null hypothesis has been debated for a long time. Some researchers think that if we cannot reject the null hypothesis then we should admit that our results are inconclusive (maybe we would have obtained a different result with a larger sample, for instance). Most researchers tend to agree with the more pragmatic view that we can 'accept' the null hypothesis, where 'accept' does not mean the same thing as concluding that the null hypothesis is 'proven' or 'true', but that we will act as if it is true until someone proves otherwise. This is the approach we will adopt on this course and the one commonly used in psychology.

Our use of two different forms of hypothesis means that we need to go through three steps, from formulating a research question, to stating first the research hypothesis and then the null hypothesis, before we are ready to design, conduct and analyse our experiment. For example:

- *Research question* – How do social factors affect the perception of pain?
- *Research hypothesis* – The sex of the researcher administering the test will affect the participants' rated perception of pain.
- *Null hypothesis* – The amount of pain reported by the participants will not be affected by the sex of the researcher administering the test.

Notice that both forms of hypothesis (null and research) are statements (not questions) about what the results of the experiment will be.

### Activity 5.2

Write research and null hypotheses for the following research questions:

(a) How does music affect learning?

(b) How does reaction time vary with amount of caffeine consumed?

(c) How does time of day affect concentration?

See the end of the chapter for possible answers.

In our discussion about what to do with the null hypothesis when we cannot reject it, you may have received the impression that just because we obtain a result, it does not necessarily follow that we obtained the 'right' result. For example, what if we obtain two samples, and it just so happens that one contains very low values and the other very high values? Even if these samples are from the same population, they may be sufficiently different to result in us concluding that they are in fact from different populations. This would lead us to incorrectly *reject* the null hypothesis. Doing this would lead to what is known as a *Type 1 error*.

Alternatively, our IV may only have a very small effect on the DV or we may have a small sample size. In either situation, our two samples might appear to be from the same population, even though they were in fact from different populations. This would lead us to incorrectly *accept* the null hypothesis. Doing this would lead to what is known as a *Type 2 error*.

For these reasons we should always be aware of Type 1 and Type 2 errors and look carefully at our data, at the statistics we calculate and *especially* at the size of our sample when drawing any conclusions.

Before we go on to look at how to use statistical tests to test the null hypothesis, there is one further distinction to be made regarding how we describe hypotheses. When we formulate our research hypothesis, we are predicting that the IV in our experiment will affect the DV or, in a correlational study, that there will be a relationship between two variables. There are two ways in which we can do this. The most basic is simply to say that there will be an effect or relationship, but we can also predict what the effect or relationship will be.

For example, imagine a memory researcher who is designing an experiment to test context reinstatement (see Book 1, Chapter 8, Box 8.2 in Section 2.2). The experiment involves providing forty trained divers with a list of twenty words that they need to learn. All the divers learn the words underwater, but whilst half are also asked to recall the words while underwater, the other half have to do so on land. The researcher could generate the following research hypothesis:

- Whether learning and test environments are matched or different will affect the number of words recalled correctly.

But, looking in the relevant literature the researcher finds many studies report that participants recalled more information when the same environment was used at both the learning and test stages than when the environment was changed. Based on these earlier findings, our researcher should expect the divers who learn and recall the words underwater to perform better than those who learn underwater but recall the words on land. In other words, they can narrow down their prediction by stating how the IV will affect the DV. A suitable research hypothesis might therefore be:

- More words will be recalled correctly when learning and test environments are matched than when they are different.

In the case of our first, more vague, research hypothesis, the researcher predicted only that there would be a difference between the conditions, but not in which direction this difference would occur (i.e. which group would recall the most words). We refer to this type of hypothesis as a *two-tailed* hypothesis.

In the second research hypothesis, the researcher predicted not only that the IV would affect the DV, but in which direction this effect would occur (i.e. which group would recall the most words). We refer to this type of hypothesis as a *one-tailed* hypothesis.

### Activity 5.3

Look again at the research questions in Activity 5.2. Imagine that there was a considerable amount of evidence already suggesting that music impairs learning, that caffeine impairs concentration, and that we can concentrate better in the morning than early evening. Write appropriate one-tailed research hypotheses.

See the end of the chapter for possible answers.

As we shall see in the next chapter, whether you have a one- or two-tailed hypothesis has implications for working out whether to reject or accept the null hypothesis. However, if you state a one-tailed hypothesis and find that the group you predicted would have the highest mean actually has the lowest mean, you must accept the null hypothesis – regardless of the results of any statistical tests. Because of the implications it has for your results, you must only ever use a one-tailed hypothesis if you have extremely good grounds (usually the results of previous research) for making a more accurate prediction.

## Summary Section 6

- The research hypothesis is a formal statement that makes a prediction; in the case of an experiment that the IV will have an effect on the DV and in the case of a correlational study that two variables are correlated.
- A two-tailed research hypothesis predicts simply that there will be a difference or that there will be a correlation.
- A one-tailed research hypothesis predicts the direction of the effect, or whether the correlation is positive or negative, but such a hypothesis should only be used if there are extremely good grounds for making such a prediction.
- We test the null hypothesis which states that the IV will not affect the DV or that two variables will not be correlated.
- Type 1 error is if we incorrectly reject the null hypothesis.
- Type 2 error is if we incorrectly accept the null hypothesis.

# 7 Hypothesis testing

We now know how to formulate a hypothesis. The next question is how do we find out whether the difference between the conditions in an experiment is due to sampling error or due to the IV (assuming we've properly controlled for all other possible confounding variables)?

It is possible to look at this question graphically. We have already seen how to produce error bar charts to display the 95 per cent confidence intervals. If the confidence intervals calculated for the two samples do not overlap at all, then it is very unlikely that the two samples are from the same population. The more the confidence intervals overlap, the more likely it is that both samples are from the same population and that the difference between them is due to sampling error.

### *Activity 5.4*

Look at the error bar charts shown in Figures 5.4 and 5.5. What do these tell you about the samples? Are they drawn from the same population or different populations?

See the end of the chapter for the answer to this activity.

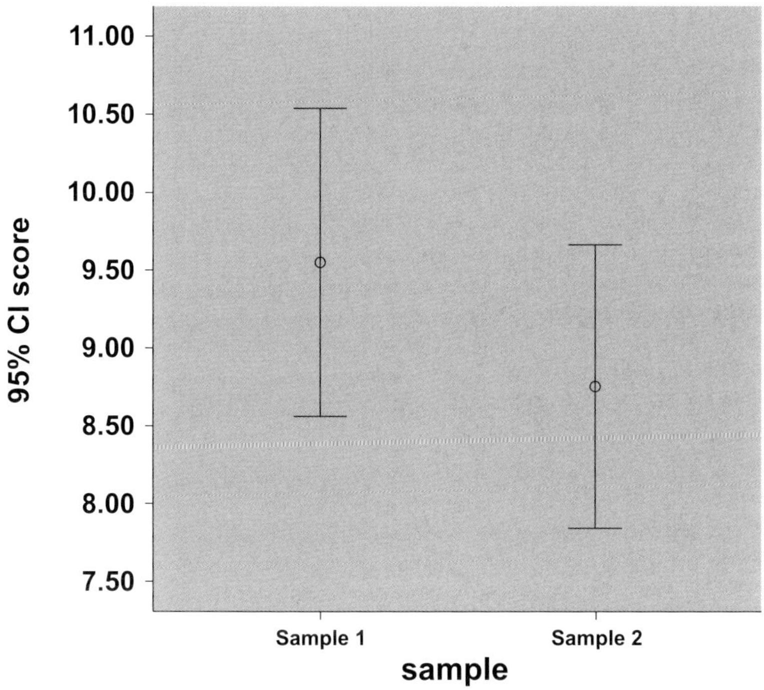


**Figure 5.4: Error bar chart 1**

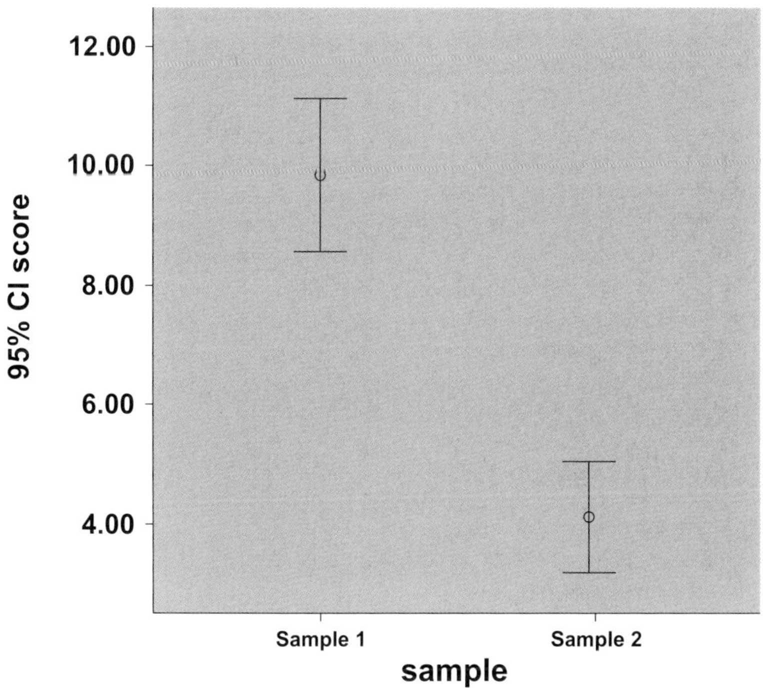


**Figure 5.5: Error bar chart 2**

Another way to test our hypothesis is to work out the *probability* of obtaining the difference between our conditions if our null hypothesis is true. In other words, we first assume that our two samples (corresponding to the two conditions) are from the same population and then work out what the probability is that the observed difference is due to sampling error.

The same logic applies to correlational studies. We formulate a hypothesis, measure the variables involved and explore the relationship between them. We then work out what the probability is of obtaining the relationship between the variables if our null hypothesis is true, i.e. if there is no relationship and hence any observed relationship between the variables is due to sampling error.

If the probability we calculate is sufficiently small, then it is unlikely that the difference or relationship we observe is due to sampling error. It therefore instead reflects a real difference or real relationship in the population. How small the probability has to be is something we shall explore in this section. First, let's look in more detail at the concept of probability, as this is clearly important in hypothesis testing.

Probability refers to the chance of something happening. If you flip a coin, the probability that it will come down 'heads' is 1 in 2, 50 per cent or .5. If you roll a standard die (the singular for dice), the probability that it will show a '4' is 1 in 6, 16.7 per cent or .167. You can see that probability can be expressed in different ways. We might say that a certain horse has a 1 in 3 chance of winning a race, that there is a 98 per cent chance of rain tomorrow, or that the chance of the next traffic light being green is .02. When using probability in research, we adopt this last method, where a value of 1 means that an event will definitely happen (the probability that 5 o'clock will follow 4 o'clock is 1) and a value of 0 means that an event could never happen (the probability of a standard die showing the number '8' is 0).

### Activity 5.5

What would a probability value of .25, .5 and .75 mean with respect to the likelihood of something happening?

See the end of the chapter for answers.

It is also possible to express the probability of one event occurring when the event is dependent on something else. For example, the probability that your front door will slam if you push it very hard may be 1, whilst the probability that it will slam if you blow on it may be 0. Likewise, the probability that the England football team will win their next game may be .06 if the opponents are Brazil and .95 if the opponents are Iceland. We refer to this type of probability as a *conditional probability*, as it is the probability of something happening that is conditional on something else.

When we are testing our hypothesis using a statistical test, we need to calculate a conditional probability. The reason for this is that we first assume that both our samples are from the same population. Having assumed this, we then work out the probability that the difference between the samples is due to sampling error. This probability is therefore conditional on the assumption that both samples are from the same population.

To recap, to test our hypothesis we need to:

- generate a null hypothesis
- assume that the *two* samples are from the same population
- calculate the probability of obtaining the observed difference between these two samples due to sampling error.

You will notice the word 'calculate' in the last of the steps above and also that we have yet to look at exactly how we could calculate this probability. You can breathe a sigh of relief, as you won't have to do this. Unfortunately (or fortunately depending on your point of view), the calculations involved in working out this probability are far too complicated and time-consuming for us to delve into, and SPSS is so much better at this sort of thing.

In the next chapter you will be introduced to *inferential statistical tests*, which allow us to draw inferences from our data. These tests calculate a *probability value* that corresponds to the chance that our results are due to sampling error. The term probability value is often shortened to $p$-value (and in fact, as you will see, is usually designated by the letters 'Sig.' in the SPSS output window).

However, working out the probability is only the first step. We also need to decide how we will interpret the probability value we calculate. For example, a researcher may work out that there is a .62 probability that the difference between the conditions was due to sampling error. Now what? Should they accept or reject the null hypothesis? To answer this question, we need to decide how small the probability of our results being due to sampling error needs to be before we reject the null hypothesis.

So that all researchers use the same value in making this decision, a probability value of .05 has been adopted. This is referred to as the *alpha value* ($\alpha$) and corresponds to a 1 in 20 (or 5 per cent) chance that our results were due to sampling error. So, if the probability of obtaining our results due to sampling error is equal to .05 ($p = .05$) or less than .05 ($p < .05$), we

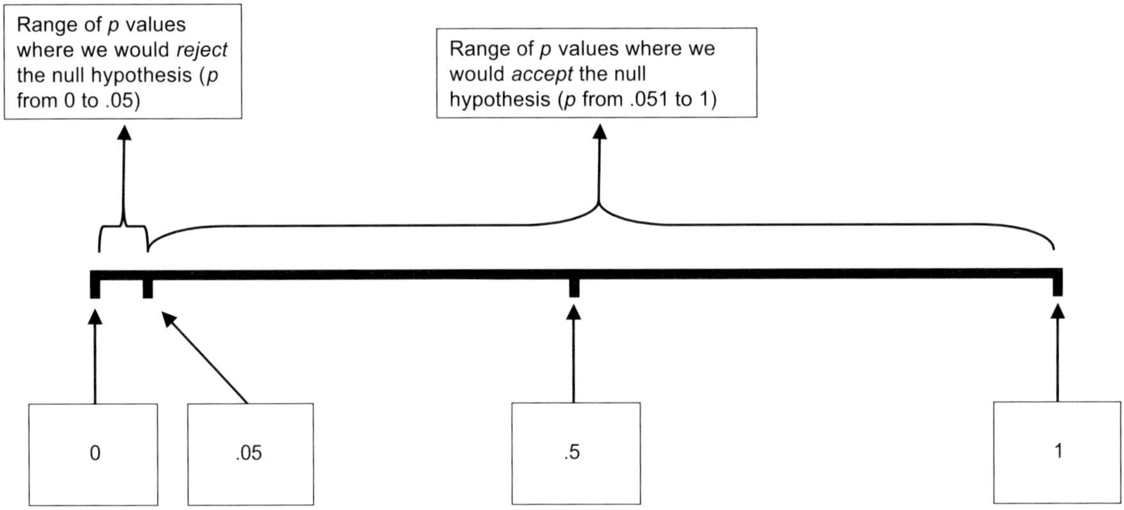


**Figure 5.6** Rejecting or accepting the null hypothesis

can reject the null hypothesis. If the probability of obtaining our results due to sampling error is more than .05 ($p > .05$), we have to accept the null hypothesis. This is summarised in Figure 5.6.

The *p*-value is therefore a very important figure, as it dictates whether we can reject the null hypothesis. We say that the *p*-value is the measure of *statistical significance*, which means it tells us whether the difference between our sample means is statistically significant or is not statistically significant (this is not the same thing as saying 'statistically insignificant', which is a term that you should avoid). If we obtain a *p*-value greater than .05, we conclude that the difference between our sample means is due to sampling error and is therefore not statistically significant. If we obtain a *p*-value equal to or less than .05, we conclude that the difference between the sample means is not due to sampling error and that it is statistically significant.

The same applies to a correlational study. If we obtain a *p*-value greater than .05, we conclude that the relationship between the variables is due to sampling error and is therefore not statistically significant. If we obtain a *p*-value equal to or less than .05, we conclude that the relationship between the variables is not due to sampling error and that it is statistically significant.

However, although the *p*-value tells us whether the difference between our conditions or the relationship between the variables is *statistically* significant, this is *not* the same thing as saying that it is significant in the sense of being important or meaningful. This is because it is possible to obtain quite a small difference between the sample means or a small correlation coefficient and still get a *p*-value that is statistically significant. So the *p*-value does not tell you about *how* different your two samples are or *how* related your variables are, just that this difference or relationship is statistically significant.

The difference between statistical significance and actual significance can be very important. For example, suppose that researchers tested the effects of a new learning-enhancement drug on students' performance by forming an experimental condition (those who received the drug) and a control condition (those who received a placebo). The mean score on the test for the experimental condition was 65.4 per cent and the mean score for the control condition was 63.2 per cent. A statistical test was employed and revealed that the difference between the conditions was statistically significant. Should the research team invest all their savings in rushing the drug to market? After all, there was a statistically significant difference between the conditions. However, if you were considering buying the drug, you might feel that the fact that the difference between the means was only 2.2 per cent is more important than whether the difference was statistically significant.

As well as our *p*-value telling us whether the difference is statistically significant, we also need to report some measure that describes how big the difference between our conditions was – or, in other words, how much of an effect the IV had on the DV. We refer to these measures as measures of *effect size* and, as we shall see in the following chapter, there is a different method of calculating effect size for each statistical test that we shall be exploring.

Before we leave the present section though, we shall return to a point made previously that the type of hypothesis we state has an effect on how we interpret our results. For some statistical tests, SPSS will calculate a *p*-value based on the assumption that you have a two-tailed hypothesis and a second *p*-value based on the assumption that you have a one-tailed hypothesis. For others, SPSS will just report a single *p*-value, and where this happens the *p*-value stated is based on the assumption that your hypothesis was two-tailed.

Basically, all statistical tests initially calculate a *p*-value assuming your hypothesis is two-tailed. To calculate the corresponding value for a one-tailed hypothesis, you just halve the *p*-value stated for the two-tailed hypothesis. In SPSS, for some statistical tests you have the option to specify one- or two-tailed probability. However, for other statistical tests it will only provide the two-tailed *p*-value, which you will have to halve yourself if your hypothesis is one-tailed. This is important in some cases, as it could make all the difference when deciding whether to accept or reject the null hypothesis.

## Summary Section 7

- To test a hypothesis, a useful first step is to produce error bar charts and look at the extent of overlap between the confidence intervals of our two samples.
- We use inferential statistical tests to calculate a probability value that corresponds to the chance that our null hypothesis is 'true'; that is, that any observed difference between the samples, or any observed relationship between variables, is due to sampling error.
- For us to reject the null hypothesis, this probability value (*p*-value) has to be as small as .05 (or 1 in 20) or lower.
- If the inferential statistical test calculates a *p*-value greater than .05, we conclude that the difference or relationship is due to sampling error, and we accept the null hypothesis.
- If the inferential statistical test calculates a *p*-value equal to or less than .05, we conclude that the difference or relationship is not due to sampling error and that it is statistically significant, and we reject the null hypothesis.
- As well as finding out whether the difference is statistically significant, we also calculate a measure of the size of the effect (e.g. how big the difference is).

| **Terms you should be familiar with:** |
|---|
| Sampling error |
| Sampling distribution of the mean |
| Confidence intervals |
| Standard error |
| Error bar chart |
| Research hypothesis (two- and one-tailed) |
| Null hypothesis |
| Type 1 error |
| Type 2 error |
| Conditional probability |
| Alpha value |
| Statistical significance |
| Effect size |

# Answers to activities

## Activity 5.1

(a) We call the histogram of the means of a large number of samples of the same population the *sampling distribution* of the mean.
(b) The sample mean is a *point* estimate.
(c) We refer to the range of values that our population mean falls into as the *confidence* interval.
(d) *95* per cent of the data falls within 1.96 standard deviation points of the mean.
(e) The standard error is calculated by dividing the *standard deviation* of our sample by the *square root* of the sample size.

## Activity 5.2

The following are possible answers – your own are likely to be different.

(a) *Research hypothesis* – Listening to Abba compared to no music whilst learning a list of words will affect the number of words recalled the next day.
*Null hypothesis* – The amount of words recalled the next day will not be affected by whether the participants learned the words whilst listening to Abba as opposed to no music.
(b) *Research hypothesis* – There will be a correlation between the amount of caffeine taken in a twenty-four-hour period and performance on a simple reaction time task.
*Null hypothesis* – Performance on a simple reaction time task will not be correlated with the amount of caffeine consumed in a twenty-four-hour period.
(c) *Research hypothesis* – Accuracy on a time-limited simple maths test will be affected by whether time of day was 10.00 a.m. or 6 p.m.
*Null hypothesis* – Time of day, 10.00 a.m. or 6.00 p.m., will not affect accuracy on a time-limited maths test.

## Activity 5.3

One-tailed research hypotheses:

(a) Listening to Abba compared to no music whilst learning a list of words will lower the number of words recalled the next day.
(b) As the amount of caffeine taken in a twenty-four-hour period increases so reaction time will decrease.

(c) Accuracy on a time-limited maths test will be better when measured at 10.00 a.m. than at 6.00 p.m.

### Activity 5.4

The error bar chart in Figure 5.4 shows that the confidence intervals for the two samples overlap substantially and that the means for each sample fall within each other's confidence intervals. This would suggest that the samples are drawn from the same population. The error bar chart in Figure 5.5 shows that the confidence intervals for the two samples do not overlap, suggesting that the samples are from two different populations.

### Activity 5.5

If 1 means that an event will definitely happen and 0 that an event could never happen, then .25 means that there is a 1 in 4 chance that the event will happen, .5 a 1 in 2 chance that the event will happen and .75 a 3 in 4 chance that the event will happen.

CHAPTER 6



# Inferential statistics

## Contents


| | | |
|---|---|---|
| | **Aims** | **164** |
| **1** | **Introduction to inferential statistics** | **164** |
| **2** | **Choosing an inferential statistical test** | **166** |
| **3** | **Analysing experiments** | **168** |
| | 3.1 The *t*-tests | 168 |
| | 3.2 The *t*-test and effect size | 171 |
| | 3.3 The paired-samples *t*-test | 173 |
| | 3.4 The independent-samples *t*-test | 173 |
| | 3.5 How to report the results of a *t*-test | 175 |
| **4** | **Correlations and associations** | **176** |
| | 4.1 The Pearson product moment correlation coefficient | 177 |
| | 4.2 Analysing two categorical variables | 180 |
| | 4.3 The chi-square ($\chi^2$) test | 181 |
| **5** | **Final word** | **185** |
| | **References** | **186** |
| | **Answers to activities** | **186** |

## Aims

This chapter aims to:

- introduce you to a range of inferential statistical tests
- explain how to select the appropriate test
- differentiate between tests of difference and tests of relationship or association.

In this study week we also show you how to perform the inferential statistical tests using SPSS (see Chapter 5 in the *SPSS Booklet*).

## 1 Introduction to inferential statistics

Over the last few weeks you've probably gathered that the numerical data we collect in quantitative research are not quite as simple and straightforward as they might at first seem. This is the final study week where we will be looking at quantitative research prior to you working on your own project, which will involve you collecting and analysing data using inferential statistics. Before looking at some of the simpler inferential statistical tests that can be used, let's briefly remind ourselves why we need to use these tests. Why don't the numbers 'speak for themselves'? What are the inferences that quantitative researchers need to make?

### Activity 6.1

Try a thought experiment: think of any three 'variables' that might be relevant in psychology. Now imagine going out and collecting data measuring those three variables. Can you imagine what the shapes of the distributions of these variables might be (i.e. what the histograms would look like)?

When you were doing Activity 6.1 it was probably quite easy to think of three variables that psychologists might want to measure. Maybe you thought of intelligence, or memory for nonsense words, or years of education, and so on. But guessing how the variable would be distributed might have made you realise that there is a step missing. First, you have to specify exactly 'who' is being tested or measured. The distribution of intelligence across everyone is going to look different from the distribution of intelligence for university students. Similarly, the distribution of age for Open University students is going to look very different from the distribution of age in a conventional university. So it is crucial to define the population that you want to describe and study. For example, university students across Europe and the USA might be the population of interest, or it might be UK and European Open University students. But notice that when you define the population you are setting the level of generalisation you will be able to make.

Doing a thought experiment as in Activity 6.1 is very different from doing a real empirical study – going out and actually measuring the variables. Perhaps whilst doing Activity 6.1 you saw that there is a problem with the *sheer number* of measures you would need to make if you were trying to measure variables in an entire population.

Quantitative research almost always uses samples of people from the population of interest rather than measuring the entire population. The Open University may well have already collected figures on the age of its students. But if a measure of the variable 'satisfaction with study at The Open University' is what you want to research, then you would almost certainly put your questions to a small sample drawn from the population of students rather than every student that is currently registered. We have seen that quantitative research has the goal of making general statements. It follows from this that quantitative research is not primarily concerned with studying individuals; rather, the whole research process is ultimately directed towards finding out about populations. But when measures come from small samples instead of the whole population to which the statement applies, there is always a degree of uncertainty about the true values of these measures in the population. It is only by using statistical inference that quantitative researchers can make estimates of population values. These estimates are still not completely certain but, with the help of statistics, can be claimed within known confidence limits (the confidence interval). Using confidence limits is a way of being clear about just how certain you can (and cannot) be.

As you read in Chapter 5, because researchers use samples drawn from the population of interest, there is always some degree of sampling error, as the values derived from the sample will not be exactly the same as those that would result from testing the entire population. The bigger the sample that is drawn, the lower the sampling error will tend to be. Sampling error is an inevitable, built-in error that has to be taken into account when deciding how to interpret the numerical findings from a study. Many quantitative studies involve a comparison (and look for a difference). For example, is there a difference between the number of words remembered by experimental group A (who were given rhyming words to remember) and the number of words remembered by experimental group B (who were given non-rhyming words)? Quite often there is a difference that can be seen by eye. For example, the mean number of words remembered by group A might be twice as many as the number remembered by group B. But how does the researcher know whether this difference is big enough to be a 'real' difference? How confident can the researcher be that the difference is not due to sampling error? Inferential statistics are needed to help the researcher decide whether the observed difference at the end of the experiment is due to sampling error or due to the effect of the experimental manipulation.

## 2 Choosing an inferential statistical test

Once you have designed and conducted your quantitative study, you will want to analyse your data to see whether to reject or accept your null hypothesis. Remember from Chapter 5, that by using a particular inferential statistical test we can calculate the probability value that corresponds to the chance that our null hypothesis is 'true' (i.e. that any observed difference between the conditions, or any observed relationship between variables, is due to sampling error). Unless this is small enough, equal to or less than .05, we cannot reject the null hypothesis.

In choosing which statistical test to analyse your data with, there are several things you need to consider. These are:

- Was your study experimental or correlational?
- What type of experimental design was employed?
- What was the level of measurement?
- How many IVs did you have?
- How many conditions were there?

Although it is possible to analyse experiments that had either more than one IV or an IV with more than two conditions, we shall not be looking at these on this course, meaning that we can concentrate on the first three questions.

You need to be very sure whether you conducted either an experimental or a correlational study, as the statistical test you will use is dependent upon this. If you are looking for a *relationship* between two variables which you have measured, then you have a correlational study. If you are looking for an effect of an IV on a DV, which might result in a *difference* between conditions, then you have an experimental study. The type of experimental design, whether between-participants or within-participants, will also influence your choice of statistical test.

The third question is also critical in deciding which statistical test to use. We know that categorical variables are measured at nominal level, where numbers are used as labels for the different categories. This includes variables such as the sex of the participant (which would entail representing male and female as '1' and '2' respectively, for example), and any question that requires a yes/no answer (so that 'yes' would be represented by '1' and 'no' by '2', for example). Data measured at ordinal, interval or ratio levels include continuous variables that can produce data of any value within a specified range and also certain discrete variables. The important point is that with such data the order of the numbers is of importance. This includes variables such as percentage correct, response time, number of errors and rating scores.

In this course we are going to focus on a particular type of statistical test that is termed a *parametric test.* Parametric tests make certain assumptions about the population from which the data have been drawn. For example, they assume that the data you collect have been drawn from a population that is normally distributed (referred to as an assumption of normality). In practice, this means checking that your sample data are approximately normally distributed (see Chapter 4). Parametric tests also assume that the variances are approximately equal (remember the standard deviation is the square root of the variance – see Chapter 3). You will see later on that SPSS checks this assumption for you (we shall cover this in the *SPSS Booklet*). There should also be no extreme scores, because the mean is very sensitive to these (see Chapter 3). If these assumptions are not met, then there are comparable inferential statistical tests termed non-parametric tests that can be used. However, when you carry out your quantitative project, you will be required to carry out a parametric test and simply comment on any extreme scores, although it is very unlikely that there will be any in your data set.

Finally, you've probably gathered that as we've been talking about the mean and variance, data analysed using a parametric test cannot have been measured at nominal level. Ideally, they will have been measured at interval or ratio level; however, studies have shown that parametric tests perform accurately with data that have been measured at ordinal level.

In the remaining sections of this chapter, we shall look at a number of simpler statistical tests. We will not show you the calculations involved in undertaking these tests, although you will learn how to carry these out using SPSS. Instead, we will concentrate on describing the purpose of each test, what statistics are involved and how to report the results. You may find it helpful to refer back to the relevant sections when working with SPSS and the *SPSS Booklet*.

### Summary Section 2

- Choosing the appropriate statistical test involves considering the type of study you conducted and how the variables were measured.
- Certain tests are parametric tests which make particular assumptions, and SPSS will check for some of these. You should check whether or not the data were measured at nominal level – if so, a parametric test cannot be used.

# 3 Analysing experiments

In this section, we shall look at how to conduct two inferential statistical tests. Both of these tell us whether there is a statistically significant *difference* between two conditions in an experiment. Both tests are called *t*-tests; one is used to analyse data from experiments employing a between-participants design and the other is used to analyse data from experiments employing a within-participants design. Both are parametric tests.

You will make use of *t*-tests to analyse data that you collect yourself for TMA 03. Although the output screen that SPSS produces for the *t*-tests can look a bit daunting, *t*-tests are one of the simplest statistical tests. As you read through this section, try to remember that what a *t*-test basically does is to tell us whether the difference between two conditions is statistically significant. Remember this simple fact, and you are halfway to understanding the *t*-test already.

## 3.1 The *t*-tests

If we have an experiment with one IV, two conditions, and the DV produces data appropriate for a parametric test, then the inferential statistical test we need to use is the *t*-test. The *t*-test is so called because it calculates a statistic referred to as $t$, which is written in italics to indicate that it is a statistic (the same applies to all other statistics, such as $p$ for probability). This statistic is representative of the amount of variation between conditions (i.e. the difference between the means for each condition) compared with the amount of variation within each condition (i.e. the standard deviation for each condition).

A *t*-test actually tests to see if the two sample sets of data are likely to have been taken from the same overall population or not. If the two samples have come from the same population, meaning that any difference between them is due to sampling error, then there will be no statistically significant difference and we cannot reject the null hypothesis. If there is evidence that we have two samples of data that have been drawn from *different* populations, then it is likely that there will be a statistically significant difference and that we must accept the null hypothesis. In this latter case, we can conclude that any differences we observe are due to a genuine underlying difference. Since the *t*-test looks for these differences, we have to have a research hypothesis that predicts that there will be a difference between the conditions and a null hypothesis that predicts that there will not be a difference.

Imagine a study where in one condition forty participants were asked to recall a list of words presented to them a day earlier, and in another condition forty participants recalled the same list but after a week. We can calculate a mean for each condition which will tell us how many words were recalled in that condition on average, and a standard deviation for each condition which will tell us how spread out (or dispersed) the scores were in that condition. What we need to do next is to assess the difference *between* the two means in respect to how the scores *within* each condition tended to vary. In other words, we need to see whether the difference between the conditions is due to sampling error or the effects of manipulating the IV.

If the variation within each condition is large (resulting in high standard deviations) and the difference between the means is small, then it is likely that this difference is due to sampling error. In other words, it is likely that sampling error alone could produce the difference between the two sample means. However, if the variation within each condition is small (resulting in low standard deviations) and the difference between the means for each conditions is large, then it is likely that there is a *real* difference between the two conditions that cannot simply be a product of sampling error.

Figure 6.1 shows fictitious data from the memory experiment described above, plotted on a histogram. You can see that the participants in the ' 1-day delay' condition are clearly recalling more words on average than the participants in the '1-week delay' condition. So there is a clear difference between the mean scores for each condition. The shape of the plot shows us that although there was some variation in each condition, the majority of participants recalled a number of words that was similar to the mean. Looking at the plots, we can also see that very few participants in the 1-day delay condition recalled fewer words than any of the participants in the 1-week delay condition. All this suggests that the difference between the

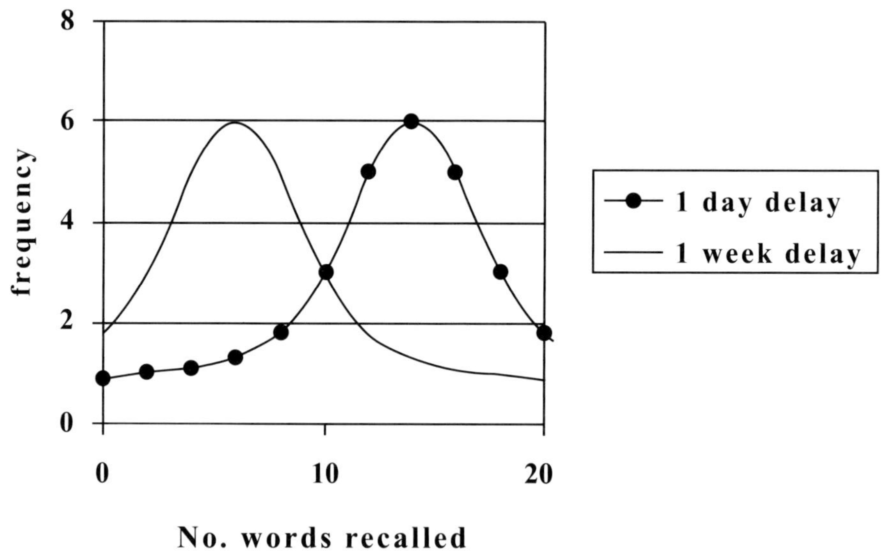


**Figure 6.1** Histogram containing data from two conditions

means is likely to be greater than the variation of scores within each condition. In other words, as there is little overlap between the plots for each condition, it is likely that the difference between the sample means is due to the IV and not due to sampling error.

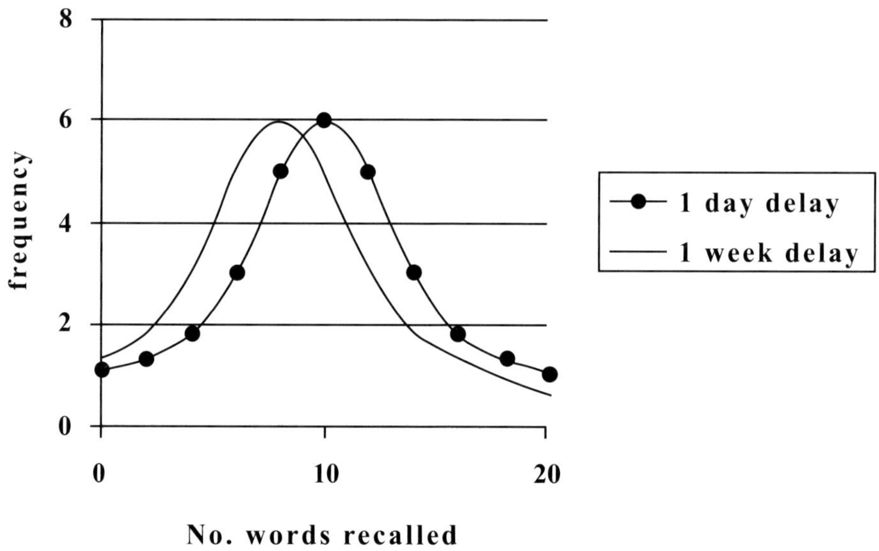


**Figure 6.2** Histogram containing overlapping data from two conditions

Figure 6.2 shows a second, different set of data from the same fictitious experiment which have also been plotted on a histogram. Here the two plots overlap to a far greater degree. You can see that although there is a small difference between the means, many of the participants in the 1-week delay condition were recalling more words than the participants in the 1-day delay condition. As the variation within each group is quite large compared with the difference between the means, it is unlikely that we are observing a *real* difference. Instead, the two samples appear to be from the same population and the difference between them is most likely due to sampling error.

The magnitude of the *t* statistic is dependent upon the relationship between the difference between the two means and the standard deviations of each mean. A large *t* value will be produced if there is a relatively *large* difference between the two means compared with the standard deviations associated with the means. A small *t* value will be produced if there is a relatively *small* difference between the two means compared with the standard deviations associated with the means. However, to tell whether the difference between the conditions was *statistically significant* we need to look at the *p*-value. Luckily for us, SPSS will calculate the *t* statistic and the *p*-value, so all we have to do is enter the data, click on a few buttons and then look at the output page.

Before we can do this, there is one more question we need to answer from those posed at the start of this section: 'What type of design was employed?' This is important, as there are two types of *t*-test, one for a within-participants design and one for a between-participants design.

The *t*-test for a within-participants design is known as the paired-samples *t*-test (or the related *t*-test, dependent *t*-test or repeated measures *t*-test).

The *t*-test for a between-participants design is known as the independent-samples *t*-test (or the unrelated *t*-test, independent *t*-test or between-groups *t*-test).

We can only use a *t*-test to analyse our data if:

- we conducted an experiment looking for a difference between conditions
- we are analysing a single IV with two conditions
- the data meet the requirements for a parametric test.

## 3.2 The *t*-test and effect size

It is sometimes tempting to rely completely on the *p*-value calculated for the *t*-test. Indeed, many published psychological studies base their conclusions entirely on whether the difference between conditions was statistically significant. However, as we explained in Chapter 5, just because a result is *statistically* significant it does not necessarily follow that it is *psychologically* significant. To overcome this it is important to report both the *p*-value and a value that represents the size of the effect (the effect size). As we shall see in later sections of this chapter, there are different ways of calculating and reporting effect size depending on the specific analysis conducted, but for now we'll concentrate on the effect size as it relates to the *t*-test.

Perhaps the simplest way of looking at the size of the effect in an experiment is to compare the means directly, but doing this will lead to a number that is dependent on the size of the mean scores. This is a problem because the mean scores will be dependent on the way in which the dependent variable was measured. For example, you would assume that a difference of 50 between the mean scores would be larger than a difference of 4, but what if these were the differences between the mean scores of 950 and 1000 (50) and of 2 and 6 (4)? The first difference (50) appears much larger than the second (4), even though in reality it represents a far smaller difference given the size of the original mean scores.

What we need instead is a way of calculating effect size that will not be affected by the size of the mean scores involved – in other words, we need a standardised way of measuring effect size. As we saw in Chapter 5, Section 5, a good way of standardising data is to use standard deviation points. The difference between two means expressed in terms of standard deviation points is known as the statistic *d*, and can be calculated by employing the following formula:

$$d = \frac{\text{Mean A} - \text{Mean B}}{\text{Mean SD}}$$

All this formula entails is subtracting the mean for one condition or group (Mean B) from the mean of the other condition or group (Mean A), and dividing the result by the mean standard deviation for the two conditions or groups (Mean SD). You can find the mean standard deviation by adding together the standard deviations of both groups or conditions and dividing the result by 2:

$$\text{Mean SD} = \frac{\text{SD A} + \text{SD B}}{2}$$

Subtracting Mean B from Mean A can sometimes result in a minus figure, and if it does then you can simply ignore the minus sign (it doesn't really matter which mean is Mean A and which is Mean B).

The result of the formula for *d* tells us the size of the difference between the two sample means, expressed in standard deviation points. The formula enables us to calculate the *size* of the effect in our experiment. The statistic *d* is therefore a measure of effect size.

Due to the nature of the normal distribution, Cohen (1988) suggests that a difference of 0.2 standard deviation points can be considered a small effect a difference of 0.5 standard deviation points can be considered a medium effect and a difference of 0.8 standard deviation points can be considered a large effect.

## 3.3 The paired-samples *t*-test

To recap, *t*-tests are tests of *difference*. They test for a statistically significant difference between two samples of data. As the name suggests, the paired-samples *t*-test sees if there is a statistically significant difference between two related samples of data (i.e. data obtained from a within-participants design). The name 'paired-samples *t*-test' is the one used by SPSS, but as we mentioned previously this test is also often known as the dependent, related or repeated measures *t*-test. (You may also see *t*-test written without a hyphen.)

We have seen that *t*-tests operate by calculating a statistic known as *t*. The value of *t* can be either positive or negative. It is important to note that the direction of *t* (+ or −) does not reflect the *magnitude* of difference; it only reflects which sample shows the larger mean. In the case of the paired-samples *t*-test, the direction of *t* (+ or −) simply tells you which condition gave the greater mean – condition 1 or condition 2. The same applies to the independent-samples *t*-test, but in this case the direction of *t* indicates which *group* showed the greater mean. In either case, as the direction of the *t* value is arbitrary (dependent upon your group coding or the order in which you entered your variables into SPSS), it is important that *you look at your means* to know the direction of difference.

### Conditions for using the paired-samples *t*-test

You can use a paired-samples *t*-test if you:

- employed a within-participants design in an experiment
- want to test for a difference between two conditions
- have data that meet the requirements for a parametric test.

## 3.4 The independent-samples *t*-test

As the name suggests, the independent-samples *t*-test determines whether there is a statistically significant difference between two *independent* samples of data (i.e. data obtained from a between-participants design). The name independent-samples *t*-test is the name used by SPSS, but as we mentioned previously this test is also known as the independent, unrelated or between-groups *t*-test.

As with the paired-samples *t*-test, the value of *t* can be either positive or negative. It is important to note that the *direction* of *t* (+ or −) does not reflect on the *magnitude* of difference; it only reflects which sample shows the larger mean. In the case of the independent-samples *t*-test, this depends only upon how you code your groups. For example, let's say you coded your groups '1' and '2'. The results of your *t*-test gave a value for *t* of 3.365

and your descriptive statistics show that the mean for group 1 is greater than the mean for group 2. Now, let's say you coded your groups the other way around (labelled group '1' as '2' and group '2' as '1'), and re-ran the test. You would now get a *t* value of −3.365 (showing that the mean for group 2 is greater than the mean for group 1), but the *magnitude* of the statistic *t* difference remains the *same*. So, the direction of the *t* value is arbitrary and depends upon your group coding or the order in which you entered your variables into SPSS. It is important that you look at your *means* to know the direction of difference.

## Conditions for using the independent-samples *t*-test

You can use an independent-samples *t*-test if you:

- employed a between-participants design in an experiment
- want to test for a difference between two groups
- have data that meet the requirements for a parametric test.

### Activity 6.2

Below, two studies are described. Decide which *t*-test you would use to analyse the data by identifying the IV, the DV and the design. (See the end of the chapter for our answers.)

*Study A*

A researcher was interested in determining whether the time of day had an effect on reaction time. Ten healthy adult participants were recruited. Each participant was asked to complete a reaction time trial in which they had to press a button as soon as a light was illuminated. The length of time (in milliseconds) between the light illuminating and the button being pressed was recorded. This trial took place at 7 a.m. Twelve hours later the participants returned and were asked to complete the reaction time trial for a second time.

*Study B*

Anti-emetic drugs are used to suppress nausea. A common side effect is that they can make people drowsy and slow down their reaction time which may be dangerous under certain circumstances (e.g. when driving). A researcher was investigating the effects of a new anti-emetic on reaction time. Twenty healthy adult participants were recruited and allocated randomly into one of two groups so that there were ten in each group. Participants in the experimental group were given the new drug and participants in the control group were given a placebo (a tablet which looked the same, but which only contained glucose). After an hour, all participants completed a reaction time trial in which they were asked to press a button as soon as a light came on. The time between the light illuminating and the button being pressed (the latency) was measured (in milliseconds).

## 3.5 How to report the results of a *t*-test

As this is a test of difference and the data are parametric, the descriptive statistics you should report are the mean and standard deviation for each condition. You can do this in a table of descriptive statistics or graphically, using a bar chart to show the means and histograms to show dispersion.

To report the result of the *t*-test itself, you must report the *t* value (the statistic that is calculated by the test), then put in brackets the degrees of freedom (see Chapter 3), followed by the *p*-value (which stands for probability and tells you how likely it is that any difference between the means from the two groups occurred by chance alone). All of these figures will be provided in the SPSS output. You also need to include *d*, the measure of effect size, which SPSS will not provide for you and which you will have to calculate by hand as shown above. You should include all of these values in your results section in a statement of results. For example, in the case of the example of a study suitable for the paired *t*-test, the results might be reported as follows:

> *The data were analysed using a paired-samples* t-*test* ($t(19) = -2.291$, $p = .04$, $d = 0.42$). *This analysis revealed the difference to be statistically significant. It was therefore possible to reject the null hypothesis and accept the research hypothesis, which stated that there will be a significant difference in reaction times measured in the morning and the evening. Taken together with an examination of the descriptive statistics, this analysis therefore shows that reaction times measured in the evening were longer than reaction times measured in the morning.*

**Note:** It is not sufficient to only look at and report the results of the inferential test; it is also necessary to examine the descriptive statistics to *determine* the direction of any difference (i.e. which condition showed the longer reaction times). For example, simply stating '*There was a significant difference between conditions*' does not tell us whether reaction times were longer in the morning or the evening. When writing a statement of results, always do so in terms of the original research hypothesis and try to *interpret* the result for your readers *in terms of the research hypothesis.*

**Also note:** If your research hypothesis was one-tailed, then there are two further points to take account of when reporting your results. First, SPSS provides the *p*-value for a two-tailed test which then needs to be halved (e.g. if $p = .06$, divide this by 2 to obtain $p = .03$). Second, if you find a significant difference, then you must check that this is in line with the difference predicted. You cannot reject the null hypothesis in favour of the research hypothesis if you predicted that performance in Condition A would be faster than performance in Condition B when in fact the opposite was shown in your results, even if the *p*-value is equal to or less than .05. This is why you have to be very cautious about formulating a one-tailed hypothesis in the first place, and should only ever do so if there are extremely good grounds.

### Summary Section 3

- The *t*-tests look to see if there is a difference between two conditions or groups, and so are suitable if an experiment was conducted.
- The paired-samples *t*-test should be used if the experiment involved a within-participants design.
- The independent-samples *t*-test should be used if the experiment involved a between-participants design.

**This would be a good point to turn to your computer and the *SPSS Booklet*. Work through Sections 1 and 2 of Chapter 5 to see how you can use SPSS to perform both types of t-tests. If it is more convenient, then you can do this at a later point in your study week.**

## 4 Correlations and associations

In Chapter 2, we introduced you to correlational studies as a different type of quantitative study from experiments, and as a way of investigating relationships between two variables. You may remember that scatterplots are used to obtain an idea of how the two variables may be related, either positively or negatively, and that correlation coefficients provide a numerical measure of the extent to which the variables are related. Because correlation coefficients tell us about the magnitude of the relationship between two variables, they are in fact a measure of effect size – they tell us how strong the relationship is.

What correlation coefficients do *not* tell us is whether the relationship is statistically significant. This may seem a little odd to you. How can a relationship that is strong and produces a large correlation coefficient (say −0.7) not also be statistically significant? Let's take an extreme example to begin with. Imagine we are trying to discover whether there is a relationship between ageing and memory. We recruit 2 participants, 1 who is 85 years of age and who scores 6 on a memory task and one who is 18 years of age and scores 36. If we were to plot these two points, they would (obviously) lie on a perfectly straight line and therefore produce a correlation coefficient of −1.

But would you be prepared to make the claim that there is a strong negative relationship between ageing and memory on the basis of this result? Probably not. The reason that you wouldn't look favourably on this result is that the sample contained only *two* people and was not, therefore, representative. By relying on just two people, we are very likely to introduce a sampling error into our results.

Now, if we performed the same observations on 50 people of different ages and found a correlation coefficient of −0.54, we should be more confident that our population is representative of the general population and therefore more confident that we have not introduced any sampling error. If we increased the number of people to 500, we could be even more confident, even though the correlation coefficient would be smaller than it was for a sample of 2 people.

When we calculate our *p*-value in a correlational study, it is telling us what the probability is that our correlation coefficient is due to sampling error. Basically, the statistical test involved looks at the size of the coefficient and *also* at how many observations we made to obtain it, and works out how likely it is that our result is due to sampling error.

So, the *p*-value tells us how likely it is that the correlation coefficient is due to sampling error, and the correlation coefficient tells us about the magnitude of the relationship between two variables and hence provides a measure of effect size. It is possible to have a large coefficient but, if you obtained this from only a few observations, a statistically non-significant result. Likewise, you can have a correlation coefficient that is quite low but that, because you had a large number of observations, is still statistically significant. It is therefore very important to report the coefficient, the *p*-value and the sample size (referred to as 'N').

## 4.1 The Pearson product moment correlation coefficient

There are several statistical tests for analysing correlational studies, but we shall be concentrating on one that is known as the Pearson product moment correlation coefficient – though thankfully this is usually shortened to 'Pearson'. The Pearson test calculates a correlation coefficient known as *r* and is a very widely used test. It is also a parametric test. As the correlation coefficient is the measure that tells us about the size of the effect (i.e. the strength of the relationship between the variables in this case), $r$ is considered to be the measure of effect size for correlation.

### Interpreting *r*

We mentioned in Chapter 2 that if the correlation coefficient is zero then there is no relationship between the two variables. If it is −1, then there is a perfect negative relationship, and if it is 1 (which is the same as +1) there is a perfect positive relationship. But what constitutes large or small effect size? Many researchers accept the suggestion of Cohen (1988) that $r = 0.10$ (or −0.10) means a small effect, that $r = 0.30$ (or −0.30) means a medium effect; and that $r = 0.50$ (or −0.50) means a large effect.

### What does this test do?

A correlation is a test of *relationship*. It provides a measure of the extent to which two variables change together, and whether or not this relationship is statistically significant.

### When can you use the Pearson product moment correlation coefficient?

You can use the Pearson product moment correlation coefficient if you:

- recorded data suitable for a parametric test
- recorded the data in the form of related pairs of scores (so that you know which two observations go together)
- want to test for a relationship between two variables
- expect the relationship between the variables to be linear (this means that when you plot the data on a scatterplot, you would expect the individual points to fall approximately on a straight line, rather than a curved line).

If the data do not meet these requirements, then it is possible to use a nonparametric correlation coefficient such as the Spearman rank correlation coefficient. This calculates the rank of each piece of the original data and then measures the strength of the relationship by calculating the Pearson correlation coefficient with these ranks. SPSS can calculate a Spearman rank correlation coefficient, and you will see Spearman as an option when you run a Pearson correlation in SPSS (*SPSS Booklet*, Chapter 5), but it is not covered in this course.

## How to report the results of the Pearson product moment correlation

There are no descriptive statistics per se for correlation. In fact, the correlation coefficient itself (*r*) is a descriptive statistic. Correlation is a test of whether two variables are related, and simply presenting the means and standard deviations for each of your variables would not describe the relationship between them. The most useful way of displaying the relationship between two variables is graphically, using a scatterplot. However, where you need to present the results of many correlations, using scatterplots can be unwieldy. In practice, scatterplots are often used as a diagnostic tool (to see if the relationship is roughly linear), but they should be used with discretion, usually only to present important correlations.

To report the results of the Pearson product moment correlation itself, you must report the correlation coefficient (*r*), the number of cases or observations (N), and the *p*-value (which tells you how likely it is that the relationship you are reporting occurred by chance alone because of sampling error). In the SPSS output, the value for *r* is labelled 'Pearson Correlation', the number of cases is labelled 'N', and the value for *p* is labelled 'Sig. (2-tailed)'. However, as you will see when using SPSS to conduct this statistical test, you can select *p* for a one-tailed test if your hypothesis is one-tailed.

You should include these values in a statement of results. Remember the fictitious study concerned with the effects of tiredness on cognitive function in newly qualified medical staff introduced in Chapter 2? The research hypothesis was that the more tired the student is, the more mistakes he or she will make. This is a one-tailed hypothesis as a positive relationship is being predicted. The two variables measured were the number of errors made in a diagnosis and the length of time that had passed since the beginning of the student doctor's shift. The results of any analysis could be presented in the following way:

> *The data were analysed using a Pearson product moment correlation (*r = *.869, N = 20,* p *=.001 for a one-tailed test). As the analysis revealed a statistically significant positive correlation, the null hypothesis was rejected in favour of the research hypothesis that the more tired the student is, the more mistakes he or she will make.*

When writing a statement of results, always do so in terms of the original hypothesis. To state simply that 'there is a significant relationship' does not tell us how tiredness is related to the number of mistakes made and therefore is of little value. You need to *interpret* the result for your readers in *terms of the hypothesis.*

## 4.2 Analysing two categorical variables

Another case where we are interested in the relationship between two variables occurs when the variables are categorical and the data measured at nominal level, and we are interested to see if there is an *association* between the variables.

For example, imagine a researcher who was interested in seeing whether there is an association between length of hair and sex. There are two categories for the variable 'sex' ('male' and 'female') and we can also categorise the variable 'hair length' into two categories ('long' and 'short', for example). Note that the categories within each variable should be mutually exclusive; you cannot be male *and* female, or have both long *and* short hair. If we present these variables *and* their categories in the form of a table (see Table 6.1), you will see that it creates four possible combinations. We call each of these combinations a contingency (as the decision as to where to place each piece of data in the table is contingent on the variables involved), and this type of table is therefore known as a *contingency table.*

**Table 6.1**

| | | **Hair length** | |
|---|---|---|---|
| | | **Long** | **Short** |
| **Sex** | **Male** | ML | MS |
| | **Female** | FL | FS |

There are two variables ('sex' and 'hair length') and as each variable has two categories, it is known as a two-by-two (usually written '2 × 2') contingency table. By tabulating the categories in this manner, you can see that there are four cells describing all possible combinations (contingencies) of the categories: males with long hair (ML), males with short hair (MS), females with long hair (FL) and females with short hair (FS). If we were to observe passers-by and record their sex and hair length, we could then place each person into one (and one only) of the cells in the table. The decision as to which cell to use would be *contingent* on our two variables: i.e. is the person male or female and do they have long or short hair?

To test for an association between sex and hair length, we need to gather a sample population of people (males and females) and simply observe (count) the numbers that fall into each of the possible contingencies (i.e. the *frequencies* of males with long hair, males with short hair, females with long hair and females with short hair). Having done so (using a sample of 100 people: 50 males and 50 females), we might find something like Table 6.2.

**Table 6.2**

| | | Hair length | | |
|---|---|---|---|---|
| | | **Long** | **Short** | **Total** |
| **Sex** | **Male** | 5 | 45 | 50 |
| | **Female** | 35 | 15 | 50 |
| | **Total** | 40 | 60 | 100 |

By looking at the table, we can see that there does appear to be an association between sex and hair length. Short hair seems to be associated more with males, and long hair seems to be associated more with females. This is OK as far as it goes, but we want to know whether this association is statistically significant.

## 4.3 The chi-square ($\chi^2$) test

To do this we make use of the chi-square test (usually written using the Greek letter 'chi' as $\chi^2$). Chi is pronounced like the 'ky' in sky and not like 'chi' as in Chi-Chi the panda. What the $\chi^2$ test does is to compare our *observed* frequencies (those we entered in Table 6.2) against the *expected* frequencies (the number of each contingency we would expect to see at chance level).

### When can you use the $\chi^2$ test?

You can use the $\chi^2$ test if you:

- recorded data at the nominal level of measurement
- want to test for an association between two categorical variables[1]
- the two variables are independent from one another (i.e. they are mutually exclusive); each participant must contribute to just one category.

The $\chi^2$ test requires that both your variables are categorical variables, but it is possible to transform continuous variables such as age or time into

[1] The $\chi^2$ test can also be used as a 'goodness of fit' test, which we won't cover here.

categories. For example, we could recode age in years into two categories so that people under 40 were in the first category and people over 40 were in the second. Note that, wherever possible, we should always *collect* data at the higher level, because we can turn 'age in years' into 'age groups', but we cannot turn 'age groups' into 'age in years'. If a participant is recorded as being 'under 40', they could be anything from newborn to a second away from their fortieth birthday.

Some find $\chi^2$ as easy to do with a calculator as with SPSS (but don't worry if you don't want to use a calculator). The calculations involved are not too complex and involve looking at the differences between each observed frequency and its associated expected frequency. For each observed frequency, you take away the relevant expected frequency, square the result and then divide by the expected frequency, and then you add these together. So, how does one obtain the expected frequencies? Let's look again at the data in Table 6.2. The expected frequency is the row total multiplied by the column total divided by the overall total:

$$\text{Expected frequency} = \frac{\text{Row total} \times \text{Column total}}{\text{Overall total}}$$

So, for our males with long hair the calculation would be: 50 times 40 divided by 100, which equals 20; for our males with short hair the calculation would be: 50 times 60 divided by 100, which equals 30; and so on. Table 6.3 shows the observed frequencies with the associated expected frequencies in brackets.

**Table 6.3**

| | | Hair length | | |
|---|---|---|---|---|
| | | **Long** | **Short** | **Total** |
| **Sex** | **Male** | 5 (20) | 45 (30) | 50 |
| | **Female** | 35 (20) | 15 (30) | 50 |
| | **Total** | 40 | 60 | 100 |

If you use SPSS rather than a calculator (which we recommend), the program will calculate the observed and expected frequencies for you from the data file. SPSS uses the difference between the expected frequencies and the observed frequencies to calculate a value of $\chi^2$. Basically, the larger the difference between the expected and observed frequencies, the larger the value of $\chi^2$ will be. To see whether the association is statistically significant, SPSS determines what the probability would be of obtaining this value of $\chi^2$ assuming that there is no association between the two variables (i.e. that the null hypothesis is true). This probability is expressed as a *p*-value in the SPSS output. If the *p*-value is equal to or less than .05 then the association between the two variables is statistically significant.

When conducting a $\chi^2$ test, it is also important that no more than 25 per cent of the cells in your contingency table have an *expected* frequency of less than 5. SPSS will check to see how many cells have an expected frequency of less than 5 and will report this figure as a footnote. When conducting a 2 × 2 $\chi^2$ test (such as that between gender and hair length described above), it is possible to overcome the problem of having more than 25 per cent of your cells with an expected frequency of less than 5 by making use of the Fisher's exact probability test. SPSS will calculate and report this test for you. All you need to do is to check the footnote and, if more than 25 per cent of your cells have an expected frequency of less than 5, you should report the *p*-value from the Fisher's exact test row of the SPSS output.

It is also possible to get SPSS to calculate a measure of effect size for $\chi^2$. This is known as Cramer's V and it acts like any other measure of effect size to tell you how strong the association between your variables is. In fact, Cramer's V is a correlation coefficient that can be used and interpreted in exactly the same way as Pearson *r* (the statistic we described in Section 4.1).

## Example of a study that might use a 2 × 2 chi-square test

A researcher was investigating the viewing habits of people who watch films at the cinema. Whilst a general census reported that horror films were as popular as romance films, the researcher hypothesised that there was an association between the sex of the viewer and the film genre. Specifically, the hypothesis was that women preferred to watch more romantic films whilst men preferred to watch horror films. The researcher conducted a survey of forty adults (twenty males and twenty females), asking them which type of film they preferred.

In this study, the researcher was testing for an association between categories of sex (male or female), and categories of film preference (horror or romance). The data were in the form of frequencies (number of males and females who preferred watching either romance films or horror films).

## How to report the results of a 2 × 2 chi-square test

The 2 × 2 chi-square test looks for an association between two categories. It uses frequency data (counts), therefore the best way to describe these data is using a table of frequencies such as those shown above (a 2 × 2 contingency table). To report the results of the chi-square test itself, you should report the value for chi-square (usually written $\chi^2$), the degrees of freedom[2] (df), the value for *p* (which stands for 'probability' and tells you how likely it is that the association you are reporting was due to sampling error) and Cramer's V (which is a measure of effect size).

You should include these values in a statement of results, such as:

> *The results were analysed using a chi-square test ($\chi^2$ = 6.465, df = 1,* p *= .01, Cramer's V = 0.402). As the analysis revealed a statistically significant association, the null hypothesis was rejected in favour of the research hypothesis that there is an association between sex and film genre preference. Women preferred watching romance films and men preferred watching horror films.*

When writing a statement of results, always do so in terms of the original research hypothesis. To state simply that 'there is a significant association' does not tell us *which* sex is associated with a preference for which film genre, and therefore is of little value. You need to *interpret* the results for your readers *in terms of the research hypothesis*, which in this case would mean stating which category (male or female) was associated with which other category (romance or horror).

**Note:** With the 2 x 2 chi-square test, but only a 2 x 2 test, it is possible to test a one-tailed hypothesis, and you would halve the *p*-value provided by SPSS. However, as we pointed out earlier you must have good grounds for specifying a one-tailed hypothesis and must check that any statistically significant association is indeed in the direction that you predicted.

## Summary Section 4

- The Pearson product moment correlation coefficient is a test of relationship and is suitable if you have conducted a correlational study measuring two variables and have parametric data.
- The chi-square test is a test of association and is suitable if you have independent categorical variables and the data are measured at the nominal level.

[2] The degrees of freedom for the chi-square test are calculated by taking the number of columns in your contingency table, minus 1, times the number of rows in your table, minus 1; in other words, (columns – 1) × (rows – 1). As the table is a 2 × 2 table this will be (2 – 1) × (2 – 1), which is 1 × 1, which equals 1. Therefore, in a 2 × 2 chi-square, the df will always be 1.

### Activity 6.3

Below are very brief descriptions of research studies; what test might be used to analyse the data?

(a) Whether concrete words are more likely to be recalled than abstract words.

(b) The relationship between age and speed of mental processing.

(c) The difference in face recognition between new and experienced police officers.

(d) The association between gender of child (boy or girl) and choice of toy (doll or Lego).

Our answers are at the end of the chapter.

## 5 Final word

The next chapter will focus on the experimental project that you will conduct for TMA 03, and subsequent chapters will look at qualitative methods. We have therefore come to the end of our coverage of quantitative methods and statistical analysis. Let us recap what we have covered. We have introduced you to:

- many important terms associated with quantitative methods
- two main quantitative methods, correlational studies and experiments
- descriptive statistics
- inferential statistics
- four statistical tests: the two *t*-tests, Pearson and the $\chi^2$ test.

As you can imagine, there are other methods used to collect quantitative data (such as observation) and many other statistical tests, and you will find that some other OU psychology courses will pick up from where we leave you here. For example, if you take either DXR222 or DZX222 you will be shown a statistical test that can deal with an IV that has three or more conditions and is an extension to the *t*-test. Figure 6.3 is a flowchart that should help you determine which test to use, based on the type and design of your study.

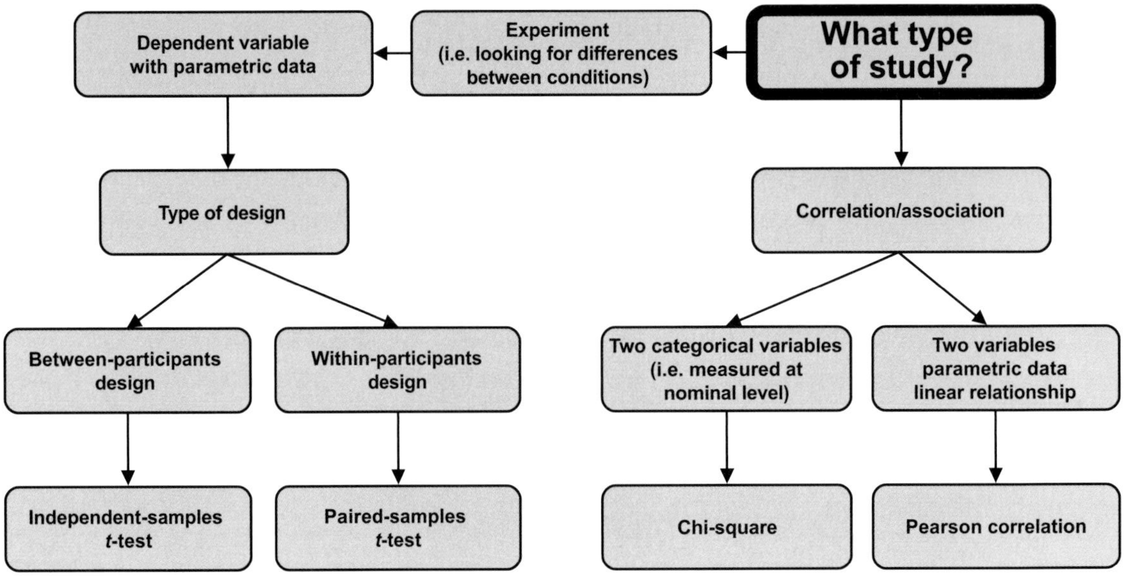


**Figure 6.3** Guide to choosing a statistical test

**Now turn to your computer and the *SPSS Booklet*. Work through Sections 3 and 4 of Chapter 5 to see how you can use SPSS to perform both the Pearson and the $\chi^2$ tests.**

# References

Cohen, J. (1988) *Statistical Power Analysis for the Behavioural Sciences* (2nd edn), New York, Academic Press.

# Answers to activities

## Activity 6.2

**Study A – paired-samples *t*-test:** In this study the researcher was interested in seeing whether there was a statistically significant difference between the two conditions; these were:

- Condition 1 – reaction times at 7 a.m.
- Condition 2 – reaction times at 7 p.m.

The design was within-participants, as each participant took part in both conditions. The dependent variable measured was a continuous variable as it consisted of the reaction time recorded in milliseconds and the level of measurement was ratio. The data meet the requirements for a parametric test.

**Study B – independent-samples *t*-test:** In this experiment the researcher was interested in seeing whether there was a statistically significant difference between the two groups; these were:

- Group 1 – who were given the new drug
- Group 2 – who were given the placebo.

The design was between-participants, as participants were randomly allocated to one of the two groups. The dependent variable measured was a continuous variable as it consisted of the response latency recorded in milliseconds and the level of measurement was ratio. The data meet the requirements for a parametric test.

## Activity 6.3

(a) Whether concrete words are more likely to be recalled than abstract words – this seems to be an experiment, looking for a difference in performance between two conditions; the dependent variable is likely to be the number of words correctly recalled, so a *t*-test seems to be the appropriate test to use. The design could be within- or between-participants, so which *t*-test is not clear.

(b) The relationship between age and speed of mental processing – this seems to be a correlational study involving the measurement of two variables. If the data are parametric, then the Pearson test is the most likely candidate. However, a scatterplot should be obtained to check that any relationship is linear.

(c) The difference in face recognition between new and experienced police officers – this seems to be a quasi-experiment looking for a difference in performance in two groups. If the face recognition task generated parametric data, then the independent-samples *t*-test is the test to use.

(d) The association between gender of child (boy or girl) and choice of toy (doll or Lego) – this seems to involve two independent categorical variables with data measured at the nominal level; therefore, the $\chi^2$ test is the only test that could be used.

CHAPTER 7

# The experimental project

## Contents


Aims 191

1 Introduction to the experimental project (and TMA 03) 191

2 Introduction to report writing 193

2.1 What goes in a report 193

2.2 Report writing: following the experimental process 197

2.3 Some other formalities in report writing 199

2.4 Your TMA 03 report 200

3 Your experimental project: the introduction and research hypothesis 201

3.1 The rationale for conducting the experiment: the introduction 203

3.2 Deciding on your research hypothesis 204

4 Designing and conducting the experiment: the method 205

4.1 Design 205

4.2 Participants 206

4.3 Materials/apparatus 206

4.4 Procedure 207

4.5 Designing and conducting your experiment 208

4.6 Your experiment: the instructions 210

4.7 Choosing your participants 211

4.8 A guide to collecting the data 213

5 Analysing the data from the experiment: the results 215

**6** **Drawing conclusions from the data: the discussion** **216**

**7** **The remaining sections of your report** **217**

7.1 Title 217

7.2 Summarising the experiment and writing the abstract 218

7.3 The references section 218

7.4 The appendices 219

**8** **Example of a report write-up** **219**

**9** **The stimuli for your experiment** **230**

**10** **Consent form to use in your experiment** **237**

## Aims

This chapter aims to:

- show you how to conduct a psychological experiment
- show you how to write a report of a psychological experiment
- provide you with the opportunity to conduct and analyse a psychological experiment yourself.

# 1 Introduction to the experimental project (and TMA 03)

So far in this course you have heard a lot about experiments. You have been introduced to the principles and terminology involved in experiments in Chapter 2 of this book and have read about experiments conducted by psychologists in Book 1 *Mapping Psychology*. You have also had the opportunity to practise your use of SPSS. Now it's your turn to carry out an experiment yourself!

This chapter will introduce you to some of the practicalities involved in conducting an experiment, give you the opportunity to collect some data and also show you how to write an experimental report. The work you will do forms the basis of TMA 03.

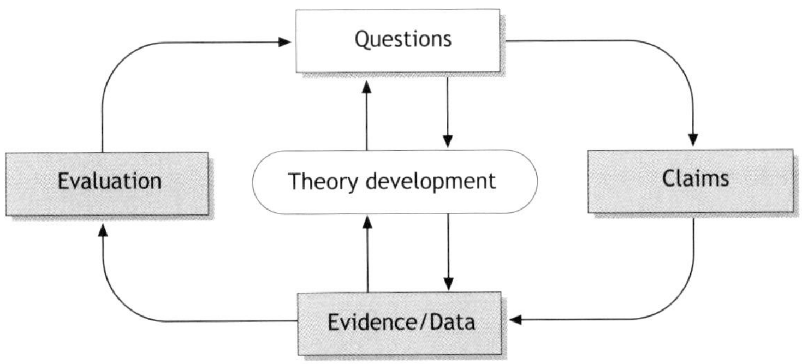


**Figure 7.1** The cycle of enquiry

You have already been introduced to the idea of the 'cycle of enquiry' that applies to the range of different research studies conducted in psychology (see Figure 7.1). This chapter (and TMA 03) will be concentrating on those parts of the cycle to do with making claims, collecting evidence/data and evaluation. As this is an experimental project, we will be focusing on:

- how we can test the claims arising from the research hypothesis
- how to evaluate the evidence we collect
- how this evidence and evaluation can be used to inform theory development and to generate new research hypotheses.

### Activity 7.1 *Design terminology*

Before we go any further, let's just quickly revise the information on experimentation that has already been covered. By now you should have a good idea about what is involved in designing and conducting an experiment. To make sure you understand the concepts and terminology, try writing a brief description of the terms listed below. If you get stuck on any of them, you can refer back to the previous chapters in this book or the glossary (but please try to work out the answers for yourself first).

Experiment

Null hypothesis

Research hypothesis

One- and two-tailed hypotheses

Experimental design

Within-participants

Between-participants

Independent variable (IV)

Dependent variable (DV)

Condition

Control

Confounding variable

Descriptive statistics

Inferential statistics

Probability value

Effect size

Sampling error

Statistical significance

Carrying out the project work outlined in this chapter should help your understanding of these concepts. In addition, the process of designing and conducting a real experiment and analysing the data from it should help with your knowledge of research and statistics. If you have been finding research methods and statistical analysis a bit daunting, remember that they are tools and concepts that have a direct, practical use and can sometimes be hard to grasp 'in theory'. Actually conducting an experiment and analysing some real data that you have collected yourself should therefore help your understanding.

Before we go into more detail about the actual project work you will undertake, we shall first introduce you to experimental report writing. Understanding what is involved in writing a report will ensure that you are aware of what information you need to make a note of in order to be able to write the report for TMA 03.

# 2 Introduction to report writing

The idea behind having a convention for writing a report is to make sure that everyone includes the essential information and describes it in a similar fashion and order. Unfortunately, different journals tend to ask authors to prepare their work in slightly different styles and authors will often, therefore, adopt a style that fits their particular study. For this reason, if you pick up a selection of psychological journals and compare the writing style, order and terminology for several different articles you will see quite considerable differences.

However, all of the articles reporting quantitative research will tend to be based on a similar report-writing model and will contain the same type of information. What we shall be doing throughout the course of this chapter is to introduce this basic experimental report-writing model and work through how and why it is the way it is. But remember, this is just one possible style of writing a report and although it has a lot in common with many published experimental reports, it also has some differences.

## 2.1 What goes in a report

Whilst you are reading through this section, try to keep in mind that one of the principal skills of report writing is to communicate complex concepts in as few words as possible. This means you should try to write with as much

**A**ccuracy,

**B**revity and

**C**larity

as you can. Also, note that a key difference between an essay and a report is that a report is subdivided into different sections. Each of these sections has a heading and it is important not only that you include all of these sections and their headings, but that you put them in the correct order. That is:

- Title
- Abstract
- Introduction
- Method
- Results
- Discussion
- References
- Appendix or appendices.

Although this is the order in which the sections should appear in the final report, it is very unlikely that you will actually come to write them in this order. Why this is will become clear in a moment when you read more about what goes in each section.

The process of writing an experimental report (referred to in the remainder of the chapter as 'report') is very reflective of the process of conducting an experiment. After all, the aim of the report is to tell people about the experiment, so we would expect it to have a lot in common with the process of conducting it. In Table 7.1 (see Section 2.2) each section of a report is linked to a corresponding part of the experimental process. But, put simply, a report should tell the reader:

- why the experiment was conducted
- what was done in the experiment
- what the results of the experiment were
- what conclusions can be drawn from these results.

To help the reader build up a picture of the experiment and address these four issues, the main body of the report is divided into four sections. These are:

### Introduction

Here we provide the reader with a summary of the research in this area that has already been conducted and explain why there was a need to conduct the experiment we are reporting (i.e. the rationale). The introduction concludes with a statement of the research hypothesis and the corresponding null hypothesis.

## Method

In this section we describe how we conducted the experiment. The key requirement is to provide enough information so that the experiment could be replicated. To help the reader understand this process, the method section is subdivided into four subsections (and you would include these as sub-headings when writing the Method section of your report):

*Design* This is where we use most of that experimental terminology that you have been reading about. We describe what design was employed; state what the independent variable (IV) and dependent variable (DV) were; explain how the IV was actually manipulated and what the conditions were; say how the DV was measured and what type of data it produced; and explain what controls were introduced in order to limit the effects of possible confounding variables.

*Participants* This section is used to answer the questions 'How many people took part in the experiment?', 'How were they selected?', and 'What were their basic demographic characteristics?'

*Materials* This description should not just take the form 'paper, pen and stopwatch'. Rather, it should provide a complete description of all the stimuli, response sheets and apparatus used in the experiment.

*Procedure* Here we describe in detail what happened and in what order. In addition, and critically for psychology experiments, we state verbatim the instructions given to the participants and how the responses were recorded. It is important to mention the use of consent forms and the debriefing of participants.

## Results

This section describes any and all calculations that were performed on the data collected in the experiment and includes a statement of which statistical tests were conducted. The descriptive statistics (e.g. means and standard deviations) and inferential statistics (e.g. the results of *t*-tests including effect sizes) must also be presented.

### Discussion

The discussion section starts with a description of the results in plain English and goes on to state what conclusions can be drawn from these results. The author should also discuss any limitations of their experiment, discuss the results in relation to previous research and look to the future in terms of what research needs to be conducted next.

So, the basic format of the main body of an experimental report is designed to make sure that all the information the reader needs to know about the experiment is included. The use of subsections is to provide the reader with easy access to particular pieces of information and reflects both the process of conducting the experiment (see Table 7.1 in Section 2.2) and the four key issues that have to be dealt with, namely:

| | |
|---|---|
| Why the experiment was conducted | = Introduction |
| What was done in the experiment | = Methods |
| What the results of the experiment were | = Results |
| What conclusions can be drawn from these results | = Discussion |

If we add four more sections to the four outlined above, we have the basic structure of the entire report. These four remaining sections are:

### The title

This should let the reader know which area of psychology is being explored and give them a very basic idea of what the experiment is looking at. It must be concise and be built around the independent variable and the dependent variable.

### The abstract

This is a short paragraph (usually no more than 150 words in length, with some journals limiting this to 100 words maximum) that goes right at the start of the report, under the title. It provides a summary of all the other sections and allows a potential reader to determine whether the report will be of interest to them. For this reason the abstract is often the section included in databases of journal articles.

### References

In describing the previous research conducted in the area and in discussing the conclusions that can be drawn, it is necessary to make 'references' to work conducted by other authors. Advice on referencing is provided in the *Assignment Booklet*.

### Appendix or appendices

This section can be used to provide examples of stimuli and questionnaires or any other material used, as well as raw data and relevant sections of SPSS printouts.

So, there we have it. An experimental report consists of eight individual sections that provide both a summarised and detailed description of the experiment conducted.

## 2.2 Report writing: following the experimental process

As indicated previously, the structure of a report has a lot in common with the process of conducting the experiment itself. When you think about it, it would be most illogical for it to be otherwise. Let's look at this similarity in more depth; it should help illuminate the process of both report writing and of conducting an experiment.

As Table 7.1 shows, the processes of conducting an experiment and of writing it up involve a series of discrete sections that follow a logical sequence. Does this mean that we should write the corresponding section of the report as we finish that section of the experiment? The simple answer is that there should be nothing to stop you doing this, but if you prefer to leave all the writing until after you have conducted the experiment, that too is alright. However, it is the case that you should not really move to the next stage of either process until you have completed the current stage to your satisfaction. For example, if you were to design and conduct the experiment before completing the literature review, you may later discover that you have missed an important detail or are repeating someone else's mistakes! Alternatively, writing the discussion before you have completed your statistical analysis would be rather pointless, as you would have no idea as to what results you had obtained.

**Table 7.1 The links between the experiment and the report**

| | Experiment | Report | |
|---|---|---|---|
| | Read books and journal articles about research in the area of interest | Provide a review of previous research | |
| *Step 1* | Work out what needs to be done next in this area | Use the review to show what you have decided to examine and why it needs to be looked at | *Introduction* |
| | Determine specifically what will be examined in the experiment | State both the research hypothesis and the null hypothesis | |
| | Work out what the most appropriate design to use in the experiment would be | Design: state the design employed and the IV and DV | |
| | Consider what problems might occur in conducting the experiment and devise a means of limiting their effects | Design: describe what controls you are including | |
| *Step 2* | Consider what ethical issues arise in conducting the experiment | Participants: consider how you will gain informed consent, what debriefing procedures you will follow, whether there are specific ethical issues arising from your research that might affect participants | *Method* |
| | Decide who to conduct the experiment on | Participants: say who took part in the experiment | |
| | Construct the stimuli you will be using in the experiment | Materials: describe the stimuli and all other materials | |
| | Conduct the experiment on the participants | Procedure: provide precise details of how the participants were tested and how they were debriefed | |

| | | | |
|---|---|---|---|
| *Step 3* | Collate the responses from the participants and enter them into SPSS<br><br>Analyse the data<br><br>Determine if these results are what you expected<br><br>Describe what the statistics mean<br><br>Work out what the statistics tell you | Describe what data were collected<br><br>Provide graphs/tables of descriptive statistics and the outcome of any inferential tests<br><br>Accept or reject the null hypothesis<br><br>Interpret your results in terms of the IV and DV | *Results* |
| *Step 4* | Compare these results to those found in previous research<br><br>Look back through the experiment and identify anything that went wrong<br><br>Work out what experiment to do next | What are the implications for research and theories in the area<br><br>Describe any problems and possible limitations<br><br>Describe possible future directions for the research area in question | *Discussion* |

Table 7.1 provides you with a clear outline of the steps you need to work through when carrying out your project work and there is a definite advantage to working through them in the order listed. You'll need to keep adequate notes as you research and conduct your experiment so that you have the key details when you come to write the report.

## 2.3 Some other formalities in report writing

There are some further formalities you need to consider when writing up psychological research and experimental research in particular. You will have already encountered some of these in connection with essay writing, but others will be new:

- Use the term 'participants' to refer to the people who took part in your research. You may find that some older journal articles use the term 'subjects' but that term is not now considered appropriate.
- Write in the third person rather than the first person. For example, instead of saying 'I then read the instructions to the participant', you might write 'The instructions were then read to the participant'.

- Write in the past tense rather than the present. For example, instead of writing 'The design of the experiment is between-participants', you might write 'The experiment employed a between-participants design'.
- Do not use gender-specific language. Avoid referring to the participants as either 'he' or 'she', unless that's a key feature of the design of the experiment.
- Do not plagiarise.

Please also bear in mind that some of these formalities are different when reporting non-experimental methods. For instance, it is common to use the first person in reporting qualitative research. You will learn about this in later chapters of this book.

## 2.4 Your TMA 03 report

You should now have a general feel for what is involved in conducting an experiment and in writing a report and are ready to read about the actual project you will be carrying out. Before we turn to this, it is worth bearing in mind that we have only looked quite briefly at what information needs to go in each section of the report. The reason for this is that it tends to be easier to get to grips with report writing when you are dealing with a real experiment and real data. Talking hypothetically as we have been is a necessary introduction, but working with a real example is a much better method. The later sections in this chapter will therefore contain notes on how to write up the specific experiment you will be carrying out for your TMA 03 assignment.

Complete instructions on what to send to your tutor are provided in the *Assignment Booklet*. For now, please note that in the *Assignment Booklet* we state that the length of your report for TMA 03 should be approximately 2000 words – this word count does *not* include title, reference section or appendices. The booklet also provides the following advice on approximate word lengths for each main section:

- Title – that captures the essence of your report and is not included in the word count.
- Abstract – up to 100 words.
- Introduction – 500 words. Remember that this needs to include your research and null hypotheses. Please also state whether this is one-tailed or two-tailed.
- Method section – 700 words. Remember that this needs to include four sections: Design, Participants, Materials and Procedure.
- Results section – 200 words (excluding graphs or tables).
- Discussion section – 500 words.
- References section – not included in word count.
- Appendices – not included in word count.

# 3 Your experimental project: the introduction and research hypothesis

As Table 7.1 shows, doing any research project involves a series of steps. The first can be quite lengthy, since you have to decide what you are researching and what your research hypothesis will be. Once you've decided on that, you have to design the experiment, as you won't be able to conduct a valid scientific investigation unless you can come up with a sound method. This method needs to be translated into the experimental design, materials and apparatus you need, including any instructions, before you can recruit participants and start to collect data. Usually, you analyse your data before you do most of the writing up, although the introduction and much of the method section can be written while, or indeed before, the experiment is being conducted.

Because this is possibly your first experiment we will be supporting you through this process and have already decided for you what you will be researching. In your experimental project you will be investigating a variation of the Stroop effect: that people find it harder to name what colour ink a word is written in if the word is the name of a colour than if the word is colour neutral. As you may remember from Book 1, Chapter 6, 'Perception and attention', this is an example of where automatic processing interferes with the information you are trying to attend to.

For your project you are being asked to investigate this further. Instead of using colour words (e.g. green) you will use colour-related words (e.g. grass). The experimental condition (the Stroop condition) will involve the colour-related words printed in a colour that is incongruent with the word. We've chosen the colour-related words to be the following:

- BLOOD: not printed in red but printed in yellow, green, orange, purple and blue
- LEMON: not printed in yellow but printed in red, green, orange, purple and blue
- GRASS: not printed in green but printed in red, yellow, orange, purple and blue
- CARROT: not printed in orange but printed in red, yellow, green, purple and blue
- PLUM: not printed in purple but printed in red, yellow, green, orange and blue
- SKY: not printed in blue but printed in red, yellow, green, orange and purple.

So, there will be a list of these words, with each word appearing five times in each of its incongruent colours. You will show the list to participants and time how long it takes them to work through the entire list, naming the colour of the ink each word is printed in.

The control condition will contain colour-neutral words. Below are the words we've chosen that we felt matched the colour-related words above:

- BLAME
- LEDGE
- GRADE
- CAREER
- PLAN
- STY

Spend a moment thinking about why we chose the words in the control condition list to use in our experiment and reflect on how these words match with the colour-related words. You will need to consider this when you write your project up. For example, you will find that each word appears in the list five times and is printed in each of the same colours as their corresponding colour-related word. You will show the control condition list to participants and time how long it takes them to work through the entire list, again naming the colour of the ink each word is printed in. Copies of both lists are provided in Section 9 toward the end of this chapter and are available to be downloaded from the course website.

The most time-consuming part of conducting experiments tends to be 'testing' or 'running' the participants – i.e. carrying out the experiment and collecting the data. To help reduce the amount of time you need to spend on this project, we carried out the experiment on sixteen participants and these data can be found in the *Assignment Booklet.* We suggest you aim to conduct the experiment yourself on at least four people, although there is certainly no harm in running more. Once you have collected your data, you should combine them with the data that we collected, which are provided in the *Assignment Booklet,* and enter them into SPSS. You then need to choose the appropriate statistical test to analyse the data and perform this test using SPSS. You should then have all the information you need to write your report.

Before thinking about recruiting participants, you need to be clear about the rationale for your experiment: why you are conducting it and what your research hypothesis will be. We shall first consider these two issues before going on in Section 4 to look in more detail at the design of your experiment.

## 3.1 The rationale for conducting the experiment: the introduction

The introduction to the report serves two principal functions:

- It provides a review of the research that has already been conducted in the area – and that is relevant to the experiment.
- It provides the rationale for why the experiment was conducted.

One important thing to remember here is that these two functions should be addressed together. An introduction *does not* provide an objective and balanced review of existing research and then at the end contain a paragraph of rationale. Instead, the rationale for conducting the experiment should be developed whilst reviewing the previous research. This means that when reviewing previous research you should keep your research hypothesis in mind and discuss things in a way that will lead logically to what you did in your experiment. By doing this you will demonstrate to the reader why your experiment is of psychological interest, and also show how it relates to existing theories and research in that area.

It is usual to begin the introduction by locating the specific area you will be examining in a broader context. Usually this means beginning by describing an area such as attention, memory or social cognition. Do not begin by providing a history or description of the whole of psychology or even of an entire perspective, such as cognitive or social psychology. After describing the area, you should begin to narrow your review down so that by the end you have reached the specific research hypothesis you will be looking at. Thus, the introduction can be seen as a funnel or upside-down pyramid, as in Figure 7.2 overleaf, starting broadly and becoming ever more specific.

Remember, though, to keep '**A**ccuracy, **B**revity and **C**larity' in mind and only include other research which is strictly relevant to your project. If possible, you should critically evaluate any research you discuss and use this evaluation to support your choice of research hypothesis and the way you have designed your study. For example, it may be that the participants in a previous study on memory tended to remember nearly 100 per cent of the items. You might point out that this would not allow any potential improvement to show through and you were therefore going to use more items or a longer testing period in your own study.

Any points you make should be supported by a specific theory or the results of a published study. You should not make sweeping statements or rely on assumptions that have not been tested empirically. The idea behind your study should be to take the next (and often very small) step in that particular field, so you should be able to build a picture that is supported by empirical evidence of all that has led to your study. Conclude the introduction by formally stating the research and null hypotheses.

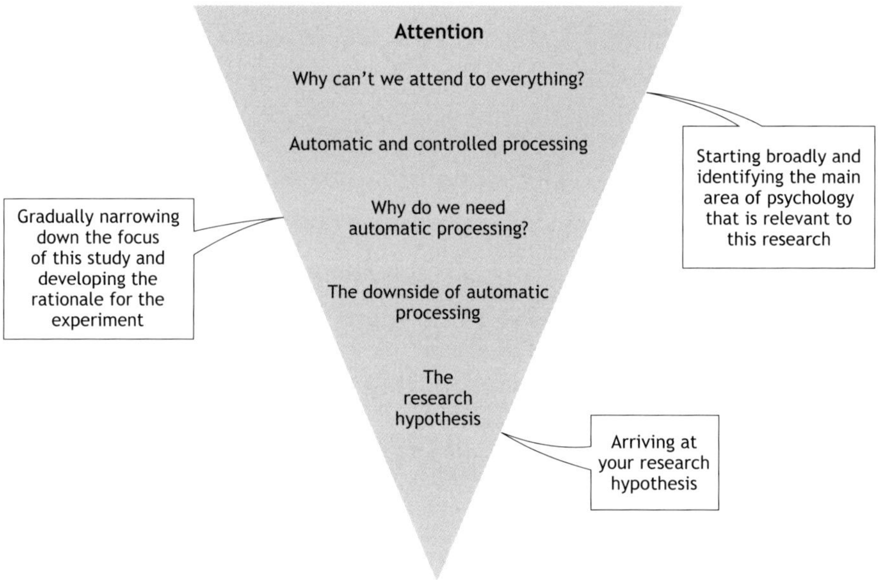


**Figure 7.2** Focusing the research question

When you write your introduction it might be useful to start by making notes on what other studies have found and concluded and then to structure these in a way that will lead logically to your research hypothesis. The rationale for conducting the study will then be clear. Keep in mind, though, the idea of an upside-down triangle: start broadly and then narrow the focus down to your specific research question. Book 1, Chapter 6 contains all the relevant information that you will need. In particular, you will need to refer to Section 2 on attention. If possible, look at that section now and make some notes.

## 3.2 Deciding on your research hypothesis

In the 1930s, Stroop carried out research into the interaction between automatic and controlled processes. Stroop found that people found it harder to name what colour ink a word was written in if the word was the name of a different colour (e.g. 'red' or 'blue') than if the word was colour neutral (e.g. 'boat' or 'table'). Thus, an apparently automatic process, reading in this case, interfered with a controlled process, naming the colour of the ink, and made completing the task at hand harder.

Pause for a moment and think about what might happen in your experiment. Do you think that there will be a difference between the two conditions? Will the participants find one of the conditions harder, thus making them take longer to complete the task, than the other? If so, which condition might they find harder and why do you think that might be? In deciding on your research hypothesis you need to think about the findings of the original experiment by Stroop and see how they relate to your experiment. You will also need to decide if your research hypothesis is one- or two-tailed. It may be helpful to revisit the section on writing research hypotheses in Chapter 5, Section 6.

# 4 Designing and conducting the experiment: the method

Before you actually start to design the experiment we shall look in detail at what information needs to be included in the method section of the report. By doing this first, you will know what information you need to report and therefore what to make a note of.

As we have already seen, the method section is subdivided into four parts and these are used to describe precisely what was done in the experiment. The key point to remember here is that you need to:

*Provide sufficient information to allow replication.*

That is to say, the description you give should allow the reader to go away and conduct your experiment. This is a very important point as replication is the fundamental method of checking the accuracy of any results reported.

To keep the layout of the report clear and to allow the reader to find the relevant information quickly, the method section is divided into four subsections.

## 4.1 Design

The design section needs to include the following information:

- The type of design employed in your experiment, i.e. within-participant or between-participant. (If the same participants were used in both conditions, then the design is within-participants. If the participants from condition 1 were not the same as those in condition 2, then the design is between-participants.)
- A statement of what the independent variable (IV) was. (The IV is the variable that you manipulated.)
- A more detailed description of the IV, including what the conditions were (i.e. how it was operationalised).
- A statement of what the dependent variable (DV) was. (The DV is the variable that you measure.)
- A more detailed description of the DV, including how it was measured and what units were used (e.g. seconds, percentage correct, or the score on a test).

- A description of all the controls introduced in order to improve the experiment. (A control is any action you took to limit the effects of any confounding variable – anything that might affect the DV other than the IV. Typical controls include making sure that all the participants received the same instructions, that they did not confer with each other and that the order of the stimuli was changed to limit practise effects.)

### Note on correlational designs

Remember that a study that is based on a correlation is *not* an experiment. In an experiment you manipulate one variable (the IV) and measure what effect this has on a second variable (the DV). In a correlational study, no manipulation is involved. Instead, the researcher observes and records variations in two variables. When reporting a correlational study, you state that the design was correlational and describe the two variables that were recorded. You do *not* label one as the IV and the other as the DV.

## 4.2 Participants

The participants section needs to include the following information about the people who took part in the experiment:

- How many people took part in the experiment.
- How these people were selected and recruited. How you gained informed consent and what you told the participants about the nature of the research.
- Whether they were 'naive' to this specific experiment and psychological experiments in general.
- Any incentive (money or course credits) that the participants received.
- An indication of who the people were – this is usually done by reporting such things as the age range and number of men and women.
- Whether you had to exclude the responses of any participants from further analysis – e.g. this could be because something went wrong in the experiment.

## 4.3 Materials/apparatus

There is a tendency for students writing their first report to simply list 'a stopwatch', 'some paper' and 'a pen' for this section. Alternatively, some students give detailed specifications of the computer they used to analyse the data. Both these practices should be avoided. Remember, the method section needs to provide the reader with all the information required to replicate the experiment. As the analysis of the data occurs after the experiment has been conducted, we do not include any equipment used to do the analysis in the method section.

Very often the most important part of the materials/apparatus section is a detailed description of the stimuli used in the experiment. So, if you were testing people's memory for lists of words, you would need to describe here exactly how these lists were constructed – not what type of pen you used, but rather how many words were on the list and what type of words they were.

You may be thinking to yourself, 'Why bother to describe these stimuli, when I could just include a copy of them in the report?' This is a good point and indeed you should put in the appendices a copy of any word lists or other stimuli, questionnaires or other materials you used. However, remember that you need to provide all the information necessary for replication, and the reader may want to replicate your study using slightly different stimuli. You therefore need to describe all the key components that guided your creation of the stimuli. This might include the number of items you used, the size/colour of the items and every other criterion you used in their creation. Also relevant are standard instructions that were read to participants, response sheets and consent forms.

Remember, although it may be tempting to simply list all the items you used, this section should be written in continuous prose just like the rest of the report.

## 4.4 Procedure

This section provides a description of what you did and of the order in which you did it. It is therefore usual to order the procedure section chronologically. Again, you need to decide what information is necessary to allow replication of the experiment and which details are not required. In general, it is usual to include the following information:

- What the participants were told before taking part in the experiment.
- Whether the participants took part individually or in groups – and if in groups, how many people there were in each group.
- The instructions that were given to the participants – a verbatim copy of these should be included here, if they are brief, or in the appendices, if they are long.
- Whether all the participants received the same instructions or whether instructions varied according to condition.
- How any stimuli were presented (e.g. by hand, one at a time, or on a computer screen).
- The order in which any stimuli were presented.
- How long any stimuli were presented for.

- The interstimulus-interval (ISI) – if there was a gap between successive presentations of the stimuli, how long this was.
- The number of items of stimuli presented.
- The approximate overall length of the experiment.
- How any decisions/responses made by the participants were recorded.
- How the participants were debriefed – i.e. what you told the participants after they had completed the experiment.

This last point is important since it relates to ethical guidelines when carrying out research. You will need to show some consideration of ethical issues when writing up your report. You may recall that these were first discussed in the Introduction to Book 1 and in Chapter 1 of this book. This might be an appropriate time to re-read the sections on ethics so that you remind yourself of some of the key issues before conducting your experiment, especially as the guidelines have a lot to say about how participants should be recruited and treated. These include informed consent, anonymity, the right to withdraw from research, and feedback and debriefing to participants. A full copy of the British Psychological Society guidelines, *Ethical Principles for Conducting Research with Human Participants,* can be downloaded from the course website.

If this list appears a bit daunting, don't worry – we will guide you through what needs to be done.

## 4.5 Designing and conducting your experiment

Now you know what the method section of the report needs to contain, you can keep careful notes of all the relevant information as you design and conduct the experiment. Your experiment is based on the Stroop effect. The first question you need to address in designing the experiment is: how are you going to test the hypothesis? We know that the Stroop effect is caused by the interaction of an automatic and a controlled process – more specifically, that participants find it very hard not to read a word that is placed in front of them, even when the task they are being asked to perform is different from that of reading. If this word is similar to the response they have to give as part of the other task (such as a colour name when the other task is to name the colour of ink), then interference will occur. As in Stroop's original experiment, the automatic process you will use is reading and the controlled process will be naming the colour of the ink. The difference is that in your experiment you will need a list of words that are colour related rather than being the actual names of colours.

But it is no good simply timing how long it takes for a participant to complete this task, as you will have no basis for comparison. You therefore need a second condition that makes use of a list of colour-neutral words that are printed in differently coloured inks. If it takes the participants longer to do the task when the words are colour related than when they are colour neutral, you will be able to conclude that the participants found this first condition harder. Later, in your discussion, you will need to consider why this happened.

Remember that the condition in which you have introduced the particular manipulation you are interested in testing (in this case a variation of the Stroop effect) is referred to as the 'experimental' condition. The condition that will give us our comparison data is the 'control' condition.

Now we have worked out what conditions we need, you need to determine which will be the best design to employ – within-participants or between participants. One of the rules of thumb in making this decision is to use a between-participants design if taking part in one condition will affect the performance of the participant in another. Within-participants designs are often useful as they can overcome some of the problems associated with individual differences, as the same participants take part in both conditions, though they do not guarantee this. In the present experiment, it is unlikely that completing one condition will give the participant practise sufficient to alter their performance in the other condition (but see the first bullet point below). **You are therefore asked to use a within-participants design**.

The next thing to do is to try to imagine what other variables might possibly affect the results of your experiment and come up with a method of preventing them. In other words, you want to introduce controls to limit the effects of any confounding variables. Below is a list of some of the confounding variables and the controls that we've thought about:

- *Possible practise effects of doing both conditions*
  Practise effects are one example of an order effect, as by using the conditions in the same order for every participant a possible confounding variable is introduced (you may recall this from Chapter 2). Hence, it will be important to counterbalance the order in which the conditions are used (i.e. for the first participant present the experimental condition and then the control condition, and reverse this order for the next participant, and so on).

- *The time taken will depend on the number of words in the list*
  The same number of words must be used in both conditions. You will be using thirty words in total in each condition.

- *Shorter words may be quicker to read*
  The words used in the two conditions are matched for length. You may have noticed that we did this when choosing the colour-neutral words.

- *Some ink colours may stand out more*

Use the same ink colours in both conditions. We've told you which colours to use but make sure you use the same hue (preferably exactly the same pen for each colour) in each condition.

- *Seeing blue ink after red ink may be easier than seeing it after green ink*
  Ensure that the order in which the different colour inks are used is the same in both conditions.
- *Repeating a word could cause a practice effect*
  As it will be necessary to use each colour-related word more than once, you must use each of the colour-neutral words the same number of times. Here each word will be used five times.

Now that we have clarified the design of your experiment, you can generate the stimuli. To assist you, we have provided you with the lists of words you will need to conduct this experiment. If you have access to a colour printer, you can download a coloured version of the lists from the course website and print them out. Alternatively, you can colour in and then use the sheets provided in Section 9 of this chapter, which includes a guide as to what colour each word should be. To help you, we have already conducted this experiment on sixteen participants and these data can be found in the *Assignment Booklet.*

So we now have a design and stimuli we can use, but before we can begin to think about the procedure, especially the instructions, we might use in this experiment, we need to consider an important and necessary step to do with recruiting participants. Part of the ethical guidelines we adhere to when conducting research requires that we obtain 'informed consent' from each participant, tell them that they may withdraw at any time during the research, and debrief them about the exact nature of the research after they have participated. As these ethical considerations are of paramount importance when conducting a psychological experiment, we have provided you with a written consent form in Section 10 (at the end of this chapter) and you must give this to each participant and obtain their signature *before they participate in the experiment.* You should also provide them with general details about what they will need to do before they participate and more detailed information once they have finished. Thus, before the experiment you might tell them that the task will involve lists of coloured words and after provide them with an explanation of the Stroop effect and how you are studying it.

## 4.6 Your experiment: the instructions

Before you can collect data you also need to know the instructions you should use so that every participant is told the same thing. We used the instructions given below when we carried out the experiment that produced the data provided in the *Assignment Booklet*, so it is important that you use the same instructions when you conduct the experiment. These instructions should be read verbatim to each participant:

> *In a moment I will place a sheet of A4 paper in front of you that contains two columns of words. You will notice that the words are written in six different colours of ink – red, blue, green, yellow, orange and purple. What I would like you to do is to say out loud the colour of the ink each word is written in. Start with the word at the top of the left column and work downwards. When you have finished all the words in the left column, start on the right column. Remember, I do not want you to read the word itself out to me, instead I want you to state what colour of ink it has been written in. You should work through the list as quickly as you can.*
>
> *To help you, here are two examples:*
>
> ***CHAIR****
>
> *For the item above you would respond 'blue'.*
>
> ***HOUSE***†
>
> *For the item above you would respond 'red'.*
>
> *Do you understand what you will be required to do?*
>
> *(If yes, then proceed to task.*
>
> *If no, go through the examples again.)*

## 4.7 Choosing your participants

You are now almost ready to collect data. So think about what type of person you want to recruit as a participant. From your knowledge of cognitive processes and experimental research, what factors do you think might be important in deciding who might be a suitable participant? Well, first and foremost the participants must be able to understand the instructions and be able to complete the task. This means they will need to be able to understand and read English well, have normal or corrected-to-normal eyesight and be able to distinguish between different colours. If you think you might have problems with getting access to fluent English speakers (e.g. if you are studying outside the UK or Republic of Ireland), you may be able to find a

* This word would need to be written in blue ink.

† This word would need to be written in red ink.

way of collecting data by phone, sending the participants the instructions and stimuli beforehand by email or post. Alternatively, you can translate the material into another language if this will help you, but be sure to mention this in your write-up.

We also know that strategies for completing tasks and cognitive processes, such as those studied by attention researchers, tend to develop with age. This means that it would be unwise to use children, even if they have good reading skills, as their cognitive processes might not be quite the same as those of an adult. Also, it would be unwise to approach adults with impairments. As it is also necessary to get permission from a parent/guardian before children or vulnerable adults are able to participate in research, we will not be using anyone under 18 years of age or vulnerable adults in this project. Perhaps one of the most important criteria to bear in mind (and one that can prove problematic for researchers who just use psychology undergraduates) is that the participants must be 'naive'. By this, we mean that they should not be aware of the hypothesis or have knowledge of the research area that could lead them to alter their responses.

Participant selection is very important and as explained above it is usual to include a summary of who the participants were when you write the report. Also, in drawing any conclusions from an experiment, we must remember who our participants were and be careful not to overgeneralise our results.

As mentioned previously, you should adhere to the ethical guidelines both when approaching participants and whilst conducting the experiment; think also about where the experiment should be conducted and consider issues involving safety and privacy. As the researcher, you are responsible for whatever happens to the participant in the experiment and so it is important that you follow the ethical guidelines with care. In particular, this entails:

- informing the participant that you are conducting a psychological experiment
- telling them why you are conducting the experiment and what participation will entail
- obtaining informed consent from all participants (in this case using the consent form provided in Section 10 and on the course website)
- providing them with an opportunity to withdraw from the experiment at any point
- debriefing them after the experiment and answering any questions they may have.

It will also be important for you to consider if there are any ethical issues arising specifically from your experiment. Can you think what some of these might be? For instance, there could be specific concerns if a participant was dyslexic or colour-blind since they might feel stressed about taking part.

Finally, you should draw up a response sheet so that you keep an accurate record of all the data you are about to collect. For example, you could construct a table that looked something like this:

| Participant | Age | Sex | Order of conditions | Condition 1 Response – to the nearest second | Condition 2 Response – to the nearest second |
|---|---|---|---|---|---|
| 1 | | | | | |
| 2 | | | | | |
| 3 | | | | | |
| 4 | | | | | |
| 5 | | | | | |
| 6 | | | | | |

## 4.8 A guide to collecting the data

So, to conduct this experiment you will need the following:

- **Instructions for participants** – as described in Section 4.6.
- **Stimuli** – two sets of stimuli, one labelled Condition 1 and one labelled Condition 2. These are to be found in Section 9 toward the end of this chapter and are available on the course website.
- **Colour printer or pens** – you will need a colour printer or set of coloured pens (or equivalent) capable of producing the following colours: green, orange, blue, red, purple and yellow.
- **Response sheet** – to record relevant details about each participant (e.g. age, sex) and how long it took them to complete the task in each condition. An example response sheet is shown above.
- **Consent form** – for participants to give their full consent to taking part in the experiment. The consent form that you should use has been provided in Section 10 at the end of this chapter.
- **Means of timing the task** – you will need to find either a stopwatch or an easy-to-read digital watch. You could also use the clock on your computer if you are conducting the experiment somewhere it is easy to

read the screen. Be very careful to record how long it takes each participant to complete both the experimental and control conditions using your pre-prepared response sheet – you should therefore record one time for the experimental condition and one time for the control condition. As it is likely that you can only really be accurate to 1 second, it would be sensible to round each response to the nearest whole second. This is what we did when we carried out the experiment.

**To conduct the experiment you should work through the following:**

1 Explain to the participant what is involved and that they may withdraw at any time they wish. Ask them to read and sign the consent form.
2 Ask the participant for the information necessary to complete the demographic questions at the top of the response sheet.
3 Read the instructions to the participant.
4 Show them the example below the instructions and make certain they understand what they are being required to do.
5 Place the sheet labelled 'Condition 1' face down in front of the participant.
6 Turn the page over, tell them to begin and start timing.
7 When they have finished the list, record how long it took them to complete the task.
8 Write this number down on the response sheet to the nearest second.
9 Now place the sheet labelled 'Condition 2' face down in front of the participant.
10 Turn the page over, tell them to begin and start timing.
11 When they have finished the list, record how long it took them to complete the task.
12 Write this number down on the response sheet to the nearest second.
13 Thank the participant and debrief them by explaining what the aim of the experiment was and answering any questions they may have.
14 Let the participant know that the data will be treated anonymously.

For the next participant, present the sheet labelled 'Condition 2' first, and the sheet labelled 'Condition 1' second. Continue to swap the order of presentation for each participant that you run.

# 5 Analysing the data from the experiment: the results

Before writing the results section, you need to analyse the data. The results section is where you tell the reader whether your prediction was borne out or not. This is done by reporting the results of both descriptive and inferential statistical tests and using these to either accept or reject the null hypothesis. We shall first look at what information needs to go in the results section so that you know what to make a note of when analysing the data from the experiment.

Below are nine steps that you will need to follow in order to include all the information that is necessary. You should try to write in continuous prose as much as possible. You should also make good use of graphs and/or tables to display the descriptive statistics and remember that it is very important to include these. Just because an inferential statistic such as a *t*-test may be more complicated than a simple mean, it does not allow you to rely on it to the exclusion of all else. Without descriptive statistics it would be impossible to interpret your results. For example, if you were to find a significant difference between the two conditions, you would still need to look at the means to know which condition produced the higher scores! It will also be important that you report the effect size, where appropriate, when presenting your results since this helps us to interpret our findings in a meaningful way.

So, it is important in your results section to do *all* of the following:

1 Restate your research hypothesis.
2 Describe the data you collected – e.g. were they measured in seconds or as a score out of a total?
3 Describe any calculations that were performed on the data before they were analysed – e.g. did you turn any totals into percentage scores or perhaps combine two numbers together?
4 Present descriptive statistics (e.g. means and standard deviations) – it is usual to do this as either a graph or a table. If you wish to include a graph and a table, avoid duplicating the same information. It may be that either a graph or a table would be sufficient.
5 Describe what these descriptive statistics show us – e.g. is the mean for one condition higher than for another? Consider whether it would be useful to include error bar charts when describing the data.
6 Say what inferential test (e.g. a *t*-test) you used in order to analyse the data.

7 Provide the results of the inferential test in the recognised manner – e.g. $t(18) = 2.14$; $p = .046$; $d = 0.96$. Remember that it may be worth commenting on the effect size.
8 Say whether this result is statistically significant or non-significant.
9 On the basis of this result, either accept or reject the null hypothesis.

We carried out the experiment on sixteen participants: their response times appear in your *Assignment Booklet*. You should now add the data from the four (or more) additional participants that you ran to the data that we have provided. Make sure that you put the data in the correct columns! Once you have added your own data, you should be ready to enter the data into SPSS.

We mentioned in the *SPSS Booklet* that the design of the experiment, whether within- or between-participants, will influence the way you set up your data file. If it is a within-participants design (like the experiment you are conducting), then you would have a column for each condition so that you can enter a pair of scores for each participant. If the design is between-participants, then you will only need to enter a single score per participant, but you will also need a column that tells SPSS which condition that participant was in. Remember that you should only ever enter data from a single participant into a single row in SPSS. This means that the number of rows in your SPSS data file should be equal to the number of participants in your study.

## 6 Drawing conclusions from the data: the discussion

The discussion section is where you draw conclusions from your results and discuss these in relation to the research and theories that you described in the introduction. A good discussion will contain the following elements:

- State what the results of your experiment were in plain English without reference to '*t*' or '*p*' values.
- Provide an explanation of the pattern of results obtained.
- Describe how your results compare with other research in the field and how they fit in with any relevant theories. You should draw on the material that you presented in the introduction.
- If you had to accept the null hypothesis, was this because the effect you hoped for does not exist, or was it because of a flaw in your experiment?

- If your results are different from those of another study, suggest reasons (based either on psychological explanations or on differences in methodology) why this may be so.
- Evaluate your experiment, pointing out anything that proved to be problematic or any confounding variables that may have affected the results. If you do find problems, suggest possible solutions to these.
- If your experiment has any bearing on applied issues, suggest how the results may be applied.
- Make suggestions for further research – i.e. given your results, what further experiments need to be conducted?

The first point above stipulates that, before you draw any conclusions from your results, you need to state what they were in plain English. The important point to include here is which condition produced the longest response times on average. Then you need to offer an explanation for the results that explains why one condition was, or was not, different from the other. This should be based on a concept that you have already mentioned in the introduction, as it is, after all, the rationale for why you chose the conditions you did.

It is very unlikely that any experiment you will ever conduct or read about will be perfect. In fact, some studies may well contain very serious flaws. However, even if you are happy with the way the experiment went, you should attempt to document any problems/limitations and possible alternative explanations of the results. Having discussed the implications and limitations of the experiment, you can then suggest some issues that future research should investigate.

# 7 The remaining sections of your report

## 7.1 Title

A good title is one that tells the reader what the report is about. Remember the importance of **A**ccuracy, **B**revity and **C**larity. 'Word list Stroop experiment' is not accurate or clear (although it is at least brief). 'An experiment using colour-associated words and neutral words to investigate whether the Stroop effect occurs with words that are not colour words' is quite accurate but not brief (and therefore not clear). Aim for somewhere between these extremes.

## 7.2 Summarising the experiment and writing the abstract

Even though the abstract is the first thing that people tend to read when picking up an experimental report, it is often the last thing to be written. In fact, it is next to impossible to write the abstract until you have designed and conducted the experiment and also analysed the data and drawn appropriate conclusions.

When you have finished all the other sections of the report, the abstract should almost write itself. All that is required is to summarize as accurately, clearly and, above all else, briefly the material you have already covered. This can often be done in about 100 words, and centres on a brief description of the experiment and its results. It is usual for the abstract to be a single paragraph and to be written in fairly plain English that does not make too much use of jargon. This means you should avoid sentences such as 'The hypothesis was ...', or 'The independent variable was ...', or statistical details such as '$p = .04$'.

Abstracts are used to give a potential reader an easily accessible summary of the paper, so that they can decide whether they want to read the whole thing. This means that abstracts have to make complete sense of the research and hence they stand alone from the rest of the report. Abstracts are then compiled into databases, which allow researchers to search through a large amount of information and identify those articles that are relevant. The Open University library contains many of these databases (both online and in hard copy).

The important points to cover in the abstract are:

- the rationale for conducting the experiment
- a very brief summary of what previous research has found (if this is important for establishing why the experiment was conducted)
- what was done in the experiment
- what the results of the experiment were (in plain English)
- the conclusion(s) that can be drawn from these results.

## 7.3 The references section

The main point here is to make certain that you include *all* the references you cite in the report. Remember to check for references in sections other than the introduction, especially the discussion. For more information on referencing, please see the advice given in your *Assignment Booklet*.

## 7.4 The appendices

As mentioned previously, one of the key aims of a report is to provide the reader with sufficient information to be able to replicate the experiment described. Key details about the materials used are included in the method section, but if possible it is a good idea to provide, in an appendix, an actual example of the stimuli or other materials used.

The same is true of the instructions. Although the key points are included in the method section, it is a good idea to include a verbatim copy of the instructions in an appendix. Many psychological experiments are very sensitive to the instructions given and you would not want someone to fail to replicate your findings just because the instructions they used were subtly different.

Use the appendices to include any information that you think is important and that is too lengthy to include elsewhere in the report.

For the purposes of this assessment, you should include a copy of the raw data and the results of your statistical analysis (i.e. a copy of the SPSS output) in the appendices. This is to allow your tutor to examine in more detail exactly what you did – if you read published articles you will notice that it is very rare to include this information. Do, though, think about which SPSS outputs you need to include. As you will be aware by now, SPSS produces a lot of information when you analyse data, so only include those outputs that are really relevant.

You will need to number your appendices clearly so that you can identify them to your reader in the body of your report. These need to be numbered in the order in which they are referred to in your report. Start with Appendix 1, then Appendix 2 and so on. Give each one a title (e.g. 'Appendix 1: Instructions'; 'Appendix 2: Raw data'). In writing about the materials, for instance, you might state that 'Examples of the word lists used in both conditions are provided in Appendix 1'.

# 8 Example of a report write-up

On the following pages you will find an example of a report write-up for an experiment that sought to investigate multiple resource versus central processor theories of attention. This is based on material that you will have covered in Chapter 6 of Book 1. We hope that this illustration will be useful when you come to write your own report. We've also added a number of comments in the form of footnotes throughout this example report, so that you can think carefully about how to structure your report.

# Multiple resource versus central processor theories of attention: the effect of varying task similarity in a dual modality task

## Abstract

*The role of task similarity was examined in an experiment employing the dual task paradigm. Previous research found that response time is longer when responses are given in the same modality than in different modalities. These results have been used in support of a multiple resource theory of attention. In the current experiment, the similarity of responses given in two modalities was manipulated. The results showed that similarity of response did not have a significant effect on response times, providing further support for a multiple resource theory.*[1]

## Introduction

A vast amount of information arrives at our sense organs and is potentially available for further processing. However, not all of this information is processed. Instead, cognitive processes select certain pieces of information for further processing and disregard others. This process of selection is referred to as *attention.*[2]

The fact that attentional processes are required suggests that the mind does not contain sufficient resources to process all of the available information.[3] This limitation was demonstrated by Simons and Levin (as cited in Edgar, 2007).[4] Using the 'change blindness' paradigm they showed that even information pertaining to someone's identity is often not processed. So why is it that so little of the available information is actually processed to any significant degree by the brain?

Kahneman (as cited in Edgar, 2007) suggested that the brain contains a 'limited-capacity' central processor, responsible for processing incoming information and integrating it into the information that is already held in

[1] Notice that, where possible, jargon is avoided and this section is kept short and succinct.

[2] Starts by identifying the broad area of attention within psychology.

[3] The beginning of developing a rationale for this study.

[4] Uses relevant research illustrations to back up the points made.

memory.[5] As this processor is limited in its capacity, it cannot process all of the information available from the senses. However, the theory that there is just a single pool of resources that is allocated to a task by a central processor cannot explain why it is sometimes possible for the brain to do two or more tasks at the same time. This issue has been explored further by using dual-task studies.[6]

Posner and Boies (as cited in Edgar, 2007) conducted a dual-task experiment, where the participants were required to perform both a visual and an auditory task. The visual task consisted of the sequential presentation of two letters. The auditory task consisted of the presentation of a simple tone. Participants had to respond by pressing a button with their right or left hand depending on the nature of the stimuli. Participants took longer to respond if the auditory tone was presented at the same time as the letter. As the participants seemed unable to make a response to the two stimuli simultaneously, this result seemed to support the concept of a single limited-capacity central processor.[7]

McLeod (as cited in Edgar, 2007) replicated the Posner and Boies study, but changed the response required for the auditory task from a manual one to a verbal one (saying the word 'blip'). Here the participants appeared capable of responding just as quickly when the two stimuli were presented simultaneously. One explanation is that the limitation in resources occurred not in perceiving the stimuli, but in responding. When the two responses were in the same mode (i.e. both manual) there was interference between the two tasks, but this disappeared when the responses were made in separate modes (i.e. one manual and one visual). Hence, it might be that the pool of resources available to make manual responses is different from the pool of resources available to make verbal responses.

If pools of resources are simply linked to the response required, then one implication of this is that it should not matter how similar the stimuli are that the participants have to respond to.[8] This idea was explored in the present experiment by making use of two different modes of both presentation (auditory and visual) and response (verbal and manual) and manipulating the similarity of the two tasks. The research hypothesis was that participants will take longer to complete two tasks that require similar responses than two

---

[5] Further development of the rationale by considering research that suggests that the brain contains a 'limited-capacity' central processor.

[6] Developing ideas, since if we have a single pool of resources, then how is it that the brain can do two or more tasks at the same time?

[7] Identifying some support for a single processor but moves on in the next paragraph to provide alternative evidence for pools of resources.

[8] Clear rationale for the experiment – intention to investigate pools of resources vs. single processor in more depth.

tasks that require dissimilar responses. This is a one-tailed hypothesis. The null hypothesis was that there will be no difference in the times taken to complete the two tasks.

## Method

### *Design*

A between-participants design was employed.[9] The independent variable was task similarity. This consisted of two conditions, a 'task similar' condition in which participants had to search a list for number-words whilst verbally responding to mathematical problems, and a 'task dissimilar' condition in which the verbal task was the same, but the participant searched a list for colour-words. In both conditions the relevant words on the lists had to be ticked (a manual response). The dependent variable was the time taken to complete the visual task. This was measured in seconds by the researcher using a stopwatch and was accurate to the nearest second.[10] To control for any differences in the way certain words are perceived, the visually presented list of words contained identical non-target words. In addition, the target words were in the same positions in both conditions. To control for the difficulty of the mathematical questions, the auditory task was also identical in both conditions. Thus, both conditions contained matched material for both the visual and the auditory tasks. The instructions given in both conditions were identical, except that in one condition the participants were asked to identify colour-words and in the other condition to identify number-words.[11]

### *Participants*

The twenty participants that took part in this experiment were all undergraduate students recruited by asking for volunteers at three tutorial sessions. Fourteen of the participants were currently studying psychology and six were studying physics. The age of the participants ranged from 18 to 56 years and there were 10 women and 10 men.

### *Materials*

A stopwatch accurate to the nearest second was used to time how long it took each participant to complete the visual task. The visual stimuli presented in each condition consisted of a list of 36 words, placed in two columns on a sheet of A4 paper. Of these words, 18 were target words,

---

[9] Design is specified.

[10] Both IV and DV have been defined.

[11] All measures taken to control for possible confounding variables have been outlined.

number-words in the case of the similar condition and colour-words in the dissimilar condition; and 18 were non-target words that were all the names of animals. Each word was used twice. The order in which the words were presented was randomised, but the same in both conditions. To the right of each word was a box into which the participant was told to place a tick. The auditory stimuli in both conditions consisted of a series of mathematical questions that were read aloud by the experimenter. Examples of the word lists and the mathematical questions are provided in Appendix 1. Standard instructions were used (Appendix 2) and all participants completed a consent form (Appendix 3).

### *Procedure*

Each participant was approached and asked if they would be prepared to take part in a cognitive psychology experiment that would take between 2 and 5 minutes. All participants who agreed to take part signed a consent form and were then tested individually. Before explaining what would happen in the experiment, the age and sex of the participant was recorded, as was whether they had any experience of psychology. The instructions for either condition 1 or condition 2 were then read. These told the participant that they would be presented with a list of words and that they should work through the list placing a tick next to each target word. They were also informed that, whilst completing this task, they would be required to respond verbally to a series of simple mathematical questions that would be read to them by the experimenter. They were told to complete both tasks as quickly as they could manage (see Appendix 2 for a copy of the instructions). Once the participant stated that they understood what was required of them, the list of words from the visual task of one condition was placed face down in front of them. The visual task was then turned over and the experimenter both started the stopwatch and began to read out the auditory task. When the participant had finished the visual task, the experimenter recorded the time this had taken. The participant was then debriefed as to the aims of the experiment and asked if they had any questions.[12]

## Results

The research hypothesis in this experiment was that participants will take longer to complete two tasks that require similar responses than two tasks that require dissimilar responses. The time it took for each participant to place a tick next to all the target words in that condition was measured to the nearest second.

---

[12] A step-by-step account of how the data were collected is provided in the procedure subsection. This would enable the experiment to be replicated.

**Table 1 Mean and standard deviation for response time in seconds**

| Condition | Mean response time (in seconds) | Std dev. |
|---|---|---|
| Dissimilar condition | 60.5 | 13.84 |
| Similar condition | 59.9 | 12.33 |

As can be seen from Table 1, the mean response times for the two conditions were very similar, with the mean time taken in the dissimilar condition being just 0.6 seconds longer than the similar condition. An independent-samples *t*-test was conducted on these data, which revealed that the difference between these conditions was not statistically significant ($t(18) = 0.102$; $p = .92$; $d = .05$). On the basis of this result the null hypothesis was accepted.[13]

## Discussion

The results of the present experiment showed that increasing the similarity between responses given in a dual modality task did not increase response times. Response times in the condition where participants had to respond verbally with a number and place a tick next to a number-word were not statistically significantly different from the condition where they had to respond verbally with a number and place a tick next to a colour-word. This result suggests that the visual and auditory tasks that the participants had to complete simultaneously interfered with each other to the same degree regardless of how similar they were.[14]

McLeod (as cited in Edgar, 2007) found a similar pattern of results, in that the modality of the response required appeared to have the greatest influence on response time. McLeod used this result as evidence for a multiple-resource theory of attention, with a separate pool of resources being available to each mode, e.g. one for verbal response and for manual. The results reported here provide further support for this theory, by showing that participants can complete tasks simultaneously, as long as the required responses are in different modes, and this is regardless of how similar these responses are.[15]

If attention were guided by a single limited-capacity central processor, then it would be reasonable to expect participants to find it harder to perform two

[13] First the research hypothesis is restated, then descriptive statistics are presented. Note that the table has been given a heading. This section ends with a statement regarding inferential analysis.

[14] The findings have been explained in plain English without statistical jargon.

[15] The findings are compared to previous related studies.

tasks at once when these tasks were similar in nature than when they were dissimilar. However, the fact that similarity had no significant effect suggests that attention is instead guided by multiple pools of resources.[16]

An alternative explanation of the results presented here could be that task similarity was not manipulated very well. After all, it is possible to argue that the manual task did not change much between the conditions as all it really involved was placing a tick next to a word. Maybe the tasks of manually ticking a number-word and verbally doing maths do not interfere with each other any more than manually ticking a colour-word and verbally doing maths.

It might also have been the case that the two tasks were not truly simultaneous and that participants managed to pause their completion of the visual task in order to listen to the auditory task. If simultaneity were removed, then there would have been no reason to expect a difference between the conditions, as the essential element of the dual-task paradigm would have been absent. As well as pausing, the participants might also have adopted a different strategy when completing the visual task. Although they were asked to place a tick next to number words in one condition, this task could have been completed equally well by simply ticking all those words that were not colours. As the participant would then have been searching for the same words in both conditions, there would have been no manipulation of task similarity.[17]

In conclusion, the results of the experiment reported here offer some support for a multiple-resource theory of attention. However, future research conducted in this area should attempt to manipulate task similarity in a more definite manner and be careful to ensure that the dual tasks are presented simultaneously.[18]

## References

Edgar, G. (2007) Perception and attention. In D. Miell, A. Phoenix, & K. Thomas (Eds.), *Mapping Psychology* (2nd ed., pp.3–50). Milton Keynes: The Open University.

## Appendices

Appendix 1: Word lists and mathematical questions

Appendix 2: Instructions

Appendix 3: Consent form

Appendix 4: Raw data (not provided here)

Appendix 5: SPSS print-out of *t*-test (not provided here)

---

[16] The findings are related to theory.

[17] Possible shortcomings/limitations are discussed.

[18] The discussion ends with a concluding statement.

# Appendix 1: Word lists and mathematical questions

**Condition I: Visual Task**

| | | | |
|---|---|---|---|
| Cat | | Green | |
| Yellow | | Goat | |
| Horse | | Sheep | |
| Rabbit | | Scarlet | |
| Scarlet | | Dolphin | |
| Green | | Brown | |
| Spider | | Blue | |
| Pink | | Rabbit | |
| Goat | | Yellow | |
| Brown | | Orange | |
| Camel | | Spider | |
| Dolphin | | Horse | |
| Orange | | Camel | |
| Blue | | Purple | |
| Red | | Dog | |
| Dog | | Pink | |
| Sheep | | Red | |
| Purple | | Cat | |

**Condition 2: Visual Task**

| | | | |
|---|---|---|---|
| Cat | | Eight | |
| Ten | | Goat | |
| Horse | | Sheep | |
| Rabbit | | Twelve | |
| Eleven | | Dolphin | |
| Sixteen | | Sixteen | |
| Spider | | One | |
| Four | | Rabbit | |
| Goat | | Nine | |
| Nine | | Four | |
| Camel | | Spider | |
| Dolphin | | Horse | |
| Two | | Camel | |
| Twelve | | Eleven | |
| One | | Dog | |
| Dog | | Ten | |
| Sheep | | Two | |
| Eight | | Cat | |

**Auditory task for both conditions**

What is:

| | |
|---|---|
| 5 × 7 | 3 × 12 |
| 35 – 18 | 20 – 11 |
| 6 × 8 | 50 – 27 |
| 21 – 13 | 4 × 7 |

| | |
|---|---|
| 9 × 7 | 17 − 8 |
| 8 × 9 | 36 − 14 |
| 32 × 3 | 36 × 2 |
| 17 − 9 | 36 − 7 |
| 28 − 19 | 16 × 3 |
| 5 × 9 | 5 × 11 |
| 36 − 23 | 42 − 8 |
| 7 × 7 | 29 − 12 |

## Appendix 2: Instructions

The following instructions were read verbatim to each participant.

### *Instructions: Condition 1*

In a moment I will place a sheet of A4 paper in front of you that contains two columns of words. What I would like you to do is to place a tick next to those words that are the name of a colour, e.g. RED or BLUE. Start with the word at the top left column and work downwards. When you have finished all the words in the left column start on the right column. At the SAME TIME as you are doing this, I will be asking you a series of simple mathematical questions. I want you to answer each mathematical question as I ask it.

Do you understand what you are required to do?

(If yes, then proceed to task. If no, go through the instructions again.)

### *Instructions: Condition 2*

In a moment I will place a sheet of A4 paper in front of you that contains two columns of words. What I would like you to do is to place a tick next to those words that are the name of a number, e.g. SEVEN or NINE. Start with the word at the top left column and work downwards. When you have finished all the words in the left column start on the right column. At the SAME TIME as you are doing this, I will be asking you a series of simple mathematical questions. I want you to answer each mathematical question as I ask it.

Do you understand what you are required to do?

(If yes, then proceed to task. If no, go through the instructions again.)

## Appendix 3: Consent form

*Cognitive psychology experiment*

*Consent form*

I have been asked to participate in an experiment that investigates an area of cognitive psychology. I give my free consent by signing this form.

- I have been informed about the research and why it is taking place.
- I understand that my participation in this research is voluntary.
- I understand that I can withdraw from the research at any time.
- I understand that my data will be anonymous.
- I understand that I will be provided with a debrief after taking part in the experiment.

Signature ______________________________

Date ___________________________________

# 9 The stimuli for your experiment

To conduct your experiment you will need to either download and print out colour versions of the stimuli from the course website or cut out and colour in the stimuli provided on the next pages – we have provided instructions as to which colour ink needs to be used for which words below.

**Condition 1**

| Word | Colour ink | Word | Colour ink |
|---|---|---|---|
| SKY | *red* | PLUM | *yellow* |
| PLUM | *orange* | BLOOD | *purple* |
| LEMON | *blue* | LEMON | *green* |
| GRASS | *red* | GRASS | *blue* |
| CARROT | *purple* | BLOOD | *yellow* |
| BLOOD | *blue* | SKY | *purple* |
| PLUM | *red* | CARROT | *yellow* |
| CARROT | *green* | LEMON | *red* |
| SKY | *green* | PLUM | *green* |
| GRASS | *yellow* | GRASS | *purple* |
| BLOOD | *orange* | CARROT | *blue* |
| LEMON | *purple* | SKY | *yellow* |
| CARROT | *red* | BLOOD | *green* |
| GRASS | *orange* | LEMON | *orange* |
| SKY | *orange* | PLUM | *blue* |

**Condition 2**

| Word | Colour ink | Word | Colour ink |
|---|---|---|---|
| STY | *red* | PLAN | *yellow* |
| PLAN | *orange* | BLAME | *purple* |
| LEDGE | *blue* | LEDGE | *green* |
| GRADE | *red* | GRADE | *blue* |
| CAREER | *purple* | BLAME | *yellow* |
| BLAME | *blue* | STY | *purple* |
| PLAN | *red* | CAREER | *yellow* |
| CAREER | *green* | LEDGE | *red* |
| STY | *green* | PLAN | *green* |
| GRADE | *yellow* | GRADE | *purple* |
| BLAME | *orange* | CAREER | *blue* |
| LEDGE | *purple* | STY | *yellow* |
| CAREER | *red* | BLAME | *green* |
| GRADE | *orange* | LEDGE | *orange* |
| STY | *orange* | PLAN | *blue* |

**Condition 1**

SKY
PLUM
LEMON
GRASS
CARROT
BLOOD
PLUM
CARROT
SKY
GRASS
BLOOD
LEMON
CARROT
GRASS
SKY

PLUM
BLOOD
LEMON
GRASS
BLOOD
SKY
CARROT
LEMON
PLUM
GRASS
CARROT
SKY
BLOOD
LEMON
PLUM

**Condition 2**

| | |
|---|---|
| STY | PLAN |
| PLAN | BLAME |
| LEDGE | LEDGE |
| GRADE | GRADE |
| CAREER | BLAME |
| BLAME | STY |
| PLAN | CAREER |
| CAREER | LEDGE |
| STY | PLAN |
| GRADE | GRADE |
| BLAME | CAREER |
| LEDGE | STY |
| CAREER | BLAME |
| GRADE | LEDGE |
| STY | PLAN |

## 10 Consent form to use in your experiment

Before conducting the experiment on a participant it is vital that you obtain their consent formally. We have provided a consent form for you to use and this can be downloaded and printed out from the course website. Alternatively you can cut out the form provided on page 239, although you will need to make one copy for every participant.

## Consent to participate

I have been asked to participate in an experiment that investigates one aspect of cognitive psychology and give my free consent by signing this form.

- I have been informed about the research and why it is taking place.
- I understand that my participation in this research is voluntary.
- I understand that I can withdraw from the research at any time.
- I understand that my data will be anonymous.
- I understand that I will be provided with a debrief after taking part in the experiment.

Signature ______________________________

Date ___________________________________

CHAPTER 8

# Qualitative research: an overview and examples

## Contents

| | | |
|---|---|---|
| | Aims | 242 |
| 1 | Introduction | 242 |
| 2 | Ontology, epistemology and methodology | 244 |
| 2.1 | Qualitative research: the often explicit role of theoretical frameworks | 247 |
| 3 | The process of doing qualitative research | 248 |
| 3.1 | Embedding research in a theoretical framework | 248 |
| 3.2 | The iterative dynamic of qualitative research and analysis | 248 |
| 3.3 | Methods and data | 250 |
| 3.4 | Transforming and analysing qualitative data | 250 |
| 4 | Qualitative data and three methods of data collection | 252 |
| 4.1 | Observation | 254 |
| 4.2 | Interviewing | 258 |
| 4.3 | Diary studies | 263 |
| 5 | Discourse analysis as an example of explicit epistemology and methodology in qualitative research | 265 |
| 5.1 | Introducing discourse analysis | 266 |
| 5.2 | Discourse concepts and discourse patterns | 268 |
| 5.3 | Doing discourse analysis | 273 |
| 6 | Concluding issues | 274 |
| | References | 277 |

## Aims

This chapter aims to:

- discuss the principles and philosophy that underpin qualitative approaches to research
- introduce you to the process of conducting qualitative research
- explore methods of data collection in qualitative research – that is, qualitative research methods
- provide you with an example of how qualitative data are analysed within one specific approach to qualitative research (discourse analysis).

## 1 Introduction

The previous chapter guided you through your quantitative research project. This chapter introduces you to qualitative approaches to research so that you can begin to get ready for doing the qualitative research project (TMA 05). Chapter 1 discussed the different research traditions from which quantitative and qualitative approaches come. Quantitative research is part of the scientific tradition, whereas qualitative research is part of a hermeneutic tradition, which is concerned with meaning and subjectivity. Hermeneutics can be traced back to the study of (religious) scripture, where 'the word', prophecy and the meanings of tales were critically described and examined. Contemporary understandings of hermeneutics are similar to these early definitions in that the focus is on the critical analysis of the meanings of accounts. Psychologists working in the hermeneutic tradition search for *subjective* and shared psychological and social meanings. This perspective is most likely to favour qualitative research methods because these allow the exploration of the subjective and broader social meanings that participants and researchers attach to their actions.

In your reading of Book 1 *Mapping Psychology*, you have come across different types of research projects that have explored a number of research questions in a variety of ways. We can step back from these research projects to consider how we generate questions, seek explanations, develop understandings and explore answers in our everyday lives. If, for example, you were interested in finding out about the well-being of a member of your family, you would generally begin by asking them how they are (in person or on the phone). This approach to gathering data involves asking somebody to express their own experiences and feelings and to give interpretations of those experiences and feelings. Alternatively, you could assess the well-being of a family member by taking their temperature and/or getting them to fill in a standardised health questionnaire. Both approaches can deliver important information, but, they are clearly situated within different perspectives (theoretical frameworks or paradigms) on how to do research, what kinds of questions to ask and what kinds of data to collect. Translating this example into a research context, we could say that if you favour the first way to gather information, you situate yourself in a perspective that is closer to the *hermeneutic* tradition, which uses a more qualitative approach. If you favour the other way of gathering information, you situate yourself in a perspective that is closer to the *scientific* tradition, which uses a quantitative approach. In a research context, you need to be clear about the perspective in which you wish to situate yourself in order to develop an appropriate research question and determine whether a quantitative or a qualitative approach is more suitable.

In this and the next three chapters we explore how using an explicitly *qualitative approach* to research works in practice. Chapters 8 to 11 will give you an overview of perspectives that adopt qualitative approaches to research, and a hands-on introduction to the process of doing qualitative research in psychology.

In order to offer a comprehensive overview of qualitative research and its theoretical background, Section 2 of this chapter will introduce you to the notion of ontology, and remind you of the importance of epistemology and methodology to research (introduced in Chapter 1). Section 3 will provide a concise overview of the process involved in conducting qualitative research. The chapter then elaborates in more detail on aspects of this process. Section 4 introduces you to qualitative data and offers a synopsis of the most popular methods of collecting qualitative data (observation, interviewing and diary studies). While these methods often share characteristics, they are distinct ways of obtaining and collecting qualitative material. Section 5 discusses in depth one specific approach to doing qualitative research: discourse analysis. In doing so it highlights the explicit role of epistemology and methodology within this perspective. Discourse analysis has been chosen as an example because it is one of the most popular approaches to qualitative research (i.e. data collection and analysis within a specific theoretical framework). However, discourse analysis is labour intensive and requires the development of expertise if it is adequately to be conducted. For these reasons, you will not be doing discourse analysis within this course. You can learn more about perspectives that adopt qualitative approaches to research in the Level 3 course on social psychology (DD307 *Social Psychology: Critical Perspectives on Self and Others*), where you also have the opportunity to apply some of these approaches. The qualitative method you will be using within this course is thematic analysis and this will be introduced in Chapter 9.

## 2 Ontology, epistemology and methodology

You may recall from reading Chapter 1 in this book that the perspective (i.e. the theoretical framework) from which research is done informs the methodology and thus the methods favoured, which thereby inform the types of knowledge generated. So, broadly speaking, research can be characterised according to whether it is qualitative or quantitative, but what this means in any specific case also depends on the overall perspective the research is situated within.

Chapter 1 has introduced you to the terms epistemology and methodology. To understand the specificity of qualitative research perspectives it is, however, helpful to introduce another theoretical term, that of ontology. Generally speaking, ontology is the study of, or the theory of the nature of, existence (i.e. of 'being'). The 'existences' or 'beings' psychology as a discipline is concerned with are human beings. Accordingly, we can say that in a psychological context ontology refers to the underlying assumptions about the nature of existence as a human being. Hence, ontology can be referred to as the theory of what, in a certain perspective, is seen to constitute a human being, or, more generally, what it is to be a person. For example, the social constructionist perspective is based on the assumption that people are social beings who are creating, and being created by, their understandings of the world around them. People are seen to do this via language and communication; that is, they are created by the discourses they are positioned in and they create and shape these discourses when drawing on them and using them. This is the ontological assumption on which social constructionism is based. Inevitably this ontological assumption is closely linked to this perspective's epistemology. This is why in this perspective researchers take an insider viewpoint and are interested in analysing people's individual experiences and meanings. The ontology underpinning other perspectives in psychology will differ from that outlined above.

So different perspectives are not just based on different understandings of epistemology (theory of knowledge), but thereby they also endorse different understandings of ontology. In other words, they operate on different understandings of what can be known, how it can be known, and what counts as evidence. By this we mean that the researcher's particular view of what constitutes the 'being' that should be examined, i.e. of what it is to be a person (ontology), of what constitutes knowledge (i.e. the epistemology they espouse), and the means by which they seek to take forward this knowledge (methodology), will necessarily inform the whole of the research process.

In summary, as you saw in Chapter 1, all research is conducted within specific perspectives and all perspectives are underpinned by particular ontological and epistemological assumptions. These in turn underpin the methodology chosen which, in turn, influences the methods favoured and so the kinds of data collected and the types of analyses performed. To understand the differences between different research perspectives, it is therefore crucial to take into account their ontological, epistemological and methodological assumptions.

Chapter 1 also introduced you to the difference between methodology and methods. Methods are techniques and tools for collecting particular kinds of data. Methodology, however, refers to the overall theoretical rationale and the principles that underpin a research question and hence influence a set of methods and data. So different perspectives may adopt similar methods, but they will treat the data generated by these methods differently, because they operate on the basis of a different methodology. Thus, while methods and the resulting data can be referred to as being quantitative or qualitative, it is important to remember that it is not the methods as such (e.g. observation or interviewing) that are quantitative or qualitative. It is the perspective within which they are used that determines whether the methods are used in a qualitative or quantitative fashion and thus whether the data collected by these methods are qualitative or quantitative.

This is why, as outlined in Section 2 of Chapter 1 of this book, psychologists working from the scientific perspective may well use the same methods as those working within the hermeneutic tradition to examine particular issues of importance (e.g. observation and interviewing). The example used in Chapter 1 was that data collected in interviews can be used in a quantitative project that relies on quantitative content analysis. Such a project could analyse the interview data by counting the prevalence and sequence of words and then conducting a chi-square test (see Chapter 6). Data from interviews are also, however, used in research situated within perspectives that entail a hermeneutic approach, where *thematic analysis, discourse analysis* or *narrative analysis* are frequently used to analyse interview data.

Chapter 1 discussed the ways in which psychologists who work from a perspective that is informed by the *scientific* model of the natural sciences (in that this model guides their ontological and epistemological assumptions) will value objectivity. They are more likely to favour methods that collect quantitative data because these allow objective forms of observation and measurement that result in numerical representations of psychological constructs. For example, the number of times people smile in a given context may be taken as a proxy measure for happiness. But this also means that 'happiness' according to this perspective is conceptualised as a psychological construct that can be examined by counting the number of smiles (i.e. it can be quantified).

In contrast, perspectives operating within the hermeneutic tradition (which explores meaning and subjectivity) take ontological and epistemological positions that necessitate the use of qualitative approaches to research and thus favour methods for collecting qualitative data. Researchers whose work is situated in a perspective that fits within the hermeneutic tradition collect rich and detailed data that can give insights into people's relation to their social context and/or their feelings. The data collected in the hermeneutic tradition often take the form of verbal or written accounts of what can then be conceptualised as psychological phenomena. For example, observers' and participants' written descriptions of what they conceptualise as happiness could be the focus of such an investigation. In this case, 'happiness' is defined as something that can be examined via the verbal or written accounts of participants. The underlying ontological assumption in this example constructs human beings as able to reflect on, and verbalise, their emotional states. In keeping with this assumption, the most appropriate way to examine 'happiness' is to collect and analyse participants' complex accounts of what it means to be happy. Further examples include: interviews with people about the reasons for their choice of partner and analyses of individuals' diaries tracing feelings of extraversion and introversion over a given week in a number of settings. In perspectives that favour qualitative approaches, human action is interpreted (analysed) by focusing on the understandings held and articulated by research participants and researchers in specific contexts at particular times.

In summary, the perspective (i.e. the theoretical framework) taken in research consists of ontological and epistemological assumptions that organise and influence all aspects of research, and so is much more than the methods chosen. The perspective taken will inform the research question that is asked; it will underpin the methodological considerations and thus guide the selection of methods that are seen as appropriate to collecting the data. Furthermore, it underpins the type of analysis used to examine the data that have been collected and so inevitably will influence the kinds of conclusions that are drawn from it.

## 2.1 Qualitative research: the often explicit role of theoretical frameworks

Chapter 1 explained that the perspectives adopted within the *scientific* tradition of the natural sciences will usually not make explicit their ontological and epistemological assumptions (theoretical framework). This is because it has a long tradition and is well established (this is why the previous chapters that introduced you to quantitative methods which are used within the scientific tradition have not explicitly mentioned ontology and epistemology). In contrast, those perspectives relating to the *hermeneutic* tradition, for example approaches based on the perspective of social constructionism (e.g. various forms of discourse analysis), often do make explicit their theoretical framework and illustrate the ontological, epistemological and methodological considerations that form the basis for their research. There are two main reasons for this. First, these are relatively new perspectives and they are intended to present new and sometimes challenging ways of thinking about the nature and the role of psychological research. Second, as we shall see in Section 5 of this chapter with regard to the example of discourse analysis, some of these perspectives have an explicit agenda to highlight and promote their theoretical framework as part of their research enterprise.

### Summary Section 2

- Ontology is the theory of the nature of existence and in the context of psychology refers to the definition of what it is to be a person. Ontological and epistemological definitions and assumptions underpin every approach to research and so guide methodology and thus the methods adopted.
- Qualitative researchers often make explicit the overall theoretical framework within which their research is situated. In most qualitative approaches to research, issues of ontology, epistemology and methodology form part of the research agenda and are thus explicitly discussed.
- Methods are techniques and tools for collecting particular kinds of data. By itself, a method cannot be either quantitative or qualitative. Whether a method (e.g. interviewing or observation) is defined as 'qualitative' depends on the perspective adopted by the researcher. The same method (e.g. interviewing) can be used in a qualitative or a quantitative fashion and might thus appear in different perspectives.

# 3 The process of doing qualitative research

This section will provide an outline of the central aspects of the qualitative research process, which are elaborated in Sections 4 and 5.

## 3.1 Embedding research in a theoretical framework

While qualitative research might appear to be a loosely organised and rather exploratory endeavour, it is crucial to understand that conducting qualitative research is not just a 'fishing trip'. It is purposive rather than random and it needs to be firmly grounded in the researcher's theoretical framework (epistemology and ontology), their understanding of the topic area, the research question(s) they generate and the sense they make of their data in relation to their research question(s). This means that all research begins with theory (i.e. it starts by establishing the theoretical framework within which a topic area is identified and research questions are developed). Researchers will usually do this by intensively reading around their topic and then following the theoretical framework adopted in the research literature that has impressed them most. Only after having gained a clear understanding of the theoretical framework they want their work to be embedded in, can they begin to narrow down their focus and to formulate specific research questions. As outlined in the previous section the theoretical framework underpins the methodological decisions and thus enables the selection of appropriate methods for collecting data that are relevant to the research question. The theoretical framework also guides the types of analysis that will be chosen to analyse and interpret the data.

## 3.2 The iterative dynamic of qualitative research and analysis

Chapter 1 in this book alerted you to the different approaches that are taken in quantitative and qualitative research. One issue that was mentioned was the fluid, ever-changing and interdependent nature of the process of qualitative research and analysis. Qualitative research and analyses are always *shaped by* and *shape* methods, theories, subjectivities and relationships in the research context. Moreover, one part of the process of developing knowledge through research *cannot exist* without the other.

In Figure 8.1, you will notice how research questions emerge at points 2 and 7 and a consideration of methods takes place at points 3 and 7. Notice how re-evaluation (point 8) involves revisiting the theoretical position from which the research started, the status of previous empirical research and the development of new research questions at other points in the cycle.

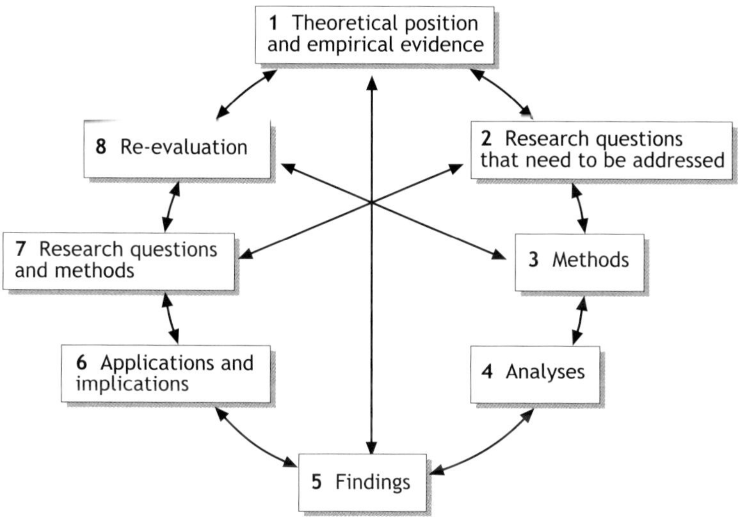


**Figure 8.1** Generating knowledge

Qualitative research is an *iterative* process, meaning that it is a dynamic process of refining questions, methods and analysis, findings and applications so that data and interpretations of them develop and change throughout the research process. The research process in qualitative research is, therefore, not linear (from questions to methods to findings). Instead, the methods we use, the analyses made and the findings drawn feed and loop back on one another. This movement and change captures the *grounded nature* of qualitative research: analyses are informed by issues of significance identified by researchers (working alone or in groups) *and* those issues that emerge as important during the course of the research. However, this must not be understood as a free-floating loop of questions inspiring data collection which inspires further questions. Research is grounded; that is, it is embedded in the theoretical framework chosen. This framework informs the kind of questions asked and guides the analysis. While research questions are sometimes revisited and refined, this process must always be made explicit and argued in relation to the theoretical framework and the context examined. Hence, qualitative research needs to proceed in a focused and rigorous fashion, with researchers discussing and reflecting on methodological and analytic decisions, arguing why certain conclusions were reached and how they relate to the research context, the research question(s) and the data collected.

## 3.3 Methods and data

There are a wide variety of methods for collecting qualitative data (see, for example, Denzin and Lincoln, 2005). Among the most popular ones are observation, interviewing and diary studies. The method of data collection researchers choose depends on the theoretical framework, the focus and their specific interest. You can imagine that if we are interested in how two people interact, for example, and elect to use observational methods, the resulting data will be very different from the data that would have been gathered if we had instead chosen to interview those engaged in the interaction. This is because particular data are produced by particular methods.

Whatever data we collect, it is impossible to focus on every aspect of them. We will inevitably select what interests us and sparks our curiosity. Establishing a clear theoretical framework and formulating a clear research question ensures that our focus is relevant to the question we are investigating. It also guarantees that the data collected are appropriate to the research question and that our analysis proceeds in a rigorous, transparent and plausible fashion rather than just producing random interpretations.

## 3.4 Transforming and analysing qualitative data

Having conducted observations, interviews or diary studies, we end up with an abundance of information. This can be in the form of 'written field notes' (from observations), recordings and transcripts of recordings (from interviews), or written texts of some kind (e.g. from diary studies). It is necessary to transform the data into a form that is amenable to analysis. Like any set of skills, learning to transform qualitative data involves hard work and persistence, whether analyses are done using computer software programs (which may be used to do an analysis of words or phrases in addition to aiding the coding of data) or manually. A number of different analytical or interpretative procedures are available for analysing qualitative data. This is partly because, while different types of qualitative research may share research purposes (such as clarifying findings, providing information, developing theories and making recommendations for policy and professional practice), the aims and procedures of analysis often differ depending on the theoretical framework within which the research is being conducted. Some researchers believe that data need only be organised in a meaningful way in order to 'let informants speak for themselves'. Other analysts are more concerned with providing a clear and convincing description of the data in relation to wider psychological concerns. The end-product here is a descriptive narrative, which often involves a summary of the data, interwoven with the analyst's descriptions and quotations from field notes. Yet other analysts are concerned with analytic interpretations that go beyond description to interpretation (e.g. in discourse analysis). Interpretations of data are linked to the methods and theories chosen. So again it is the theoretical framework that underpins and guides the analytic choices.

In qualitative research it is common in the initial stages of the analysis to feel daunted by the amount of data amassed and to wonder how any sense can be made of it. However, just as quantitative researchers make sense of the array of numbers they generate by using statistical procedures, in qualitative approaches there are techniques available to help in interpreting the information.

Some of the same principles apply in both qualitative and quantitative analysis. For example, it is important to 'get to know your data'. In quantitative analysis you need to start by looking carefully at the data in order to understand what the numbers represent (see Chapter 3), and, similarly, in qualitative analysis you need to understand what the data you have collected represent. This means that you need to prepare yourself by reading around the topic. Good researchers prepare themselves thoroughly by familiarising themselves with their research area prior to conducting the research. It is important to remember that qualitative research is grounded in the researcher's understanding of the topic area and the sense they make of this in relation to their research question. During analysis it is thus important to read and reread the data (e.g. interview transcripts and/or field notes).

## Summary Section 3

- It is important to embed qualitative research into a theoretical framework and to recognise that qualitative analysis is a dynamic process.
- Knowledge generation is a cyclical, iterative and interactive process and it is important that qualitative researchers make explicit the decisions they make, throughout the research process, and explain why these decisions were taken.
- Qualitative data take a variety of forms. Interpretations of data alter during the research process, dependent to an extent on the selected

method as well as the personal and theoretical interests of the researcher. There is interplay between analysis and all other aspects of the dynamic process of research.

- Qualitative researchers adopt different positions and have different intentions when analysing their data. These positions and intentions are informed by differences in ontology, epistemology and methodology. Some researchers aim to 'let informants speak for themselves', some are concerned to make convincing descriptions, and others take a more interpretative approach.

## 4 Qualitative data and three methods of data collection

Table 8.1 identifies the qualitative studies you have met so far in DSE212.

**Table 8.1 Qualitative research studies featured in Book 1**

| Chapter | Research studies introduced |
|---|---|
| 1: Identities and diversities | Kuhn and McPartland (1954): Twenty Statements Test |
| | Marcia (1966): Semi-structured interviews |
| 3: Three approaches to learning | Keogh *et al.* (2000): Observation of joint activity and talk |
| | Mercer (1995; 2000): Classroom observation, transcripts and thematic analysis |
| 6: Individual differences | Stern (1985): Observation of babies' temperaments by mothers |
| 7: Perceiving and understanding the social world | Joffe (1999): Semi-structured interviews and thematic analysis related to HIV risk |

As Table 8.1 shows, in Book 1 you have already come across varied types of qualitative data. Qualitative researchers gather naturally occurring data from everyday contexts, often from the social worlds they are part of.

Qualitative data take many forms based, for example, on observable behaviours and/or the spoken or written word. As the Introduction to Book 1 pointed out, qualitative researchers work with observational data, people's inner experiences and symbolic data. If we are interested in what people actually do, we may ask them, but may prefer to observe them. Observational data are sometimes of everyday interactions observed in real time or on video, television or film. These may be real life or fictional, one-to-one (such as nurse–doctor, cashier–customer), or group-based – a family or work team, for example. Data gathered through observation will take the form of written descriptions of what the researchers saw (these are often referred to as field notes) and can include diagrams and videos of both the context and the interactions within it. As you saw in 'Three approaches to learning', for example, Mercer (1995) collected observational data on children's classroom behaviour along with fifty hours of classroom talk which was transcribed and analysed qualitatively.

If, on the other hand, we are interested in what people say they do or feel and/or how they have understood particular experiences or events, an interview is the most appropriate method of gaining data. Interviews are usually audio-recorded with permission, and then transcribed verbatim to provide written data, which are easier to work with than audio recordings. Song lyrics, or the contents of a lesson or meeting, for example, can be recorded and transcribed in the same way. The study by Marcia (1966) showed that data from semi-structured interviews can be analysed in both quantitative and qualitative ways. Interviews can also be transcribed and coded using computer systems as in Joffe's study (1999).

Existing written data produced for purposes other than research may also be explored. For example, psychologists sometimes analyse personal documents such as autobiographies, letters, diaries or memos. Alternatively, there are many readily available published texts. Newspapers, magazines, policy documents and prospectuses may provide relevant sources of data. The chapter 'Language and meaning' in Book 2 (*Challenging Psychological Issues*) provides an in-depth examination of several studies which use existing written data as sources. In this chapter, we focus on diary studies as an example of already-existing data.

In Sections 4.1 to 4.3 we introduce you to three different methods of collecting qualitative data: observation; interviewing; and diary studies. These methods are approaches to generating data that aim to capture the complex, contextual, rich, meaningful quality of psychological phenomena as they are expressed and described by people. Hence, these methods produce data from inner experiences and symbolic data. As explained in Section 2, within qualitative research perspectives qualitative methods are not simply seen as tools chosen by a researcher. Instead, the researcher is primed to consider research aims and research questions within the social contexts in which they are produced.

## 4.1 Observation

Observation involves paying particularly detailed attention to chosen aspects of our world, for example by focusing on activities and processes representative of people's everyday lives. Often these will be social contexts and activities with which people are already engaged.

*DVD Programme 1, 'Observation', gives two examples of observation being used as a method in psychological research on learning and problem solving. If you haven't seen this, or want to refresh your memory of the material, now would be a good time to look at it.*

Observation is one of the most common methods of data collection. Depending on the perspective it is embedded within and the related research question being explored, it can take many forms. It can be both qualitative and quantitative, and so can be set up and analysed somewhat differently depending on the perspective taken. A *structured observation* is likely to involve noting the frequency of particular behaviours that the researcher has conceptualised as indicative, for example of leadership qualities or collaborative actions. The resulting data are usually subject to statistical analysis. You saw an example of this kind of research in DVD Programme 1 'Observation' that depicted the work of the researchers at Strathclyde University who studied children's pedestrian behaviour. In contrast to that, in this chapter we focus on *unstructured naturalistic observation*. This is a qualitative approach that avoids disturbing the activities that are observed in a setting. This approach focuses on the way people interact and collaboratively produce meaning in activities that can be observed in a chosen context. You saw an example of this kind of approach in the DVD programme 'Observation' that depicted the work of researchers from The Open University studying children's collaborations in a school setting. This approach collects data that inevitably have very high 'ecological validity', because if everything goes to plan the data collected depict people behaving naturally in everyday settings.

Gold (1958) outlines different roles that observers may adopt in their chosen setting. These vary from *participant observer* (openly observing while also taking an active part in the setting), through to *complete observer* (openly observing while in no way participating in the setting), with various positions between these two extremes. Clearly, the position the observer takes influences the nature of the setting. If, for example, the observer adopts the position of a participating observer, any intervention has the potential to undermine the 'naturalistic' or 'everyday' nature of the activities and processes of the research context and will impact on the data collected. The position of the observer will also influence the nature of the data collected. If, for example, the observer adopts the position of 'complete observer' and thus remains outside the actual setting, certain details or specificities of the practice observed might escape them because they are not participating. Participants may also change their behaviour when they know they are being observed by a detached researcher.

### Activity 8.1

Imagine you have volunteered to take part in research that involves you being followed around and observed by a researcher while you are grocery shopping. Do you think that your behaviour will be influenced by that knowledge? If so, in what way? Take about five to ten minutes to jot down some points describing how far your behaviour while grocery shopping would be 'as usual' and how it might be 'different from usual'. Also try to imagine your possible thoughts when shopping while being observed.

One of the purposes of observation is to make explicit what we see going on within our chosen context. The aim of observation is to gain a rich (i.e. detailed and contextualised) understanding of what is occurring. As researchers, this means making a detailed observation of the setting. However, there are two central issues that we must bear in mind as researchers. First, we need explicitly to acknowledge that we can never be entirely 'neutral' in our descriptions. It is always possible to provide multiple descriptions of any action or event. For example, the same person following a certain course of action might be called efficient by one person whereas another might call them officious. So, when observing, taking notes and describing (i.e. taking field notes), we have to be aware of the implications of our descriptions and reflect on them.

Second, as researchers we can never observe and take notes about 'everything' we might be able to see. So before embarking on an observation it is crucial to establish a clear understanding of the aim and the focus of the observation. The aim might be an initial exploration of a context to start off the research process and generate questions (in this case a very broad approach might be useful), or the aim might be to collect data that are intended to 'answer' the research question (in this case a very specific approach, guided closely by the research question would be appropriate). The focus of the observation determines what specific aspects within a context we are interested in and thus will focus on and which ones are not at the centre of interest and might thus be given less attention. Establishing and maintaining a clear focus will enable a detailed look at the context in question and ensure that the data collected (i.e. field notes taken) are specific and relevant to the research question.

When writing our field notes, our task, as researchers, is to generate descriptions that are illuminating about a given context, with a focus on their relevance to the research question(s). Taking field notes (i.e. 'writing down what you see') might appear to be an easy, almost intuitive task, and it is not difficult to learn. However, it is a highly skilled task requiring effort, attention and reflection. Good field notes follow the aim and the intended focus of the research and generate detailed data that are relevant to the research question. To get used to note taking, it is advisable to try to get general practise as well as conducting a 'pilot' observation of the context that will be observed for the research project.

Observation is often used alongside other methods (e.g. interviews) and can serve a variety of aims and purposes within a research project. Depending on the role we have decided to give observation in our research project, the intention can be either to explore a context to generate research questions (pilot exploration), or to narrow down the research focus and identify the most relevant questions, or to provide an answer to a research question. The initial commitment is often to exploration, to look afresh at familiar settings or to gain a good understanding of a previously unfamiliar context – to make the familiar strange or the strange familiar. Where observation is used to explore a context in general in order to generate research questions, the researchers could ask themselves very generally: What do you see going on? What aspects of what you notice would it be useful to focus on? What questions might be asked? What are your interpretations? Such exploratory approaches often bring to the surface unexpected data and thus offer new insights, often within very familiar settings. This is what 'making the familiar strange' means.

It is worth noting that when observing we are working directly with our conscious awareness. However, it is also possible that some unreflected preconceptions that we hold about an activity or context, or even a current personal concern, will influence what we perceive and how we perceive it. For example, if you are currently worried that your own child is unhappy at school, you may be unable to recognise the degree to which other children might be happy and enjoying school if you are observing them in a school setting. We are often not aware of our motivations and of the degree to which even our explicit personal concerns and worries might influence our perceptions and interpretations. Chapters 6 and 7 in Book 1 discussed how our perception might be influenced by our motivations, schemas and the biases we inevitably hold. Hence it is important to reflect as much as possible upon personal issues that may not only guide and inform, but also distort and bias, our observations.

### Activity 8.2

Imagine you are a researcher conducting research in a large supermarket. For this imaginary observation, note down the descriptors you might use if you were observing parents who are grocery shopping with their children. Do you think it makes a difference that you yourself are/are not a mother/father? If so, to what extent do you think that your own position and experience might influence the kind of things you notice, the way you might note them down and interpret them? Spend about two or three minutes noting down some ideas in answer to these questions.

Now imagine you could reverse your position. If you are a mother/father imagine you did not have any children, and if you are not a mother/father try to imagine you did have children yourself. Note down the things you might perceive now. Once you have thought of a few points, compare these notes with the ones you made initially. How do the things you imagined you would have observed and the way you interpreted them differ? How difficult/easy was it for you to imagine yourself into the 'reverse' position and 'ignore' your own experience?

Look at your notes and consider the words and phrases you have used to describe your imaginary observation. Looking at them now do you think they might imply a certain 'view' of the people/context you have 'observed'? Can you think of different words/descriptors you could have used instead of the ones you have chosen? You might, for example, have noted that a mother responded *impatiently, angrily, harshly* to her child's demands to buy sweets. But you could also have noted that she was *firm, setting clear boundaries* or that she was *upset* and *at the end of her tether.*

When analysing our observations (e.g. from our field notes), we need to bear in mind that observation does not give direct access to other people's experiences. However, through shared cultural knowledge we may be able to make interpretations based on our observations. As mentioned above with regard to observing and taking notes, when analysing observations we cannot escape our cultural knowledge, values, beliefs and experiences, nor can we step outside the social context. Differing cultural knowledge might, however, lead to divergent interpretations of an observation. As researchers, when analysing observations, it is crucial to try and reflect upon our cultural knowledge and to develop an awareness of the ways in which cultural knowledge and social context influence our judgements. In reflecting in this way, we may well be able to benefit from this knowledge and turn it into an explicit tool for analysing and understanding specific contexts. Crucially, we can also ask those people we have observed what they experienced.

Remember the actor/observer effect, discussed in Chapter 7 of Book 1. According to attribution theory, as observers we are taking an outsider's perspective and may be tempted in our analysis to overemphasise people's dispositions to act in particular ways. Alternatively, when we are participant observers, we have an insider's perspective and may focus too much on the influence of the social setting on our actions (for further discussion see Book 1, Chapter 7, Section 3.3).

In summary, when observing we need to be clear about the aim and the focus of the observation in order to collect data (field notes) relevant to the research, rather than ending up with a set of random observations. We need to reflect upon the potentially implicit assumptions and motivations that always guide and colour our perceptions. We also need to be aware that our descriptions are never entirely 'neutral', because the way we describe something (i.e. the words, phrases, formulations we choose) always carry some kind of implicit meaning. As this cannot be avoided, it needs to be made explicit and reflected upon in order to avoid merely imposing preconceived understandings onto the observed context. Such an instance would result in a situation where the observer creates a reality that bears little relation to what is going on in the setting.

## 4.2 Interviewing

Nearly all of us have had experience of interviews in one form or another, be it for a job, a market research survey or applying for a bank loan. In an interview, questions with specific purposes are posed to gather information from the interviewee. The context and aim of an interview can differ widely, ranging, for example, from the police interviewing witnesses and suspects of crime through to a clinical psychologist interviewing a patient for the purpose of clinical diagnosis. Here we shall discuss interviewing in the context of research.

A research interview has famously been described as 'a conversation with a purpose' (Bingham and Moore, 1959). In conducting research, the interviewer identifies a research question(s) and selects a number of topics that will enable her/him to elicit information surrounding the question(s) and find appropriate research participants or informants to interview. The data are then analysed to address the research question(s) and to consider other questions that follow from the accounts given in the interview.

### *Activity 8.3*

Think about a psychological topic that a researcher might be able to explore via an interview. Note down the topic and formulate four questions that you think would help to get a potential interviewee talking about the issues you want to know about. Spend five to ten minutes doing this.

Now think of interviews you have recently seen on television (in the news or in films), heard on the radio or possibly experienced yourself. Thinking about these examples, can you imagine what kind of questions are likely to elicit long and elaborate answers from an interviewee? On the other hand, what kind of questions are likely to elicit very short answers or even silence the interviewee? Jot down a few ideas about these two types of questions.

Return to the four questions you formulated initially and imagine you are the person being asked them. Spend a few minutes imagining what your answer would be to each of the four questions (or ask a family member of friend to pose these questions to you). Does the way the questions are formulated elicit a long and elaborate answer from you? Is it difficult to relate to and answer these questions? Do you feel comfortable answering these questions in detail?

Keep your notes from this activity for later reference.

### Comment

You may have noted that forced choice or closed yes/no questions often elicit very short answers as they do not invite elaboration. Open questions will usually spark longer and more complex responses. In some contexts, 'why-questions' may be perceived as challenging and may produce defensive or short responses. In contrast, 'how-questions' are more likely to encourage elaborate responses.

*You can see two research interviews that produce long, narrative-type answers in DVD Programme 4, 'Interviewing and thematic analysis'. You will use one of those interviews in your own qualitative methods project for TMA 05.*

## Interviews in qualitative research

This subsection provides an introduction to interviews in qualitative research, and contrasts them with other interviews used in psychology and elsewhere. It also illuminates some of the assumptions and the controversies involved in interviews used in qualitative research, so that you can recognise these before you start doing your project.

As discussed above, interviews are extensively used within psychology, and are sometimes used in quantitative research. Like observation, interviews can be used in the exploratory stage of a research project, as pilot interviews; that is, as a means to gather a broad range of material to give researchers insights into how they can develop their main project. These pilot interviews can help researchers ascertain what key questions need to be asked and to ensure that the research being carried out is meaningful to the participants and does not merely reflect the researcher's interests or some consensus in the relevant literature. Hence interviews can be a very useful starting point for further research. They can also be a way of providing ongoing feedback about the results of a particular project.

However, while interviews could, for example, be an addition to quantitative research projects, they have a central role in qualitative research and are frequently used within qualitative research projects. Where interviews are conducted within the hermeneutic tradition, the emphasis is on analysing how a particular person understands an issue. The interview is therefore concerned with exploring meanings to gain a detailed understanding of how individuals experience, perceive and interact with their social context. In this sense, interviews in qualitative research differ from, for example, job or market-research interviews and require different skills. The main reason for this is that research interviews follow an entirely different agenda. For example, most formal job interviews are relatively structured, employing predetermined questions that reflect the requirements of a specific job and ensure that all candidates are treated equally. Their explicit aim is to select the best candidate for a particular job; hence they are structured to ensure the same relevant and fair questions are asked of all applicants. Applicants, on their part, know that they are being judged on the basis of their answers. In contrast, a qualitative research interview will aim to illuminate issues raised and formulated in the research question. It will be exploring the participant's own complex understanding of a situation, context or role they are in and thus will give encouragement and allow plenty of space for them to elaborate what they want to say. It is therefore important to try to create an atmosphere where participants do not feel they are being judged for the answers they give.

The data that emerge from qualitative interviews should provide richness (an abundance of detail and depth) of information that is compatible with the perspectives of the hermeneutic tradition and thus the principles of qualitative research. These principles are concerned with a search for meanings that individuals assign to their lives and experiences. Consider Activity 1.1 in Book 1, Chapter 1. The activity asked you to write down ten responses to the question 'Who am I?' A given response might include: a mother, a daughter, tall, tired and 37 years old. This activity tells us something about who the person thinks they are but does not provide any depth of information. In an interview, such responses could be followed up and the meanings of the brief descriptions can be explored. For example, consider the descriptor 'mother'. To understand this term in depth we would need to know what this particular person means by it. Although it is on the surface fairly obvious, in a real-life context motherhood is experienced in many different ways: as troublesome, exciting, tiring, or all of these, for example. The point is that what motherhood means will almost certainly be different across different women because each of them will have personal experiences that shape their perceptions of motherhood. A qualitative interview allows the researcher to explore, acknowledge and use this variety, in order to gain a greater depth of understanding of what the term 'mother' means to each interviewee and in different social contexts.

Interviews in qualitative research can be more or less structured, ranging from completely open explorations of a topic area to semi-structured interviews that are arranged around specific questions. However, the interviewer will always have a specific focus and research interest that underpin and inform the interview. As a result of reading the relevant literature, discussing their interests with others and pilot work, the researcher arrives at one or several research questions. The researcher then prepares a set of interview questions that will act as a basis for exploring the area of interest staked out by the research question(s). The precise format of the interview will differ according to who is being interviewed, how questions are asked and how they are responded to. There is a deliberate attempt to try to get the participant to provide insights into their own reality, thus allowing the interviewer to explore the participant's viewpoint (Hollway and Jefferson, 2000). Where possible, interviews will be followed up, so that interpretations and analyses can be tried out with the participant, and to provide the participant with time to reflect on what it is that they have said.

Note that there are inevitably power imbalances in an interview situation; it is the interviewer who is nominally in control of the situation and to a large extent determines the length and direction of the interview. It is also often difficult for the participant to refuse to answer questions. This is because in our everyday interactions we are used to responding to questions, either as a matter of politeness or respect for the person asking, or because implicitly we assume that not giving an answer might be seen as stupid. Hence, it is important to reflect upon how we ask questions and what kind of questions we ask. These points need to be carefully considered when looking at interviews as a method in psychological research, and they should form part of the process of reflexivity, which will be discussed in Chapter 10.

Take another look at the questions you formulated for Activity 8.3 and consider them again in the light of the discussion above.

---

*Kvale (1996) describes two metaphors for the activity of research interviewing. The first of these views the interviewer as a miner, seeking buried treasures that may be revealed if the right questions are asked. The second views the interviewer as a traveller, on a journey resulting in a tale that can be told to others on their return. The second view recognises the journey as one of mutual discovery, where the person interviewed may change as a result of the experience, and the interviewer may also change. In this case, the process of doing an interview is more of a joint construction, involving both the researcher and the participant. From this viewpoint interviewing does not simply solicit and record the views of the participant, but is an active construction of an account that is as much produced by the questions and comments of the interviewer as by the participant's account.*

---

As mentioned above, there are different types of interviews. In qualitative research, the most common is probably the semi-structured interview technique (see Book 1, Chapter 1, Featured Methods Box 1.2). In a semi-structured interview, the researcher normally identifies a number of topics around which questions are framed for the participant. The actual questions asked will depend on the responses of the participant, as the researcher will follow up and probe responses to elicit meanings. This does not mean that the interviewer fires a battery of questions at the participant, but rather that the questions encourage the participant to talk about experiences, feelings and events in an everyday manner. In doing this, the researcher is more likely to gather rich data and, importantly, space is made for the participant to develop and expand on their meanings within the interview.

### Interviews are situated in particular contexts and co-constructed

Many things influence the nature of interview data, not least the relationship between the researcher and the participant. Remember that all conversations, including interviews, are *interactions*: each person is actively involved in the process and therefore the data will change according to the nature of the interaction. Think about this using your own experience. In discussing a particular topic with, say, your mother, it is unlikely that you will discuss the same issues as you might with a close friend. In addition, the issues you discuss with a close friend may change according to the mood you are in, the mood the friend is in, and perhaps whether you are discussing the topic on the bus or in the privacy of your own home. This is one of the reasons why data from interviews can never provide a complete picture of a topic as it is seen by the interviewee. Within qualitative research, researchers acknowledge that the interview is always dependent on its specific context and the two people participating in it. Many researchers talk about interviews as co-constructed between the interviewer and interviewee. Think back to our example about motherhood and identity. The data gathered with a given participant will change over time and place, each account representing the experiences and feelings of the participant at that time. This illustrates one strength of the interview as a research method from the qualitative perspective – repeated interviews can give access to the complexity of identity as it is experienced by showing it to be fluid, multiple and a product of personal experience and interpretation.

## 4.3 Diary studies

Diary studies are another method of collecting rich qualitative data. These include any personal accounts written by the research participant over a period of time. Such documents may be explicitly solicited to explore a particular research question where participants are asked to keep time limited diary entries – perhaps daily for a week or a month – about particular events, experiences or understandings. Qualitative researchers search for meanings emerging from the accounts and also make clear their part in constructing and analysing their research.

### Activity 8.4

Note down what you believe to be the advantages and disadvantages of keeping a diary during an event or period of change. As you read through the rest of this section, compare your notes with the issues raised here.

Personal statements already in existence may be explored with a particular research question in mind. It is possible to collect diaries and letters of people living in the past, as Thomas and Znaniecki (1958) did to explore what it was like to be a Polish peasant in Europe and the USA in the 1950s. Whatever form is used, diaries in qualitative approaches to research are about illuminating stories, making explicit people's lived experience. Such accounts offer insights into the ways in which particular people perceive and construe their world. The focus is on their subjective experience. Personal accounts are not simply a record of what 'actually happened': truths vary, but such accounts offer insights into the ways in which the author understood what was going on, at the time the account was written.

The 'unfolding stories' within diaries can be explored in a variety of ways, often, but not always, by researchers working at a much later time and in a different social context from that of the author. As diaries are kept over time, whether it is a week, a month or a year, they offer us the opportunity to note and track changes occurring during the time span of the entries. They allow us to explore the richness of people's past and present. The longitudinal nature of diaries, even if merely written over the course of a week, also makes available contradictions and variability in understandings within the entries as well as threads of continuity and coherence. Patterns are likely to emerge within single diary accounts (that is, those kept by a single author) as well as across and between sets of accounts from different people.

Solicited diary entries, specifically focusing on day-to-day understandings of interactions, are often used to explore how relationships are experienced from the viewpoint of those within the relationship. In an innovative diary study, Wilkinson (1987) recruited pairs of people who had never previously met and requested that they meet on a regular basis over a four-week period. Each recorded their impressions of the other as well as commenting on what they thought was the other's view of them. Analysis of participants' accounts revealed the very different perspective and understanding each person offered of the same relationship. For example, 'S' believed that she could make a friend of 'D', as she considered that they had mutual interests and liked to talk. 'D', however, felt differently and commented that she experienced a barrier between herself and 'S'. She felt that 'S' treated her as a child (Wilkinson, 1987).

Existing accounts in diaries offer the possibility of exploring the author's life from our present-day social context. However, this may be far removed from the author's intention. Rereading accounts from different social contexts often highlights new meanings and can offer historical insight. A classic example is the diary of Hannah Cullwick (a Victorian maidservant), asked to write a diary by her employer, who later became her husband. This diary was initially interpreted by Stanley (1984). Later it was reinterpreted by Swindells who questioned the authenticity of Hannah Cullwick's voice in the diary. Swindells claimed that as Hannah was writing for someone else's purpose, namely her employer/husband who gained sexual pleasure from reading about women immersed in dirt and hard work, she was not free to allow her own voice to be fully present. Swindells's conclusion is that researchers must take on the responsibility of 'analysing the conditions of their [diary authors'] lives' (Swindells, 1989, p. 65). This example illustrates the need to be aware of the social context of both author and interpreter and the danger of accepting at face value and as unproblematic the version of reality represented in diaries.

Clearly, there are multiple ways, even within diary methods, in which lives may be studied and construed, and each has different implications. Those who record their experiences in response to a request may well develop their own agenda. Participants may, consciously or not, reorganise their lives for the duration of the diary entries, to be more engaging, more dramatic in terms of the research topics, or they may put a gloss on events in ways that they consider sound more interesting. As in the example of Hannah Cullwick, diaries are rarely a stream of consciousness but constructed for purposes over and above the research. Qualitative researchers consider that meanings are always socially embedded and are actively constructed. As a result, the social context and conditions in which the diary was written and in which it is interpreted need attention during analysis. Whose voice is dominant, that of the interpreter or the author?

### Summary Section 4

- Section 4 has introduced you to qualitative data and outlined different methods of collecting qualitative data. It has introduced you to the general qualitative approaches of observation and interviewing, and more specifically to the approach of diary studies (as an example of data collection for textual analysis). All of these methods aim to generate rich data that are illustrative of the meanings and experiences in participants' lives.
- The section has highlighted issues that arise when collecting, transforming and interpreting qualitative data in the context of qualitative research perspectives. It has, for example, highlighted the importance of reflecting on the words and phrases used to take field notes during an observation, the power imbalances between interviewer and interviewee, the nature of the questions asked during an interview, or contextual issues that may arise in diary studies (e.g. at what time and for what purpose were the diaries written originally?). We need to be aware of these issues, reflect upon them and discuss their relevance for our research project as a whole.

## 5 Discourse analysis as an example of explicit epistemology and methodology in qualitative research

Section 4 introduced you to a variety of ways to collect qualitative data. Yet, as explained earlier (Section 3), data collection is only one specific aspect of research, and overall a research project is always embedded within a broader perspective (i.e. theoretical framework) (Section 2). Researchers working within the hermeneutic tradition, and thus employing methods to collect qualitative data, often make explicit the particular ontological and epistemological positions on which their research is based. By this we mean that the researchers' particular view of their object of enquiry, i.e. how they conceptualise the nature of what they are looking at (what it is to be a person), what constitutes knowledge and the means by which they should approach this knowledge (epistemology), will necessarily and explicitly inform the methods that they use. Researchers will explicitly elaborate on and discuss these issues. We would like to illustrate this next by providing an exemplary account of one qualitative approach to research, namely that of discourse analysis.

Researchers working within the social constructionist perspective base their research on the epistemological assumption that knowledge is constructed in discourse. That is, they assume that knowledge is constructed in stories – private, public, individual and collective discourses about ourselves and others – and that these stories allow us to communicate and form our identities. Hence, they also assume that people inherently construct discourse and are constructed by discourse (this is the perspective's ontological assumption). If they follow these ontological and epistemological assumptions, researchers are likely to adopt a *discourse analysis* approach because this focuses on and analyses the private and collective discourses and narratives people engage in and tell about themselves and others. Choosing this particular approach and type of analysis is part of the methodological consideration of the researcher. As part of their research they will not just describe their method (e.g. qualitative interviews) but will also explain the underlying methodological considerations that inform their approach (e.g. discourse analysis). In this context they might elaborate on issues of ontology and epistemology in order to explain why, for example, discourse analysis is the most appropriate approach to analysing their data.

## 5.1 Introducing discourse analysis

Discourse analysis is an approach to doing qualitative research that emerged in the mid-1980s. It is associated with the development of *discursive psychology* and tries to take a systematic approach to the study of people's talk in interviews and in other contexts. It focuses on the ways in which people *make meaning* and looks closely at how their talk is put together. Next, we introduce some of the main concepts that discourse analysts use when building systematic analyses of how people make meaning. Any discourse analyst will have considered the central aspects of the qualitative research process outlined in Section 3 of this chapter before collecting and beginning to analyse their data. We will address some of the concerns that discourse analysts take into account when conducting research, but we do not seek to cover all the different types of discourse analysis employed.

## Activity 8.5

You have already encountered the terms 'discourse analysis' and 'discursive psychology' at several points in the course. Look back at Book 1, Chapter 1, Section 5.2 (you will encounter a more elaborate introduction later, in Book 2, Chapter 2, Section 4). Try to write down several broad conclusions about the process of making meaning in discourse analysis and discursive psychology.

## Comment

The discussion of discourse analysis in Books 1 and 2 presents the following key features. Broadly speaking, these key features express the ontological, epistemological and methodological considerations on which discourse analysis is based:

1. People make choices about how to describe things including themselves.
2. These choices are related to the broader social history of the community in which people live and what is taken for granted in that context. What is taken for granted is a consequence of power relations.
3. Meanings emerge in social interaction.
4. Words and accounts are forms of social action.
5. Words do things such as construct realities or make things real, create identities and positions for people, construct memories, intentions and emotions.

Based on this conceptualisation of what it is to be a person (ontology), discursive psychology focuses on people's meaning making and use of language in interaction, because this is the best way to find out about how they express themselves and experience themselves and others within the social world (epistemology). Accordingly, the methods used to collect qualitative data are those considered to be most appropriate to give an insight into this (methodological consideration). Discursive psychology often uses data recorded in natural settings and data from interviews or discussion groups. These data are usually transcribed, meaning that the analysis will be performed on a written account of conversations or interviews.

The last time you systematically analysed language was probably when you were in school studying your own or a foreign language. Perhaps you did some grammatical analysis at that time and took apart sentences in terms of the verbs, the nouns, the adjectives, and so on. You may have studied poetry or novels and analysed things like the use of metaphor and similes. In a similar way, discourse analysis tries to pay careful attention to how a piece of text like the transcribed record of an interview or a conversation *works* to produce the effect or the meaning it does. But, of course, our interest here is in social psychology not linguistics. We are not interested in grammar in itself or in literary style, but rather in the social and psychological dimensions of making meaning and the consequences for people and for society as a whole. A different set of concepts is therefore needed for the analysis. Grammatical concepts like 'noun' and 'verb' and stylistic concepts like 'simile' do not get at the kinds of pattern in the data which are most relevant to the research questions discursive psychologists want to ask.

What concepts might be more useful and what kinds of patterns in talk and text do they pick out?

## 5.2 Discourse concepts and discourse patterns

This section reviews five broad concepts that discursive psychologists use a great deal when doing discourse analysis: *participants' orientations, voice, narrative, interpretative repertoires* and *subject positions*. They have been taken from a number of different traditions of research on language and discourse found in the social sciences. You will encounter two of these in more detail when you read Section 4 of Chapter 2, Book 2.

### Participants' orientations

The term 'participant orientation' comes from research on discourse conducted by conversation analysts and ethnomethodologists. This concept focuses on the activities accomplished in conversation and the turn-by-turn organisation of the talk. Any kind of interaction between people, whether it is in an interview or an ordinary conversation, goes back and forth and is constructed jointly, turn by turn. It has what are often called dialogical properties (from the word 'dialogue'). One person says something, this utterance sets a frame for the conversation and begins to define what is going on. Someone else responds, their response shows how they have interpreted what is happening and changes the frame or the context again.

Note that in discourse analysis both the interviewer and the interviewee are seen as participants. Unlike many other qualitative approaches, discourse analysts see the interviewer's utterances as equally open to investigation because they set the context for what happens. Interview questions are not just a neutral procedure for getting information that can then be ignored in the analysis. Working out the participant orientations is sometimes very straightforward and quite mundane and sometimes it gives fascinating insights into what is going on. If we ask the general question, 'Where is the meaning produced?, we have to answer that the meaning emerges from the back and forth of the interaction and is produced jointly by all the participants. It emerges *in between* the participants. In other words, we could say it is created *inter-subjectively* – it is not just a product of one mind or subjectivity but is produced by the changing situation constructed by all the participants.

## Voice

According to the dramatist Dennis Potter 'the trouble with words is that you do not know whose mouth they have been in' (cited in Maybin, 2001, p. 68). Dennis Potter is saying something noteworthy about discourse: namely that our words are never entirely our own. When we speak our words are populated with the voices of others and with the previous contexts in which words have typically been used. Often these are the voices of people who are significant to us (perhaps the voices of parents, teachers, friends, politicians we admire, partners, and so on). Parents of small children, for instance, often worry that they sound just like their own parents even though they may be trying hard not to repeat the mistakes of an earlier generation. Sometimes the voices we draw on are the official or recognised voices in our culture for doing certain activities. Think, for instance, of the typical voice and whole style of presentation of the television newsreader and how we might imitate this if asked to 'put on' that style. Indeed, the process of being educated is a process of learning how to use certain languages (and the voices that go with them) that one did not know before. Certainly, we also have our own individual voice as we struggle to make our own meanings and express our own views. But it is also revealing to ask what other voices we might be speaking with and in what contexts we might have picked them up and what meanings they carry with them.

These points about 'voice' have emerged from the work of the Russian discourse scholars Mikhail Bakhtin and Valentin Volosinov, and looking at when speakers use reported speech is a good (and the simplest) way of further investigating this aspect of discourse (Maybin, 1994). This is often found in narratives in the 'he said then she said' form. Reported speech is not necessarily a literal description of what someone actually said. The point is that speakers do not report faithfully the words of someone else but tell a story with a certain message, and the voices of others are enlisted to support that aim. It is possible to analyse how we might recruit these voices, exactly when we bring them out to speak for us, and how we inflect them with new meanings for the new contexts in which they are used. Also note that we can use our own internal monologues and dialogues in this way.

## Narrative

A third analytic concept often used by discursive psychologists is that of narrative, which came originally from traditions of narrative analysis found in sociolinguistics. This concept focuses on the way in which people order and structure their talk. Stories are a perennial feature of conversation and everyday life – they are a way of organising events, presenting oneself, forming bonds in a community through shared experience, creating entertainment and passing on information (Jaworski and Coupland, 1999).

Discursive psychologists are most interested in the self-presentational functions of stories and how they organise people's psychology. Indeed, if we ask the most basic question about identity – 'Who are you?' – the answer is actually often a collection of stories. In a sense we are all walking records of all our life events. This record is often organised as a set of narratives about what kind of people we are, what our personalities are like and the things that have happened to us throughout our lives that can be used to account for where we are now. How those stories are organised and their 'flavour' (the kinds of evaluations of ourselves and others they contain) are crucial to our sense of well-being. This is why some psychologists are convinced of the benefits of narrative therapy – working with people to develop better, more enabling and empowering stories and narratives of key events in their lives.

Within cultures, there are clear and recognisable kinds of stories that are told at various points. For example, having recovered from a serious illness or surviving a serious accident, it is common for people to tell stories of 'a fresh start', of 'having been given a new life', and of seeing and appreciating their life, family and friends in a completely different way. It is possible to identify in people's accounts a number of stories or narratives. Narrative researchers use a variety of techniques for analysing narratives (Bamberg, 2006). However, the sociolinguist William Labov (see Jaworski and Coupland, 1999), argued on the basis of his research into narrative that typical well-formed narratives have five features:

1. An abstract: narratives often begin with an anticipatory summary of the plot of the story.
2. An orientation: something that sets the scene for the listener.
3. A complicating action: something that creates a puzzle or a problem that needs solving.
4. An evaluation: it works towards a positive or negative evaluation of the situation being described.
5. A result or resolution: there is an outcome to the story and the complicating action.

Narrative analysis is not a precise art. These five features are sometimes mixed together in the same utterance. In addition, many narrative analysts do not focus on analysing the structure of narrative in the way Labov does, or do not concentrate only on discourses. The narrative perspective is increasingly influential in the social sciences and asserts that social life is bound together by stories (Riessman, 2007). Bowker (1993) suggests that an 'age of biography is upon us': where stories infuse a variety of private/public and individual/collective contexts that make up the fabric of social reality. People reflect upon their life experiences and retell narratives of childhood, building upon the stories told to them by loved ones and it is through listening to anecdotes that we all get to know other people and come to formulate opinions of them. Knowledge, whether it is scientific, political, psychological or commonsensical, is imparted through the construction of plausible stories. Stories are a central component of human experience (this is the ontological assumption) and of the construction of reality (e.g. Plummer, 2001) (this is the epistemological assumption). They not only reflect our experiences but also are crucial to the construction of how we see other people and ourselves. It has been argued that a core of the human condition is a reliance on storytelling. We are *homo narrans* (storytelling people) – telling stories in order to impose structure and give meaning to our lives (Bruner, 2003). If telling stories is a large part of what we do, i.e. is a central feature of what it is to be a person (underlying ontological assumption), then it makes sense to use it as a method for illuminating the experiences and realities of narrators (Bamberg, 1997; Bruner, 1987).

### Activity 8.6

Write a 150-word account of your life that you would be happy to give to a total stranger as a way of introducing yourself. Now consider the following:

1 Why have you included some things/events/experiences and not others?

2 What could a reader infer about you and your social position from reading your story?

3 In addition to a snapshot of your life as an individual, what could the reader learn about life in the twenty-first century from your story?

Narrative analysis is the collection, writing-up and presentation of stories and of the ways in which those stories are told (Georgakopolou, 2006). Narrative forms include autobiography, biography, life story, oral history and life history. Life stories allow personalised insights into social worlds, so that theories of the social world, both 'lay' and 'academic', can be assessed from these individual standpoints. Life stories investigate some of the meanings held not only by narrators but also in the culture. Through individual accounts, narrative analysts can rigorously and systematically examine the ways in which material, social, cultural and political conditions shape individuals' lives and their views of themselves (McAdams, 2006).

### Interpretative repertoires

A fourth concept discourse analysts use is the notion of 'interpretative repertoire' (developed by Potter and Wetherell, 1987). This concept (like narrative analysis) focuses on the more global organisation of talk as opposed to the more fine grain perspective of 'participants' orientations'. You will find a more detailed definition of interpretative repertoires in Section 4 of

Chapter 2, Book 2. Essentially, these are a way of picking out the familiar arguments and ways of making sense that one sees over and over again, and which tell us something about how a society or a community or a social group taken as a whole make sense of social life. In other words, they allow us to identify the taken-for-granted cultural resources found in talk.

One way of identifying interpretative repertoires is by analysing the ways things are typically described and then considering the social and psychological implications of these dominant representations. What versions of the social world do these buy into? This mode of analysis has been important to critical psychologists interested in tracing how power relations in broader society impinge on people's everyday identities and understandings. Interpretative repertoires can be picked out through identifying the clichés, proverbs and familiar metaphors produced in talk.

One of the curious features of everyday discourse is that the interpretative repertoires people draw upon are usually not consistent. They are highly variable and clash with each other (Potter and Wetherell, 1987), and these clashes lead to dilemmas (Billig *et al.*, 1988) because things can be described in different ways and these ways are evaluated differently in different contexts. For instance, in research with young men talking about sexuality, Wetherell (1998) and Edley (2001) note all the available repertoires evident in the young men's talk. The young men went back and forth in their talk while also constructing versions of themselves as responsible and respectful of women. At the same time they said that women also 'fancied a bit', and there was a notion that you were a 'lucky lad' if a girl was 'willing'. Each of these different interpretative repertoires constructed a different kind of identity for the young men involved (and, crucially, the young women) and also created some major dilemmas. In summary, analysing the different ways in which things can be represented is an important part of understanding the social psychology of a situation.

## Subject positions

The final analytic concept we wish to introduce is the notion of 'subject positions' (this will be explained in more detail in Section 4.2, Chapter 2, Book 2). This concept is used in various ways but goes back to some developments in social theory and the ideas of the French theorists Louis Althusser and Jacques Lacan. Discourse is full of positioning work. Every time a person tells a narrative, and usually each time they use an interpretative repertoire from the stock available in their culture, they position themselves, and often others as well. These positions construct an identity, a self and a subjectivity. Subject positions are evident when we study participants' orientations turn by turn and analyse the different voices on which they draw.

One of the most interesting things about subject positions in discourse is that they set up rights and responsibilities as well as identities. If one positions oneself, for instance, as a good host, then social actions follow from that. Similarly, if someone repeatedly positions themselves as a stoical person, gamely facing difficult situations and transitions and working out a solution each time, this is likely to be an effective and constructive form of subject positioning that has real consequences for their identities and how people see them.

## 5.3 Doing discourse analysis

The five concepts for analysing discourse (participants' orientations, voice, narrative, interpretative repertoires and subject positions) discussed above can be used to identify patterns in people's talk. Doing complete discourse analysis, however, would depend on the research questions being asked and the kind of research project this discourse belonged to. It is worth dwelling on the purpose of the research a little more. What discourse analysis can reveal depends on the questions that are asked. Discourse analysis can be used to address quite a wide range of issues. One strand is relatively global and this is where investigations of interpretative repertoires and dilemmas come into play. This strand would usually involve analysis of a large sample of material – as many as eighty interviews, for example, around a theme like the ways in which a majority ethnic group represent and talk about a minority ethnic group (Wetherell and Potter, 1992). Here the focus is not on any one individual but on the meaning-making processes of a whole community (i.e. how they 'make sense') and the implications of the patterns in their talk for understanding how racism operates, for instance, in the society and culture as a whole.

A second strand of discourse analysis research is much more focused on the individual. Narrative analysis, for instance, might be applied to interviews with young boys and young men (e.g. in a study of how boys construct their masculine identities – Frosh *et al.*, 2001). The interviews will be analysed to pick out all the narratives around particular episodes and then the patterns and subject positions in these are analysed to reveal insights about the psychology of masculinity. Alternatively, the focus could be just on one person's life history to reveal everything about the ways in which they typically create meaning.

Finally, some discourse analytic research is more interested in the organisation of social interaction itself. For instance, research focused on participants' orientations, and using other concepts from conversation analysis and ethnomethodology, can tell us about how discourse and social interaction are organised in settings like courtrooms or clinics or in the cockpits of aeroplanes. This has had important consequences for improving communication in these key places.

Although discourse analysis is an approach in its own right, that is explicitly based on specific epistemological and methodological assumptions, it shares with all other kinds of qualitative research an embeddedness in the perspective it takes (in this case, social constructionism), and it cannot be understood in separation from the research questions developed. This impacts more widely on issues such as the number of interviews that are done or the kinds of raw data that are collected.

It is important to note that discourse analysis is only one of many different approaches to doing qualitative research. For example, other approaches include grounded theory (Glaser and Strauss, 1967), ethnomethodology or ethnography. You can learn more about the wide range of qualitative approaches to research in the Level 3 social psychology course DD307.

### Summary Section 5

- Discourse analysts often explicitly discuss their theoretical framework and methodological decisions because discourse analysis employs and promotes a specific understanding of what it is to be a person and how best to investigate people's meaning making, experiences and interaction.
- Discourse analysis takes as its starting point the ways in which text and discourse provide different ways of constructing action and versions of self.
- Central analytic concepts include participant's orientations, voice, narrative, interpretative repertoires and subject positions.

## 6 Concluding issues

The next chapter will introduce you to the process of conducting qualitative research in more detail and you will have the opportunity to get some hands-on experience of analysing qualitative data. As mentioned earlier, it is not intended that you should use any of the more complex approaches discussed in this chapter (e.g. discourse analysis). In order to provide you with a simple and accessible first experience in qualitative research and analysis, you will be introduced to thematic analysis. Thematic analysis is not a complex approach to research and/or analysis in its own right, but it can be understood as a generic technique of categorising and sorting qualitative data that allows first interpretations to be made. Hence, even though in actual research projects it is unlikely to be the only analytic tool used, it is an ideal starting point for learning about analysing qualitative data and gaining an initial understanding of how qualitative research is organised. The example of thematic analysis will serve to illustrate in more detail, and on a basic level, how it is possible to make sense of data and formulate meaningful analyses.

While the following chapter will mainly focus on issues of analysis, it is crucial to bear in mind how the whole process of undertaking qualitative research is organised. This is why we would like to conclude this chapter with a systematic summary of the central steps that need to be followed and the most crucial issues you need to reflect upon when conducting a qualitative research project (see Box 8.1).

### 8.1 The process of conducting qualitative research

It is important to remember that qualitative research is not just a 'fishing trip'. It is purposive rather than random and is grounded in the researcher's theoretical framework (ontology and epistemology), their understanding of the topic area, the research question they generate and the sense they make of their data in relation to their research question.

In essence this means that all qualitative research begins with theory; that is, all research begins with the researcher's attempt explicitly to situate himself/herself within the theoretical framework they favour and that, in their consideration, allows them to generate the most interesting research questions.

When planning and conducting a qualitative research project, the researchers will always try to follow these steps:

1 Researchers start by thinking about and situating themselves within a research perspective they favour. They do this by reading about the topic area that interests them and by finding out about the research perspective applied in the literature and studies that impress them most. Hence, while reviewing the literature they will aim to find and specify their research topic as well as determining the perspective (i.e. theoretical framework) they would like to situate their research in. Crucially, they will make sure they understand and follow the theoretical framework underpinning the research literature on the basis of which they wish to develop their own study.
2 Researchers think of and formulate a research question (or several research questions). They do this by specifying their topic area and thinking about what interests them within this topic area and how they could find out about the aspect that interests them. It is crucial to make sure that the research question(s) makes sense within, and relates to, the theoretical framework

they have chosen (see step 1). Furthermore, the research question(s) must be focused and specific. If the question(s) is (are) vague or too broad, it will be difficult to devise methods and to collect relevant data. Even though the research question(s) might be revised and specified further during the research process (as explained in Section 3 of this chapter), it is important that researchers are very clear about the focus and intention of the research from the start. It is thus crucial to think carefully about the initial research question(s) and to make explicit why and how they were formulated.

3 Researchers choose the methods they wish to employ. They do this by considering which methods are appropriate within their perspective (i.e. those methods used by other researchers in their field). From those methods available within the chosen perspective, they will use those most appropriate for their research question(s) (e.g. if they are interested in how people express certain experiences, they are likely to conduct interviews rather than doing an observation).
4 Researchers collect data and transform it into a form that is most approachable for analysis (e.g. interview data will be transcribed because a written account is easier to work with).
5 Researchers analyse data using the analytic tools available within the perspective they have chosen (e.g. narrative analysis or discourse analysis, etc.). The analytic tool you will be introduced to in the next chapter is thematic analysis.
6 As outlined in Section 3 of this chapter, qualitative research is always an iterative process. While analysing the data, the researchers will re-evaluate the theoretical position, reconsider the status of previous research (literature) in the light of the findings, and possibly revise and specify the research question(s) in view of the first analytic findings (please go back to Section 3 and look again at Figure 8.1).
7 Finally, researchers formulate and discuss their analytic findings (e.g. the analytic categories or themes they found).

These seven steps are only a very broad outline that is meant to illustrate the stages involved in a complete research process. The next chapter will focus mainly on data analysis (i.e. it will focus on steps 5 to 7). However, this summary should help you see that research is a process involving a number of steps that include, but are not limited to, data collection and analysis. Don't worry though, as in Chapter 10 we will provide full guidance regarding the project work that you will undertake for TMA 05.

# References

Bamberg, M.G. (ed.) (1997) 'Oral versions of personal experience: three decades of narrative analysis', *Journal of Narrative and Life History*, Special Issue, vol. 7.

Bamberg, M. (2006) 'Stories: big or small. Why do we care?', *Narrative Inquiry*, vol. 16, no. 1, pp. 139–47.

Billig, M., Condor, S., Edwards, D., Gane, M., Middleton, D. and Radley, A. (1988) *Ideological Dilemmas*, London, Sage.

Bingham, W. and Moore, B. (1959) *How to Interview*, New York, Harper International.

Bowker, G. (1993) 'The age of biography is upon us', *Times Higher Education Supplement*, 8 January, p. 9.

Bruner, J. (1987) 'Life as narrative', *Social Research*, vol. 54, pp. 11–32.

Bruner, J. (2003) *Making Stories: Law, Literature, Life*, Cambridge, MA, Harvard University Press.

Denzin, N.K. and Lincoln, Y.S. (2005) *The Sage Handbook of Qualitative Research* (3rd edn), London, Sage.

Edley, N. (2001) 'Analysing masculinity: interpretative repertoires, subject positions and ideological dilemmas' in Wetherell, M., Taylor, S. and Yates, S.J. (eds) *Discourse as Data: A Guide for Analysis*, London, Sage/Open University Press.

Frosh, S., Phoenix, A. and Pattman, R. (2001) *Young Masculinities: Understanding Boys in Contemporary Society*, London, Palgrave.

Georgakopolou, A. (2006) 'Thinking big with small stories in narrative and identity analysis', *Narrative Inquiry*, vol. 16, no. 1, pp. 122–30.

Glaser, B.G. and Strauss, A.L. (1967) *The Discovery of Grounded Theory: Strategies for Qualitative Research*, Hawthorne, Aldine.

Gold, R.L. (1958) 'Roles in sociological field observations', *Social Forces*, vol. 36, pp. 217–23.

Hollway, W. and Jefferson, T. (2000) *Doing Qualitative Research Differently*, London, Sage.

Jaworski, A. and Coupland, N. (1999) 'Introduction: perspectives on discourse analysis', in Jaworski, A. and Coupland, N. (eds) *The Discourse Reader*, London, Routledge.

Joffe, H. (1999) *Risk and the 'Other'*, Cambridge, Cambridge University Press.

Keogh, T., Barnes, P., Joiner, R. and Littleton, K. (2000) 'Gender, pair composition and computer versus paper presentations of an English language task', *Educational Psychology*, vol. 20, no. 1, pp. 33–44.

Kuhn, M.H. and McPartland, T.S. (1954) 'An empirical investigation of self-attitudes', *American Sociological Review*, vol. 19, pp. 68–76.

Kvale, S. (1996) *InterViews: An Introduction to Qualitative Research Interviewing*, London, Sage.

McAdams, D.P. (2006) *The Redemptive Self: Stories Americans Live By*, Oxford, Oxford University Press.

Marcia, J.E. (1966) 'Development and validation of ego-identity status', *Journal of Personality and Social Psychology*, vol. 3, pp. 551–8.

Maybin, J. (1994) 'Children's voices: talk, knowledge and identity' in Graddol, D., Maybin, J. and Stierer, B. (eds) *Researching Language and Literacy in Social Context: A Reader*, Clevedon, Multilingual Matters/The Open University.

Maybin, J. (2001) 'Language, struggle and voice: the Bakhtin/Volosinov writings' in Wetherell, M., Taylor, S. and Yates, S. (eds) *Discourse Theory and Practice*, London, Sage/The Open University.

McAdams, D.P. (2006) *The Redemptive Self: Stories Americans Live By, Oxford, Oxford University Press.*

Mercer, N. (1995) *The Guided Construction of Knowledge*, Clevedon, Avon, Multilingual Matters.

Mercer, N. (2000) *Words and Minds: How We Use Language to Think Together*, London, Routledge.

Plummer, K. (2001) *Documents of Life 2: An Invitation to a Critical Humanism*, London, Sage.

Potter, J. and Wetherell, M. (1987) *Discourse and Social Psychology: Beyond Attitudes and Behaviour*, London, Sage.

Riessman, C.K. (2007) *Narrative Methods for the Social Sciences*, London, Sage.

Stanley, L. (ed.) (1984) *The Diaries of Hannah Cullwick, Victorian Maidservant*, New Brunswick, NJ, Rutgers University Press.

Stern, D.N. (1985) *The Interpersonal World of the Infant: A View from Psychoanalysis and Developmental Psychology*, New York, Basic Books.

Swindells, J. (1989) 'Liberating the subject? Autobiography and women's history' in Personal Narratives Group and Barbre, J.W. (eds) *Interpreting Women's Lives: Feminist Theory and Personal Narratives*, Bloomington, IN, Indiana University Press.

Thomas, W.I. and Znaniecki, F. (1958) *The Polish Peasant in Europe and America*, New York, Dover Publications.

Wetherell, M. (1998) ' Positioning and interpretative repertoires: conversation analysis and post-structuralism in dialogue', *Discourse and Society*, vol. 9, pp. 431–56.

Wetherell, M. and Potter, J. (1992) *Mapping the Language of Racism: Discourse and the Legitimation of Exploitation*, London, Harvester Wheatsheaf.

Wilkinson, S. (1987) 'Exploration of self and other in a developing relationship' in Burnett, R., McGhee, P. and Clarke, D.D. (eds) *Accounting for Relationships: Explanation, Representation and Knowledge*, London, Methuen.

CHAPTER 9

# Doing thematic analysis

## Contents


Aims 282

1 Introduction 282

2 What is thematic analysis? 282

2.1 Banal or informal thematic analysis 283

2.2 Epistemology and ontology 285

3 The process of doing thematic analysis 286

3.1 Research questions 286

3.2 Analysing data through thematic analysis 289

3.3 Thematic analysis by two researchers 297

3.4 The constituents of high-quality research 303

4 Concluding issues 306

References 306

Appendix: Interview transcript 307

# Aims

This chapter aims to:

- demonstrate one technique for analysing qualitative data – thematic analysis
- equip you with the tools to carry out a thematic analysis of interview data.

# 1 Introduction

The previous chapter gave you an overview of qualitative research and introduced you to a variety of qualitative approaches to research. This chapter has a more practical focus. It narrows the focus on qualitative research to thematic analysis, the method of analysis you will be using for your qualitative research project (TMA 05), which will be discussed in Chapter 10. The main aim of this chapter is to introduce you to thematic analysis, demonstrate how it can be done and to allow you an opportunity to do a practice thematic analysis before you analyse interview data in this way for TMA 05. It starts by explaining what thematic analysis is before outlining the process involved in doing it and presenting examples of thematic analysis of the same interview by two researchers. The final part of the chapter presents some practical steps that can be taken to make thematic analysis systematic and open to scrutiny. The chapter should not be treated as an exhaustive account of the techniques involved in thematic analysis, but rather as a guide to the principles and assumptions that underpin thematic analysis and an exploration of how researchers' theoretical ideas affect the analyses they conduct. You will need to refer to the appendix to this chapter, which is an interview transcript (complete with line numbers) as you work through the chapter.

# 2 What is thematic analysis?

Thematic analysis is a way of organising interview and other written qualitative material to draw out meanings in the form of *themes*. Themes are recurrent topics, ideas and statements that are identified by seeing the patterns in ideas or experiences from one person or across several people. These patterns are then brought together into a single category and labelled by an expression from the data or a phrase devised by the researcher. Some people refer to this as a process for 'encoding' or 'indexing' qualitative information, using words rather than numbers, while others avoid calling the process encoding since coding has quantitative associations. Thematic analysis is the most commonly used form of qualitative analysis and many researchers do a form of thematic analysis first before undertaking more detailed analyses using other analytical tools or techniques. Its popularity means that researchers often do thematic analysis without spelling out all the steps they took to arrive at their themes. However, as in all processes of research and analysis, it is important to be systematic. There are techniques that can be applied to ensure that qualitative analysis is both rigorous and demonstrably so, even if the final result will always be unique because different researchers bring their different understandings and experience to their analyses. Some approaches to qualitative research take specific perspectives. For example, you have already seen that discourse analysis situates itself within a specific and complex theoretical framework. This is not the case for thematic analysis, which is not associated with a particular perspective or theoretical framework, but is an analytic technique used by people from a range of different perspectives. However, any research is embedded within a theoretical framework (perspective) and thematic analysis is informed by ideas about the nature of language and assumptions about ontology (i.e. what it is to be human).

## 2.1 Banal or informal thematic analysis

Thematic analysis is a routine part of everyday life. For example, many cultures tell stories that have a proverb attached. Aesop, who was enslaved in sixth-century BCE Greece, told fables that have a moral. The moral or proverb is a condensation of the story that constitutes a thematic analysis of it.

### Activity 9.1

As you read the following Aesop's fable, try to work out what the proverb it is telling might be:

**THE FOUR OXEN AND THE LION**

*A Lion used to prowl about a field in which Four Oxen used to dwell. Many a time he tried to attack them; but whenever he came near they turned their tails to one another, so that whichever way he approached them he was met by the horns of one of them. At last, however, they fell a-quarrelling among themselves, and each went off to pasture alone in a separate corner of the field. Then the Lion attacked them one by one and soon made an end of all four.*

*(Aesopfables.com, 2007)*

The proverb associated with this story is a well-known aphorism: 'United we stand, divided we fall'. This is the theme of the story.

While knowing proverbs that are common in our cultures may be seen as passive knowledge that we have picked up without making any effort, we also make active use of thematic analysis in our everyday lives. In order to illustrate this, consider the following everyday example. Imagine you meet a friend, whom you have not seen for a number of months, in a restaurant one night. In the three hours or so you spend together you discuss a range of subjects, exchanging experiences and feelings about the events of your lives during the time you have not seen each other. The next day you meet another friend, who knows you both. She asks how the restaurant friend is and you relate the details of the previous evening's conversation. It is unlikely that you will repeat the news exchanged in the order and manner in which it was discussed the previous night. Instead, you will order the information and relate it according to your own understanding, perhaps using quotes from your friend to illustrate your points. For example, you might talk about her relationships: she has a new partner and says she is happy but you detected some problems because she didn't want to talk about that too much. You might discuss her job, which she said is going well but you think she looks tired and so perhaps the job is difficult. In doing this you are engaging in a form of informal data analysis: you are restructuring the actual event and explaining it. Furthermore, you are explaining it in a way that relates to the sorts of questions that you want answered about your friend. In a similar way, themes in thematic analysis are identified in relation to specific research questions.

All of us engage in this informal type of research, and therefore also in informal data analysis, on a daily basis. In order to maintain our sense of the world, we constantly arrange incoming information into themes and use our existing knowledge and experiences to make sense of it (see the discussion of schemas and memory in Book 1, *Mapping Psychology*, Chapter 8). In relating information to others, we order it and elaborate upon it to ensure that our audience understands the points we wish to communicate. To this extent each one of us is already experienced in the art of thematic analysis. We could say that informal thematic analysis is a banal, or everyday, process. In analysing research transcripts, thematic analysis is employed in a more formal way and therefore the process requires breaking down so that the mechanism for achieving analysis can be understood and applied in a more systematic way as part of formal research.

### Activity 9.2

The appendix to this chapter contains an extract from an interview by an undergraduate psychology student, who was exploring facets of what it means to 'age successfully' (i.e. to be healthy and happy in old age). The interviewee/participant is a retired nursing sister, a woman in her seventies to whom we've given the pseudonym 'Jess'.

Read through the interview transcript now and try to identify and note down two themes related to the question of 'successful ageing' that seem significant to you. Please save these so that you can look back at them later on.

Identifying themes is the first step in doing thematic analysis of qualitative data. Since we have everyday experience of thematic analysis, this process is perhaps simpler than first appears. However, the identification of themes in research is guided by theory, including epistemology, ontology and more specific theories about the subject of the research.

## 2.2 Epistemology and ontology

All research is informed by epistemology (the theory of knowledge) and ontology (the theory of the nature of existence, which in this case is the theory of what it is to be a person). One reason that thematic analysis is so widely used, however, is that it can be utilised by researchers who work from within different theoretical frameworks and perspectives. It can be employed within a social constructionist theoretical framework as part of what has been termed the 'turn to language'. This involves viewing language as constructing the ways in which we see the world, rather than as simply reflecting reality (see Book 1, Chapter 1, Section 5.2 for a discussion of this). However, it is also employed by those who take a realist, rather than social constructionist perspective, which treats what people say as reflecting reality. In both cases, thematic analysis is concerned with producing detailed analyses of meanings. The ontology that underpins thematic analysis considers that people are sense making and able to reflect on their experiences. This means that thematic analysis rests on the assumption that people both produce meanings and read them (i.e. make sense of them). Language is central to these processes of meaning making and meanings can be seen as organised into themes, which are produced in talk and writing.

The examples of thematic analysis given in this chapter start from a social constructionist theoretical framework (which assumes that people construct meanings through language) and ontology (which assumes that people are meaning making). However, despite sharing these broad theoretical perspectives (and so assumptions about epistemology and ontology), the examples also illustrate how using different theoretical frameworks in relation to the specific subject matter of the research produces different emphases in analysis of the same material.

### Summary Section 2

- Thematic analysis is a way of organising interview and other written qualitative material to draw out meanings in the form of themes.
- Themes are recurrent topics, ideas and statements that are identified by seeing the patterns in ideas or experiences from one person or across several people.
- Thematic analysis is an everyday, banal or informal process, which is employed in a more formal way in research. It is widely used because it can be employed by researchers who work from within different theoretical frameworks.
- Researchers who do thematic analysis share ontology that people are meaning making and reflect on their experiences.

# 3 The process of doing thematic analysis

This section deals with the practicalities of doing research. It discusses the research process from the setting of the research question to doing analyses of interview transcripts. It does not detail the process of doing interviews since you will not be doing these in DSE212, but instead, allows you to spend more time becoming familiar with thematic analysis.

## 3.1 Research questions

Research questions are at the heart of any research. A good research question helps to guide the research process, whereas an irrelevant research question can lead to poor and irrelevant research. Developing the overall research question to guide the research process takes time and thought because research questions differ from spontaneously arising everyday questions in two ways. First, research questions are developed from theoretical understandings of particular issues and from readings of the background literature so that research does not 'reinvent the wheel'. For that reason, it is important that anybody starting research situates themselves within a perspective. For those new to research, this can seem a daunting task. However, researchers generally situate themselves in the perspective adopted by the literature that has most impressed them and that they want to draw on. In order to do your research, therefore, you will need to ensure that you are clear which theoretical framework is being employed in the literature you read. Once you have done this, you can think about a research question that makes sense within this framework.

Second, research questions have to be posed in ways that allow them to be answered through research – that is, they have to be feasible. This means that, for example, all the topics discussed in a research interview should be guided by the overarching research question. Research questions thus provide both a theoretical and a practical focus to the research undertaken. They also assist researchers in identifying the topics to be discussed in the interview, which guide the analysis. It is only when the research question has been devised that it is possible to work out what kind of method would fit with your theoretical framework and answer your research question. When students first start to do research they sometimes find it difficult to understand that it is not acceptable to select a theoretical framework after data collection. However, there is a logical sequence to the research process that makes it coherent: the theoretical framework in which researchers situate themselves has an impact on the research question they devise, which then affects the methods chosen.

While it is essential to follow the sequence described above, qualitative research is frequently an iterative process – meaning that researchers may go back to an earlier stage in the research in response to what has been learned. This means that, sometimes, the research question is adapted or refined once some data have been collected. However, please note that, although you can refine your research question after data collection has started, it is crucial that your initial question is well embedded within a theoretical framework and so makes sense within that framework. The question must also be specific enough to allow a precise focus for collecting the data, otherwise it is not possible to know what, for example, to ask when conducting an interview or what to look for when analysing data. The following quotation provides an example of a piece of research where the initial research question was modified after an initial period of data collection.

> *Morse's [1992] initial research question was 'What is the role of gift-giving in the patient-nurse relationship?' ... Morse and her research assistants conducted semi-structured interviews with nurses. During the initial*

> *stages of data analysis, it became clear that gift-giving was merely a way of negotiating a certain type of relationship. It played a symbolic role that could potentially be played by other actions. This led Morse to broaden the focus of the study and to ask 'How does the nurse–patient/patient–nurse relationship develop?' ... They conducted further interviews, this time with nurses who had themselves been patients ... .*
>
> *(Willig, 2001, p. 41)*

In a similar way, researchers may refine or adapt their research question if all the themes they identify as a result of their initial examination of interview data seem irrelevant to it. For example, if their research focus was on age and all the themes they identified were about gender, they may well consider changing their research question. The process of refining or even changing the initial research question is a crucial part of qualitative research and, indeed, the insight that a change in focus has become necessary can be considered a finding in its own right. Any change to the research question must be well documented and argued so that readers can understand, and be convinced of, the rationale for the change. It is important to remember that, for the study to be coherent, any new research question will have to be embedded within the same theoretical framework as the first one.

There is a difference between a research hypothesis, which is generally used in quantitative research, and a research question. You will recall that a research hypothesis makes a prediction about the result. In the case of an experiment the hypothesis predicts that manipulating independent variable 'A', will lead to change in dependent variable 'B'. Research questions in qualitative research do not make predictions. As we have pointed out, qualitative research is about exploring people's experiences and understanding social practices. It is centrally concerned with the *interpretation* of meanings. The research question in the study of successful ageing that you began to consider in Activity 9.2 reflected this by focusing on experiences and meanings. It was: How does a woman in her seventies construct what it means for her to live a happy and worthwhile life at her age (i.e. what it means to age successfully)? This research question is underpinned by a social constructionist epistemology and an ontology which starts from the assumption that people reflect on their experiences. Based on media reports and on reading health literature, the student who conducted the interview had previously taken it for granted that ageing is an unhappy process of deterioration in skills and health and reduced social contacts. She got the idea for the study from reading the psychological literature on ageing. From that literature, she arrived at a theoretical understanding that ageing is not necessarily problematic or unhappy. She therefore could not have devised a research question that made theoretical sense and was answerable and interesting, without reading the literature and thinking about the theoretical perspective in which it was located. Understanding how a qualitative research question is developed from theory and relevant literature and how it guides both methods and analysis is central to an appreciation of the goals of qualitative research.

## 3.2 Analysing data through thematic analysis

There are three post-interview stages necessary to conducting successful thematic analysis: transcription; familiarising yourself with the data (in this case, the transcript); and coding (or indexing). Each of these takes time and effort, but each contributes to the production of high-quality thematic analysis. Each is detailed below.

### Stage 1: Transcription

When interviews are the method used in a research project, the interviews themselves provide the 'raw data'. It is normal practice to record interviews and to produce typed transcripts by transcribing the interview and numbering each line from beginning to end.

#### *Activity 9.3*

Spend a few minutes thinking about and jotting down the different types of information available in an audio or video recording of an interview which may no longer be available when the interview is transcribed.

You may have noted that information such as tone of voice, length of pauses and non-verbal information may well be removed when interviews are transcribed. Transcription conventions vary depending on the kind of analysis that will be conducted and, in particular, on the level of analysis to be done. It is possible, for example, just to record the words said, but it is also possible to spend more time transcribing people's ums, ers, hesitations, pauses, laughter, etc. These differences in transcription mean that the same interview can provide different kinds of information. This can be important because different emphases can change the meaning of an account. Hancock (1998) argues that good quality transcribing is not simply transferring words from the recording to the page, because when people are in conversation, part of what they communicate comes from how they say what they are saying. Tone and inflection show various feelings and meanings. In the quotation below, Hancock gives an example of how recording emphasis and intonation can change dramatically how we read the meaning of the phrase: 'He was alright':

> *'He was ALRIGHT' (He was alright, I liked him)*
>
> *'HE was alright' (He was alright but I wasn't so keen on the others)*
>
> *'He WAS alright' (He used to be but he isn't now)*
>
> *'He was alright?' (Well, you might think so but I don't)*
>
> *By listening and noting the intensity and feeling in the interviewee's voice it is possible to detect the following:*
>
> - *Positive/negative continuum: Whether something was seen as good or bad.*
> - *Certainty/uncertainty: How sure the interviewee was about what he said.*
> - *Enthusiasm/reluctance: How happy or supportive the interviewee was about the topic being discussed.*
>
> *(Hancock, 1998, p. 15)*

In any research project you will need to decide whether the additional information you gain from recording emphasis and emotion is important to addressing your research question and so worth the effort of spending time doing detailed transcription. You may also choose to use a method, like audio recording, which gives less information than video recording, but is less intrusive and so ethically preferable or more practicable in a particular research project. Research participants may also have preferences for, or objections to, particular kinds of recording.

The level of transcription (and so of analysis) to be done will depend on the research question and how much information is required to answer it. However, because it is extremely time-consuming to transcribe non-linguistic detail, many researchers concentrate only on recording the words. It is therefore a good idea to keep a copy of the audio, or videotapes to enable you to refer back to this information. When researchers are transcribing their data, many find it useful to jot down their reactions to, and reflections on, it. This is because the information available from an audio or video record is different from that evident in a written transcript.

### Stage 2: Familiarisation

Having completed the transcript, your next step is to keep your research question (i.e. the focus of your research) in mind as you read through the interview transcript. Researchers always need to read a transcript a number of times to familiarise themselves with the participant's responses and to think about how they relate to the research question/focus of the research. Thinking about what your participant has said and, later, to how your themes relate to the research question or focus is central to producing good analysis since you may identify themes that are interesting, but have nothing to do with your research focus. In research projects, many themes are put aside at this stage as noteworthy, but irrelevant to the research project currently being done. If, however, a researcher found that most of the themes they came up with were not related to their research focus, they might consider that the research question was not as relevant as they had first considered and, since the research process is iterative, might go back and refine it. The reading and rereading of the transcript is central to the analytic process as it helps you to become familiar with the data, attending to the participant's words in detail in order to present an accurate record. Remember that the aim of the analysis is to draw out meaningful themes from the participant's own words. It can also be useful to think of the link between the interview and the transcript. The raw data – the audio or video record – comes between the interview itself (which is no longer accessible) and the transcript from which you are working. It can be helpful to return to the raw data at various points during the analysis to 'check out' your interpretations by seeing whether they still seem justified once you can see and/or hear extra-linguistic cues.

## Stage 3: Coding

Once you have read through the transcript several times you can begin the process of *coding* (or indexing) the data. In simple terms, coding is the process of giving labels or codes to your textual data – this can be words, sentences or meaningful 'chunks' of the transcript. It is possible to distinguish different levels of coding, the term 'level' referring to the amount of interpretation being applied to the data. Langdridge (2004) discusses three levels of coding: *first order* (descriptive); *second order* (combining descriptive codes); and *third order* or pattern coding, which is thematic analysis.

First-order coding is the lowest level of coding. Here, your aim is to organise and categorise the data in the transcript by capturing chunks of meaning and giving them codes or labels. This process is purely descriptive with minimal interpretation. In order to do this you will need to read through the transcript several times looking for ideas which appear and may recur in the text. You may well need to change or revise the labels or codes that you first devise if they seem not adequately to capture the meaning that you intend. You are likely to find that you end up with quite a lot of descriptive codes at this stage. Some will be more relevant to your research question than others.

## Example of first-order coding

In the coded extract presented below, the analytic focus is on what Jess says about coming to terms with life after the death of her husband and developing and maintaining an active and busy life on her own. The student whose research project the extract comes from identified the following codes and developed a key for them so that she could mark up the extract that follows in order to make visible how she arrived at her analyses and so that she could easily see which quotations illustrate which of her themes.

---

### *Key*

CT = coming to terms

SR = self-reliance

CR = caring responsibilities

APl = attachment to place

CPe = connection to people

*Note:* A full stop in brackets (.) shows a short pause.

**Interviewer:**

I'm very interested in your ideas and what you think is important in maintaining an active and busy life. Please take your time to, sort of think about it.

**Jess:**

Yes, hmmm, (.) well, since I retired and after the death of my husband (.) I had a lot to sort out, but came to terms with it **CT**, to realise that I had to stand on my own two feet (.) **SR** and, err, I was not interested in any further – any work, it wasn't, you know, sort of at all necessary and I felt that I had served my time in the profession. I was, however, part way involved looking after my mother-in-law – **CR** who was a great mother-in-law and she lived till she was 91, but, erm, she died peacefully in hospital, and I have still, since then, kept a very good rapport with my sister-in-law who lives nearby. We meet up each week **CPe** and go out for days, etc. etc. Err, after my husband died, erm, but it was prior to this, erm, it was when my mother died, in the village where I was brought up there was my nephew who lived in this house. So, when my mother died, my nephew was on his own (.) and my husband and I went up once a month just to see all was well and to see to his domestic chores. **CR** Being a man, not the least bit domesticated.

**Interviewer:**

[*laughs*]

**Jess:**

and I, we, I did this and after my husband died I still went up once a month **CR** and my nephew and I – he was like a son to me **CPe** [...] Because, after my husband died (.) – I can remember to this day, about six months afterwards, saying, 'Jess, you've got to go on holiday'(.) and I walked across the road, [*chuckles*] to the travel agents, I knew the girl in there.

**Interviewer:**

Yes.

**Jess:**

I said, 'Have you got any flights to Jersey?' This is where I used to go on holiday (.) **APl**

**Interviewer:**

Yes.

**Jess:**

with my husband, you see, before we started travelling to France. I loved France. **APl** She said, 'Yes, there are some flights.' I said, 'Well, I'll ring you back in an hour.'

**Interviewer:**

Yes.

**Jess:**

And I rang up my friends Barbara and Will that keep a guest house. **CPe**

**Interviewer:**

Yes.

**Jess:**

Er, in Jersey, a private hotel. I rang up Barbara – 'Jess', she said, 'just come.'

**Interviewer:**

Ah lovely.

**Jess:**

And I've been going there twice a year since, till they retired from the hotel. I still keep in touch with them, **CPe** and I found another hotel, I've been going twice a year ever since (.) Even after Richard died, you know, I thought 'I've got to go back.' **APl**

**Interviewer:**

Good for you.

**Jess:**

And one year I went three times. I felt as if I had to get away (.) and come to terms with things (.) **CT**

**Interviewer:**

Yes.

**Jess:**

And funnily enough I found the peace and quiet on that island (.) to get myself gathered together. **CT**

**Interviewer:**

Yes.

**Jess:**

To sort myself out and realise (.) that life has got to go on **CT** (.) You can't just sit back.

---

In the above example you can see that the transcript has been 'coded' in a way that simply describes what Jess says. Jess refers to her connection to people – family and friends – and these are coded **CPe**. She also refers to her attachment to important places (**APl**) including France and Jersey and to her caring connections and responsibilities (**CR**). Note that there is little attempt to interpret or to explain at this stage – you are simply aiming to catch and label the main ideas within the data. You may well find that as you proceed with the analyses, you need to change and revise the labels you use to capture the meaning of your participant's words. Remember, too, that while the student has demonstrated that her 'coding' does come from the data, there may well be additional themes that another researcher might highlight.

## Second-order coding

At the second level of coding your aim is to go beyond simple description of the data and begin to interpret the meanings of your participant's words. This will usually involve devising labels that encompass some of the first-order descriptive codes and so capture the meaning of larger segments of the data, but they could be additional codes that you may not have noticed before, but which begin to interpret, rather than simply describe, what your participant has said. These are all superordinate constructs in that they are more generic than the first-order descriptive codes. At this stage you are likely to reduce the number of codes you use as the data are sorted into broader and more encompassing categories.

An example of a second-order descriptive code that captures the meaning of large segments of data from the above transcript extract is the 'importance of activity'. This descriptive code incorporates some of the data that has been first-order coded as 'connection to people' and as 'self-reliance'. Jess refers to a variety of activities in the interview, including meeting up with old colleagues (line 64, see full extract in appendix), taking holidays (lines 29–48), and interests at home (lines 76–9). These different activities can be coded together into a superordinate construct (that constitutes a second-order code) to show the importance of engagement in activity for Jess.

A further example of a superordinate construct is 'emotional connections', which combines connections to people and attachment to places. Jess refers to family connections (e.g. mother-in-law, sister-in-law and nephew) (lines 10–17), to friends (line 36) and to ex-colleagues (line 64). She also makes reference to a variety of places which hold special meaning for her. She does not bring these issues together. However, as we begin to interpret the transcript, we can begin to see the importance of connections to people and places in giving meaning to Jess's life.

## Third-order coding and thematic analysis

Third-order coding and thematic analysis are the final stages of coding and involve drawing out the overarching themes within the data. At this higher level, your task is to identify superordinate constructs that are more global and which identify larger-scale patterns than those you identified in second-order coding. These are the themes that give thematic analysis its name and which capture the meaning of your descriptive and interpretative codes. You are likely at this stage to reduce your overall number of themes down to a few key ideas, in a similar way to the example in Section 1.1 about reporting your meeting with one friend to another mutual friend. This process is also known as pattern coding, as you are looking for patterns within the data. This is the basis of thematic analysis – the drawing out of overarching themes which represent more general concepts and patterns and often incorporate several of your lower-level codes together with the identification of quotations that exemplify them.

In the excerpt from the interview transcript above, Jess talks about the importance of activity in her daily life as a way of dealing with feelings and creating meaning for herself. For example, in lines 24–6 she says '*after my husband died (.) – I can remember to this day, about six months afterwards, saying, 'Jess, you've got to go on holiday'*. Later in the interview she says '*And one year I went three times. I felt as if I had to get away (.) and come to terms with things*' (lines 47–8). Later still (in the full extract, but not in the excerpt above), she explicitly combines the ideas of coping through activity when she says *'There are days (.) I do feel empty. But I look at it and say, (.) 'Get up and do something.'* (lines 56–9). The overall meaning of this recurrent idea is captured by the third-order code (or theme) 'use of activity to give meaning and direction'. This theme captures the meaning of the second-order code 'importance of activity', but it is superordinate to it (and so third order) in that it also indicates the function that activity is serving and that Jess is using it strategically. A great deal of what she says in the interview can be understood through this third-order code: 'use of activity to give meaning and direction'.

In order to carry out higher-level coding it is helpful to stand back from your data and try to summarise the main ideas which recur in the transcript. This means that you will need to develop a *narrative* or story that links the themes together for the write-up of the project.

### Activity 9.4

Now read through the completed transcript of the interview again (in the appendix to this chapter) and carry out your own thematic analysis starting with familiarisation, then applying descriptive (first-order) and higher-order (second- and third-order – or pattern) coding. For the purpose of this exercise, you should narrow down the focus of the research question to: What issues does Jess identify as important for her in maintaining an active and busy life? Keep this research focus clearly in mind when reading through the transcript. Please note down your themes and keep them for later use. You might also want to consider whether you identified different themes from those you noted in Activity 9.2 since you have now read more about thematic analysis and are addressing a narrower research question. We have allowed time for you to complete the thematic analysis described above by making this chapter shorter than the others in this book because this activity is invaluable preparation for your own qualitative project work.

## 3.3 Thematic analysis by two researchers

The previous chapter introduced the idea that insights gained from qualitative data will depend as much on the theoretical position of the researcher or research group as on the focus or purpose of the research. It pointed out that the aims of analysis often differ and that this is at least partly because researchers sometimes take different ontological, epistemological and theoretical positions. This means that, while researchers do frequently agree on aspects of analysis, different researchers can 'read' the same interview transcript in different ways. In Boxes 9.1 and 9.2, two researchers do third-order, thematic analysis of Jess's interview transcript. Both researchers have done their thematic analyses from a social constructionist theoretical framework and a shared ontology (that humans are reflective, meaning making and interpreting). However, they differ in the more specific theories they employ and so produce some themes in common as well as somewhat different readings of the same data. The fact that qualitative analyses produce different readings does not mean, however, that researchers simply make intuitive guesses about how to interpret their data. The final part of this chapter (Section 2.4) discusses ways in which researchers can ensure that they produce high-quality, systematic thematic analyses.

As you read what Researcher 1 has written (in Box 9.1), note that she takes a *humanistic theoretical approach* (described in Book 1, Chapter 9) and so focuses on notions of agency and positive engagement with the world.

**9.1 Researcher 1: Thematic analysis of Jess's interview transcript**

The following themes emerge, for me, on initial reading of this transcript. First, the underpinning sense of *connectedness* to people and places over time [Theme 1]. Jess is clearly involved with her family across generations, she was, '*... involved looking after my mother-in-law – who was a great mother-in-law*' [lines 9–10]. Since her mother-in-law's death Jess has:

> *... kept a very good rapport with my sister-in-law who lives nearby. We meet up each week and go out for days ... [lines 12–14].*

She mentions that after her own mother died:

> *... my nephew [who lived with her mother] ... was on his own (.) and my husband and I went up once a month just to see all was well ... after my husband died I still went up once a month and my nephew ... he was like a son to me [lines 16–23].*

Friends too are clearly a feature of her life:

> *... I have good friends who I sometimes go out to dinner with, or they invite me down to lunch and my way of repaying their hospitality is, I take them out for a meal ... [lines 88–91].*

She also often meets with old colleagues. In terms of places, Jess offers us the extra information that her mother died, '*in the village where I was brought up*' [line 16], indicating perhaps its importance to Jess. '*... Jersey, ... where I used to go on holiday (.) ... with my husband*' [lines 29–32], clearly was and is important to her. After a break from holidaying in Jersey, seemingly of a good few years, she decided six months after her husband died to return and she says, '*I've been going twice a year ever since*' [line 44].

She also at this time renewed her connections with old friends on Jersey:

> *... I rang up my friends Barbara and Will, that keep a guest house ... she [Barbara] said, 'just come' [lines 36–40].*

Jess's sense of *agency* and *ability to take action* [Theme 2] also feature strongly in my reading – she appears to be decisive and clear about what she needs to do:

> *... after the death of my husband (.) I had a lot to sort out, but came to terms with it, to realise that I had to stand on my own two feet (.) ... I was not interested in any further ... work, it wasn't ... necessary and I felt that I had served my time in the profession [lines 4–9].*

She later states that she has no financial problems. The fact that she juxtaposes this with caring for her mother-in-law is interesting. Seemingly from the start of this new chapter, which began with the death of her husband, she was clear about not needing in any sense to do paid work. There are numerous examples of her telling herself that she has to do something to make herself feel better. For example:

> *I can remember to this day, about six months afterwards, saying, 'Jess you've got to go on holiday'(.) And I walked across the road, [chuckles], to the travel agents [lines 24–27].*
>
> *There are days (.) I do feel empty ... But I look at it and say (.) [slaps her wrist] 'Get up and do something' [lines 56–59].*

She is also clear and seemingly comfortable about making some changes:

> *... I won't cook now like I used to [for friends]. I've not the same interest in it. I will cook for myself [lines 91–92].*

Jess seems very *positively engaged with life* [Theme 3]. The tone of the transcript is very lively, with diverse interests evident. She goes '*... out every day* *and I often meet up with old colleagues*' [line 64]. In addition she spends time alone at home:

> *I like to do the puzzles and ... word games ... I read ... I'm quite cosmopolitan in what I read [lines 76–82].*
>
> *I am not a television addict ... I prefer to listen, you know, to music ... But not the Radio One, you know. [chuckles] I like to hear discussions [lines 77–82].*

*(Manning, 1998)*

Researcher 2's theoretical framework is *feminist* (see Book 2, *Challenging Psychological Issues*, Chapter 3). She therefore highlights gender issues; for example, to do with caring and mothering and connectedness and interdependence (see Box 9.2).

### 9.2 Researcher 2: Thematic analysis of Jess's interview transcript

On reading the transcript, a number of themes emerge.

#### (i) Loss and change

The interviewee refers on a number of occasions to loss in her life and subsequent changes:

> *... and after the death of my husband (.) I had a lot to sort out, but came to terms with it, to realise that I had to stand on my own two feet (.) and, err, I was not interested in any further – any work, it wasn't, you know, sort of at all necessary and I felt that I had served my time in the profession [lines 4–9].*
>
> *Errr, after my husband died, erm, but it was prior to this, erm, it was when my mother died, in the village where I was brought up there was my nephew who lived in this house. So, when my mother died, my nephew was on his own ... and I, we, I did this and after my husband died [lines 14–22].*
>
> *Because, after my husband died (.) – I can remember to this day, about six months afterwards, saying, 'Jess, you've got to go on holiday' [lines 24–26].*
>
> *Even after Richard [her nephew] died, you know, I thought 'I've got to go back' ... and one year I went three times. I felt as if I had to get away (.) and come to terms with things [lines 44–48].*

### *(ii) Caring/mothering*

The participant clearly has taken on and currently takes on roles that involve looking after others and relating to others from a maternal standpoint:

> *... my nephew was on his own (.) and my husband and I went up once a month just to see all was well. And see to his domestic chores. Being a man, not the least bit domesticated ... I did this and after my husband died I still went up once a month and my nephew and I – he was like a son to me [lines 17–23].*

There is clearly a gendered component to this, the notion of the nephew being a man:

> *And see to his domestic chores. Being a man, not the least bit domesticated [lines 19–20].*

### *(iii) Social networks*

The interviewee mentions friends, family and colleagues as potential sources of social support:

> *But I have good friends who I sometimes go out to dinner with, or they invite me down to lunch and my way of repaying their hospitality is, I take them out for a meal because I won't cook now like I used to [lines 88–91].*
>
> *I go out every day and I often meet up with old colleagues [line 64].*

### *(iv) Independence*

The participant recognises her position and status following her changing circumstances: retirement, family bereavement, caregiving, etc:

> *And funnily enough I found the peace and quiet on that island (.) to get myself gathered together ... To sort out myself and realise (.) that life has got to go on (.) You can't just sit back ... There are days (.) I do feel empty ... But I look at it and say (.) [slaps her wrist] 'Get up and do something' [lines 50–9].*
>
> *Y'know I'm quite content with life ... I don't and I'm going to be quite honest with you have any financial problems but then on the other hand I don't lead a social life so I don't have to spend a great deal on clothes, you know and that sort of thing [lines 83–8].*

*(Manning, 1998)*

Table 9.1 brings together the themes identified in the two analyses so they can easily be compared. In order to aid comparison, the themes are not presented in the order in which the researchers wrote about them, but reordered.

**Table 9.1 Comparison of the two researchers' thematic analyses**

| Researcher 1's themes | Researcher 2's themes |
| --- | --- |
| Connectedness – the extent to which Jess feels involved in relationships over time | Social networks – the support Jess experiences through her relationships |
| | Loss and change – losing people has resulted in changes in Jess's life |
| Positive engagement with life – Jess is lively with diverse interests | Caring/mothering – Jess looks after people, she mothers them |
| Agency and ability to take action – Jess is decisive and clear | Independence – Jess reflects on her current status and how she feels |

When the two thematic analyses are presented alongside each other, we can see that no themes are labelled in exactly the same way across the researchers. Nonetheless, it is possible to see that there are some areas that both researchers have highlighted, but that there are some differences in what they focus on – both in terms of overall themes and in terms of emphasis. As discussed above, qualitative research entails an interaction between the account produced by a participant and the meanings the researcher assigns to the data. You and the two researchers have each read the transcript and analysed themes focusing on the issues Jess identifies as important in maintaining an active and busy life. In order to do this, you have all used your own experiences and knowledge.

## Activity 9.5

Reread Boxes 9.1 and 9.2 looking particularly at the quotations each researcher uses to devise the themes they label and which are listed in Table 9.1 as well as the ways they describe those themes. Can you see any overlaps and/or differences between their analyses? Look back at your notes from Activities 9.2 and 9.4. Are there similarities and/or differences between the themes you initially picked out and those picked out by the researchers?

Although the two researchers have different styles for writing up their themes, it is important to note that they identify the same excerpts from the transcript as being central to addressing the research question. Not surprisingly, then, there are commonalities in the themes they analyse. For example, links can be made between the 'connectedness' theme (Researcher 1) and the 'social networks' theme (Researcher 2), or between 'positive engagement with life' (Researcher 1) and 'social networks' (Researcher 2). Similarly 'agency and ability to take action' (Researcher 1) can be viewed as having similarities to 'independence' (Researcher 2). However, there are important differences. Researcher 1 (Box 9. 1) tends to focus on Jess more as an individual and so includes a focus on agency and taking action, while Researcher 2 (Box 9.2) considers Jess more as a relational being and so has themes of 'loss and change' and 'caring/mothering'. It is important to note, however, that Researcher 1 has identified the theme of 'connectedness' while Researcher 2 has identified the theme of 'independence'. They thus seem to have some different emphases in their analyses, as well as having analysed some related themes. Of course, the researchers had more time to do their thematic analysis than you did and are experienced qualitative analysts who are familiar with the process described above. However, you might find that some of the themes you identified also overlapped with some of theirs, even if you labelled them somewhat differently.

As you read the two analyses, you can gain a greater understanding of the interpretations by thinking about the theoretical positions of the two researchers. While they do not discuss their theoretical frameworks in the short presentations of their thematic analyses, the researchers' different interpretations are likely to have arisen from their different theoretical frameworks. Researcher 1 focuses more on theories that emphasise human agency, while Researcher 2 focuses more on those that emphasise connectedness and interdependence. This is because Researcher 1 takes a *humanistic approach* (described in Book 1, Chapter 9) and so the notions of agency and positive engagement fit with this wider theoretical standpoint. Researcher 2 often uses *feminist principles* to understand the world and this emerges in the consideration of caring/mothering and its gendered component. If an attachment theorist were to conduct thematic analyses of the same interview, they would also focus on ties of affection, but would be more concerned with the impact of these ties on what Jess does and how she feels. It follows, then, that the interpretation of qualitative data involves some understanding of both the participant and the researcher. In qualitative research, the researcher is treated as an integral part of the interpretative process. So it is not only the experiences and beliefs of the participant that emerge from the thematic analysis but also the theoretical commitments of the researchers. For this reason, *reflexivity* – the process of researchers reflecting on how they have affected the research done (e.g. the questions asked in interviews and the issues focused on in analyses) – is important in qualitative research. This process is made easier if researchers are clear about the theoretical framework that informs their research. In studying any form of qualitative analysis you should keep these issues in mind and try to be as aware of the theoretical standpoints of the authors of the research (including yourself when you do research) as you are of the data you are analysing.

## 3.4 The constituents of high-quality research

Unlike the results of a statistical test, there is no right or wrong result of thematic analysis. Rather it is an interpretation of data, and interpretations are bound to vary between people and across space and time. This means that quantitative ways of assessing reliability and validity are not appropriate. For those new to qualitative analyses, this may seem to indicate that *any* reading of qualitative data is appropriate. This is, however, not the case. There are ways in which it is possible to check whether analyses are appropriate and plausible. Good qualitative analysis focuses on the research question and is consistent with the epistemological, ontological and theoretical frameworks from which the question arises. The analyses are not free-floating but can be demonstrated by reference to the transcript. In addition, they should not ignore examples that run counter to the themes identified, but should explain them or use them to revise and refine the themes. Throughout the analysis, the themes identified should be contextualised in relation to other research findings in the literature as well as to the data. For example, the theme of connectedness might be related to Mary Ainsworth's ideas about attachment beyond infancy. Ainsworth suggests that 'feelings of responsibility in caring for others in the family and/or a sense of family solidarity were important factors in successful resolution of mourning the loss of a family member' (1989, p. 714). Jess clearly feels both connected to her nephew and responsible for him after her husband's death. In addition, Ainsworth encourages the use of interview studies to research attachment beyond infancy – something that has been done in the study of Jess's ageing.

Overall, analyses should be able to demonstrate that they are plausible, convincing and fruitful in communicating the richness of the participant's experiences in ways that simply reading the transcript is unlikely to. Good analysis, therefore, explores the participant's meanings and enlarges understanding of the research topic while presenting sufficient data (e.g. quotations from transcripts) to make the basis of analyses clear and convince the reader (or allow them to disagree). While the two researchers presented above draw slightly different conclusions, each presents a convincing case and demonstrates how they have reached their conclusions. This is even more important when researchers are working with several transcripts from a number of participants and reading across them.

Since different people do thematic analysis in different ways, it is difficult to be entirely prescriptive about what constitutes a 'good' or 'bad' analysis.

However, researchers use criteria such as those in Box 9.3 to evaluate their qualitative analyses. Please note that these criteria will not be relevant to your thematic analysis since you will not be designing your own research study or working out a research question and will only be analysing themes from one participant (see Chapter 10). The box is presented so that you can see how researchers ensure that their thematic analyses are systematic and so that you can use the criteria presented for future reference.

### 9.3 Criteria for good thematic analysis

- *The variability in the data is represented.* If more than one person has been interviewed, this might mean that a range of views are represented. But even if the sample consists of only one person (as in the example above), contradictions, changes of mind, etc. should be included and fitted within codes or themes.
- *The transferability of findings* is established by clearly describing the characteristics of the sample (the interview participants in this case) so that readers can see the sorts of people from whom they have been produced. Many qualitative researchers (e.g. Silverman, 2000) suggest that the qualitative equivalent of statistical generalisability involves establishing the representativeness of a single participant or small sample on the basis of comparing them with similar others.
- *Dependability of the analyses* is established by providing an audit trail – i.e. enough information and quotations for it to be clear that the themes analysed are justified by the theoretical framework, the data and the literature.
- *Credibility and confirmability* are demonstrated by giving examples and/or checking interpretations with other researchers and sometimes with participants. All qualitative researchers aim to present sufficient quotations from their data and to locate their findings in the literature clearly enough to convince their readers that their analyses are plausible.
- *Evidence that the sample used, the data collected and the analyses done* are appropriate to the research question should be presented in the write-up.

As you do your own thematic analysis, ask yourself the following questions to help you evaluate what you produce:

- To what extent does the analysis you have done provide an answer to the research question? Does it instead, or in addition, raise new questions that require to be researched?
- Are the themes clearly labelled and described?
- Do the themes reflect the meanings that have emerged rather than the topics raised by the researcher during the interview? To illustrate this important point, look again at the transcript extract and the analyses in

Section 3.3, Boxes 9.1 and 9.2 above. The themes identified reflect the analysts' interpretations of the content of the participant's answer not the initial question asked, which was about how to maintain an active and busy life ('What do you think is important in maintaining an active and busy life?').

- Is the meaning of each theme clearly described, with sufficient quotations from the transcript to support the meaning?
- Have all irrelevant themes and quotations (i.e. those that do not relate to the research focus) been excluded? Remember that if all the themes and quotations you identify are irrelevant, you should reconsider, and perhaps refine or adapt, your research question.
- Does the analysis interpret the data as well as describing them?
- Is the interpretation grounded in theory?
- Has the analysis taken account of counter instances (e.g. where a participant contradicts themselves or makes a specific exception to a general point) in the transcript and considered omissions (i.e. things you might expect to have been said that have not been said)?
- Have you considered how your understandings and theoretical commitments have had an impact on the analyses you have produced (i.e. have you been reflexive)?

## Summary Section 3

- Several different stages are involved in carrying out thematic analysis, and there are different levels at which the data can be 'coded'.
- In thematic analysis researchers will bring different theoretical and epistemological perspectives to the analysis.
- As a result, different researchers are likely to produce different analyses of the same data.
- A good qualitative analysis must, however, be grounded in theory, address the research question it sets out to address and be able convincingly to demonstrate that it is rooted in the data (e.g. in the transcripts). In order to do this, it is important to consider how the researcher's views and experiences affect the interpretations they make (i.e. reflexivity).

# 4 Concluding issues

This chapter introduced you to the process of conducting thematic analysis and allowed you to try it out for yourself. Having done so, you have a good grounding in the basics of qualitative analysis and are now ready to move on to doing the thematic analysis that constitutes TMA 05. The chapter that follows explains the task you will do for TMA 05 and places the thematic analysis in the context of the whole process of undertaking qualitative research.

# References

Aesopfables.com (2007) *Aesop's Fables: Online Collection* [online], http://www.aesopfables.com/cgi/aesop1.cgi?2&TheFourOxenandtheLion (Accessed 13 February 2007).

Ainsworth, M.D. (1989) 'Attachments beyond infancy', *American Psychologist*, vol. 44, no. 4, pp. 709–16.

Hancock, B. (1998) *Trent Focus for Research and Development in Primary Health Care: An Introduction to Qualitative Research* [online] Nottingham, Trent Focus Group, http://faculty.uccb.ns.ca/pmacintyre/course_pages/MBA603/MBA603_files/IntroQualitativeResearch.pdf (Accessed 19 February 2007).

Langdridge, D. (2004) *Introduction to Research Methods and Data Analysis in Psychology*, Harlow, Prentice Hall.

Manning, A.C. (1998) 'Successful ageing: experiences, reflections and observations of older proactive women', Unpublished BSc thesis, Manchester Metropolitan University.

Morse, J.M. (1992) 'Negotiating commitment and involvement in the patient–nurse relationship' in Morse, J.M. (ed.) *Qualitative Health Research*, London, Sage.

Silverman, D. (2000) *Doing Qualitative Research: A Practical Handbook*, London, Sage.

Willig, C. (2001) *Qualitative Research in Psychology: A Practical Guide to Theory and Method*, Buckingham, Open University Press.

# Appendix: Interview transcript

*Note:* A full stop in brackets (.) shows a short pause.

---

**Interviewer:**

I'm very interested in your ideas and what you think is important in maintaining an active and busy life. Please take your time to, sort of think about it.

**Jess:**

Yes, hmmm, (.) well, since I retired and after the death of my husband (.) I had a lot to sort out, but came to terms with it, to realise that I had to stand on my own two feet (.) and, err, I was not interested in any further – any work, it wasn't, you know, sort of at all necessary and I felt that I had served my time in the profession. I was, however, part way involved looking after my mother-in-law – who was a great mother-in-law and she lived till she was 91, but, erm, she died peacefully in hospital, and I have still, since then, kept a very good rapport with my sister-in-law who lives nearby. We meet up each week and go out for days, etc. etc. Err, after my husband died, erm, but it was prior to this, erm, it was when my mother died, in the village where I was brought up there was my nephew who lived in this house. So, when my mother died, my nephew was on his own (.) and my husband and I went up once a month just to see all was well and to see to his domestic chores. Being a man, not the least bit domesticated.

**Interviewer:**

[*laughs*]

**Jess:**

and I, we, I did this and after my husband died I still went up once a month and my nephew and I – he was like a son to me [...] Because, after my husband died (.) – I can remember to this day, about six months afterwards, saying, 'Jess, you've

got to go on holiday'(.) and I walked across the road,
[*chuckles*] to the travel agents, I knew the girl in there.

**Interviewer:**

Yes.

**Jess:**

I said, 'Have you got any flights to Jersey?' This is where I
used to go on holiday (.)

**Interviewer:**

Yes.

**Jess:**

with my husband, you see, before we started travelling to France.
I loved France. She said, 'Yes, there are some flights.'
I said, 'Well, I'll ring you back in an hour.'

**Interviewer:**

Yes.

**Jess:**

And I rang up my friends Barbara and Will that keep
a guest house.

**Interviewer:**

Yes.

**Jess:**

Er, in Jersey, a private hotel. I rang up Barbara – 'Jess', she said,
'just come.'

**Interviewer:**

Ah lovely.

**Jess:**

And I've been going there twice a year since, till they retired
from the hotel. I still keep in touch with them, and I found
another hotel, I've been going twice a year ever since (.) Even
after Richard died, you know, I thought 'I've got to go back.'

**Interviewer:**

Good for you.

**Jess:**

And one year I went three times. I felt as if I had to get away (.)
and come to terms with things (.)

**Interviewer:**

Yes.

**Jess:**

And funnily enough I found the peace and quiet on that island (.)
to get myself gathered together.

**Interviewer:**

Yes.

**Jess:**

To sort myself out and realise (.) that life has got to go on (.)
You can't just sit back.

**Interviewer:**

Absolutely.

**Jess:**

There are days (.) I do feel empty.

**Interviewer:**

Yes.

**Jess:**

But I look at it and say (.) [*slaps her wrist*] 'Get up
and do something.' What else can you do? (.) I make a point in
going out every day.

**Interviewer:**

That's good.

**Jess:**

Come hail, rain, thunder, snow or what.

**Interviewer:**

Yes. Yes.

**Jess:**

I go out every day and I often meet up with old colleagues.

**Interviewer:**

Yes. 65

**Jess:**

Or. Even some of them that are still practising. 66

**Interviewer:**

Yes. 67

**Jess:**

And it's very interesting to hear the comments and observations 68
and particularly if some of them have been in hospital, and how 69
things have, you know, have changed. 70

**Interviewer:**

Yes. 71

**Jess:**

And it's nice when they come and, you know, talk to you. 72
The odd time I've met a consultant that I know and they always 73
come and speak to you. 74

**Interviewer:**

Oh that's very good. 75

**Jess:**

I have my interests here at home, I like to do the puzzles and 76
the word games here. I read, I am not a television addict. 77
I can go for a couple of days on end and never look at television. 78
I prefer to listen, you know, to music. 79

**Interviewer:**

Yes. 80

**Jess:**

But not the Radio One, you know. [*chuckles*] I like to hear 81
discussions (.) I'm quite cosmopolitan in what I read (.) 82
Y'know I'm quite content with life. 83

**Interviewer:**

Yes, that's marvellous. 84

**Jess:**

I don't and I'm going to be quite honest with you have any financial problems but then on the other hand I don't lead a social life so I don't have to spend a great deal on clothes, you know and that sort of thing. But I have good friends who I sometimes go out to dinner with, or they invite me down to lunch and my way of repaying their hospitality is, I take them out for a meal because I won't cook now like I used to. I've not the same interest in it. I will cook for myself.

---

CHAPTER 10

# The qualitative project: from research design to analysis

## Contents

Aims 314

1 Introduction 314

2 The background to the project 315
- 2.1 Why pre-recorded data? 319
- 2.2 Transcription 321

3 What you have to do in the project 323
- 3.1 Reading the literature and watching the interview 323
- 3.2 Carrying out the thematic analysis 324

4 The importance of reflexivity in qualitative analysis 328
- 4.1 Using reflexivity to avoid over-interpretation and misinterpretation 330
- 4.2 Doing reflexive analysis 331

5 A final word 332

References 333

Appendix: Additional reading material on attachment 335

## Aims

This chapter aims to:

- introduce the constituent parts of the qualitative research project conducted for TMA 05
- explain the elements of thematic analysis necessary to doing TMA 05
- demonstrate the importance of reflexive analysis in qualitative analysis.

## 1 Introduction

As you have seen, there are many different ways of analysing the data produced by interviews. The project that you will undertake for your next assignment (TMA 05) requires you to do qualitative analysis, specifically thematic analysis. The purpose of this project is to give you some experience in carrying out thematic analysis and to get you to think about some of the wider issues involved in qualitative research, including the need to take a reflexive stance. This should help to hone your skills in critical appraisal of psychological research methods generally and, more particularly, deepen your understanding of qualitative analysis and specifically of thematic analysis.

For your qualitative project you will be carrying out a thematic analysis of a qualitative research interview. This project should be informed by your reading of Chapter 9 and those sections of Chapters 1 and 8 of this book that focus on ethics, interviews and analysis. You will also need to refresh your memory of Section 3 in Chapter 1, 'Lifespan development', of Book 2, *Challenging Psychological Issues*, as this provides some theoretical background on attachment theory, which is necessary to your project. You will find additional reading material on attachment in the appendix to this chapter, and the British Psychological Society (BPS) *Ethical Principles for Conducting Research with Human Participants* can be accessed from the course website.

---

*This chapter introduces you to the constituent parts of the qualitative project. It first explains what you will be doing and how the data that you will analyse have been produced, before explaining in detail what you need to do in order to carry out the thematic analysis. The final section explains why reflexive analysis is important and explains how to do your own thematic analysis. Reflexive analysis is central to the thematic analysis you will be doing and should permeate all stages rather than be a stage on its own.* ***You will, therefore, need to read the whole chapter through to get a good understanding of what you should be doing in TMA 05 before going back and reading through each section again in detail.***

The chapter that follows (Chapter 11) will deal with how to write up your project.

## 2 The background to the project

The project you will do for TMA 05 requires you to conduct a thematic analysis of a short interview that has already been conducted by a researcher and has formed the basis of a dramatised interview with an actor. This interview has been video-recorded and is part of Programme 4 on the DVD. It has been transcribed for you to use and the transcript is available on the DSE212 course website for downloading and printing out.

You may remember that Chapters 1, 8 and 9 all explained that research is a coherent process in which different levels of theory are interlinked, i.e. perspectives, methodology and methods are all consistent with each other. More specifically, all research is embedded within a theoretical framework (or perspective) that is underpinned by epistemology (theory of knowledge) and ontology (the theory of the nature of existence and so what it is to be a person). The methodology (theory of methods) adopted is the overall theoretical rationale and provides the principles that define how a research question and methods of data collection and analysis are embedded within a perspective. Even though your main task in TMA 05 is to analyse data, the analysis has to be consistent with the theoretical framework and methodology within which the data have been produced. In other words, the specific thematic analysis you will be doing has to be located within the broad theoretical framework adopted by the researchers who collected the data.

Chapter 9 made clear that thematic analysis is popular because it can be used by researchers who take different foci or are even situated within different perspectives. There is no one specific perspective that is associated with thematic analysis. This does not mean, however, that it is possible to avoid situating the project within a theoretical framework. Researchers who do thematic analysis have to decide on the perspective, and on the particular focus and approach they will take to their research before they devise their research question. The researchers who conducted the interview on which you will do thematic analysis started from an approach associated with the social constructionist perspective – that is, one that views the world as constructed in language.

### Activity 10.1

**Have another look at Section 2.2 of Chapter 9. What ontology is identified as commonly shared by those who do thematic analysis?**

### Comment

In order to do thematic analysis, researchers have to share a broad ontological position that treats people as able to reflect on their experiences, to make sense of them and to produce accounts in language (talk or writing), in which meanings are organised into themes (although speakers and writers may well neither intend nor recognise these themes). These meanings can be particular to individuals, but may be shared across individuals or social groups. The researcher who designed the research project in which you will take part (by doing thematic analysis) took up this ontology.

You may recall from your reading of Chapters 1, 8 and 9 that an important characteristic of qualitative research, which distinguishes it from the quantitative approach, is that there are no 'variables' to be measured and therefore no specific hypotheses to be tested. Instead, a qualitative researcher will typically identify an area of interest which he or she wishes to explore (i.e. the 'research focus') and will formulate a question or a series of questions that will guide data collection (e.g. by determining the topic to be discussed with participants in an interview). These questions will then serve as the focal point for analysis. For instance, the researcher may begin with a broad research topic, such as the ways in which identities are constructed in families. However, this subject is rather wide to investigate as it stands, and the researcher will most likely have more specific interests in particular aspects of family relationships that they will want to investigate. There are many different kinds of families and the researcher may concentrate on one family type. They may, for example, choose families that are single-parent, extended and/or 'mixed' in terms of culture, religion and/or 'race'. Having decided on the kinds of family to research, the researcher will need to decide whose experiences they wish to focus on within a family, e.g. adult siblings; mothers; fathers; grandparents; stepchildren. Qualitative research is concerned with exploring the experiences of people within a specific context and one of its main principles is that interpretations of meaning (individual or shared) are central to what it means to be human. The research question should, therefore, reflect this by asking about experiences and meanings rather than making predictions as would a quantitative research question.

Chapter 9 explained that research questions are devised from reading the literature and from theoretical understandings of issues that have social relevance. The research question devised for this research project was developed after reading literature on attachment (discussed in Section 3 of Chapter 1, in Book 2). That literature discusses John Bowlby's ideas that secure attachments are important to later development and that children develop 'internal working models' of the world, which help them to understand who they can turn to when they need security and how those people are likely to react (Main *et al.*, 1985). Bowlby (1973, p. 203) describes internal working models as follows:

> *Each individual builds working models of the world and of himself* [sic] *in it, with the aid of which he perceives events, forecasts the future, and constructs his plans. In the working models of the world that anyone builds a key feature is his notion of who his attachment figures are, where they may be found, and how they may be expected to respond. Similarly, in the working model of the self that anyone builds a key feature is his notion of how acceptable or unacceptable he himself is in the eyes of his attachment figures.*

Bowlby suggested that the internal working models developed in childhood are stable over time and so carry over into adulthood – mostly unconsciously. They become more complex and sophisticated as children develop and their content can be changed, updated and elaborated as circumstances change. However, if internal working models do alter, changes happen gradually and with difficulty (Pietromonaco and Barrett, 2000). Therefore, on the dimension of fixity and change that you encountered in the commentaries in Book 1 *Mapping Psychology*, internal working models are generally relatively fixed over time, but not absolutely so, in that they can be modified, depending on circumstances.

Hazan and Shaver (1987) studied more than 600 adults' self-reports about their romantic relationships by getting them to fill in a 'love quiz' in a local newspaper. The researchers found that adults described themselves in ways that they (the researchers) analysed as showing different types of attachment pattern. Some appeared to be comfortable with having close relationships and did not have particular fears that they would be rejected by others. Other adults were more preoccupied with the possibility of rejection and liked to maintain close relationships, while yet others were uncomfortable with being close to others and found it difficult to depend on people. These adult relationships were affected by childhood experiences, in that those who reported that their childhood attachments had been secure and not characterised by loss and separation seemed more likely to report that they felt comfortable with having close relationships. Childhood experiences do not, however, *determine* adult relationships. Main and Goldwyn (1984) found that adults could have 'earned security' – that is, security in relationships does not have to be achieved though attachments in childhood but can be attained later in life through strong and positive adult relationships. The *Adult Attachment Interview* devised by George *et al.* (1984) focuses on adults' accounts of their 'early attachment experiences and their effects and ... elicit[s] memories of childhood experiences with key attachment figures' (Barrett, 2006, p. 75). The analysis of these accounts is concerned with how adults are able to make sense of, and talk about, those experiences and key relationships in the present, rather than with how they actually were in childhood. This fits with Main and Goldwyn's ideas that it is possible to attain 'security' later in life.

From their review of the attachment literature, the researchers who conducted the research which provided the interview data you will be analysing for your TMA 05 project decided to make their research focus the ways in which adults construct their attachment relationships and experiences. The research question they devised is: 'How do adults perceive that significant others in their lives (i.e. people who are or have been important to them) have affected their development?' Having developed the research question, the researchers had to consider carefully the methodology that would be appropriate in order to come up with methods that fitted both with the literature and with the perspective they drew upon, which was a social constructionist perspective. This means that the ontology they adopted viewed humans as able to talk about the meanings of their experiences. This broad perspective (i.e. theoretical framework), together with the more narrowly focused attachment theory, provides the overall theoretical rationale (i.e. methodology) for the methods of data collection and analysis. Interviews are an ideal method of data collection within the perspective selected and for studying adult attachment, since they allow the analysis of adult constructions of the meanings of their relationships.

As you will see on the video recording that you will use for your thematic analysis, the researchers chose a mode of interviewing that encourages and enables research participants to talk at length and tell stories about their experiences. It would, however, be pointless to select a method of data collection that allowed participants to talk at length and then to use a method of analysis that could not represent that potential complexity. Thematic analysis is underpinned by the ontology selected for this particular study (in that it is about the analysis of meanings as themes) and can fit with the study's epistemology. For that reason, thematic analysis is better suited to the study provided for TMA 05 than, for example, quantitative content analysis would be, since content analysis focuses on counting how frequently particular words occur in a transcript or other written text. If you look at the quotation below, you can see that quantitative content analysis would be inappropriate for your analysis, since the study for which the data you will be analysing was collected is situated within a social constructionist perspective and so is not well suited to a quantitative approach:

> *[Quantitative] content analysis is a research tool used to determine the presence of certain words or concepts within texts or sets of texts. Researchers quantify and analyze the presence, meanings and relationships of such words and concepts, then make inferences about the messages within the texts, the writer(s), the audience, and even the culture and time of which these are a part.*
>
> (*Busch* et al., *2005*)

The study for which you will be analysing some interview data is coherent, in that the perspective or theoretical framework is consistent with the methodology, which guides the data collection and data analytic methods. You may remember from reading Section 3, Chapter 1 of Book 2, that attachment is often studied from an alternative perspective; one that assumes it is possible to analyse 'real' (rather than socially constructed) attachment relationships in infancy using the Strange Situation laboratory procedure and rating infants' behaviours when they are reunited with their caregivers following periods of separation, and in adulthood by the procedure called the Adult Attachment Interview, which is a structured interview where answers are rated according to a standardised protocol.

## 2.1 Why pre-recorded data?

The data for your project come from one of two filmed interviews – one of which was with Chloe, a white, 50-year-old British woman and the other with Assan, a 35-year-old man originally from the Middle East (both names have been changed to protect the participants' identities). The interviewees you see on the film are actors. However, what the actors say is based on actual recorded research interviews conducted with the two research participants. These participants gave their informed consent for their interview material to be used in this way but, by asking actors to play them, their anonymity is maintained for ethical reasons. The filmed interviews were edited to produce a short extract and both are available on DVD Programme 4, 'Interviewing and thematic analysis'. The first interview extract is presented to allow you to get some idea, before you conduct your own thematic analysis on the second interview extract, of how the experienced researcher who did the interviews would begin the process of thematic analysis.

There are limitations in looking at interview material that has been produced for a DVD in this way. For example, you cannot know whether this edited version of the interviews focuses on what you would have considered to be important if you had been present. You should bear this in mind when it comes to your project. No camera can capture everything that is going on at the time of recording and so the video recording produced is necessarily selective. It may seem, therefore, that it would be preferable to allow you to conduct your own interviews, or even entirely to design your own research study so that you gain experience of devising a coherent project. There are, however, two sets of reasons why we have deliberately chosen to ask you to carry out a qualitative analysis of an interview that we provide you with, rather than asking you to carry out a project based on interviews you have done yourself:

1 **Ethical reasons:** Ethical considerations are *always* important in carrying out research. By using pre-recorded material we have ensured that the interview you will analyse conforms to ethical principles of informed consent, confidentiality and anonymity. The participants have given their full permission for their interviews to be used in this manner, and are aware that you will be studying them, but that they will remain anonymous. The research also conforms to the BPS *Code of Ethics and Conduct* and *Ethical Principles for Conducting Research with Human Participants*, which set out the main responsibilities; of psychologists. These are: respect; competence; responsibility and integrity (see the discussion of ethics in the Introduction to Book 1 and in Chapter 1 of this book, and the link to the code and principles on the course website).

2 **Time and workload constraints:** Interviewing normally requires extensive preparation, including reading the relevant background literature, making decisions about the research focus, devising the research question, deciding who to interview, accessing interviewees, obtaining their informed consent to participate in your study, and gaining ethical consent from official organisations if and when necessary. This can take months to do. In addition, transcribing, analysis and writing up are all very time-consuming. The necessity of fine-tuning these different elements of research means that carrying out research interviews is a skilled process, and there is not sufficient time for you to develop these skills and to be introduced to the theory and practice of qualitative research in time to complete TMA 05.

Analysing secondary material in this fashion means that you will miss out on the experience of carrying out an actual interview. It also means that you do not have the opportunity to design your own study or to take responsibility for situating yourself in a perspective, formulating a research question and selecting a methodology, research method and method of analysis. All these decisions have been taken by the course team and implemented by the researchers who did the interviews. The constraints of time and workload discussed above would, however, have been magnified if you had to devise a study yourself, from start to finish. The advantage of being presented with a pre-recorded interview and its transcript is that it allows you to concentrate only on learning the skills of analysis and to do a more detailed thematic analysis than you would otherwise have the opportunity to do. At the same time, the fact that the interview is video recorded allows you to see parts of the research process in which you are not actively involved and so to include them in your write-up of the project (discussed in Chapter 11). You will have opportunities to carry out an interview project if you do the Level 3 social psychology course (DD307).

## 2.2 Transcription

Much qualitative research involves the analysis of texts. Although many qualitative researchers analyse written material (newspaper articles, official documents, diaries, etc.), the 'raw data' in the majority of qualitative research studies consist of audio recordings (e.g. semi-structured interviews, naturally occurring conversation, accounts, recollections, etc.). These 'raw' data are then transcribed and the transcript constitutes the partially processed data from which the analyses are done. The data for your project are on the second interview in Programme 4 on the DVD and we have provided you with a transcript on the course website so that you can focus on data coding, analysis and writing up the project. However, it is important to think about the nature of the transcript you will be using, so this section discusses some of the issues involved in transcription before you do your thematic analysis. Should you decide to continue your studies in psychology, you will have the opportunity of transcribing qualitative data on the Level 3 social psychology course, DD307.

As you saw in Chapter 9, transcription is a process of converting spoken discourse (and sometimes visual material) into written form. A transcript is a representation of an interview that reduces the information potentially available in the actual interview setting to a manageable form, in order to facilitate analysis. At its simplest, it involves writing down what people are saying. However, there are different ways of transcribing data, and the choice of transcription method is closely related to the type of qualitative research you are doing. For instance, *conversation analysis* is an analytic method which focuses on the precise details of conversational interactions and *how* people talk (e.g. the way in which participants in a conversation take turns when they talk, or how people deal with 'awkward' situations which arise during an interaction). A conversation analyst would need to transcribe an interview in detail, including, for example, details of intonation, speed and loudness as well as the length of pauses. This level of detail is not, however, necessary for your purposes, in that *thematic analysis* focuses on the content of what people are saying, rather than extra-linguistic details.

Transcription is very time-consuming and can be hard and frustrating work, particularly if the recording is poor, but the time and effort used to produce an accurate transcript is a valuable investment. For example, any transcription requires repeated listening to the recording and paying detailed attention to what participants are saying. This is an excellent way of getting to know the data. In that sense, transcription is the first stage of analysis during which important early insights will be gained. Unfortunately, for this project you will not have the time to create your own transcription, which is why we have provided one for you. However, if you choose to take one of the associated project courses (DXR222 or DZX222), you will have the opportunity of doing transcription within a small group, or on your own on DD307.

Transcription makes analysis much easier because it allows you to read the material at your own pace, to highlight sections and to cut and paste extracts that you consider especially relevant to your analyses. Having a transcript in electronic format enables you to scroll easily through the material and to use the 'search' function to look for certain words. This can save time, particularly when large studies are conducted, involving hundreds of hours of interviews and thousands of pages of transcript.

## Summary Section 2

- Research is a coherent process that requires a consistent perspective (theoretical framework), underpinned by epistemology (theory of knowledge) and ontology (the theory of what it is to be a person). The methodology (theory of methods) adopted is the overall theoretical rationale and the principles that define how a research question and methods of data collection and analysis are embedded within the perspective.
- The research interview that has been dramatised and video-recorded for you to analyse was conducted by researchers working within a social constructionist perspective. Hence it is underpinned by ontology that views human beings as able to reflect on, and talk about, the meanings of their experiences.

- Attachment theory is the specific theory that informs the study on which the project is based. Together with the perspective within which the researcher is working, attachment theory informs the methodology of the study, which guides the methods of data collection (in-depth interviewing) and of data analysis (thematic analysis).
- The qualitative project you will undertake for TMA 05 is limited to data analysis for ethical reasons as well as time and workload constraints. This has the advantage of allowing a more detailed engagement with thematic analysis.
- The transcript of the interview provided is of the words used, rather than extra-linguistic details since that level of detail is unnecessary to thematic analysis.

# 3 What you have to do in the project

As discussed in Section 1, the research question devised by the researchers for this project is: 'How do adults perceive that significant others in their lives (i.e. people who are or have been important to them) have affected their development?' This is therefore the research question you will work with. You will see in the DVD interviews that the interviewer posed a closely related question to the two participants: 'Can you tell me about your early relationships with significant others that you think have affected your development as a person?' This question guided the interview itself and, as discussed above, is underpinned by attachment theory. You will need to revisit the material covered in Section 3, Chapter 1 in Book 2 and read through the additional reading material we provide in the appendix to this chapter in order to understand how this question is related to the research literature and, later, to get ideas about the themes you can analyse from th interview.

## 3.1 Reading the literature and watching the interview

To carry out this project, you will need access to a DVD player. There are two qualitative research interviews in Programme 4 on the DVD you have been sent and it is the second interview that you will focus on for your own thematic analysis. Before you start your analysis, you will need to watch the interview carefully as it includes an introduction showing the interviewee being asked for their consent to participate in the study. It therefore establishes that the interview conforms to ethical codes. There is a short section at the end of the interview where you can see the interviewer reflecting on the interview and her response to it. This part of the interview will, therefore, be worth watching carefully because it should help you to think about the issues you may wish to consider when doing your own reflexive analysis – which will form part of your thematic analysis.

A crucial step in any qualitative analysis is to become familiar with the data that you will be analysing. We would strongly suggest that, after having read Section 3, Chapter 1 of Book 2 and the literature in the appendix to this chapter, you next watch the entire programme on the DVD from start to end. Then find the time to watch the second interview quite a few times. It is a good idea to print a copy of the transcript of this second interview (available on the DSE212 course website) so that you have this to hand when watching this interview.

### *Activity 10.2*

Watch the second videoed interview at least three times so that you gain some familiarity with the material. In between viewings, think carefully how the interview relates to attachment theory and research on it presented in the lifespan chapter. Make a note of your thoughts and any responses you have to the material as you go along, as these are likely to be useful when it comes to writing up the reflexive analysis section of your project (reflexivity will be discussed later in this chapter). Remember, too, that the theoretical framework within which the project is situated is social constructionist. Given that the related ontology is about humans as meaning making and emotionally motivated, you should pay particular attention to the personal experiences expressed and the meanings the participant produces as well as the emotional tone of what is said. There is no need to focus on whether or not the participant is telling the truth, since this is irrelevant to the social constructionist perspective.

## 3.2 Carrying out the thematic analysis

For this project, you should code the data in the way demonstrated in Chapter 9, which you practised when reading the chapter. Remember that your aim is to provide a succinct summary of the material that brings out the participant's meanings, so that the research question can be addressed.

## Preparing for analysis

There are various ways in which you can address the research question in your analysis because the research participants discuss a number of areas. For example, they both talk about their relationships with their fathers. They also discuss later adult relationships with partners and with other key people who have played important roles in providing security in their lives. One possibility is that you could explore this interview material by looking at the impact of early relationships on current ones in relation to Bowlby's ideas about internal working models and the importance of a safe and stable attachment for later development. A second possibility is that you could choose to focus your analysis in relation to the research question by looking at the effects of separation and loss and the impact of these experiences at the time and on subsequent relationships. You could, instead, situate the research question in relation to the work of Ainsworth (1989) and of Hazan and Shaver (1987) on the impact of secure and insecure childhood attachments on later (romantic) relationships. Another possibility would be to look at the interviews in terms of Main and Goldwyn's ideas about 'earned security' (1984) – the concept that security does not have to be achieved though attachments in childhood but can be attained later in life through strong and positive adult relationships. You could alternatively choose to focus on an aspect of attachment theory you find in your reading that is not mentioned above. Whichever of these approaches you take, you will need to ensure that you address the research question by focusing on the experiences of the interviewees and situating your analysis within an attachment theory theoretical framework, making it clear which literature you are using to situate your analysis.

If you have access to a photocopier, you may find it helpful to take some photocopies of the transcript, or to print out a second copy so that you can write on one while keeping a clean copy. Read through the transcript a few more times to familiarise yourself with the interviewee's responses and think about how they relate to the research question. Mark those sections of the interviews that relate specifically to the research question in pencil so you can easily return to them in the future. Note that there may be quite a lot of material which appears to be superfluous (e.g. digressions, repetitions, material that is not essential to the main story being told, or that is not directly relevant to your focus in addressing the research question). Try to ensure that you identify all those sections which may be relevant. You can be rather more selective later on in the process. **Remember that you only need to consider the second interview!**

## Coding the data

Having marked up relevant sections of the transcript, the next step is to begin the process of coding the data. Start by giving labels or codes to the interviewee's words (as demonstrated on Jess's interview in Chapter 9). Remember that first-order coding is purely descriptive and you are aiming at this stage simply to categorise the data by capturing relatively small chunks of meaning. Try to use labels that are meaningful in relation to what the participant has said, rather than ones that mean something to you but are difficult for anybody else to see how they are relevant. You are likely to end up with quite a lot of codes at this stage. You may also find that you need to revise your codes in order to capture the meaning of the interviewee's words. This is perfectly acceptable.

## From first-order codes to themes

When you have worked through the transcript and completed your first-order coding, return to the transcript and try to interpret the meanings of the participant's words. At the second level of coding, your aim is to go beyond simple description of the data. This can involve descriptive codes that capture the meaning of bigger segments of the data (i.e. applying superordinate constructs). At this stage you will probably find that you are reducing your large number of initial labels down to a smaller number of ideas.

You can then move on to the final stage of third-order coding or thematic analysis. At this level, your task is to identify superordinate constructs or themes which capture the meaning of your descriptive and interpretative codes. Themes can be seen as recurrent topics, ideas or statements, which ideally come up on a number of occasions in the material presented. In order to carry out this level of analysis it is helpful to stand back from your data and try to summarise the main ideas that recur in the interview. Remember that your themes or headings should try to capture the interviewee's words and preoccupations as well as being relevant to the research question.

## Providing evidence for your themes

When you have identified your themes, go back through the transcript and mark each bit of the dialogue that can be related to each of your identified themes (remember that any part of the interview may illuminate more than one theme). One way to relate what the interviewee says to these themes is with a variety of different-coloured highlighter pens (marking each separate theme clearly in a different colour) so that you can see at a glance where each theme is represented in the transcript. Other researchers like to cut up a duplicate copy of the transcript (this is where photocopies would be useful), making little stacks of quotations that illustrate each theme.

Others use 'post-it' notes to indicate relevant material. Having done this, you will need to go back to your material and look at what has *not* been categorised by this procedure. The remaining material may be irrelevant to your themes or it may suggest that further themes are needed.

### Reviewing your thematic analysis

When you have reduced the material to a number of key themes which relate to the research question, reread the transcript in its entirety to see if there is anything that you have overlooked and whether there are any contradictions in the themes. This is not necessarily problematic since people often say contradictory things. However, you should show that you have noted the contradictions and aim to provide an interpretation of them. Remember that you need to illustrate your themes by reference to quotations from the transcripts. You may decide during the process of doing the analysis that the initial themes require adjustment after you have given them further thought, or they may need to be changed in the light of your analysis. What you are aiming for is a relatively small number of themes (about three) which capture the material in the interview, are relevant to the research question and are clearly supported by quotations from the transcripts.

Having identified three or four recurrent issues which have emerged from the interview and which capture important aspects of your interviewee's experiences and the meanings he or she has given to them, you then need to consider these in the light of the research question and the theoretical material, from Bowlby, Ainsworth and others, which you have used to underpin your analysis. You may wish to consider whether your themes are broadly supportive of the claims made by these theorists about the nature of attachments. You may instead have found that the interviewee's words and experiences appear to contradict particular aspects of these theoretical views. Think carefully at this stage about what you have found and how it relates to the material in Section 3 of Chapter 1, Book 2.

As explained in Chapter 9, there is no one, definitive way of carrying out thematic analysis and so no one set of 'right' answers to the research question that you should be aiming for. However, there are right and wrong ways to conduct, argue and present your analysis. Your tutor will be looking for evidence that you have systematically read the transcript and are familiar with the material in it. You should demonstrate that your analysis is firmly rooted in your data and that you have written up your analysis clearly so as to enable readers to understand how you have approached the transcript. Your overall aim is to convince readers that your analysis both makes sense and provides a new way of understanding what has been said.

## Summary Section 3

- Reading Section 3 on attachment theory in Chapter 1 in Book 2 and additional reading in the appendix to this chapter is crucial to understanding how the research question is related to the research literature. It is also crucial to helping you to get ideas about the themes that can be derived from the interview.
- It is important to become familiar with the data to be analysed. Initially, this involves repeated watching of the interview with the transcript in front of you and the epistemology and ontology in mind. Later in the analytic process, you may focus on the transcript, rather than watching the video recording.
- The aim of the analysis you will undertake is to answer the research question. There are, however, various ways in which this can be done because the research participant discusses a number of areas that are relevant to the attachment literature. It is important to show how your analysis relates to the literature.
- It will be helpful to have at least two copies of the transcript of the second interview so that you can write on one or cut it up and divide it into different themes. We recommend you follow the process of first-, second- and third-order coding demonstrated in Chapter 9 and discussed above. At the end of the process of coding, you will need to review your themes to ensure that they are relevant to your research focus. You will also need to provide evidence for your themes and relate them to the attachment literature.

# 4 The importance of reflexivity in qualitative analysis

One of the distinguishing features of quantitative research is the assumption that the results of a study are independent of the qualities or the characteristics of the researcher who conducted it. This is because quantitative research is situated within the scientific tradition and linked to perspectives that aim for objective data. It is understood that anyone who follows a set of procedures (usually outlined in the method section of a report or a journal article) would or should come up with the same set of findings and the same conclusions. When this does not occur (i.e. when a study cannot be replicated) a quest begins to find various 'extraneous' or 'confounding' variables that might account for the difference in findings. Hence, where the criteria for 'objectivity' are not met (e.g. the study cannot be replicated), we need to reflect upon any factors potentially affecting reliability and validity.

In contrast, this kind of replicability is not relevant to the kind of qualitative analysis undertaken in perspectives related to the hermeneutic tradition. Instead, it is recognised that different researchers bring different theoretical and personal insights into their analysis and that conclusions would not necessarily be shared by those who favour different theoretical perspectives. In the book *Analyzing Race Talk*, the editors Van den Berg *et al.* (2003) asked a dozen scholars from different areas of conversation analysis, discourse analysis and sociolinguistics to analyse the same set of interview transcripts (from a study by Wetherell and Potter, 1992). Each scholar approached the material in a different way and explored the interviews from their own perspective. Different questions were asked about the content of the interviews, different insights were produced and different conclusions were reached. This reflects the fact that either these researchers were drawing on different theoretical frameworks, which led them to ask different questions and meant that different issues in the text were relevant. In addition, they either employed different rationales to examine those questions or, if they shared the same theoretical framework, they were interested in addressing different research questions. This example demonstrates why qualitative researchers do not stipulate a 'right' way to do research and why no two DSE212 students will come up with exactly the same analysis, although they are analysing the same interview and addressing the same research question.

You may recognise the concept of reflexivity as a central principle of George Kelly's personal construct theory that you read about in Book 1, Chapter 9. According to Kelly (1955) our research, like all that is ours, is inevitably part of our personal construct system: we cannot stand apart from it and hold it at a distance. We are actively engaged with our own research. Reflexivity is about acknowledging our centrality as researchers in the whole process of research from the initial choice of research focus through to analysis and writing up. It involves reflecting upon and analysing, rather than attempting to minimise, our subjective involvement in the process. Qualitative researchers in psychology are increasingly emphasising the impact of the researcher's reflexivity on the research produced. Many qualitative researchers claim that engagement with reflexivity heightens awareness and fine-tunes our analyses because attending to the 'affective component of research' provides an important source of insight (Denzin and Lincoln, 1998; King, 1996; Willig, 2001).

At the heart of the idea of reflexivity in research lies the recognition that the researcher plays a significant part in the production of meaning throughout the various stages of research. This is perhaps most obvious when we think about the interview situation, where we can often see clearly where interpersonal dynamics between the researcher and interviewee have influenced what is said and how it is said. This dynamic can also affect what is *not* said.

Although part of the acquired skill of a qualitative researcher is to try not to let his/her own understandings and opinions about the research topic override what the research participant is saying, it is acknowledged that nobody can ever 'empty' themselves entirely of feelings and opinions. By acknowledging this, researchers can reflect on what they bring to the research process and how their own thoughts, feelings and experiences might influence it.

## 4.1 Using reflexivity to avoid over-interpretation and misinterpretation

A great temptation for inexperienced (and enthusiastic) researchers is to engage in 'wild analysis' of their data! This is where the analyst sees instances of what they are looking for everywhere in the interview material. They over-interpret or misinterpret the data to produce meanings that were not originally either intended or presented by the interviewee. This can partly result because it is difficult for novice qualitative researchers to understand that not having one right way to do analysis does not mean that anything that comes to mind is acceptable as analysis. If you were carrying out qualitative research from start to end, one way to avoid 'wild analysis' might be to return to your interviewee with your thematic analysis to 'check out' your interpretations and themes. Sometimes in qualitative research, participants are interviewed again at a later stage and this would also be an opportunity to share your interpretations with interviewees or to check them through further questioning. Clearly, this is not possible within the scope of TMA 05. However, you can systematically reflect on what you bring to the analysis of data and how this may affect your interpretations and therefore the production of research knowledge. When you have finished your analysis, you can also stand back and read through your final report for the TMA, paying attention to what the way you have written about the research participant says about you as well as about them. If that seems a difficult notion, it is worth thinking about buying presents for other people. An editorial in the *The Economist* in 2001 helps to make the point:

> *At the simplest level, giving gifts involves the giver thinking of something that the recipient would like – he tries to guess her preferences, as economists say – and then buying the gift and delivering it. Yet this guessing of preferences is no mean feat; indeed, it is often done badly. Every year, ties go unworn and books unread. And even if a gift is enjoyed, it may not be what the recipient would have bought had they spent the money themselves.*
>
> (Economist, *Editorial, 20 December 2001)*

Not surprisingly, then, many analysts consider that gift-giving says more about the giver, and how they understand their relationship with the recipient, than it does about the recipient.

Reflexivity implies attentiveness to what your work says about you and willingness to attend to and theorise your part in the research process. Paying attention to this helps remind us that we are not impartial or objective observers of the 'truth'. Importantly, it alerts us to the fact that we can easily introduce misinterpretations and mistakes into the analysis of qualitative research data.

## 4.2 Doing reflexive analysis

Activity 10.3 is designed to help you to understand how to do your own reflexive analysis as part of your thematic analysis for TMA 05.

### Activity 10.3

When you first watched the second interview in the DVD Programme 4 we suggested that you 'make a note of your thoughts and any responses you have to the material' on the transcript (in Activity 10.2). You did not choose the focus of research or conduct the interview. Nonetheless, you are likely to have reactions to what you see and hear in the interview. We suggest that, as you conduct your thematic analysis of the data from the second interview, you continue to think about and keep notes on your reactions to what the interviewee has said. As you watch the interview again, reread the transcript and code the data continue to pay attention to your responses to the experiences described in the interview. Are there moments in the interview when you feel bored, irritated, uninterested, empathic? Are you surprised or puzzled by what the interviewee says? How do you think these responses might have shaped your interpretation of the data?

### Comment

In this kind of reflection it is important to look closely at your own assumptions about people, their lives and experiences. Part of this involves thinking about points of identification between you and the interviewee; that is, in what ways do you think that you and the interviewee are similar in some way or share similar experiences? Are there points at which you think that you are very different from one another? This reflection will help you think about how your own beliefs and experiences – whether similar to or different from those of the interviewee – may have influenced your analysis.

## Summary Section 4

- The idea of reflexivity in research gives recognition to the part played by researchers in the production of meanings in their research.
- Rather than trying to minimise the researcher's involvement in their research, reflexive analyses attempt to recognise it, reflect upon it and so make it a tool for helping to situate analyses.
- Analysing reflexivity can help qualitative researchers avoid the dangers of over-interpretation and misinterpretation of their data.

# 5 A final word

By now it may seem that there is a lot to remember about how to do this qualitative analysis project. Learning a new method of analysis (or even doing some new analyses with a familiar method) can seem daunting, especially when, in many ways, it is different from what you have done before. However, once you have started the analysis you will find that it gradually gets easier and that you will learn a lot. Many people find that the process is good fun. We hope that you enjoy doing this project and that, through carrying out a small-scale piece of research using a qualitative method, you will end up better appreciating the advantages and disadvantages of using this kind of research in psychology.

Most of the material in Box 10.1 is reproduced from Chapter 9 in order to provide a quick checklist to enable you to evaluate your own thematic analysis.

### 10.1 Checklist for evaluating your thematic analysis

As you do your own thematic analysis, ask yourself the following questions to help you evaluate what you produce:

- To what extent does the analysis done provide an answer to the research question? Does it instead, or in addition, raise new questions that require to be researched?
- Are the themes clearly labelled and described?
- Do the themes reflect the meanings that have emerged rather than the topics raised by the researcher during the interview?
- Is the meaning of each theme clearly described, with sufficient quotations from the transcript to support the meaning?
- Have all irrelevant themes and quotations (i.e. those that do not relate to the research focus) been excluded? Remember that if all the themes and quotations you identify are irrelevant, you should reconsider, and perhaps refine or adapt, your specific research focus (the overall research question has been decided for you but you will have chosen to address this question in a certain way).
- Does the analysis interpret the data as well as describing them?
- Is the interpretation grounded in theory?
- Has the analysis taken account of counter-instances (e.g. where a participant contradicts themselves or makes a specific exception to a general point) in the transcript? Has it considered omissions (i.e. things you might expect to have been said that have not been said)?
- Have you considered how your understandings and theoretical commitments have had an impact on the analyses you have produced?
- How have your reactions to the interview data and the interview as well as your own positioning affected your analysis (i.e. have you included reflexivity in your write-up)?

Chapter 11 aims to take you through the stages of writing up the qualitative project (TMA 05).

## References

Ainsworth. M. (1989) 'Attachments beyond infancy', *American Psychologist*, vol. 44, no. 4, pp. 709–16.

Ainsworth, M., Blehar, M., Waters, E. and Wall, S. (1978) *Patterns of Attachment: A Psychological Study of the Strange Situation*, Hillsdale, NJ, Erlbaum.

Barrett, H. (2006) *Attachment and the Perils of Parenting: A Commentary and a Critique*, London, National Family and Parenting Institute.

Bowlby, J. (1973) *Attachment and Loss: Vol. 2, Separation: Anxiety and Anger*, New York, Basic Books.

Busch, C., De Maret, P.S., Flynn, T., Kellum, R., Le, S., Meyers, B., Saunders, M., White, R. and Palmquist, M. (2005) *Content Analysis* [online], Writing@CSU, Colorado State University Department of English, http://writing.colostate.edu/guides/research/content/ (Accessed 15 February 2007).

Denzin, N.K. and Lincoln, H.S. (1998) *Collecting and Interpreting Qualitative Materials,* London, Sage.

George, C., Kaplan, N. and Main, M. (1984) *Adult Attachment Interview,* Berkeley, CA, Department of Psychology, University of California.

Hazan, C. and Shaver, P.R. (1987) 'Romantic love conceptualized as an attachment process', *Journal of Personality and Social Psychology,* vol. 52, pp. 511–24.

Kelly, G.A. (1955) *The Psychology Of Personal Constructs*, New York, Norton

King, E. (1996) 'The use of the self in qualitative research', in Richardson, J.T.E. (ed.) *Handbook of Qualitative Research Methods for Psychology and the Social Sciences,* Leicester, BPS Books.

Main, M. and Goldwyn, R. (1984) 'Predicting rejection of her infant from mother's representation of her own experience: implications for the abused-abusing intergenerational cycle', *Child Abuse and Neglect,* vol. 8, pp. 203–17.

Main, M., Kaplan, K. and Cassidy, J. (1985) 'Security in infancy, childhood, and adulthood: a move to the level of representation', *Monographs of the Society for Research in Child Development,* vol. 50, no. 1/2, pp. 66–104.

Pietromonaco, P. and Barrett, L.F. (2000) 'The Internal Working Models concept: what do we really know about the self in relation to others?', *Review of General Psychology,* vol. 4, no. 2, pp. 155–75.

*The Economist* (2001) 'Is Santa a deadweight loss? Are all those Christmas gifts just a waste of resources?, 20 December [online,] www.economist.com/finance/displayStory.cfm?Story_ID=885748 (Accessed 9 January 2007).

Van den Berg, H., Wetherell, M. and Houtkoop-Steenstra, H. (eds) (2003) *Analyzing Race Talk: Multidisciplinary Perspectives on the Research Interview,* Cambridge, Cambridge University Press.

Wetherell, M. and Potter, J. (1992) *Mapping the Language of Racism: Discourse and the Legitimation of Exploitation,* Hemel Hempstead, Harvester Wheatsheaf.

Willig, C. (2001) *Introducing Qualitative Research in Psychology: Adventures in Theory and Method,* Buckingham, Open University Press.

# Appendix: Additional reading material on attachment

*American Psychologist*
April 1989; 44(4): 709–716

## Attachments Beyond Infancy

*Mary D. Salter Ainsworth*
*University of Virginia*

**Note**: *Editor's note.* This article was originally presented as a Distinguished Professional Contributions award address at the meeting of the American Psychological Association in Atlanta in August 1988.

*ABSTRACT: Attachment theory is extended to pertain to developmental changes in the nature of children's attachments to parents and surrogate figures during the years beyond infancy, and to the nature of other affectional bonds throughout the life cycle. Various types of affectional bonds are examined in terms of the behavioral systems characteristic of each and the ways in which these systems interact. Specifically, the following are discussed: (a) the caregiving system that underlies parents' bonds to their children, and a comparison of these bonds with children's attachments to their parents; (b) sexual pair-bonds and their basic components entailing the reproductive, attachment, and caregiving systems; (c) friendships both in childhood and adulthood, the behavioral systems underlying them, and under what circumstances they may become enduring bonds; and (d) kinship bonds (other than those linking parents and their children) and why they may be especially enduring.*

My major contribution to psychological knowledge has focused on infants' attachment to their mothers. There were two chief aspects to this research: first, a normative account of the development of attachment during the first year of life, through direct observation of the behavior of infants and their mothers in the natural environment of the home, and second, an examination of individual differences in the qualitative nature of the attachment. The latter entailed identifying three major patterns of behavior in a laboratory situation at the end of the first year and relating these patterns to the nature of mother–infant interaction at home. It has been very gratifying to me that my work on individual differences engaged the interest of many able researchers who greatly expanded our knowledge of infant–parent attachment and in so doing did much to validate the concepts and findings that emerged from my own pioneer work.

So far, most of the research on attachments beyond infancy has been concerned with individual differences—and especially with the issue of the continuity of patterns of infant–parent attachments over time. For example, Sroufe (1983) and his able associates established the coherence in development of these patterns in regard to various aspects of cognitive and socioemotional development in the preschool years. Main and her associates (e.g., Main, Kaplan, & Cassidy, 1985; Main & Goldwyn, in press) developed several procedures for assessing attachment patterns in the sixth year and devised an adult attachment interview with procedures to classify adults according to their "state of mind in regard to attachment." This body of research already has provided strong evidence of the continuity of patterns of attachment over time, and of cross-generational influences. However, no further detail about studies of individual differences beyond infancy can be given in the present article. It deals with theoretical issues regarding attachments and other affectional bonds *beyond* infancy to provide a normative context for an understanding of individual differences.

The great strength of attachment theory in guiding research is that it focuses on a basic system of behaviour – the attachment behavioral system – that is biologically rooted and thus species-characteristic. This implies a search for basic processes of functioning that are universal in human nature, despite differences attributable to genetic constitution, cultural influences, and individual experience. We have made substantial progress toward understanding what these basic developmental processes relevant to attachment are in infancy; now we need to find out what they are throughout later phases of development. That is the first major topic of this article.

The second major topic concerns long-lasting interpersonal relationships that may involve affectional bonds. These include the attachments of the child to parents, the bonds of parents to a child, bonds with other kin, sexual pair bonds, and the bonds that may occur between friends. These classes of bond differ from one another in regard to the role played by the attachment system and its interplay with other basic behavioral systems.

[...]

## Attachment of the Child to Parents Beyond Infancy

Here I am concerned with the normative shifts in the nature of a child's attachment to parent figures beyond infancy. At some time between the child's third and fourth birthdays, he or she becomes capable of what Bowlby (1982) termed a "goal-corrected partnership." He suggested that this developmental phase was triggered by certain cognitive advances, which Marvin (1977; Marvin & Greenberg, 1982) promptly began to investigate and elaborate. The onset of simple cognitive perspective-taking enables the child to begin to grasp something of the parents' motivations and plans, and thus the child becomes more able than before to induce parents to change their plans so that they more closely agree with the child's own plans. Although language began to develop in the previous phase, now the further improvement of the child's language skills helps both the child and parents better communicate their plans and wishes to each other and thus to facilitate their negotiation of mutually acceptable plans. Confidence in the stability of this mutual understanding becomes built into the child's working model of his or her relationship with the mother figure,[1] and enables him or her to tolerate separation from that figure for longer periods and with less distress. Meanwhile, the child has achieved a qualitative advance in locomotion, from uncertain toddling to assured walking and running, presumably contingent on neurological development. This enables the child to venture farther away from his or her secure base to explore an expanded world and to connect with playmates and generally with a wider variety of people, including strangers.

It seems certain that another major shift takes place with the onset of adolescence, ushered in by hormonal changes. This development leads the young person to begin a search for a partnership with an age peer, usually of the opposite sex – a relationship in which the reproductive and caregiving systems, as well as the attachment system, are involved. Much more research is required before we have a good understanding of the normative changes implicit in adolescence, or indeed of other important developmental shifts before it. In this, one must be alert to the fact that key changes in the nature of attachment may be occasioned by hormonal, neurophysiological, and cognitive changes and not merely by socioemotional experience.

[1] By the term *mother figure*, I mean the person who has been the child's principal caregiver and thus has become his or her principal attachment figure, whether this is the mother, the father, or a parent surrogate.

### *Child-Parent Attachment During Adulthood*

There is reason to believe that a sense of autonomy from parents is normally achieved early in adulthood, presumably as a result of processes that operate gradually from infancy onward through adolescence. However, research into such developmental processes beyond the preschool years is as yet sadly lacking. On the other hand, there is good reason to believe that even an optimum degree of autonomy does not imply cessation of attachments to parent figures. Even though the individual is likely to have found a new principal attachment figure when a sexual pair bond is eventually established, this does not mean that attachment to parents has disappeared. Most adults continue a meaningful association with their parents, regardless of the fact that the parents penetrate fewer aspects of their lives than they did before. Moreover, a person's response to the death of a parent usually demonstrates that the attachment bond has endured. Even after mourning has been resolved, internal models of the lost figure continue to be an influence. However, there is little systematic knowledge of the nature of these continuing attachments to parents.

Thus, for example, we do not know to what extent a parent and an adult child can enter into a symmetrical relationship in which each, in some ways and at some times, views the other as stronger and wiser, so that each can gain security in the relationship and can give care to the other. Or do old dispositions persist for parents to feel themselves stronger and wiser than their children and/or to be so viewed by them? It is generally believed to be malfunctional for the parent of a young child to reverse roles and to seek care, support, and security from the child, but it seems likely that some role reversal might be healthy should a parent become impaired through illness or old age. Systematic research into such issues is needed.

Another issue involves children's relationships to parent surrogates to whom they may become attached and who may play an important role in their lives, especially in the case of children who find in such relationships the security they could not attain with their own parents. Such surrogates might include an older sibling, another relative such as a grandparent, an especially perceptive and understanding teacher or athletic coach, and so on. As potential attachment figures, these deserve research attention. In the case of older persons, attachment figures cast in the parental mold might include mentors, priests or pastors, or therapists. Bowlby (e.g., 1988) held that in psychotherapy the therapist should assume the role of an attachment figure, who by inspiring trust can provide a secure base from which patients may confidently explore and reassess their working models of attachment figures and of themselves.

These secondary or supplementary attachments may differ from primary attachments in their longevity, that is, in their continuing pervasiveness in the life of a person. The therapeutic relationship is a case in point. It may be very influential for a limited period in a person's life, but when therapy has been terminated, the active relationship usually ceases. To be sure, the therapist and his or her influence may continue to be valued, and the representational model of the relationship may persist. In that sense the attachment continues, even if the active connection has ceased.

## Other Affectional Bonds Throughout the Life Span

Now I will consider affectional bonds other than attachments to parents and surrogate parent figures and will focus on types of bonds that are likely to be represented in all cultures, namely, those that are species-characteristic and may be assumed to have evolved because they yielded survival advantage.

Affectional bonds are not synonymous with relationships. They differ from relationships in three ways. First, affectional bonds are, by definition, relatively long-lasting; relationships may or may not endure. Second, relationships are dyadic. Affectional bonds are characteristic of the individual, not the dyad, and entail representation in the internal organization of the individual person. Third, as Hinde (e.g., 1976) has pointed out, the nature of a relationship between two individuals grows out of the total history of their interaction. This interaction is likely to be varied, involving a number of categories of content. Thus, a relationship is likely to have a number of components, some of which may be irrelevant to what makes for an attachment or indeed any kind of affectional bond.

I define an "affectional bond" as a relatively long-enduring tie in which the partner is important as a unique individual and is interchangeable with none other. In an affectional bond, there is a desire to maintain closeness to the partner. In older children and adults, that closeness may to some extent be sustained over time and distance and during absences, but nevertheless there is at least an intermittent desire to reestablish proximity and interaction, and pleasure – often joy – upon reunion. Inexplicable separation tends to cause distress, and permanent loss would cause grief.

An "attachment" is an affectional bond, and hence an attachment figure is never wholly interchangeable with or replaceable by another, even though there may be others to whom one is also attached. In attachments, as in other affectional bonds, there is a need to maintain proximity, distress upon inexplicable separation, pleasure or joy upon reunion, and grief at loss. There is, however, one criterion of attachment that is not necessarily present in other affectional bonds. This is the experience of security and comfort obtained from the relationship with the partner, and yet the ability to move off from the secure base provided by the partner, with confidence to engage in other activities. Because not all attachments are secure, this criterion should be modified to imply a seeking of the closeness that, if found, would result in feeling secure and comfortable in relation to the partner.

[...]

### *Bonds With Siblings and Other Kin*

Older siblings may, on occasion, play a parental, caregiving role with one or more of their younger siblings and thus may become supplementary attachment figures for them. When two or more siblings are separated from their principal attachment figure and are cared for in the same setting, the distress of each may be somewhat diminished by interaction with the other (e.g., Heinicke & Westheimer, 1965). When a child's parent dies, the child's feelings of grief and abandonment may be alleviated by the care he or she receives from an older sibling who plays a protective, caregiving role. Indeed this role may actually help the older sibling to feel more secure himself or herself, whether because caregiving makes the older sibling feel less helpless or because it diverts the sibling from his or her own feelings of distress or grief.

Ainsworth and Eichberg (in press) found evidence that both feelings of responsibility in caring for others in the family and/or a sense of family solidarity were important factors in successful resolution of mourning the loss of a family member. Further, in many societies (and in some families in our own society) it is common for older siblings to be expected to assume some responsibility as caregivers for their younger brothers or sisters, even when there has been no loss or major separation (e.g., Konner, 1976). However, there has been little systematic research into siblings as attachment figures.

Among the few studies that have been done is one by Stewart (1983), who reported that approximately half of his sample of three- and four-year-old children acted to provide reassurance, comfort, and care to their younger siblings when their mothers left them alone together in a waiting room setting. He later confirmed this finding in a study (Stewart & Marvin, 1984), in which the separation from the mother took place in a modified "strange situation." Whether the older sibling displayed caregiving behavior to the younger was found to be strongly related to the older sibling's conceptual perspective-taking ability, and this in turn was related to the younger sibling's use of the older one as a secure base from which to explore the unfamiliar situation. Thus, even a child of preschool age may serve as an attachment figure to a younger sibling.

Siblings close in age may also be playmates, especially when both are beyond infancy, and some of these may become friends, perhaps best friends, with the same sort of symmetrical, cooperative, reciprocal, mutually trusting relationship earlier described as characteristic of close friendships. This implies a secure attachment component to such sibling friendships.

On the other hand, many sibling relationships are characterized by ambivalent feelings rather than mutual cooperation and trust, and yet are likely to constitute enduring affectional bonds. Whereas friends who had once been close may drift apart as their interests shift and they become less congenial, bonds with kin tend to be much more persistent, even though they may be more ambivalent. One may account for the longevity of kinship bonds in various ways – sociological, biological, and psychological.

Cultural practices tend to regulate relations among kin in such a way as to foster in the individual a sense that he or she can rely on kin as allies or for substantial help when needed, as Weiss (1974) implied. Indeed many people feel that they can ask material help from kin that they would hesitate to seek from friends, however close and congenial. In turn, they feel morally obliged to provide such help to kin when it is demanded. Such attitudes make kin especially important in a person's social network.

The biological explanation is based on the principle that the key dynamic of evolution is neither individual survival nor even species survival, but gene survival. Thus, an individual organism, which shares half of its genes with each of its offspring, promotes the survival of its genes by promoting the welfare of its offspring, and in this regard stands to gain more than by supporting the welfare of others who are more distantly related or not related at all. Siblings, who also share a relatively large proportion of genes, tend to promote the survival of their genes by promoting each other's welfare (and thus survival), and so on, to a lesser extent with kin less closely related.

Another, more psychological, explanation of kinship bonds rests on a shared background of experience within the family or other kinship group. Thus, despite current differences in activities and interests and despite rivalries or other causes of ambivalence, siblings have a background of shared experience over a relatively long period of time, which not only promotes similarities in their perception of situations and in value systems that influence their decisions, but also promotes mutual understanding, without necessarily requiring explicit communication. By extension, these same dynamics may also hold with other kin less closely related.

Indeed, the sharing of experience over a long period of time is important not only in kinship bonds but also may play a role in all affectional bonds that are especially lasting. In enduring marriages, shared experiences are pleasant to talk about and connote a basis of mutual understanding that, in turn, contributes to security and mutual trust. Even after a husband and wife have agreed to divorce, they may still find themselves tied by a long history of shared experiences in which they find pleasure, despite mutual hostility, divergent aims, disparate interests, and new bonds that compete with the old. Like congeniality of interests and activities, shared experiences with friends contribute to the feelings of understanding and being understood that are so focal to close friendships.

[...]

*Child Psychiatry and Human Development*
Fall 1997; 28(1): 33–43

# Bowlby's Legacy to Developmental Psychology

*Inge Bretherton, PhD*
*University of Wisconsin - Madison*

*ABSTRACT: In formulating attachment theory, Bowlby made a number of important conceptual contributions to our understanding of human development. Discussed here are the balance (rather than the conflict) between attachment and exploration, the concept of internal working models, and the parent as a psychological secure base. In addition, Bowlby's "theory of reality" is examined, integration of Bowlby's and Erikson's ideas regarding attachment and culture is suggested, and Bowlby's open-minded approach to theory construction is acknowledged.*

John Bowlby (1907–1991) revolutionized our thinking about the infant–mother relationship and about the importance and function of close relationships in general. Trained as a psychoanalyst in the object relations tradition, he drew on concepts from ethology, cybernetics, developmental psychology and cognition to formulate a new theory, attachment theory. He presented the broad outlines of the theory in three seminal papers to the British Psychological Society in the late 1950s and then spent the next 20 years expanding and elaborating his ideas in three volumes respectively entitled *Attachment, Separation and Loss.*

The impetus for theory development came from a report on the mental health of homeless children in postwar Europe that Bowlby had been commissioned to write for the World Health Organization. Based on his extensive review of the then available literature on institutionalized children who had been separated from parents for a variety of reasons, Bowlby concluded that to grow up mentally healthy "the infant and young child should experience a warm, intimate and continuous relationship with his mother (or permanent mother substitute) in which both find satisfaction and enjoyment." A theory was needed that could explain the nature of the bond whose disruption had such adverse effects on young children. Bowlby rejected then current notions that infants love their mothers because mothers are the purveyors of sensual (oral) gratification. His new theory proposed that infants are social from the beginning, and that, in the course of the second half of the first year of life, infants' "attachment behaviors" become focused on a particular individual or small number of individuals. The evolutionary function of infant–mother attachment is believed to be protection from danger, both physical and psychological. In what follows, I will highlight just a few of the many major contributions Bowlby's theory made to developmental psychology.

[...]

## Internal Working Models

Another major legacy is Bowlby's thinking about the development and function of internal working models (representations) of self and parent or primary caregiver in relationship. He proposed that patterns of relating acquired in the early parent–child relationship are internalized and form the basis for how an individual enters and subsequently maintains other close relationships. Healthy patterns of relating to attachment figures, he contended, depend on open (nondefensive) emotional communication between child and parent that makes continuous updating and refinement of internal working models possible. By contrast, miscommunication, especially deliberate miscommunication wherein a parent tries to falsify a child's actual experience, leads to internal contradictions within working models. Under these conditions, suggested Bowlby, a child will create two segregated sets of working models of self and parent: one set that is accessible to conscious awareness and is compatible with what the child has been told and a second one, inaccessible to awareness, that represents the child's experience unaltered by parental interpretations. Because it is unconscious, this second set will be hard to modify. As Bowlby put it:

> '*Thus the family experience of those who grow up anxious and fearful is found to be characterized not only by uncertainty about parental support but often also by covert yet strongly distorting parental pressures: pressure on the child, for example, to act as caregiver for a parent;* or to adopt, and thereby to confirm, a parent's false models – of self, of child and of the relationship. *Similarly the family experience of those who grow up to become relatively stable and self-reliant is characterized not only by unfailing parental support when called upon but also by a steady yet timely encouragement toward increasing autonomy, and* by the frank communication by parents of working models – of themselves, of child and of others – that are not only tolerably valid but are open to be questioned and revised ... *inheritance of mental health and mental ill health through the medium of family microculture ... may well be far more important, than is their inheritance through the medium of genes.*'

In recent years, empirical studies – especially those using the Adult Attachment Interview and other representational assessments of attachment, have corroborated Bowlby's claim that open communication is one of the hallmarks of secure attachment and that insecure attachment is often characterized by an inability to discuss attachment experiences openly and coherently with nonjudgmental interviewers. These studies support the assumption that insecure individuals' internal working models are fragmented while secure individuals' working model are better integrated and hence facilitate easier access to attachment-related information.

## The Psychological Secure Base

Contained within the earlier quotation about parent–child communication is Bowlby's suggestion that parents function not only as protectors from physical danger, but as secure bases for a child's exploration of the inner world. In most of his work, Bowlby discusses this function in negative terms by dwelling on the adverse consequences likely to ensue when a parent engages in deliberate misinterpretations of attachment-related events that he or she does not want the child to understand and then places a taboo on the discussion of that event or related topics. Yet it is not self-evident why self-deception or simple failure to understand on the part of the child cannot also play a role in the construction of inadequate working models. When Bowlby highlighted the implications of misleading parent–child communication about traumatic situations as a risk factor for psychopathology, he did not sufficiently consider the young child's inability to make sense of such events. Children may misinterpret what they are told because their background knowledge is insufficient, and conversely, parents may inadvertently fail to clarify misunderstandings or explain procedures at an age-appropriate level.

The positive side of parent–child dialogue has been neglected because of attachment theory's emphasis on optimal parenting as primarily supportive and responsive to infant signals. This perspective fails to acknowledge that in responding to a child parents also exert an active teaching influence whether or not they mean to do so.

An alternative view of the parental role as psychological secure base can be derived from social constructivist ideas beginning with William James, James Mark Baldwin, George Herbert Mead, Lev Vygotsky, and more recently exemplified by Barbara Rogoff. Under this view the parent is an active *guide* who – for better or worse – transmits his or her own patterns of relating to the child. This occurs initially through nonverbal interaction but increasingly also through dialogue about past, future, and hypothetical experiences. The child does not passively take in what he or she is told, but filters parental communications through his or her own developing system of understandings and, indeed, often seeks interpretations from the parent.

Katherine Nelson, also taking a social constructivist stance, reviews a variety of helpful studies on parent–child conversations about past, present, and future which illustrate this point. These studies underscore the vital role parent–child dialogue can play in structuring not only the content but even the organization of child memory, and hence by inference the child's internal working model of self and the world. Miller, Hoogstra, Mintz, Fung, and Williams provided a striking example of these processes at work when parents familiarize children with cultural products such as story books. In a detailed case study, they describe a 23-month-old child who requested rereadings of a story that had troubled him, and then reworked the story in conversation with his mother until he had come to terms with the various upsetting story issues that did not accord with his own experience of families. Interestingly, once the child had worked out his personal concerns about the story, the retellings ceased.

[...]

*Attachment & Human Development*
March 2005; 7(1): 31–49

## Anna's story: A qualitative analysis of an at-risk mother's experience in an attachment-based foster care program

*Molly D. Kretchmar, Nancy L. Worsham, & Natalia Swenson*
*Gonzaga University, Spokane, USA*

**Abstract:** *This study chronicles an at-risk mother's experience in an alternative foster care program. Influenced by attachment theory, the Children's Ark reunited children with their mothers in a supervised home environment while also providing residential support, intensive therapy, and education. After losing custody of her infant Kindra[1], 18-year-old Anna[1] participated in the Ark for 2 years, after which she regained custody of Kindra. We assessed Anna and Kindra at multiple times using a variety of instruments, including a semi-structured interview, the Adult Attachment Interview, and the Strange Situation procedure. Anna moved from a profoundly insecure state of mind to a secure one, while Kindra moved from a resistant to a secure attachment. Qualitative analyses of Anna's interviews documented growth in her capacity to use the important relationships at the Ark as secure bases and to welcome rather than fear intimacy with Kindra. The qualitative analyses also described growth in Anna's capacities for reflective functioning and positive changes in her internal working model. We conclude with an analysis of the process of change from the perspective of attachment theory.*

[...]

### Qualitative analyses, results, and interpretation of semi-structured interviews

The researchers coded all semi-structured interviews using qualitative analysis techniques (e.g., Miles & Huberman, 1984; Rubin & Rubin, 1995). The two principal investigators and one highly skilled undergraduate research assistant analysed the data using the process described below. We focused on the question: 'What helped?' That is, what helped Anna move from losing custody of her child to self-sufficiency and positive caregiving, and ultimately to regaining custody? We explored this question in two ways: first, we examined the things that Anna described as important changes or as having had a positive impact on her. We called this 'what' part of change 'content analysis'. Next, we looked at events that Anna may or may not have described directly but that we inferred had helped her. This included evidence of psychological changes (e.g., changes in depression, reflective functioning), changes in significant relationships, changes in sense of self, and so forth. This allowed us to further examine the 'how' part of change that we termed 'process analysis'.

We followed a series of steps in completing the analyses: (1) read the entire transcript without taking notes or coding to get a sense of the whole story; (2) read again for content analysis as described above and marked themes and passages; (3) read again for process analysis using the attachment theory lens by focusing on several primary constructs (e.g., secure base, internal working model, reflective functioning) and marked themes and passages; (4) compiled all three coders' notes by indicating the themes and passages all three identified, two identified, and one identified. There was a high level of convergence, and we discussed areas of discrepancy; (5) compiled tables to examine processes of change over time.

Most of what we present below focuses on the process analysis described above and is organized around the attachment constructs examined. Space constraints preclude a full presentation of the content analysis. Of note, the content and process analyses converged over time. That is, Anna developed such an astute awareness and capacity to analyse her own experience of change that her explanations matched and added insight to our own (see below). Consistent with strategies of qualitative research, we preserve Anna's story by supporting identified themes with her own words[2].

[...]

### *Internal working model*

As described by Bowlby (1969/82), the internal working model reflects thoughts and feelings about the self and about the self in relation to others. Anna spoke of her feelings of low self-worth, anxiety, depression, and self-doubt. Although her words over time indicated an ongoing struggle with her sense of self, she showed improvements in this area. Her words also indicated a growing capacity to read others' cues, a new understanding of relationships (e.g., that some are safe), and an ability to define and protect her own boundaries (see Table V).

**Table V: Reflections of changes in Anna's internal working model**

***Time 1*** **(intake) Feelings of worthlessness/low self-esteem**: My self-esteem definitely, my sense of self worth ... I always feel like I don't, I don't deserve anything.

***Time 4*** **Struggling with sense of self**: I've been doing very, very well with trying to treat myself with some respect, and there's times when I just get so, I get feeling very lonely and so alone that I just feel like 'oh, I don't care' ... Why should I be nice to myself if I'm gonna be alone and nice to myself?

***Time 5*** **Childhood effect on current view, struggle in relationships**: The connection and the sense of connection that I had with my parents was, with my father, I had none. With my mother, I had one, but it was built on ideas and beliefs, not really truth and reality ... it was me compromising myself so that I could have some degree of connection with my mom.

***Time 7*** **Working on relations and attachment issues, more authentic self**: I am really working on my relationships. 'Cause I really believe that that is the core issue for me ... is my relationship with people in general, and learning how to maintain relationship because one of my fears is you know, moving out and losing whatever relationships I have here.

***Time 8*** **(discharge) Changing view of relationships, self as separate**: I'm a lot happier now than I have ever been in my life. I feel a lot stronger now. I feel like I'm able to define who I am and let other people know that. Whereas before, I didn't know who I was, and therefore I just let other people choose for me. *(re: relationship with Kindra)* But then learning that that wasn't the only way ... learning a lot of things about relationships that I never knew made it easier for me to be able to be in relationship with her.

### *Mother as a secure base for child*

Upon entry, Anna reported a basic notion of the importance of providing security for her child. She clearly wanted to act as a secure base, but her anxious caregiving disrupted the relationship. Based on her childhood history and in the absence of intervention, we would expect Anna to carry forward her own insecurity into her relationship with Kindra (Kretchmar & Jacobvitz, 2002; Oliver, 1993; van IJzendoorn, 1992).

An early videotaped interaction with Anna and Kindra, processed with the interviewer at the Time 7 interview, was especially revealing in terms of this intergenerational process. The video began with Anna holding 6-month-old Kindra, both of them very still, nearly frozen. Anna commented: 'But see there. I'm totally gone. I have nothing to do with her except trying to keep her calm.' The interviewer asked about the importance of keeping Kindra calm (using the metaphor, 'like skating on thin ice'). Anna responded: 'That was such a big issue for me. When she was able to play, I would never face her toward me, I would always hide ... It was like, do NOT break it [*re: the ice*].' The interviewer asked: 'Were you scared of her then?' Anna stated: 'Oh yeah, big time. Big time scared of her. I was very scared.' As proposed by Main and Hesse (1990) frightened and/or frightening caregiving is a likely precursor to disorganized attachment, as the caregiver is simultaneously a source of comfort and a source of fear.

Of note, although we might have expected Anna to show frightening or hostile caregiving toward Kindra based on Anna's own history, Anna did not articulate nor display such concerns. It is possible that any hostility that Anna felt became translated into a helpless and even dissociative stance, as evident in the stilling behavior discussed above (see Lyons-Ruth, Bronfman, & Atwood, 1999). Further, Anna's early caregiving behavior seemed more consistent with what Lyons-Ruth and Spielman (2004) described as a helpless–fearful profile than a hostile profile, both of which are 'alternate behavioral expressions of a single underlying hostile–helpless dyadic internal model' stemming from early maltreatment (Lyons-Ruth & Spielman, 2004, p.325).

As Anna experienced movement in other areas (e.g., experiencing security and support herself, enhanced capacity for reflective functioning) her ability to act as a secure base increased markedly. For example, she began to enjoy intimacy with her child (see Table VI, Time 6), rather than fear it, and continued to support her child's exploration (see Table VI).

**Table VI: Anna's increasing ability to act as a Secure Base (SB) for Kindra**

***Time 2*** **Emerging SB for child**: I want her (*Kindra*) to grow up happy and that is not what I grew up. I don't know how my parents raised me so I would grow up to question myself so much and to not be happy; I stay clear in terms of doing things differently with her. (*re: what do you enjoy most about Kindra*) I know that I am there for her; she is also there for me.

***Time 4*** **Increased signs of secure child**: (*re: reunion with Kindra*) Yesterday I went to the doctor, and she was very upset that I left ... And when I came back, Janet was holding (*Kindra*) up to the window. I ran up to the door, and I walked inside and she was kinda leaning back against Janet, and she looked at me with biggest open-mouthed smile, and she held out her hand ... and Janet got her down and she walked over to me just holding out this truck (*laughs*) I mean it wasn't like 'look what I have' it was like 'I'm so glad to see you, I wanna share what I'm ...'

***Time 6*** **Welcoming intimacy**: (*re: describing relationship with Kindra*) Um, I'd say close ... a lot more intimate ... the biggest thing about our relationship though, is that it's not scary anymore.

***Time 7*** **SB for child**: (*re: describing relationship with Kindra*) The relationship that I had with her when she was first born is nothing, we have nothing like the relationship we had before. And that's because I wanted different things from our relationship then, and I didn't understand what our relationship was supposed to be ... when she was first born, I wanted her because I needed something.

***Time 8*** **(discharge) SB/relationship with child**: (*re: what changed her relationship with Kindra?*) Um, I think the major thing that contributed to it was ME being able to change my relationship with myself ... learning how to, to be in relationships with people ... learning a lot of things about relationships that I never knew ... made it easier for me to be able to be in relationship with her.

[...]

## Notes

1 In order to protect the privacy and respect the confidentiality of the mother and child represented in this paper, their names have been changed. Further, the mother provided full consent to her and her daughter's participation in every assessment used in this study, and the consent process was reviewed with the mother at each assessment. Finally, the mother read a complete draft of this manuscript prior to its submission in order to confirm that it was an authentic representation of her experience and that she was comfortable with its contents.

2 Throughout this paper, direct quotations have been slightly edited for enhanced readability.

*American Psychologist*
October 2000; 55(10): 1093–1104

# Attachment and Culture: Security in the United States and Japan

*Fred Rothbaum, Tufts University*
*John Weisz, University of California, Los Angeles*
*Martha Pott, Tufts University*
*Kazuo Miyake, Hokkaido University*
*Gilda Morelli, Boston College*

*Attachment theorists maintain that cultural differences are relatively minor, and they focus on universals. Here the authors highlight evidence of cultural variations and note ways in which attachment theory is laden with Western values and meaning. Comparisons of the United States and Japan highlight the cultural relativity of 3 core hypotheses of attachment theory: that caregiver sensitivity leads to secure attachment, that secure attachment leads to later social competence, and that children who are securely attached use the primary caregiver as a secure base for exploring the external world. Attachment theorists use measures of sensitivity, competence, and secure base that are biased toward Western ways of thinking: The measures emphasize the child's autonomy, individuation, and exploration. In Japan, sensitivity, competence, and secure base are viewed very differently, calling into question the universality of fundamental tenets of attachment theory. The authors call for an indigenous approach to the psychology of attachment.*

> *'When most investigators [have] ... a common cultural perspective or ideological position, the effect may be to retard or to corrupt the search for scientific knowledge by collectively blinding them to alternative conceptions.'*
>
> *(Spence, 1985, p.1285)*

In this quotation from her 1985 American Psychological Association presidential address, Janet Spence argued that Western[1] theories of achievement, although assumed to have universal significance, are in fact deeply rooted in American individualism. Criticisms about ethnocentrism have also been leveled against Western theories of control and self, and attempts to develop culturally specific theories of these phenomena have been made (e.g., Baumeister, 1986; Markus & Kitayama, 1991; Weisz, Rothbaum, & Blackburn, 1984a, 1984b).

In this article, we make similar criticisms of psychology's most influential theory of relatedness: attachment theory. We argue that Western investigators have been blinded to alternative conceptions of relatedness, because they tend 'to construct other cultures in terms saturated with Western ideals and preconceptions' (Gergen, Gulerce, Lock, & Misra, 1996, p. 497; see also Bruner, 1990). The attachment perspective has dominated academicians' understanding of relatedness for the past 20 years, as evidenced by the many articles published (e.g., 662 entries in a 1999 psycINFO search), and has 'spawn[ed] one of the broadest, most profound and creative lines of research in 20th century psychology' (Cassidy & Shaver, 1999, p. x). Moreover, it has served as an ideological basis for parent intervention programs and therapeutic interventions (Bowlby, 1988; Lieberman & Zeanah, 1999; Slade, 1999). If, as we suggest, the concepts that frame this theory are deeply rooted in a Western perspective, then the theory and these derivative interventions require renewed scrutiny through the lens of culture.

[...]

## Competence in Children

### *Exploration, autonomy, and efficacy*

U.S. children who are classified as securely attached as infants are later more likely to be willing and able to venture forth on their own. Securely attached children are more autonomous, more likely to persist in problem solving, have higher self-esteem and ego resilience, and engage in more versatile and positive exploration than do their insecure counterparts (Grossman, Grossman, & Zimmermann, 1999; Weinfield et al., 1999). Insecurely attached children not only score lower on these indexes of competence, but they score higher on dependency–widely regarded as a marker of failure to successfully individuate (Weinfield et al., 1999).

[1] The term *Western* as used here refers to the United States, Canada, and Western European countries. Because most of the studies conducted in these countries primarily use mainstream middle-class samples, these are the samples to which the findings reported here pertain.

In their review of the evidence on attachment and social competence, Weinfield et al. (1999) concluded,

> *Overall, these findings on dependency, self-reliance and efficacy suggest that early attachment history does contribute to a child's effectiveness in the world. Children with secure histories seem to believe that, as was true in infancy, they can get their needs met through their own efforts and bids. In contrast, children with anxious histories seem to believe that ... they must rely extensively on others who may or may not meet their needs.*
>
> *(p.77)*

In this quotation, the authors' focus on individuation and on related qualities, such as self-reliance and efficacy, seems to lead them to devalue reliance on others as a way of meeting one's needs. The path of relying on others, so often devalued in the West, is often favored, even prescribed, in Japan (Azuma et al., 1981; Lebra, 1994; Rothbaum et al., in press). For example, Japanese preschoolers' group-oriented accomplishments are much more encouraged and valued than are their individual accomplishments (Lewis, 1988; Peak, 1989). Dependence on others as a way of meeting one's needs and coordinating one's needs with the needs of others (e.g., social fittedness or accommodation) are seen as essential to the goal of social harmony, which is highly valued in Japan (Kitayama, Markus, Masumoto, & Norasakkunkit, 1997; Roland, 1989; Weisz et al., 1984a, 1984b).

[...]

## Competence in Adulthood

Western adults who are securely attached show higher levels of social competence than do adults who are insecurely attached (ambivalent, resistant, or preoccupied). This finding takes on added significance when combined with the attachment theory claim that secure attachments in infancy and adulthood are related (Bowlby, 1979; Hazan & Shaver, 1994). Adults who are securely attached show greater competence in several areas: They have greater comfort with autonomy and greater valuing of it; indeed, attachment theorists refer to securely attached adults as 'autonomous.' They have a more positive view of self. They have a greater willingness to verbally communicate with their partners, a lesser likelihood of avoiding discussion of strong affect, and a lesser likelihood of showing signs of distress related to disagreement with attachment figures. They also assess others more realistically, rather than idealizing their partners and past relationships (Allen & Land, 1999; Bartholomew & Shaver, 1998; Feeney, 1999).

There is evidence that all of these aspects of 'competence,' which are associated with security in the West, are seen more negatively by Japanese:

'From [an East Asian] perspective, an assertive, autonomous ... person is immature and uncultivated' (Fiske, Kitayama, Markus, & Nisbett, 1998, p.923). In Japan, self-enhancement is less common and less valued, and self-criticism and self-effacement are more common and more valued. People are expected to respectfully and empathically preserve harmony by avoiding any expression of discord or direct expression of wants, and adherence to values of filial piety makes negative comments about parents inappropriate (Fiske et al., 1998; Kitayama et al., 1997).

The dissimilarity between Western and Japanese ideas about consequences of security is clearest with regard to independence. There is substantial evidence in the West that secure adults tend to be less dependent: They are less likely to be clingy and to rely on others to meet their needs, less anxious about gaining acceptance from others, have less of a preference for unqualified closeness, and are less likely to experience love as involving union (Bartholomew & Shaver, 1998; Feeney, 1999; Hazan & Shaver, 1994). In Japan, dependence (i.e., interdependence), seeking of acceptance and commitment, and desire for union are more common and more likely to be associated with competence (Fiske et al., 1998) and presumably with security.[2]

[...]

## Attachment and Exploration

The concept of secure base was originally intended (Ainsworth, 1963) and is sometimes used to refer to infants' sense of safety in all aspects of engagement with the world. However, the majority of attachment researchers use the concept of secure base to refer to the link between attachment and exploration (e.g., Cassidy, 1999; Kobak, 1999; Posada et al., 1995). Although acknowledging that the attachment system can be linked to other behavioral systems, including affiliation and sexual mating, these investigators presume that attachment is most closely linked to exploration (Ainsworth, Bell, & Stayton, 1971). They claim that infants who are sufficiently protected and comforted by the presence of caregivers are better able to use their caregivers as a secure base from which to explore their environment.

Our analysis of the secure base focuses on this attachment–exploration link. We maintain that attachment theorists' conceptualization of the secure base reflects the Western emphasis on exploration and the belief that

[2] We are not suggesting that most Japanese are insecurely attached. Two characteristics of insecure-ambivalent people that are not at all common among Japanese individuals are uncertainty about caregivers' availability caused by caregiver inconsistency and difficulty regulating negative affect. Our point is that Japanese children and children classified as insecure in the United States share several salient qualities. Perhaps this is why many Japanese are classified as insecurely attached (Miyake, Chen, & Campos, 1985; Takahashi, 1990).

exploration leads to individuation – which is viewed as a healthy, positive outcome. As noted by Seifer and Schiller (1995), 'Secure base behavior provides a context in which differentiation of self and other can take place' (p.149). Japanese experts are less likely to emphasize a dynamic that is so centered on individuation. On the basis of her study of attachment in Japan, Takahashi (1990) concluded that 'mothers' effectiveness in serving a secure base function well represents the quality of attachment only in the American culture, in which social independence or self-reliance is emphasized' (p.29).

Observations of infants in different cultures (and different species) suggest that there may be a biological basis to the link between attachment and exploration (van IJzendoorn & Sagi, 1999). It is adaptive for human young to explore and to do so only as long as a caregiver is available to respond if needed. However, there is evidence that the extent to which exploration occurs, and the primacy of the link between attachment and exploration, varies across cultures.[3] In five separate studies, Japanese babies were observed to engage in less exploratory activity than were U.S. babies (Bornstein, Azuma, Tamis-LeMonda, & Ogino, 1990; Bornstein, Toda, Azuma, Tamis-LeMonda, & Ogino, 1990; Caudill & Schooler, 1973; Caudill & Weinstein, 1974; Shand & Kosawa, 1985). Another study found that Japanese babies explored much less than U.S. babies when left alone in the Strange Situation and manipulated toys less often when their mothers returned (Takahashi, 1990). Moreover, Japanese babies were more oriented to their mothers in circumstances involving both distress and positive emotions, and U.S. infants were more oriented to the environment in those circumstances (Bornstein, Azuma, et al., 1990; Miyake et al., 1985).

[...]

[3] Several studies have found greater exploration in the United States than in other cultures, including Mayan culture (Gaskins, 1996), Tanzanian culture (McGillicuddy-De Lisi & Subramanian, 1996), and Argentinian culture (Bornstein, Haynes, Pascual, Painter, & Galperin, 1999). Gaskins (1996) noted that the motivation to master and explore, although valued in the United States, 'would be considered by Mayan caregivers a negative characteristic for infants' (pp. 361–362).

CHAPTER 11

# Writing up your qualitative research report

## Contents


- Aims 358
- 1 General guidance 358
- 2 Reporting thematic analysis 360
- 3 Structuring your qualitative report 362
- 4 Example of a report write-up 367
- 5 A final word 377
- References 377

## Aims

This chapter aims to:

- provide general guidance on writing up your qualitative research report
- reflect on different report-writing conventions
- demonstrate ways in which to write up thematic analysis
- outline the different sections for your qualitative report.

## 1 General guidance

Report writing has already been described in detail in Chapter 7. You should return to this for the basic framework of a write-up, and the philosophy behind it. There are important differences between quantitative and qualitative reports, however, and these need to be kept in mind when you produce your report of the qualitative project that you have just completed.

Please note the following points:

1. Qualitative research focuses on answering research questions rather than testing hypotheses.
2. It tends to talk about the *process of analysis* or findings, rather than results. This is explored further in the next section of this chapter.
3. It gives prominence to thinking about the whole process of carrying out and writing up research, in particular through the inclusion of a reflexive analysis in the write-up.
4. The use of 'I' is permitted in qualitative reports.

One important difference that you may have already spotted should you have accessed journal articles via the Open University online library, is that quantitative researchers aim for a formal writing style and will almost always use the third person (hence avoiding the use of 'I/we'). By using the third person, they are following a convention that emphasises the objective and scientific nature of the research process along with the neutrality of the researcher. In contrast, many qualitative researchers embrace the use of 'I/we' in their writing, as the research is seen as not just the participant's story but also a product of the researcher. This difference in language style reflects the underlying assumptions in both types of research about the role of the researcher and his/her impact on the research process.

Therefore, you may find it more appropriate to write in the first person, recognising your own social, psychological and demographic position in the research process and reflecting on whether this might have affected the way in which you examined and analysed the material. It is difficult to stand back and look at qualitative material as an outsider. And so a danger is that you may be tempted to draw on your subjective understandings without acknowledging this. This should be avoided, regardless of whether writing in the first or third person (see Section 4 on reflexivity in Chapter 10 for suggestions for ways to avoid this danger).

The aims of achieving accuracy, brevity and clarity are as important when writing a qualitative report as when writing a quantitative report – remember your aim is to communicate your findings and your thoughts about them to your readers. In a qualitative study you should aim to provide sufficient detail to allow the reader to pick up your report and clearly understand what you have done. However, it is also important to acknowledge that a different researcher may have come to different conclusions from the material analysed. Hence, as mentioned above, when writing up qualitative reports there is a tradition of separating out the discussion into two sections, one of which is the conventional discussion, and the other a 'reflexive analysis'. We will look at these in more detail later on in this chapter but, briefly, the 'reflexive analysis' section considers your thoughts and feelings as a researcher about the research process itself.

You might also find the following tips helpful:

1 A good piece of general advice is to make a brief plan for your report, which should help it to remain structured. Your research question should remain at the forefront, and it is often useful to write it down on a card, and to stick it in front of you throughout the process, to enable you to remain focused on your substantive area.
2 You should try to review your report a day or so after you have written it. This may be difficult, because you will inevitably be writing to tight deadlines. If possible, however, try to finish your report slightly before the cut-off date, and then put it to one side for a few days, turning to something else in the interim. Then return to it, and reread it. The gap of a few days will help you to view what you have written with more detachment than would otherwise be the case and enable you to produce an improved report as a result.
3 Whether you find you have time to do this or not, it is always helpful to get somebody who is unfamiliar with the research to look at the report to see if they understand what you have written. This is something that academic writers regularly do. For example, a number of colleagues looked at and commented on a draft of this chapter before a final copy was produced. An added advantage of this process is that other people may be able to make positive contributions to your analysis by shedding a different light on it from a new angle. Their comments may enable you to make improvements based on their reflections.

## 2 Reporting thematic analysis

Section 3 of this chapter will provide guidance on writing the different sections of your qualitative report. Before doing so we focus here on one particular section of your report – the *analysis* section – in which you describe the thematic analysis that you conducted. Rather than refer to results, qualitative reports refer to analysis or to findings. The first thing that you need to note is that the analysis section of the report will be longer than a corresponding section in a quantitative study. What you are doing is not simply reporting the results of a statistical analysis, from which you can extract conclusions about the relationship between variables in terms of a predetermined hypothesis. In the words of Potter and Wetherell (1987), what you are doing is presenting 'analysis and conclusions in such a way that the reader is able to assess the researcher's interpretations' (p. 172). You must demonstrate the whole reasoning process, situate your research question and discussion within a theoretical framework, justify your reading and interpretation of the material and include relevant examples.

Potter and Wetherell (1987) illustrate the difference between qualitative and quantitative research processes using a simple analogy. Quantitative research, they argue, is a bit like baking cakes from a recipe. There are clear-cut stages which are followed in chronological order. For a recipe to work, the sequence of steps must be adhered to, and ingredients added at the right time. Within this culinary analogy, writing up would be comparable to laying out the cake on a tray, to be served to dinner guests. It is the last stage of the research process, by which the hard work is presented to an interested or hungry audience.

Qualitative research, according to Potter and Wetherell (1987), is less like baking and more like riding a bicycle. Apart from getting on and off, there isn't a single, straightforward set of procedures to be followed in a set order. You often need to do several things at once in a carefully coordinated way. Also, when you buy a bicycle, it does not come with instructions about how to ride it: you must learn the skill through experience! Qualitative research is a bit like that: there isn't a clear set of sequentially ordered procedures for extracting meaning from a transcript or well-ordered steps for the researcher to follow. Right until the end of your write-up you will need to go back to your transcript and look over the comments you jotted in the margins or on 'post-it' notes, etc. You will find things that you missed the first time round and your opinion on the meaning and the significance of specific extracts may well change. Some things that seemed obvious at the start of your analysis will turn out not to be so. Remember that qualitative research is frequently an iterative process.

Consider the following thoughts on qualitative research from Billig (1997). In this paragraph he is referring specifically to discourse analysis, although his words also apply to thematic analysis and other qualitative methods:

> *There can be no detailed description of procedures, which can be followed precisely in order for analysts to build up a composite picture. So much depends upon the details of the material collected and the theoretical hunches of the analyst. However, one point can be stressed: the analysis is achieved through writing. One does not do the analysis, and then write up the results. Instead, one begins writing and tries to arrange the material through writing. One should not underestimate the difficulty of this task. Nor should one offer the comfort that it becomes easier with experience. There is no substitute for drafting and redrafting, trying out ways of analysis, and then abandoning them. In short, progress can be judged by the volume of unsatisfactory drafts in the waste-paper basket ...*
>
> *(Billig, 1997, p. 48)*

So, don't forget the importance of writing. If qualitative research is like riding a bicycle, then writing is like balancing: whatever else you are doing, you must balance – from the moment you get on the bike, right until you get off it! Of course, as the quotation from Billig (1997) above implies, it may not always be easy to decide when to get off. Billig's implication is that you should continue writing and rewriting up to the point when further drafting reveals no further insights, as long as time permits. It is therefore vitally important not to leave your TMA until the last minute!

When writing up a piece of qualitative research, one thing that you will have to do is to illustrate your analysis with examples or extracts from your transcript. It is very important to strike a balance between the number of quotations and the analytical comments you make. Your analysis section should *not* consist mainly of quotations, which would therefore mean that you do not include sufficient analysis. At the same time, important points you make should be illustrated with examples.

It is very unlikely that you will be able to include all the quotations which you selected at the coding stage. This poses the question: what constitutes the best quotation to use? Apart from the obvious criteria concerning relevance, here are some thoughts, once again from Billig:

> *In going through the pages of transcripts, some passages seem to leap out; they might be filled with humour, irony and surprise; they might make the analyst smile. This is the sort of passage, which you, the analyst might wish to tell your friends, for it makes a good story. And this is precisely the sort of passage to include in the analysis. If your theories are encouraging you to include the dull passages, and to omit*

> *the 'good stories', then get some better theories. After all, analysts, at all stages of qualitative research, have to back their own judgment. And can there be a better guide than the feeling that there is a good story to tell?*
>
> *(Billig, 1997, p. 54)*

The point that Billig is making is that when writing up a qualitative piece of research, you do not have a prescribed and definitive methodology to rely upon. You cannot assume that anyone else tackling the same transcript using the same analytic method would have arrived at the same conclusion, in the way that a quantitative researcher can be confident that anyone else would count the same number of words or measure the same heart rate. The interpretation you provide (albeit theoretically informed and grounded in data) is your own, and it is up to you to convince the reader that there is something in what you are saying. One way of doing so is to tell a good, convincing story, and this involves choosing relevant quotations to support this story. Insights you make about the transcript must be *evidence-based*. Don't expect the reader to take your word for it: you must show them *where* things are in the transcript and *what* led you to your particular conclusion if they are to be convinced by your analysis.

We shall now look at all the different sections that will make up your report.

# 3 Structuring your qualitative report

You have already been introduced to the structure of writing a report in Chapter 7 and you may find it helpful to look again at the relevant sections in that chapter and indeed the feedback you received from your tutor on TMA 03. Here we draw attention to the particular conventions of a qualitative report. Your report of the qualitative analysis you have undertaken, and the research project from which it came, should be not more than 2500 words in length. All researchers, whether quantitative or qualitative, have to write their research reports to word lengths that journals specify, so it is a useful skill to learn to write up research to a preset length. It should report on the whole process (i.e. on how the research question came about, the relevant theoretical background as well as the thematic analysis you undertook) and should include the nine sections covered below.

## Title (not included in word count)

Try to make sure that this fits the analysis you have done. It should give the reader an indication of what is to follow.

## Abstract (about 100 words)

As a matter of general advice, it is often a good idea to write the abstract last, so that it really is acting as a brief summary of your whole project. Remember that your study should be described as a qualitative thematic analysis of an interview.

## Introduction (about 550 words)

This section should review the relevant literature, structured so that it presents an argument that shows why your research question appropriately arises from the literature. It should start by describing in a few sentences the perspective (theoretical framework) within which the research was conducted and making explicit the epistemological and ontological assumptions underpinning that perspective. The reader will then be able to see how the research question is embedded in that perspective as well as how it may relate to previous research in this particular area. The research question should be stated clearly at the end of this section. We have provided information relevant to the introduction for your report in Chapter 10, in the first part of Section 2 and in the Appendix.

## Method (about 200 words)

The method section in a qualitative report is often quite short and is not subsectioned. (You may remember that in the quantitative report you did for TMA 03, you divided the method section into several subsections and you probably wrote quite a bit more than 200 words.) In this project, you are analysing pre-existing material. You should make this clear to the reader in this section. Include a brief description of who was interviewed and who carried out the interviews. You should acknowledge the ethical issues involved in the research even though you have not addressed them yourself, as the interviews have been carried out for you. You will also need to give a clear account of the way in which you carried out your thematic analysis, from familiarisation through to first-order and higher-level coding, so that the reader can use the same techniques on the transcript material, and can understand how you arrived at your themes.

## Analysis (about 650 words)

Please see Section 2 of this chapter for full advice on writing this part of the report. The key point to note is that the emphasis is on the understandings that have been gained from the findings of the research. This section needs to:

- Remind the reader of your research question.
- Give a general picture of what you have found (e.g. the major themes were identified, as follows ...).
- Present the themes that you have arrived at.
- Provide supportive quotations for each theme – remember these should be actual quotations from the transcript, with the line numbers clearly stated, so that the reader can easily find where they occur in the interviews. Note that the quotations count in the word length for this section – choose carefully what to include!
- Give a commentary that makes links between the quotations, making clear which points seem to be well established and which are more speculative. For example, a theme which occurs 'throughout the interview' (which you would demonstrate did occur throughout the interview by indicating the many line numbers in the transcripts where it recurs) might be well established, whereas an interesting point which was only mentioned once in the interview might be more speculative.

## Discussion (about 600 words)

As outlined in Chapter 7, the discussion section should clearly state what you have found. You should link the themes to the literature and the research question covered in the introduction, coming to a conclusion as to how the findings from the interview fit with the literature and how they answer the research question. As you are looking at a research question centred on the topic of 'attachment', you might discuss how *your findings* relate to those of previous researchers. You may also want to consider the influence of certain methodological issues; for instance:

- The demographic characteristics of the interviewee or interviewer – did these have a bearing on your findings?
- Are there time, space and/or methodological differences between the study you are writing up and the literature you have cited (e.g. US versus UK context or changes over time)?
- The retrospective nature of the accounts – how might this influence your findings? Think about how people tend to produce consistent narratives about their lives – to make sense and give meaning to experiences which in themselves might appear confusing or contradictory.
- What do you think the participant did not say that you might have expected according to the theoretical framework(s) that led to your research question?
- Were there any unexpected findings and how did you interpret these?

- Are there any findings that could be interpreted in different ways? It should be acknowledged that you cannot draw a simple conclusion based on such findings.
- What general implications can be drawn from this research?
- If you were redoing the study (including the data collection), what changes might you make?

Any or all of the above may be of importance (and there could be other points that are not included in the list above).

## Reflexive analysis (about 300 words)

We have seen that reflexivity is an important critical component of qualitative research, allowing the reader to see some of the researcher's story. As mentioned previously, a major difference between quantitative and qualitative reports is that the latter include a separate reflexive analysis section following the discussion section. This is a short section and, before writing it, you may find it helpful to look back through the notes you made while carrying out the project work. Think about how your own positioning may have influenced the analysis, the discussion of findings and any conclusions reached. You may, for example, consider whether the fact that you either have or have not had similar experiences to those of the participant affected your interpretations (either positively or negatively). Section 4 of Chapter 10 provides ideas about how to analyse your reflexivity in relation to the project you are writing up.

## References (not included in the word count)

This section is as important as the other sections of your report and needs to be done to the standard format (see the *Assignment Booklet* for guidance on referencing conventions). The task of producing your reference section will be much less tedious if every time you cite a source you make a note of it, so that you can ensure that your final list is comprehensive and so that you have a full list of the references you have used and do not have to engage in time-consuming searches for them. Both experienced and new researchers often neglect this and are then forced to spend long periods searching for references when they have otherwise finished a piece of writing.

## Appendices (not included in the word count)

You should include a copy of your annotated transcript and any notes you have made on how you identified your key themes. This will help your tutor to see how you have done your analysis and which specific parts of the transcript you have related to which particular themes in your analysis.

## General points to consider

We have already mentioned that it is a good idea to read your report a day or so after finishing it (if time permits of course!). The idea is that you will be more detached when rereading it and be able to make improvements. To finish this section, we would like to highlight the elements that combine to make a good qualitative research report.

Crucially, the study needs to be grounded in a relevant perspective (e.g. social constructionism) and theory (attachment theory in this case). This needs to be clearly stated and argued in the report. For their methodological considerations to be sound, the qualitiative researcher will also have ensured that the method they have used is appropriate to the ontology and epistemology of the perspective they have chosen. Here all of these decisions have been made for you (including the choice of thematic analysis as a method of anlysis). However, when writing the report you need to explain these choices (as if you had made them), and relate them to the thematic analysis you have done. Your report should have theoretical coherence and your discussion should relate back to the perspective and background theory outlined in your introduction.

It is easy in qualitative research to find yourself getting lost in description. After all, you are selecting evidence in the form of quotations to illustrate and support the themes you have identified and this can take up a large amount of your available words. However, as we explained in Section 2 of this chapter, qualitative analysis should go beyond mere description; you need to strike a balance between the number of quotations and the analytical comments included. It is very important that you do not engage in 'wild analysis' (see Chapter 10, Section 4.1). You should, therefore, ensure that you can demonstrate why your analysis is justified, through quotations and citing line numbers of the transcript, even though you cannot quote everything you might like.

Also important is a strong reflexive thread. As we have seen, reflexivity involves showing a constant awareness that the account presented will be the researcher's (i.e. your) story as well as the participant's. This means that researchers should make as explicit as possible the processes by which the material and analysis have been produced and should think about, and show through their writing, how they have influenced the research from conception through to analysis. In your case, you have only influenced the analysis and you should focus your reflexive analysis on this.

Linked to reflexivity is transparency. There is wide agreement amongst qualitative psychologists that the research process needs to be as transparent as possible. In practice, this means that you should attempt to include as much detail as is possible in the report about the stages of the research process. The function of this high level of detail is to enable the reader to trace the stages of the research and to see how the analysis has been carried out. See Chapter 9, Box 9.3 on criteria for good thematic analysis.

Finally, good qualitative research should also be ethically sound. It should involve informed consent, mutual respect, responsibility and integrity. Although most of the ethical issues have been dealt with for you in this case, you need to maintain respect for the participant and so demonstrate responsibility and integrity in how you write up your report and, in the method section of your report, you should show your awareness of ethical issues and reflect on how they have been addressed.

## 4 Example of a report write-up

On the following pages you will find an example of a very good report write-up for a thematic analysis of a series of interviews with a married couple, aimed at addressing the research question of whether the couple's life context affects their experiences. This is based around material covered in Chapter 1 of Book 2 *Challenging Psychological Issues*. It is, of course, not based on the interview that you will be analysing, but it is a TMA report written by a DSE212 student who has kindly given permission for us to use it in this way for teaching purposes. We have treated it ethically by not identifying the student and by ensuring that our evaluative comments are respectful to the student and the work.

We hope that this illustration will be useful when you come to write your own report. We have added a number of comments in the footnotes throughout this example report so that you can think carefully about how to structure your own report. Note that this report is not intended to be a 'perfect' model and that at certain points we have included comments indicating how it might be improved. So it is important that you look at the footnotes as you read the report.

## A qualitative study[1] showing what influence context has on a person's life, using thematic analysis

### Abstract

This study examines the contextual development view that context influences an individual's life. More specifically, the researcher explores the argument that an individual can influence self-development. A qualitative, textual analysis was carried out on two pre-existing, edited, filmed semi-structured interviews. Thematic analysis showed that context does have influence on an individual's life, and that an individual can influence self development.[2]

### Introduction

Lifespan psychology aims to understand the factors influencing human development and the extent to which this is predetermined, or subject to change and agency.[3] Initial work focused on the key stages of development in childhood and subsequent affects on later life – implying that the environment could only influence the speed of development but not alter its nature, which is undermined by the culturally-specific aspects of these theories (Shaffer; Kincheloe and Steinberg; as cited in Wood, Littleton and Oates, 2002). Other research considered how the context, particularly relationships, influences development. Attachment theory focused on the relationship between children and parents (Main, Kaplan and Cassidy; as cited in Wood et al., 2002), which provide the child with security (Ainsworth, Blehar, Waters and Wall; as cited in Wood et al., 2002). Hazan and Shaver (as cited in Wood et al., 2002) had over 1,200 replies to a published 'love quiz', asking numerous questions about current and past relationships. The findings suggested that early childhood experience impacted on parental behaviour – consistent with the meta-analysis of van Ijzendoorn (as cited in Wood et al., 2002), though life events and cultural context are more potent influences (Zimmerman et al.; as cited in Wood et al., 2002). Horizontal relationships between siblings and peers are

[1] Remember that you must not refer to a qualitative study as an 'experiment'.

[2] Notice that the abstract is kept short, simple and concise, providing a brief summary of the study's method, data and main findings.

[3] Note that the introduction starts immediately with the literature review. We recommend that you first describe the perspective adopted by the researchers undertaking the study, and make explicit the epistemological and ontological assumptions underpinning the perspective. This need not be very long and two or three sentences should suffice.

important in the development of cognitive skills, a sense of self, social and cultural understandings (Piaget; Fein; Mead; as cited in Wood et al., 2002), as is evident from the observational studies of children (Dunn; Abramovitch, Corter, Pepler and Stanthorpe; as cited in Wood et al., 2002). However, there is a danger that these are over-generalised from patterns in particular societies (Shaffer; as cited in Wood et al., 2002) and Mead's work may be too simplistic (Wood et al., 2002).[4]

The contextual development approach – reflected in much contemporary research into relationships, but contrasting with ideas in attachment theory (Wood et al., 2002) – suggests development is affected by the context of a person's life (Bronfenbrenner; as cited in Wood et al., 2002) and is influenced by dynamic interactions within and between internal and external variables and levels of explanation. Moreover, each human differs in genetic endowment and environment, so the interactions between these factors will be unique for each person. It proposes that individuals can influence self-development through decisions, social networks, interrelationship with the environment and experience (Ford and Lerner; as cited in Wood et al., 2002).[5]

Little research has explored the influence of context (including self-development, adaptation and change) on a person's life. This study aimed to address this, using thematic analysis of a transcript and videotape of semi-structured interviews to explore reality from the participants' viewpoint. In recognition of the theories into the importance of context on a person's development, this was done within the meanings of the research question: 'Does the context of Tony's and Jo's life influence experience?'.[6]

[4] This paragraph sets the scene for the research, locating it within a particular area of psychology (lifespan psychology) and introducing the key theories underlying the research question (e.g. context, attachments, life events). Notice that all of the points made are supported with reference to prior research studies and/or theories.

[5] In this paragraph the writer is narrowing down the focus to their specific area of interest: the contextual development approach and how people interact with their environment, or context, which may in turn influence self-development.

[6] The final paragraph of the introduction identifies the precise rationale for the study – in this case a gap in the prior research. The writer explains how they will attempt to fill this gap without going into too much detail on the method, as this will come in the following section. The introduction ends by stating the research question.

## Method[7]

The researcher, a psychology student at The Open University,[8] analysed pre-existing material (edited extracts from filmed, semi-structured interviews) comprising a videotape (Video 1, Research Methods in Psychology, Band D, 'Interviewing') and a transcript supplied by The Open University (Banister, 2002), with each line numbered in sequential order from beginning to end (see Appendix 1). The method was selected because it enabled the researcher to explore reality from the participants' viewpoint (Banister, 2002). The transcript only provided a partial picture of the interviews so additional notes were produced by the researcher (see Appendix 2).

The participants (a married, middle-aged couple from Leeds) were provided by The Open University, which gained consent from the participants to use the interview material for the purpose of the research. It was assumed that the participants were properly briefed/debriefed and offered the right to withdraw from the research at any time (Banister, 2002).[9]

The participants were interviewed together, successively; by three different interviewers (only the first was known to the couple). The first two interviews explored a similar subject matter, the third reflected on the experience of the previous interviews – providing an 'insider' viewpoint (Banister, 2002).

Condensation, categorization and narrative structuring techniques[10] were used in a thematic analysis of the first two interviews – referring to the videotape and transcript (noting recurrent topics, ideas and statements) the major themes: cultural influences; choice and agency; change and stability,

[7] Remember that it is not usual to subsection the method in qualitative reports.

[8] Note that some information about the researcher is typically appropriate in qualitative research, as the findings will come from an interaction between the experiences and insights of the researcher themselves and the experiences reported (in this case) by the interviewees. We will return to this issue when we come to the reflexive analysis section of the report.

[9] Remember that relevant ethical issues must always be considered.

[10] You won't recognise these terms but these techniques are similar to ones outlined in Chapter 9.

were identified. Each line of dialogue relating to a theme was highlighted; using different colours for each theme (see Appendix 1) – easing reference but limiting one colour per line/quote.[11]

## Analysis[12]

In reviewing the texts, and taking into consideration the research question:[13] 'Does the context of Tony's and Jo's life influence experience?', three main themes were identified:

(i) Cultural influences

### *Interview One*

Both Tony and Jo acknowledge how culture influenced early experience, and still permeated their lives – parental values (Tony) and (Jo) [lines 54–67], war (Tony) and (Jo) [lines 26 and 45–6] and restricted career options (Jo) [lines 72–6]:[14]

> *... It's part of our background, it's the Victorian work ethic.*
>
> *(Tony) [lines 54 and 9]*

[11] Notice that, although the method section should not be subsectioned like a quantitative report, much of the same information is given when appropriate. In this example, the participants (interviewees), the method used (semi-structured interviews), the materials (video footage and textual transcripts), and the 'procedure' used by the researcher to turn the interviewees' responses into data that can be analysed (last paragraph of the section) are all described. All of this enables the reader to know what was done and how it was done, which is the primary purpose of a method section.

[12] Remember: this section is not a 'results' section, although it presents findings.

[13] It's generally advisable to remind your reader of your research question at this point.

[14] See how, throughout the analysis section, the writer explains the themes that have emerged in relation to the data. Line references to the transcript are given in support of points and selected illustrative direct quotations are given. In this report the writer has selected short quotations which map very clearly onto the themes that have been identified. The art of deciding which quotations to select is something which is developed through experience, but you may wish to reflect on the second quotation from Billig (1997) in Section 2 of this chapter. Remember, though, that quotations are included within your word count so you may have to be selective.

*Interview Two*

Tony and Jo noted the different cultural influences between generations, with references to 'our day' (Tony) [lines 116 and 140] and changes in opportunity and standards (Tony) and (Jo) [lines 137–58]:

> *... Well I think it's very different today ...*
>
> *(Tony) [line 137]*

(ii) Choice and agency

*Interview One*

It was clear that choice and agency were important to Tony and Jo, whether it was limited career options (Tony) [lines 80–5] and (Jo) [lines 72–6], (self) education (Tony) and (Jo) [lines 25–47] or separation from family (Tony) [line 35] and (Jo) [lines 45–6]:

> *... suppose I am self-educated I've read an awful lot obviously ...*
>
> *(Tony) [line 41]*

*Interview Two*

Tony and Jo relayed how choice and agency had impacted on their experience throughout life, delaying marriage (Tony) [line 116], career opportunities versus family commitments (Jo) [lines 142–8] and maintaining individual identity (Tony) and (Jo) [lines 117–31]:

> *... No we've encouraged each other to keep up our own interests ...*
>
> *(Jo) [line 119]*

(iii) Change and stability

*Interview One*

Change was a key feature for both – separation from family (Jo) [lines 45–6], education (Tony) [lines 24–41] and (Jo) [lines 43–7], and differences between generations (Tony) [lines 80–2) and (Jo) [lines 71–7]:

> *... I had a very disrupted childhood ... moved round the country.*
>
> *(Tony) [lines 24–6]*

*Interview Two*

With change and separation explored again (Tony) and (Jo) [lines 89–99 and 137–52], a stable environment for the family, both as parents ... it's the base that you create ... because children like stability ... (Jo) [lines 153–4] and as a couple (individual interests, working towards a shared identity) (Jo) [lines 119–20] became important.

The above is in line with the contextual development theory that each human differs in genetic endowment and environment, with the interactions between these being unique for Tony and Jo, who had similar and different experiences of change and were influenced by the interactions of these variables (Bronfenbrenner; as cited in Wood et al., 2002). A functionalist approach would explain how Tony and Jo adapted to their environment in order to survive (Wood et al., 2002) but Ford and Lerner (as cited in Wood et al., 2002) would suggest how they influenced their own development. While attachment theorists Ainsworth et al. (as cited in Wood et al., 2002) would suggest that Tony and Jo's early vertical relationships impacted on their sense of security and stability, with van Ijzendoorn (as cited in Wood et al., 2002) predicting this would influence their parenting style (and Main et al.; as cited in Wood et al., 2002, suggesting the style type), Zimmerman et al. (as cited in Wood et al., 2002) would base it on the life events and cultural context discussed, as the more potent influence.

## Discussion[15]

The aim of this study was to see if the context of Tony's and Jo's life influences their experiences. Within theme (i) cultural influences, it can be seen that Tony and Jo's life had been affected by context, which is consistent with the contextual development theory that each human differs in genetic endowment and environment, with the interactions between these being unique for Tony and Jo – who had similar and different experiences of change and were influenced by the interactions of these variables (Bronfenbrenner; as cited in Wood et al., 2002). For example, they both had a strong work ethic, being influenced by their parents, in the context of Methodist/Victorian values and the change in cultural values in society over time would account for the contrasting experience of their children.

Tony and Jo considered a number of opportunities for choice and agency (theme, ii), within the context of their lives. A functionalist approach would explain how Tony and Jo adapted to their environment in order to survive (Wood et al., 2002) but Ford and Lerner (as cited in Wood et al., 2002) would suggest how they influenced their own development. For instance, Tony polished his skills, manipulated situations and educated himself for a

[15] It is sometimes difficult to know where your analysis should end and your discussion begin. Indeed, you may come across some published papers where these sections overlap or are combined. In this report, the last paragraph of the analysis section falls somewhere between giving a commentary on what was found (analysis) and linking themes to the literature (discussion) and could equally well have been placed at the beginning of the discussion rather than the end of the analysis. The student did not lose marks for this.

successful career and Jo adapted her lifestyle to support her children and provide a stable family life.[16]

The above can explain how both Jo and Tony seemed to have adapted to a dynamic context in theme (iii) change and stability. In contrast to all the change, Tony and Jo have provided a stable environment within the family, for themselves and their children. Ainsworth et al. (as cited in Wood et al., 2002) would suggest that Tony and Jo's early vertical relationships impacted on their sense of security and stability. Van Ijzendoorn (as cited in Wood et al., 2002) proposed this would influence their parenting style, with type suggested by Main et al. (as cited in Wood et al., 2002). However, there is little in the material about these relationships, so it is difficult to imply whether this is the basis of their parenting style. Certainly, from these theories, one would suggest that they both had a secure style (acknowledging the importance of relationships to them, richly describing examples of both positive and negative experiences, with insights into influences on the self) (Main et al.; as cited in Wood et al., 2002). However, Zimmerman et al. (as cited in Wood et al., 2002) would base it on the life events and cultural context discussed (such as understanding the importance of stability, and experiencing so much change) as the more potent influence.[17]

In conclusion, it can be seen from the above findings that context does influence Tony and Jo's lives – who also have an influence on their own development. This is in line with the theoretical approach of contextual development. The extent and depth of the influence is not known, though it seems to permeate all aspects discussed, and may guide future studies. Also, contrasting their experience with that of their children provided an interesting insight into the influence of changing contexts on experience, and may guide future studies in gaining a further understanding of this. If, as the above suggests, a person is influenced (but not determined) by childhood experience and the ongoing context of life, and able to effect self-development, it could have implications for the policy and work of agencies

[16] Throughout the discussion, the writer explains what they have found in their study and discusses their findings in relation to the literature. The themes that were described in the analysis are explained here in terms of the theories and research which the writer has read about. References to the sources of these theories and studies are given throughout the text.

[17] Notice also that the writer considers some of the limitations of the study (e.g. not knowing about the interviewees' experiences as parents) that could be addressed if another similar study was conducted.

such as those involved with disaffected/disadvantaged youths, offenders and education and training in general.[18]

## Reflexive analysis

It should be noted that this is a personal interpretation of the materials reviewed; other researchers would apply their own interpretation. Having experienced an unconventional education, I may have been influenced by Tony's background and the concept of agency, and contributed to the construction of meanings throughout the research process.[19] Also, it is likely that edited interviews may not produce the material needed for the research and analysing secondary material means that I missed out on some of the experience of the interview. In addition, cameras are selective and restricted. Further, the presence of a camera crew will inevitably affect the interview process more than an unobtrusive audiotape. Plus, the interviewee's account is a complex product of the context – particularly the relationship between the interviewee and interviewer. In this case, both interviews differed in style because the participants knew one of the interviewers better than the other. That the participants were interviewed together, and the interviewer could influence the (framework, length, quality and direction of the) interview are also noteworthy – and may have made it difficult to refuse to answer questions, especially being filmed. Furthermore, there are limitations involved in carrying out research. For example, in the third interview (an insider viewpoint of the interview process) Tony admitted that he tried to keep off subjects that he doesn't really want to discuss and frame his answers to seem interesting, which would influence the quality and authenticity of his responses. Finally, although the focus of the research was on verbal

[18] Here the writer ends the discussion with a few concluding observations, including possible directions for future research and/or applications of the findings.

[19] Remember that at the beginning of the method section the writer gave us some information on who they, the researcher, were. Here the writer reflects on how an aspect of themselves that they see as potentially relevant might have influenced the outcome of the analysis and the interpretations made. It is not always easy to identify which characteristics might be relevant. For example, Tony and Jo are a married heterosexual couple. Could the researcher's own sex (or gender), relationship status, sexual orientation or other characteristics have also had an influence?

interactions it might be worth considering to what extent this affected the findings. Analysis of non-verbal interaction may have added to the research, suggesting future work could include scrutiny of, for example, body language (what leg posture and hand movements signify) and the impact of the seating positions.[20]

Word Count: 2,254[21]

## References[22]

Banister, P. (2002). *Methods Booklet 5, Qualitative Project.* Milton Keynes: The Open University.

Wood, C., Littleton, K., & Oates, J. (2002). Lifespan development. In T. Cooper & I. Roth (Eds.), *Challenging Psychological Issues* (pp. 1–64). Milton Keynes: The Open University.

## Appendix 1[23]

Appendix 1 contained the transcript of the interviews, annotated with the researcher's insights and with the themes colour-coded.

## Appendix 2

Appendix 2 contained the researcher's notes, including insights into the non-verbal communication present in the video but not included in the transcript and the researcher's own reactions used to inform the reflexive analysis.

[20] After the previous comment, the writer takes a slightly different turn in their reflexive analysis – considering the perspective of the interviewees (e.g. differing familiarity with the interviewers, avoiding certain 'uncomfortable' topics). These are all valid points, of course, but would have been better placed as part of the discussion (e.g. analysing non-verbal cues in future research in case interviewees avoid saying certain things). Remember that the purpose of the reflexive analysis section is for the researcher to consider their own role in, and influence on, the research. For example, the writer could have considered whether their own sex etc. had an influence. Note, however, that if the researcher themselves had conducted the interviews, then their differing familiarity with Tony and Jo would most likely have made them more aware of the impact on their analysis.

[21] It is important to remember to add the word count. Doing so will also help you to ensure that you do not inadvertently make the TMA too long or too short.

[22] It is, of course, vitally important to provide a references section detailing the sources that you have cited in support of your points. Note that the author refers to an earlier edition of Book 2 than the one you are reading.

[23] We have omitted the full text of the Appendices here, for reasons of space. However, you should include the appropriate Appendices with your TMA. The Appendices do not count towards your word count.

# 5 A final word

You have now reached the end of this particular exploration of research methods in psychology. Both here and in the featured methods boxes of Book 1, *Mapping Psychology* we have introduced you to many of the diverse ways in which psychologists have approached and conducted research. The chapters in this book introduced you to the different types of data and the different ways in which those data may be analysed, and they should also have helped you to acquire some of the tools necessary to conduct your own investigations. Should you decide to continue your study of psychology, you will find that the other psychology courses offered by The Open University will extend your knowledge and research skills. Above all, we hope that you have enjoyed the exercises and the practical work that you have carried out and that you also enjoy doing TMA 05 and learn a lot from it.

# References

Billig, M. (1997) 'Rhetorical and discursive analysis: how families talk about the Royal Family' in Hayes, N. (ed.) *Introduction to Qualitative Methods*, Sussex, Lawrence Erlbaum.

Potter, J. and Wetherell, M. (1987) *Discourse and Social Psychology: Beyond Attitudes and Behaviour*, London, Sage.

# Glossary

**Alpha value** Usually, the probability value of .05 is the alpha value used in inferential statistics as the measure of significance. This value has been adopted as the threshold for accepting the null hypothesis (test result is greater than .05), or rejecting it (test result is equal to or less than .05).

**Bar graph** A graph often used to visually compare differences between the means of separate groups or conditions. The x-axis represents the different groups and the y-axis represents the means. Each mean is drawn as a vertical bar, and because the means are from different categories (groups or conditions) the bars are not joined.

**Baseline measure** The effect of the control condition on the dependent variable against which the effect of the experimental condition can be compared to give the size of the difference between the two conditions.

**Behavioural data** Data produced from measuring behaviour. These can cover a wide range of activities such as reaction times (e.g. time taken to press a buzzer) and memory (e.g. number of words correctly recognised) as well as less well-defined behaviours such as problem solving which might be described qualitatively.

**Between-participants design** An experimental design where different participants complete each condition, so more participants are needed than for a within-participants design. Also known as independent groups design, independent samples design, or independent measures design. Can help eliminate confounding variables such as demand characteristics since participants' understanding of the whole experiment is restricted, but does not reduce the influence of individual differences.

**Bimodal distribution** A distribution with two modes. The distribution is described by two symmetrical bell-shaped curves that appear joined, with two peaks representing two values for the mode.

**Categorical data** Data that have been classified into discrete categories which are measured at the nominal level. Numbers are often used as labels (e.g. male = 1, female = 2), but the order numerically is of no importance.

**Categorical variable** A variable which is measured at the nominal level; data produced are grouped into mutually exclusive and distinct categories.

**Cause and effect** The aim of any experiment, a general law which can be established when an isolated, independent variable is manipulated to cause a measurable effect on the dependent variable.

**Chi-square test** A statistical test used to analyse data measured at nominal level. This test allows one to look for associations between two categorical variables, by comparing the observed frequencies against the expected frequencies (see contingency table). The test calculates the statistic $\chi^2$ and Cramer's V provides a measure of effect size.

**Coding** The process of assigning or converting material to a code for the purpose of identification, classification or analysis.

**Complete observer** A researcher who openly observes but does not participate in the research setting.

**Condition** In an experiment, the different forms of the independent variable created from its being manipulated. Very often an experimental condition and a control condition are set up, so that the effects of each can be measured and compared, with the control condition giving a baseline measure.

**Conditional probability** The likelihood of something happening that is dependent on something else.

**Confidence interval** The range of values within which a population mean is likely to fall. Confidence intervals are specified by stating the lower and upper bounds of the range. For normally distributed data, we can be 95 per cent certain that the population mean will fall within 1.96 standard deviation points of a sample mean. This allows us to judge whether two samples are from the same population where any difference between them is simply due to sampling error.

**Confounding variable** A variable, which is not the independent variable, that affects the dependent variable in one condition more than another – hence *confounding* the results. Researchers strive to eliminate confounding variables through good experimental design.

**Content analysis** A quantitative method of analysing data. For example, data from an interview will be analysed by counting the prevalence and sequence of certain words and these are sometimes analysed using a chi-square test.

**Contingency table** Table used in studies looking for an association between independent (mutually exclusive) categorical variables. The table presents the number of observations in each possible combination, or contingency, of each category. If there are two variables (gender; film preference) each with two categories (male/female; horror/romance), then the number of observations in each possible combination of categories would be presented in a 2 × 2 contingency table.

**Continuous variable** A variable that can produce data of any value (including decimal places) between the highest and lowest points on a scale; e.g. time taken to recall items in a memory test.

**Control condition** The condition of the independent variable which is in all respects but one identical to the experimental condition – nothing is introduced to cause the dependent variable to change. The control condition can then be used to give a baseline measure.

**Controls** Techniques used in an experiment to eliminate the foreseeable effects of any confounding variables.

**Conversation analysis (CA)** An analytic method which focuses on the precise details of conversational interactions and on how people talk – for example the orderliness, structure and sequential patterns of interaction.

**Correlation** The relationship, or association, between two variables whereby if the value of one changes so does the value of the other. One variable cannot be said to *cause* the other to change.

**Correlation coefficient** A numerical measure between −1 and +1 where the size of the number indicates the strength of the relationship between the two variables in a correlation, or the effect size. A value of 1 shows a perfect positive correlation while a value of −1 shows a perfect negative correlation. If the correlation coefficient is 0, there is no relationship between the two variables at all.

**Counterbalancing** A control introduced to eliminate practise effects as a confounding variable in a within-participants experiment, whereby different participants undergo the conditions in a different order from one another.

**Cramer's V** A measure of effect size reported when using the chi-square test.

**Data** Information collected during a study that has been documented in a suitable manner ready for communication or analysis.

**Debriefing** The procedure where participants are given previously undisclosed information about a research project following completion of their participation.

**Degrees of freedom (df)** A concept often defined as the number of scores whose values are free to vary. Degrees of freedom take account of the size of a sample, the number of variables, and the number of conditions in a study, and are reported with most inferential statistics.

**Demand characteristics** Potentially a confounding variable. Introduced when participants do not respond naturally in an experiment, but react as they think they are expected to. The influence of demand characteristics may be reduced by using a between-participants design, as participants take part in only one condition.

**Dependent variable (DV)** The variable that is measured in an experiment, whose values result from manipulating the independent variable.

**Descriptive statistics** A set of statistics used to summarise and present numerical data (e.g. mean and standard deviation).

**Discourse analysis** Focuses on the ways in which people make meaning – discourse is unravelled in microscopic ways to see what it consists of and how it is put together to accomplish different actions.

**Discrete variable** A variable that can produce data of only certain values, such as only whole numbers, between the highest and lowest points on a scale; e.g. the number of items recalled in a memory test can only be measured in whole numbers.

**Double-blind testing** In drug trials particularly, the process of not informing either the participants or the drug administrator whether they are dealing with the real drug or not, to avoid confounding variables such as demand characteristics.

**Ecological validity** The extent to which a study reflects naturally occurring or everyday situations. Ecological validity is often low in laboratory experiments where control of confounding variables is, however, higher.

**Effect size** The magnitude of the effect the independent variable has on the dependent variable or the size of the relationship between two variables. In experimental designs, the statistic *d* is a standardised measure of effect size, calculated by subtracting one sample mean from the other and dividing the result by the mean standard deviation. A correlation coefficient is also a measure of effect size, as is Cramer's V which is a measure of effect size for a chi-square test.

**Empirical evidence** Evidence based on some form of experience such as that gained through experimentation, observation, surveying or interviewing.

**Epistemology** Epistemology is the 'theory of knowledge'. It refers to the principles of what can be known and how we can know it; that is, how we can find out about it.

**Error bar chart** A graph used to present confidence intervals. The upper and lower bounds of the confidence interval are represented by single lines above and below the mean, which is drawn as a single point.

**Evidence** Information presented to determine or demonstrate the truth or the plausibility of an assertion, a consequence of the way that information is gathered, documented and analysed. Anecdotal evidence is informal argument based on personal experience or hearsay. In quantitative research, scientific evidence serves to either support or counter the truth and validity of a hypothesis and is established through empirical analysis such as statistics. In hermeneutic research, evidence means drawing plausible inferences from patterns of meaning implied in the data.

**Experiment** A research method used to investigate a hypothesis about the effect of the independent variable on the dependent variable. As far as possible the experimenter attempts to control for any other variables that might influence the dependent variable.

**Experimental condition** A form of the independent variable created from its being manipulated. Unlike control conditions, something is introduced to the experimental condition as the possible cause of change in the dependent variable.

**Experimental design** See 'between-participants design' and 'within-participants design'.

**Experimenter effects** Potentially, a confounding variable. Introduced by the experimenter or researcher exerting an influence, consciously or unconsciously, reducing objectivity. Experimenter effects can be overcome by ensuring all participants are treated in the same way as each other (e.g. each participant is read the same instructions), and by limiting experimenter contact with them as far as possible.

**Fatigue effects** Introduced when a study takes a long time to run and participants become tired. Fatigue can affect responses as the study progresses, particularly if the participants are young children or elderly people. Fatigue effects can sometimes be limited in experiments by using a between-participants design, so no individual participant is required to complete the whole experiment.

**First-order coding** The organising and categorising of data in a transcript by capturing chunks of meaning and giving them codes or labels. The process is purely descriptive, with minimal interpretation.

**Fisher's exact probability test** A statistical test used instead of the chi-square test when an expected frequency of less than 5 occurs in more than 25% of the cells of a 2 × 2 contingency table.

**Generalisability** The extent to which research findings may be applied to a larger population and/or other situations.

**Generalisation** To establish general laws or statements which apply across participants and specified conditions.

**Habituation** Introduced when the same stimulus or task is presented to the same participants many times. Participants become increasingly used to responding to the stimulus or performing the task, which may obscure the effects of the independent variable. Habituation can sometimes be limited by using a between-participants design, or by simply reducing the number of responses required of participants.

**Hermeneutic** The theory and practice of interpretation, involving the analysis of meanings in subjective accounts.

**Histogram** A graph showing the number of occurrences, or frequency, of each value in a data set across the range (hence also known as a frequency distribution). The y-axis represents frequency and the x-axis represents the data range. Each value is drawn as a vertical bar and, because data are continuous, the bars are joined together.

**Hypothesis** A statement making a prediction about the results of a study.

**Independent samples *t*-test** A parametric test of difference used in inferential statistics to analyse data produced by an experiment with a between-participants design and which has two conditions. This test may also be called the unrelated *t*-test, independent *t*-test or between-groups *t*-test.

**Independent variable (IV)** The variable that is manipulated in an experiment, to investigate a potential effect on the dependent variable that is measured.

**Individual differences** Introduced when, for example, different participants are allocated to different conditions in an experiment, so that the naturally occurring variations between people may obscure the effects of the independent variable. The influence of individual differences may be reduced by firstly ensuring the sample is large enough, by randomly allocating participants to each condition, and/or by using a within-participants design.

**Inferential statistics** These involve statistical tests which allow conclusions to be drawn from numerical data generated by research. The tests calculate a statistic, from which a probability value can be derived telling us the likelihood of any difference of relationship being due to sampling error.

**Informed consent** The permission granted by a participant after he or she has received comprehensive information about the study.

**Inner experiences** The private monologues (thoughts), feelings, sensations and process experienced by individuals either at a conscious or unconscious level.

**Insider viewpoint** A viewpoint gained from introspection, interviews and analyses, where the researcher tries to see and think about the data through the eyes of the participant generating the data.

**Interpretation** A representation of the meaning or significance of something.

**Interpretative repertoires** A term associated with discourse analysis. Interpretative repertoires are 'turns of phrase' or arguments that people typically employ to describe or explain things. These are systematically related sets of terms that are commonly used in society because they are developed from particular historical contexts and have become part of the common sense of a culture or a particular institution. They are often organised around metaphors. This means that interpretative repertoires are a way of picking out the familiar arguments that tell us something about how a society, community or social group make sense of social life. In other words, they allow us to identify the taken-for-granted cultural resources found in talk.

**Interval level scale** A numerical scale where the intervals between measurements are specified and constant but the scale does not contain a true zero (e.g. Celsius temperature measurement scales), so the numbers used are arbitrary representations (e.g. 80 degrees Celsius is not twice as hot as 40 degrees).

**Interview** A 'conversation with a purpose', interviews provide in-depth information or understanding about a particular research issue or question. Structured interviews consist of a list of specific quotations where the interviewer does not deviate from the list or inject any extra remarks – data from these are usually quantified. In qualitative, semi-structured or unstructured interviews, the interviewer adjusts questions to the interviewee response and may inject their own opinions and ideas – the focus is on gathering rich complex meanings.

**Laboratory experiment** An experimental study that takes place in a controlled, laboratory environment. Although ecological validity may be low, it is easier to control for confounding variables in the laboratory than in the field.

**Longitudinal** Involving the collection of data about an individual or group over a long period of time.

**Lower bound** The lowest value in a confidence interval. For a 95% confidence interval, this is calculated by multiplying the standard error by 1.96 and subtracting the result from the sample mean.

**Material data** Direct evidence from bodies and brain, for example when measuring biological reactions (e.g. hormone levels) or using brain-imaging techniques.

**Mean** A descriptive statistic that is a measure of central tendency; an average calculated by dividing the sum of values in a data set by the number of values. The mean is usually reported if data are measured at interval or ratio level.

**Mean deviation** A measure of dispersion used in descriptive statistics to describe the average variation from the mean of each individual value in a data set. The mean deviation is calculated by subtracting each value in a data set from the mean and then calculating the average. However, the standard deviation is the more generally accepted measure of dispersion reported.

**Meaning** The content, intentions and expressions carried by the words or signs exchanged by people in communication. Also definitions, interpretations and values, a reference of equivalence or difference.

**Measurement error** The discrepancy that may arise between scales of measurement used (e.g. for rating scales in self-reports) and the actual value of the measurements.

**Measures of central tendency** The collective term for the descriptive statistics, mean, mode and median, which describe the central values, or average, of a range.

**Measures of dispersion** The collective term for the descriptive statistics, range, mean deviation, variance and standard deviation, which describe the spread of data.

**Median** A measure of central tendency used in descriptive statistics; an average calculated by finding the middle value in a data set. The median is usually reported if an ordinal level scale is used, or if there are outliers in the data set (extreme scores or values).

**Methodology** The 'theory of methods'. It refers to the overall theoretical rationale and the principles that define how a research question, a set of methods, procedures of data collection and analysis are embedded within a theoretical framework; i.e. how they relate to the ontology and epistemology that underpins the choice of methods.

**Methods** Techniques and tools for collecting and analysing kinds of data.

**Mode** A measure of central tendency used in descriptive statistics; an average calculated by counting the most frequently occurring values in a data set. The mode is reported if a nominal level scale is used, giving the category with the highest frequency count.

**Narrative** A narrative is a story which gives an account of a sequence of fictional or non-fictional events. Discourse analysts focus on the ways in which the stories are told while researchers interested in life history focus on biography.

**Naturalistic field experiment** An experimental study that takes place outside the laboratory, in an environment where the variables, while still controlled, occur naturally.

**Negative correlation** A correlation where the relationship between the two variables is positive, represented by a correlation coefficient between −1 and 0. As one variable increases in value, the other decreases.

**Negative skew** A spread of data with more values lower than the mean than higher. The distribution is described by a non-symmetrical, bell-shaped curve which peaks to the right.

**Nominal level scale** A number is used as an arbitrary label to distinguish between mutually exclusive and distinct groups of data, as is the case with categorical variables.

**Normal distribution** A regular spread of data where the mean, median and mode have similar values and which commonly occurs with natural phenomena such as height, weight or shoe size. The distribution is described by a smooth, symmetrical, bell-shaped curve with the mean at the highest point.

**Null hypothesis** In an experiment, a formal statement that asserts that a named independent variable will not affect a named dependent variable. It states that any difference between the groups or conditions is due to sampling error. In a correlational study, it is a statement which asserts that there will be no relationship between two named variables and that any relationship observed is due to sampling error. Using statistical tests we can decide whether the data we collect allow us to reject or accept the null hypothesis.

**Objective data** Data which are assumed to have only one interpretation and not be biased by the views of the researcher.

**Observation** A research method where the observer notices, watches and scrutinises significant details of an event which are then recorded within a framework of previous knowledge and ideas.

**One-tailed hypothesis** A research hypothesis which states the direction of the effect or correlation, for example whether the named independent variable will cause values measured for the dependent variable to increase or decrease. A one-tailed hypothesis should only be stated if there are extremely good grounds for making a directional prediction.

**Ontology** Ontology is the study of, or the theory of the nature of existence (i.e. of 'being'). In a psychological context, ontology refers to the underlying assumptions about the nature of existence as a human being. Hence, ontology can be referred to as the theory of what, in a certain perspective, is seen to constitute a human being, or, more generally, what it is to be a person.

**Operationalise** The process of converting or defining variables of interest that allows them to be measured or manipulated.

**Order effects** Potentially a confounding variable introduced when the same participants are allocated to more than one condition in an experiment and conditions are run, or materials are presented, in the same order for each participant. This means the effects of the independent variable cannot be isolated. Order effects may be avoided by counterbalancing, by randomising elements of the materials, or by using a between-participants design.

**Ordinal level scale** A numerical scale where numbers are used to imply order or rank.

**Outsider viewpoint** A viewpoint gained from using methods, such as the experiment, to collect data which can be 'seen from the outside' without recourse to introspections or people's own accounts of their mental states.

**Paired samples *t*-test** A parametric test of difference used in inferential statistics to analyse data produced by an experiment with a within-participants design and which has two conditions. This test may also be called the related *t*-test, dependent *t*-test, or repeated measures *t*-test.

**Paradigm** A thought pattern and set of practices that define a discipline during a particular period – that is, the beliefs about what should be studied, what types of questions should be asked and how the investigations should be carried out and interpreted. In this course (DSE212) the term 'paradigm' is used synonymously with 'perspective' or 'theoretical framework'.

**Parametric test** Parametric tests are inferential statistical tests which make certain assumptions about the population from which the data are drawn, e.g. that the population is normally distributed. With parametric tests the data cannot have been measured using a nominal level scale. The *t*-tests are an example of a parametric test.

**Participant** A person who takes part in a psychological experiment or study. Previously the term 'subject' was used, so you may come across this term in older publications.

**Participant observer** A researcher who openly observes while also taking an active part in the research setting.

**Participants' orientations** A term associated with discourse analysis. Activities accomplished in conversation – for example, when a person says something, this utterance (orientation) sets a frame for another person's response which shows how they have interpreted what is happening (their orientation), and which changes the frame or the context again.

**Pearson product moment correlation coefficient** A parametric test used to analyse data from correlational studies when a linear relationship between the variables is expected. This test calculates a correlation coefficient known as '*r*', which is considered to be the measure of effect size, or the strength of the relationship between variables.

**Perspective** A theoretical framework that informs the types of questions asked, methods favoured and thus the types of knowledge produced.

**Pie chart** A circular diagram used to display subsets of a whole data set, where each subset is represented as a proportion (as 'slices of a pie').

**Placebo effect** The effect, particularly in drug trials, that occurs when participants in the control condition of an experiment are given a placebo (a harmless substance that looks like the drug being tested) – they still experience the apparent effects of the drug.

**Population** The group or set of individuals or entities, defined by some characteristic(s) about which statistical inferences are to be drawn, usually based on a random sample taken from the population.

**Positive correlation** A correlation where the relationship between the two variables is positive, represented by a correlation coefficient between 0 and 1. As one variable increases in value, so does the other.

**Positive skew** A spread of data with more values higher than the mean than lower. The distribution is described by a non-symmetrical, bell-shaped curve which peaks to the left.

**Positivism/positivist model** The belief that the world as it is given to observation is the way the world actually is.

**Practise effects** A type of order effect. A confounding variable introduced when the same participants are allocated to more than one condition in an experiment and conditions are run in the same order for each participant. Participants become more 'practised' as the study progresses. This means the effects of the independent variable cannot be isolated. Practise effects may be avoided by counterbalancing, or by using a between-participants design.

**Probability** The likelihood of something happening. In research, probability is expressed numerically, so that a value of 1 equates to an event definitely occurring, and a value of 0 equates to an event never occurring.

**Probability value** The value calculated by a statistical test as the measure of significance. It gives the level of likelihood that differences or relationships are due to sampling error. This is often written as '*p*-value'. A probability value of .05 has been adopted as the threshold for accepting the null hypothesis (test result is greater than .05) or rejecting it (test result is equal to or less than .05) – see 'alpha value'.

**Qualitative analysis** Qualitative researchers critically immerse themselves in their data – they sort, organise, conceptualise, refine and interpret the data. The aim of qualitative analysis is to generate rich descriptions of common patterns and themes and theorise about how and why these relations appear as they do. Theories are contextualised in relation to the context the participants create (e.g. in what they say and do) and in relation to the research context. They are also, however, related to the context of how others have articulated the evolving knowledge in the literature.

**Qualitative methods** Methods used to access and understand the meanings that participants give to the phenomena of interest – for example interviewing, observation, ethnography, discourse analysis, participant observation, focus groups.

**Qualitative research** Research that describes and develops theories of how people in their natural settings understand the world and construct meanings. Explanations always refer to a specific time and context. Multiple realities and viewpoints are assumed and researchers consider themselves an explicit part of the data gathering and analysis. Reflexive analysis thus forms a crucial part of the analysis.

**Quantitative methods** Methods that investigate psychological properties that can be counted or measured and statistically analysed. Examples include experiments, questionnaires and observational studies.

**Quantitative research** Research that relies upon measurement and numbers, and which aims to make general statements about a population.

**Quasi-experiment** An experimental research method where the independent variable occurs naturally (e.g. age, height, sex) and cannot be manipulated by the researcher.

**Random allocation** The arbitrary assignment of participants to each condition of an experiment, usually introduced as a control for potential confounding variables such as individual differences.

**Range** A measure of dispersion used in descriptive statistics, calculated by subtracting the smallest value in a data set from the largest.

**Ratio level scale** A numerical scale where the intervals between measurements are specified and constant. Similar to an interval level scale, but where the zero point is a true zero and numbers used are not arbitrary representations.

**Reflexivity** The process of researchers reflecting on how they may have influenced the research that was conducted, i.e. the process of identifying how a researcher's involvement influenced, acted upon and informed the research, including the questions asked, the analysis conducted and the conclusions drawn.

**Reliability** The extent to which a measure or test always produces the same results for an individual over time and across situations.

**Replicability** The extent to which a study can be repeated with a different sample and still produce similar results.

**Research hypothesis** Also known as an 'alternative hypothesis' or, in the case of an experiment, an 'experimental hypothesis'. In an experiment, a formal statement that predicts that a named independent variable will have an effect on a named dependent variable. In a correlational study, a statement which predicts there will be a relationship between two named variables. In experiments and correlational studies it is actually the null hypothesis that is tested.

**Research question** Research questions define and specify the focus of interest. In qualitative research, they are always embedded in a theoretical framework; i.e. they are underpinned by the epistemological and ontological assumptions of the respective research perspective and thus provide both a theoretical and practical focus to the research undertaken.

**Sample** A subset of a population (see 'population').

**Sampling distribution of the mean** The spread of a number of sample means taken from the same population, which will form a normal distribution if enough means are plotted.

**Sampling error** The naturally occurring difference between the values derived from testing a sample of participants in a study and testing the entire population from which the sample was drawn. Increasing the sample size may reduce the error.

**Scatterplot** A graph showing the relationship between two variables (represented by the axes), whereby the corresponding data values are plotted as single points. The pattern of points produced may suggest a correlation exists between the variables if they appear to fall in a straight line. The pattern of points will slope upwards from left to right for a positive correlation, and downwards from left to right for a negative correlation. Also known as scattergram or scatter graph.

**Scientific** The rigorous, systematic and empirical study of observable behaviour using experiments, observations or correlational studies and statistical analysis.

**Second-order coding** Following on from first-order coding, the researcher identifies codes that capture the meaning of larger segments of the data. This reduces the number of first-order codes as the data are sorted into broader and more encompassing categories.

**Single-blind testing** In drug trials particularly, the process of not informing participants whether they are receiving the real drug or not, to avoid demand characteristics.

**Social constructionism** A theoretical perspective that emphasises the ongoing building of self-perception and world views by individuals in dialectical interaction with society; for example, identities are not fixed and the exclusive result of biology but highly contingent on social and historical processes.

**Standard deviation** A measure of dispersion used in descriptive statistics to describe the spread of values in a data set in relation to the mean. The standard deviation is calculated by finding the square root of the variance (see 'variance'). It is the most accepted measure of dispersion and should always be reported if the mean is stated.

**Standard deviation points** Related to the standard deviation of a data set, so that two standard deviation points is the value for the standard deviation multiplied by 2, and so on. Because each standard deviation point is always at the same point on a normal distribution curve, either side of the mean, they may be used to predict the likelihood of a value. Importantly for statistical calculations, 95% of the data falls within 1.96 standard deviation points of the mean.

**Standard error** The standard deviation associated with the sampling distribution of the mean. The standard error is calculated by dividing the standard deviation of a sample by the square root of the sample size. Calculating the standard error allows the population mean to be calculated within a 95% confidence interval.

**Standardised measure** A measure that is the same no matter how large or small the numbers involved. For instance, the statistic *d* is a standardised measure of effect size, calculated by subtracting one sample mean from the other and dividing the result by the standard deviation. This gives a more meaningful result that can be compared across studies.

**Statistical significance** In inferential statistics, if it is found that the results are not due to sampling error, then the null hypothesis can be rejected and the results (either the difference between conditions or the relationship between the variables) can be said to be statistically significant. A probability value of .05 has been adopted as the threshold for accepting the null hypothesis (test result is greater than .05) or rejecting it (test result is equal to or less than .05) – see 'alpha value'.

**Structured observation** The noting and recording of the frequency of behaviours, usually subject to statistical analysis.

**Subjective data** Data based on or influenced by personal experiences, thoughts, feelings, opinions.

**Subject positions** A term associated with discourse analysis, but used more widely. The identity, opinion or stance that is constructed when a person draws on a particular interpretative repertoire from the stock available in their culture.

**Superordinate constructs** Superordinate (or super-ordinate) constructs subsume lower-order codes or constructs. In order to do this, they tend to be more abstract or conceptual than lower-order constructs and to bring together two or more lower-order constructs. For example, rain, sleet and biting wind are simple descriptions that can be subsumed into 'bad weather' or 'dramatic weather' or 'brooding day'. All of these are superordinate constructs of the description.

**Symbolic data** Symbolic creations of minds, such as texts or art.

**Thematic analysis** The process where qualitative data, for example interview transcripts, are reorganised into categories and themes.

**Themes** Recurrent topics, ideas and statements that form patterns which can be brought together into a category.

**Theoretical framework** See 'perspective' or 'paradigm'.

**Theory** A logical model or framework for describing or conceptualising the behaviour of a related set of natural or social phenomena.

**Third-order coding** The identification of superordinate constructs – the themes – which capture the overarching meaning of second-order codes and so are necessarily broader. The process is also known as pattern coding since the overarching themes represent more general concepts than second-order codes and often incorporate several lower-level codes. This drawing out of overarching themes and the identification of quotations that exemplify them is the final part of the process of thematic analysis.

***t*-tests** Parametric tests of difference, used in inferential statistics to determine whether the difference between two conditions in an experiment is statistically significant. *t*-tests produce a statistic referred to as '*t*' which compares the variation between conditions (i.e. the difference between the means) and the variation within the conditions (i.e. the standard deviation for each). The particular *t*-test used depends on the design of the experiment.

**Two-tailed hypothesis** A research hypothesis which states a difference or a relationship but does not state a particular direction, for example that the named independent variable will affect the dependent variable to either increase or decrease the values.

**Type 1 error** Where the null hypothesis is rejected incorrectly when it should have been accepted.

**Type 2 error** Where the null hypothesis is accepted incorrectly when it should have been rejected.

**Unstructured naturalistic observation** A qualitative approach committed to avoiding disturbance of the activities that are being observed.

**Upper bound** The highest value in a confidence interval. For a 95% confidence interval, this is calculated by multiplying the standard error by 1.96 and adding the result to the sample mean.

**Validity** The extent to which a measure or test measures what it claims to.

**Variables** Things or properties that we can measure and which have values that can *vary*; for example, attributes (e.g. attractiveness) and characteristics (e.g. height).

**Variance** A measure of dispersion used in descriptive statistics to describe the mean of squared deviation values (calculated by subtracting the mean from each value and squaring the result – squaring avoids any negative values). It is usually used as a step on the way towards calculating the standard deviation. Variance is calculated by dividing the sum of squared deviation values in a data set by the number of values.

**Voice** One focus of discourse analysts is the different voices that people bring into their narratives. According to the linguist Bakhtin, when people speak their narratives are populated with the voices of others – typically those who are significant to the person; for example, parents, teachers, friends, partners, people who are influential.

**Within-participants design** An experimental design which uses the same participants in each condition, so fewer participants are needed than for a between-participants design. Also known as paired samples design or repeated measures design. Can reduce the effects of individual differences, but those of demand characteristics and/or order effects have to be taken into consideration.

# Index

Psychological Research Methods
ABC (accuracy, brevity and clarity), in report writing 193–4, 203, 217, 359
abstract writing
  experimental reports 194, 196, 200, 218
  qualitative research reports 363
actor/observer effect 257–8
adolescents, self-concepts and the Twenty Statements Test 24
Adult Attachment Interview 318, 319
Aesop's fable, and informal data analysis 284–5
age groups, statistical measurement of 85–7
Ainsworth, M. 303, 325, 327
alpha value, and hypothesis testing 157–8
Althusser, L. 272
anonymity of participants 34
appendices
  in experimental reports 194, 197, 200, 219, 225–9
  in qualitative research reports 365
attachment theory
  and the qualitative research project 317–18, 323, 325, 328
    additional reading material on 355–56
  thematic analysis of 302, 303
Bakhtin, M. 269
banal thematic analysis 283–5, 286
bar graphs 106, 112–16
  axes 112, 116
  error bar charts 146–7, 154–5
  legends/keys 114, 116
  titles and sub-titles 115–16
baseline measures in experiments 62
Bashir, M., interview with Diana, Princess of Wales 28, 30–1
behavioural data 6, 11–12, 44
  measurement of 82
between-groups *t*-tests 173–4
between-participants design 67, 68, 70–1
  and the experimental project 216
  and inferential statistical tests 167, 168, 171
  and sampling error 134
Billig, M. 361–2
bimodal distributions 125–6
biological psychology 3
Bowker, G. 270
BPS *see* British Psychological Society (BPS)
Bowlby, J. 317, 325, 327
brain-imaging techniques 10, 39–40
British Psychological Society (BPS), on ethical issues 33, 36, 37, 314, 320
Busch, C. 319
categorical variables
  analysing 180–1
  and the chi-square test 181–2
  measurement of 83, 84, 167
cause and effect
  and correlational studies 52–3
  and experiments 59, 66
central tendency measures 87–93, 99, 100
  and normal distributions 116–17
  and sampling error 133
  and skewed distributions 124
  *see also* mean; median; mode
change blindness research, measurements 80, 81
children
  ethical issues in research with 38
  and the experimental project 212
  and fatigue effects in experiments 69
  self-concepts and the Twenty Statements Test 24
  word recall tasks, statistical representations of 87–91, 107–12, 112–16
chi-square tests 181–4, 245
  reporting results of 183–4
*Code of Ethics and Conduct* (BPS) 33, 36, 320
cognitive psychology 3
Cohen, J. 51, 172
complete observers 254–5
computer software, for qualitative data analysis 250
conditional probability, and hypothesis testing 157
conditions in experiments 60–2
confidence intervals 130, 132, 140–7, 154, 165
  calculating 142–7
    error bar charts 146–7
    standard error 145–6
  lower bound 146
  upper bound 146
confidentiality issues 34
confounding variables
  in the experimental project 209
  in experiments 64–6, 70
  and sampling error 135
consent issues in research 33–4, 37, 38
content analysis 6–7, 245, 319
contingency tables 180–1, 184
continuous variables, measurement of 82–3, 84, 167
control conditions in experiments 60–2
conversation analysis 321–2
correlational studies 12, 45–53, 72, 166
  correlation coefficients 50–3, 176–80
    Pearson product moment 177–80
    Spearman rank 178
  defining correlation 45–9
  and the experimental project 206
  and experiments 55
  and hypotheses 149, 150–1, 152
    testing 156
  sampling error in 135
  scatterplots in 47–50, 50, 51, 53, 135, 176, 178
counterbalancing in experimental design 68
Cramer's V, and the chi-square test 183
Criminal Records Bureau (CRB) checks 38
Cullwick, H. 264
cycle of enquiry 4

data
behavioural 6, 11–12, 44, 82
defining 5
interpretation 82
levels of measurement 81–2, 93, 97, 100
and methodology 6–8, 11, 39
objective 11–12, 39, 44
subjective 20, 39
symbolic 6, 7, 20, 29
types 6
*see also* material data; qualitative data
data analysis 80, 276
and the experimental project 215–16
and the qualitative research project 318
*see also* thematic analysis
data sets, and descriptive statistics 85–7
degrees of freedom, in descriptive statistics 98–9, 100
demand characteristics, in experimental design 68
dependent *t*-tests 171, 173
dependent variables (DVs)
in the experimental project 205, 206
in experiments 58–60, 61, 63, 64, 65, 66, 70, 71
and hypotheses 148, 149–50, 151, 152, 153
and hypothesis testing 159
inferential statistical tests of 166
measuring 79, 81–2
and sample means 141
and sampling error 133, 139–40
and *t*-tests 168, 174
descriptive statistics 78, 84, 85–93
data sets 85–7
degrees of freedom in 98–9, 100
and the experimental project 215
measures of central tendency 87–93, 99, 100, 116–17
measures of dispersion 93–8, 100, 116
and *t*-tests 175
*see also* distributions; graphs
deviation scores
in descriptive statistics 94–8
*see also* standard deviations
dialogical properties, and discourse analysis 268
diary studies 243, 246, 250, 253, 263–5
longitudinal nature of 263–4
and social context 264–5
subjectivity of 263
disability
and discourse analysis 27–8
subjective analysis of 22
discourse analysis 6, 7, 27, 243, 245, 247, 251, 265–74
concepts and patterns of 268–73
interpretative repertoires 271–2, 273
narrative 27, 269–71, 273
participants' orientations 268, 273
subject positions 272–3
voice 269
Diana, Princess of Wales interview 28, 30–1
and discursive psychology 266, 267
global stand of 273
individual stand of 273
newspaper articles 27–8
and thematic analysis 283
discrete variables, measurement of 82–3, 84, 167
discursive psychology 266, 267
dispersion, measures of 93–8, 116, 133
distributions 106, 116–26
non-normal 123–6
*see also* normal distributions; sampling distributions
double-blind testing 62, 69
drug studies, experimental and control conditions in 61–2
DVs *see* dependent variables (DVs)
ecological validity 18, 32, 79
defining 106
and observation 254
Edley, N. 272
effect size
and the chi-square test 183
and *t*-tests 171–2
Eisen, M. 24
embeddedness 4, 7
emergent findings, qualitative analysis of 25, 26
empirical approach 10–11, 131
epistemology 7, 9, 11, 28, 39, 243, 244–7, 248, 252, 265–6, 275
defining 5
and discourse analysis 267, 271, 274
and the qualitative research project 315, 322
and thematic analysis 285–6, 297, 303
error bar charts 130, 146–7
and hypothesis testing 154–5
*see also* sampling error
errors in measurement 80
essays, and report writing 194
ethical issues 32–8
children in research 38
examples of psychological studies reflecting 32, 36–7
in experimental research 210, 212
report writing 198
in qualitative research 314, 320, 324
report writing 367
and quasi-experiments 63–4
*see also* participants
*Ethical Principles for Conducting Research with Human Participants* (BPS) 33, 36, 37, 314, 320
ethnomethodology 273, 274
evidence 7
evidence-based report writing 362
evolutionary psychology, and experiments 54
expected frequencies, and the chi-square test 182, 183
experimental project 39, 185, 191–238
abstract 218
appendix/appendices 219
data analysis 215–16
design terminology 192
discussion 216–17
ethical issues 210, 212
introduction and rationale for report writing 203–4
method 205–14
data collection 213–14
design 205–6
designing and conducting the experiment 208–10
giving instructions 210–11
materials/apparatus 206–7
procedure 207–8
response sheet 213

participants 201, 206, 207, 210–13, 214
references section 218
report writing and the experimental process 194, 197–9
and the research cycle 191–2
research hypothesis 201–5, 215
stimuli for 230–1
title 217
experimental report writing 193–200
abstract 194, 196, 200, 220
appendix/appendices 194, 197, 200, 225–9
discussion 194, 196, 200, 224–5
example of 219–29
and the experimental process 194, 197–9
formalities in 199–200
introduction 194, 200, 220–2
method 194, 195, 200, 222–3
order of writing 197
references 194, 196, 200, 225
results 194, 195, 200, 223–4
title 194, 196, 200
TMA 03 report 200
word lengths for each section 200
writing styles 193
experimenter effects, in experimental design 69
experiments 6, 9, 10, 26, 54–71, 72
baseline measures 62
conditions of 60–2
confounding variables in 64–6
defining 54–7
dependent and independent variables in 58–62, 63, 64, 65, 66, 67, 70, 71, 72
experimental design 66–71
advantages and disadvantages of 69–71
important elements of 67–9
types of 67
and hypotheses 149
inferential statistical tests of 166–7, 168–76
laboratory 54, 79
naturalistic field 55
quasi-experiments 63–4
and real-life situations 18, 79
sampling error in 133–5
social categorization 12–16, 54
familiarisation stage, in thematic analysis 290–1
fatigue effects, in experimental design 69
featured methods 3
feminist approach, to thematic analysis 299–301, 302
field notes 26, 250, 253, 255, 256, 257, 258
filing methods materials 3
Fisher's exact probability test 183
frequency distributions 107
*see also* histograms
'fuzzy' issues 39
generalisability 17–18, 106
and degrees of freedom 98–9, 100
and thematic analysis 304
George, C. 318
Gergen, K. 21
gift-giving, and reflexivity 330–1
Gold, R.L. 254
Goldwyn, R. 318, 325
graphs 107–16, 126
pie charts 85–6
*see also* bar graphs; histograms
grounded theory 27, 274
habituation, in experimental design 69
Hall, S. 21–2
Hancock, B. 289–90
Hawthorne effect 57
Hazan, C. 317, 325
hermeneutic tradition 8, 9, 11, 20, 22–3, 40–1, 242–3, 245, 246, 265
and discourse analysis 27
and interviews 260
histograms 86–7, 106, 107–12, 116
axes 107
and bimodal distributions 126
constructing on SPSS 107, 111
distribution of variables on 164
frequency of values 107, 108, 111
and normal distribution 118, 119–22
problems with 111–12
and sampling distributions 138, 141
and *t*-tests 169–71, 175
hostility/favourability index 78–9
Howell, D.C. 98
humanistic approach, to thematic analysis 297–9, 301, 302
hypotheses 26, 40, 130, 148–54
one-tailed 153, 154, 159, 175–6, 179, 184
research question 151–2
two-tailed 153, 154, 159
Type 1 error 152, 154
Type 2 error 152, 154
*see also* null hypothesis; research hypotheses
hypothesis testing 130, 154–60
error bar charts 154–5, 160
experimental project 201
and probability value 157–9, 160
identity, and discourse analysis 267, 270, 272–3
identity research
objectivity in 8
subjectivity in 8, 21–2
imaging technology, data gained from 10
independent groups/samples/measures 67
independent-samples *t*-tests 173–4
independent *t*-tests 173–4
independent variables (IVs)
and confidence intervals 146
in experiments 58–62, 63, 64, 65, 66, 67, 70, 71
experimental project 205, 206
report writing 195
and hypotheses 148, 149–50, 151, 152, 153, 154
and hypothesis testing 159
inferential statistical tests of 166
and sampling error 133, 135
and statistical testing 139–40, 141
and *t*-tests 168, 169, 174
individual differences, and experimental design 66, 68, 69–70
inferential statistics 84, 130, 131, 157, 164–87
analysing two categorical variables 180–1
chi-square tests 181–4
choosing a test 166–8
correlations 176–80
and the experimental project 215–16
*see also* *t*-tests
informal thematic analysis 283–5, 286
informed consent of participants 33–4, 37, 210
inner experiences 6, 253

insider viewpoints, and subjectivity 20, 21, 23, 29, 40, 44
interpretative repertoires, and discourse analysis 271–2, 273
interval level data measurements 81, 93, 167
interviews 6, 7, 243, 246, 253, 258–63, 265
as co-constructed 262–3
and discourse analysis 266, 268
Diana, Princess of Wales interview 28, 30–1
experimental and control conditions in 60, 62
metaphors for research interviewing 261–2
open/unstructured 27
pilot 259–60
qualitative analysis of interview material 26–7
in qualitative research 259–62
recordings 250
and reflexive analysis 329
rights of participants 35
semi-structured 22, 26–7, 252, 253, 261, 262, 321
structured 26, 261
thematic analysis of interview transcripts 289–90, 297–303, 307–11
qualitative research project 314, 318–22, 323–7
transcripts of recordings 250
type of questions asked 258–9
iterative dynamic, of qualitative research 248–50, 276, 287
IV *see* independent variables (IVs)
Jefferson, G. 28
Joffe, H. 253
jury decision making, experiments on 57
Kelly, G. 329
knowledge generation, and qualitative research 249, 251
Kuhn, M.H. 24
Kvale, S. 261
laboratory experiments 54, 79
Labov, W. 270
Lacan, J. 272
Langdridge, D. 291
language
and discourse analysis 27–8
and social constructionism 21, 22, 244, 316
and thematic analysis 285
lifespan development, and the qualitative research project 314, 317, 323, 327
lower bound confidence intervals 146
McPartland, T.S. 24
Main, M. 318, 325
Marcia, J.E. 253
material data 6, 7, 10, 11–12, 39–40, 44
measurement of 80, 82
mate selection research, measurements 80–1
mean 86, 89–90, 92, 94, 99, 131
in bar graphs 112–15
and bimodal distribution 126
and confidence intervals 132
measures of dispersion 94–8
and normal distribution 116, 117, 123
population mean 140, 141–3
sample means 140, 141, 146, 147
sampling distribution of the 131, 137–8, 141, 143, 145
and sampling error 131, 133–4
and statistical testing 131–2
*t*-test scores 169–71, 172, 174, 175
measurement 78–85
categorical variables 84, 85
continuous variables 82–3, 84
and data analysis 80
discrete variables 82–3, 84
error 80
levels of 80–2
reliability of 79
validity of 79
*see also* central tendency measures
median
in descriptive statistics 90, 91, 92, 93
and normal distribution 116
Mercer, N. 253
methodology 40, 41, 224–7, 243, 248, 252
and data 6–8, 39
defining 5, 11
and discourse analysis 267, 274
and qualitative research 315, 318, 322, 323
report writing 366
methods
and data types 6
defining 5, 247
and methodologies 6–7, 245
of qualitative data collection 252–65, 276
minimal group experiments 14–15, 54, 78–9
misinterpretation, and reflexive analysis 330–1
modal scores, and bimodal distribution 126
modal values on histograms 109
mode
and bimodal distribution 126
calculating 90–1, 92
and normal distribution 116
Montemayer, R. 24
Morse, J.M. 287–8
motivation, and experiments 56–7
narrative analysis 27, 245, 269–71, 273
naturalistic field experiments 55
negative correlations 50, 52, 53, 179, 180
negative skewed distribution 123–5
neuropsychology, and material data 39–40
newspaper articles, discourse analysis of 27–8
nominal level data measurements 81, 92–3, 100
and the chi-square test 181
and parametric tests 167, 168
non-normal distributions 123–6
normal distributions 116–23, 126, 131, 141
calculating confidence intervals 143–5, 146
and parametric tests 167
note-taking, and qualitative analysis of observation 26
null hypothesis 130, 150–1, 152, 153, 154
and the chi-square test 183
and the experimental project 215, 216
and inferential statistical tests 166, 169, 176
testing 156, 157, 158, 159, 160
objectivity 2, 8–9, 10, 11–19, 39, 44–5, 329
features of objective data 11–12
and operationalisation 79

research goals of 12–17
and statistics 17–19
observation 6, 8, 12, 243, 245, 254–8, 265
aim and focus of 255–6
complete observers 254–5
and consent of participants 34
and cultural knowledge and values 257
data collection through 250, 252, 253
and experiments 55
exploratory approaches to 256
field notes 26, 250, 253, 255, 256, 257, 258
participant observers 254–5, 258
personal issues in 256–7
pilot observations 256
qualitative analysis of 26
structured 254
one-tailed hypotheses 153, 154, 159, 175–6, 179, 184
ontology 20–1, 243, 244–7, 248, 252, 275
and discourse analysis 267
and the qualitative research project 315, 316, 318, 322, 324
and thematic analysis 285–6, 297, 303
open questions 259
open/unstructured interviews 27
operationalisation, and measurement 79, 85
order effects
in experimental design 67–8
in the experimental project 209
ordinal level data measurements 81, 83, 93, 97, 167
outsider viewpoints, and objectivity 44
paired-sample design 67
paired-samples *t*-tests 171, 173
paradigms 4
parametric tests 167, 168
Pearson product moment correlation coefficient 188–80
*t*-tests 168–76
participant observers 254–5, 258
participants 33–8
anonymity of 34
children as 38
consent forms for 229, 237–8
and experimental design 66–71
in the experimental project 201, 206, 207, 210–13, 214, 237–8
and experimental report writing 195, 199
feedback and debriefing of 35–6, 37
informed consent of 33–4, 37, 210
orientations in discourse analysis 268, 273
random allocation of 14–16
in experiments 61, 63–4
right to withdraw from research 35, 37, 38
and sampling error 134–5
pattern (third-order) coding, in thematic analysis 295–6, 296, 297–303, 326
Pearson product moment correlation coefficients 177–80
reporting results of 179–80
personal construct theory 329
personality research 44
correlational studies of 45
measuring variables in 82–3
PET (positron emission tomography) scans 10, 40
pie charts 85–6
pilot interviews 259–60
pilot observations 256
placebo effect 61, 62
populations
population mean and confidence intervals 140, 141–147
samples of 98–9, 131–2, 132
and the null hypothesis 151
populations of interest 132, 165
and sampling distributions 136–8
and statistical testing 138–40
population standard deviations 99
positive correlations 50, 52, 53, 179, 180
positive skewed distribution 123–5
positivist model 3, 4
Potter, D. 269
Potter, J. 360
power relations
and discourse analysis 267, 272
in interviews 261
and research with children 38
practice effects
in the experimental project 206, 209
in experiments 66, 67
probability, and hypothesis testing 156–8
psychoanalytic theory, and research participants 36
psychological tests 6
*p*-value
and the chi-square test 184
in correlational studies 177, 179
and hypothesis testing 157–9, 160
and *t*-tests 175–6, 181
qualitative data 20, 25, 250–1
interpretations of 251–2
methods of data collection 252–65, 276
transforming and analysing 250–1
qualitative research 2, 10, 39, 40, 242–76
analysis 25–8
characteristics of 360–1
ethical issues in 34, 35, 314, 320, 324
grounded nature of 249, 251
and the hermeneutic tradition 8, 9, 11, 20, 22–3, 40–1, 242–3, 245
iterative dynamic of 248–50, 276, 287
and knowledge generation 249, 251
methods *see* diary studies; discourse analysis; interviews; observation; thematic analysis
process of conducting 275–6
and quantitative research
data and methods 24–5, 29, 245–6
differences in report writing 358–9
reflexivity in 302–3, 305, 314–15, 328–32, 361
research focus 316
and research questions 275–6, 316, 316–17, 318, 325
and subjectivity 8, 9, 20–9
theoretical frameworks 247, 251, 275–6, 315
embedding research in 248
*see also* epistemology; ontology

qualitative research project 314–56
background 315–23
checklist for evaluating 332–3
ethical issues 314, 320, 324
process 323–8
carrying out the thematic analysis 324–7
reviewing thematic analysis 327
watching the interview 323–4
and reflexive analysis 314–15, 328–32
and the research question 316–17, 318, 323, 328
reviewing 327
time and workload constraints 320–1
transcripts 321–2, 323, 326–7, 328
use of pre-recorded data 319–21
qualitative research report writing 258–77
abstract 363
analysis 363–4
appendices 365
discussion 364–5
ethical issues 367
evidence-based nature of 362
example of 367–76
general guidance 358–9
including quotations 361–2
introduction 363
method 363
reading over the report 259, 366
references 365
reflexive analysis 359, 365, 366
reporting thematic analysis 360–2
and theoretical framework 266, 363
title 363
transparency 366–7
use of the first person 358–9
word length 362
quantitative research 2, 10, 22–3, 39, 40, 45
comparisons with thematic analysis 303
and content analysis 6–7
experimental report writing 193–200
interviews in 260
and objectivity 8, 9, 12
and observation 254
and qualitative research
data and methods 24–5, 29, 245–6
differences in report writing 358–9
and the scientific tradition 3, 4, 7, 8, 11, 40–1, 45, 242, 243, 245, 328–9
and statistics 17–19, 164–6
*see also* correlational studies; distributions; experiments; graphs; statistics
quasi-experiments 63–4
questionnaires 6, 8, 12
reliability of 79
systematic self-reports in 44
quotations, in qualitative research report writing 361–2
random allocation of participants 14–16
in experiments 61, 63–4
random samples 17, 130
range, in descriptive statistics 86–7, 94, 100
ratio level data measurements 81, 82, 83, 97, 167
real-life situations, and laboratory experiments 18
recording data, objectivity in 16–17
reflexivity
in interviews 261
in qualitative research 314–15, 328–32, 361
avoiding over-interpretation and misinterpretation 330–1
report writing 359, 365, 366
thematic analysis 302–3, 305, 331–2
related *t*-tests 171, 173
reliability, defining 106
repeated measures design 67
repeated measures *t*-tests 171, 173
replicability in research studies 16
and qualitative analysis 329
report writing *see* experimental report writing; qualitative research report writing
representative samples 17–18
research hypotheses 130, 149–50, 151–2, 152–3, 154
and the experimental project 192, 201–5, 215
and research questions 288
and statements of results 184
and *t*-tests 175–6
research questions
and hypotheses 151–2
in qualitative research 275–6, 316–17, 318
thematic analysis 286–9, 291, 303
and the qualitative research project 316–17, 318, 323, 325, 328
samples 17–19, 130
generalising to the population 98–9
sample means 140, 141, 146, 147
sample size
and hypotheses 152
and normal distribution 121
reducing sampling error 136
sample standard deviations 99, 132
sampling distributions 130, 131, 136–8
of the mean 131, 137–8, 141, 143, 145
and statistical testing 138
sampling error 130, 131, 132, 133–5
and confidence intervals 146
and correlational coefficients 177
and hypotheses 148, 149–50, 154
and hypothesis testing 156, 157–8, 160
and inferential statistics 165–6
reducing 136
and statistical testing 139–40
and *t*-tests 169, 171
scatterplots
in correlational studies 47–50, 50, 51, 53, 135, 176
and Pearson product moment correlation 178, 179
Schatzman, L. 26
scientific tradition 3, 4, 7, 8, 11, 40–1, 45, 242, 243, 245, 247, 328–9
self-concepts, and the Twenty Statements Test 24–5
self-knowledge, and research participants 36
self-reports
and measurement error 80
and objective research 44
semi-structured interviews 22, 26–7, 252, 253, 261, 262, 321
Shaver, P.R. 317, 325
single-blind testing 61–2
skewed distribution 123–5

social categorisation (minimal group) experiment 12–16, 19, 54, 78–9
social constructionism 4, 244, 247
  and discourse analysis 266, 274
  and identity research 21–2
  and the qualitative research project 316, 318, 319, 324
  and thematic analysis 285
*Social Psychology: Critical Perspectives on Self and Others* 243
social setting, and experiments 56–7
Spearman rank correlation coefficient 178
SPSS 130, 167–8
  calculating confidence intervals 142, 148
  and the chi-square test 182–3
  constructing bar graphs 115, 116
  constructing histograms 107, 111, 116
  and correlation coefficients 178, 179
  and experimental reports 216, 219
  and *t*-tests 168, 171, 173, 175, 176
squared deviation scores 95–7
square roots 97
  and confidence intervals calculations 145, 146
standard deviation points 143–4, 147, 172
standard deviations 87, 100, 131
  and bar graphs 112
  calculating 97–8
  and confidence intervals 143–5
  and degrees of freedom 99
  and parametric tests 167
  sample standard deviations 99, 132
  and sampling distribution 131
  and sampling error 131, 133
  and standard error calculations 145–6
  and *t*-tests 168, 169, 171
standard error calculations 145–6, 147
Stanley, L. 264
statistical testing 130, 131–2, 138–40
  and hypotheses 150–4
  hypothesis testing 130, 154–60
  inferential statistics 166–84
statistics
  and correlational studies 45
  generalisability 17–18, 98–9, 100, 106, 304
  importance of 84
  and objectivity in research 17–19
  statistical significance and hypothesis testing 158–9
  summary of key points underlying 130, 131–2
  *see also* descriptive statistics; inferential statistics
Stokoe, E. 28
Strange Situation 319
Strauss, A.L. 26
Stroop effect
  in the experimental project 201–2, 204–5, 208–10
  measurement of response time 81–2
structured interviews 261
structured observations 254
subjectivity 2, 4, 8–9, 10, 19, 20–9, 39, 44, 246
  and diary studies 263
  research goals 20–9
subject positions, in discourse analysis 272–3
Swindells, J. 264
symbolic data 6, 7, 20, 29, 253
systematic self-reports, in objective research 44
Tajfel, H., social categorisation experiment 12–16, 19, 54, 78–9
Tesch, R. 22
test-retest reliability 45
thematic analysis 27, 39, 243, 245, 252, 274–5, 282–311
  banal or informal 283–5, 286
  coding stage 291–6
    first-order coding 292–4, 296
    in the qualitative research project 326, 328
    second-order coding 295, 296
    third-order coding 295–6, 296, 297–303
  defining 282–3
  epistemology and ontology 285–6, 297, 303
  evaluating 303–5
    checklist 332–3
  familiarisation stage 290–1
  reflexivity in 302–3
  and research questions 286–9, 291
  theoretical frameworks 286, 287, 297
    feminist 299–301, 303
    humanistic 297–9, 301
  transcripts 289–90, 296, 303, 305, 307–11
  two researchers 297–303
  writing up 267, 360–2
    example of 367–76
  *see also* qualitative research project
theoretical assumptions 3–4
Thomas, W.I. 263
transcription, and thematic analysis 289–90
*t*-tests 168–76
  and effect size 171–2
  independent-samples 173–4
  paired-samples 171, 173
  reporting results of 175–6
Twenty Statements Test 22, 23–5, 39, 252
twin studies, correlational 45, 53
two-tailed hypotheses 153, 154, 159
Type 1 error 152
Type 2 error 152
unrelated *t*-tests 173–4
unstructured interviews 27
unstructured naturalistic observations 254
upper bound confidence intervals 146
validity
  defining 106
  ecological 18, 32, 79
  measuring 79
Van den Berg, H. 329
variables
  in correlational studies 45, 46–53, 176
  distribution of 164–5
  in the experimental project 209–10
  in experiments 58–62, 63, 64–6, 67, 70, 71, 72
  measurement of 78–85, 167
  operationalisation of 79, 85
  in quasi-experiments 64
  *see also* categorical variables; confounding variables; dependent variables (DVs); independent variables (IVs)

voice, and discourse analysis 269
Volosinov, V. 269
Wetherell, M. 272, 360
Wilkinson, S. 264
within-participants design 67, 68, 69–71
  and the experimental project 209, 216
  and inferential statistical tests 167, 168, 171, 173
  and sampling error 134
workplace productivity, experiments on 57
writing up research *see* experimental report writing; qualitative research report writing
written data 253
  *see also* diary studies
Znaniecki, F. 263

# Acknowledgements

Grateful acknowledgement is made to the following sources:

## Text

Page 336: Salter Ainsworth, M.D. (1989) 'Attachments beyond infancy', *American Psychologist*, Vol. 44, No. 4, April 1989, pp. 709-716. Copyright © American Psychological Association. Adapted with permission; Page 343: Bretherton, I. (1997) 'Bowlby's legacy to developmental psychology', *Child Psychiatry and Human Development*, Vol. 28(1), Fall 1997, Springer; Page 347: Kretchmar, M.D. et al (2005) 'Anna's story: a qualitative analysis of an at-risk mother's experience in an attachment-based foster care program', *Attachment & Human Development*, Vol. 7(1), March 2005, pp. 31-49, Taylor & Francis Ltd; Page 352: Rothbaum, F. et al (2000) 'Attachment and culture: security in the United States and Japan', *American Psychologist*, Vol. 55, No. 10, pp. 1093-1104. Copyright © 2000 by the American Psychologist Association. Adapted with permission.

## Photograph

Page 31: Copyright © BBC